RICHARD WAGNER

HIS LIFE AND HIS DRAMAS

AMS PRESS
NEW YORK

Richard Wagner

RICHARD WAGNER

HIS LIFE AND HIS DRAMAS

A BIOGRAPHICAL STUDY OF THE MAN AND AN EXPLANATION OF HIS WORK

BY

W. J. HENDERSON

AUTHOR OF "THE STORY OF MUSIC," "WHAT IS GOOD MUSIC?"
"SOME FORERUNNERS OF ITALIAN OPERA," ETC.

SECOND EDITION REVISED

G. P. PUTNAM'S SONS
NEW YORK AND LONDON
The Knickerbocker Press
1923

Reprinted from the edition of 1923, New York and London
First AMS EDITION published 1971
Manufactured in the United States of America

International Standard Book Number: 0-404-03239-7

Library of Congress Catalog Number: 70-137240

AMS PRESS INC.
NEW YORK, N.Y. 10003

TO

ROBERT EDWIN BONNER

PREFACE TO NEW EDITION

MUCH musical experience has been gained since this book was published in 1901. The excursion of "Parsifal" into the world, begun at the Metropolitan Opera House in 1903, has extended through several lands. Familiarity with the great lyric dramas has become a common possession of music lovers. An entire generation of opera patrons, fed from infancy on Wagnerian music, has reached maturity. The ancient battle for acceptance of "the art work of the future" is almost forgotten. A few white-haired opera goers and the members of fashionable society, who have always been hostile to every serious art aiming at something other than their entertainment, continue to complain when the name of Wagner appears in the programs. The broad world of art, letters and music and the circles of polite culture are, as usual, deaf to their murmurings. Wagner is performed as a matter of course.

But just at this point we find a reason for an endeavor to reawaken interest in Wagner's personality, his art theories and his disclosure of them in the theatre. Wagner is performed as a matter of course. That is his new misfortune, for to nineteen persons in every twenty his works are operas, just as Verdi's "Aïda" and Gounod's "Faust" are. For the public attitude the public itself, at least in so far as New York is concerned, is not to blame. In the United States representations of the Wagnerian drama are given almost exclusively at the Metropolitan Opera House. At the moment of this writing a German company is preparing to offer productions of the works according to the manner of Berlin; but little is to be expected from this, for in Germany perfunctory and inadequate presentations of Wagner dramas are quite as common as they are here, and the public is just as oblivious to the man's purposes.

The Germans should not be too severely censured for their misconceptions of Wagner, since many of them have originated in the festival theatre of Bayreuth. The performances there in recent years have represented the ideas of Cosima, not Richard, Wagner, and the court of last resort in all disputes has been her son Siegfried. He has been called upon again and again to declare how his father wished this or that done in "Der Ring des Nibelungen." As the young Siegfried was six years old when the tetralogy was produced, he, of course, understood his father's artistic principles perfectly. Owing partly to the teachings of Bayreuth and perhaps quite as largely to the long established German attitude toward the lyric declamation of the stage, Wagner's dramas have been badly sung in Germany almost always. To this day Germans, not only in Germany, but those long resident in the United States, where the dramas have been sung ravishingly, rather resent this kind of performance and yearn for their own prized style of "Wagner singing."

It was not, of course, anything of this kind that troubled Wagner in his later years, when he realized that his designs were not comprehended by the world and that operatic artists could not bring their art into harmony with his. Despite the prevalence of unmusical singing of Wagner's works, the impersonators of his characters have climbed to a higher level than that which they occupied in his day. They understand him fairly well and when they are willing, as some of them are, to obliterate their own ambition and sink themselves in the lucent glory of Wagner's imagination, they render unto Cæsar that which is Cæsar's.

But it is nevertheless undeniable that the majority of singers keep a close eye on the opportunities to make points in the old-fashioned way. The conductors often fail in their study of the deeper significance of the scenes in the dramas and therefore misconceive the spirit of their movement and kill them by dull and incongruous tempi. Stage managers apparently believe that when they have caused the fire to illumine the sword in the tree at the sounding of the first note of the sword motive in the first act of "Die Walküre" or have perfected a striking scheme of lighting for the unveiling of the Grail in "Parsifal" they have done for the Wagnerian drama all that its creator conceived and the union of the arts tributary to the drama stands forth in all its convincing beauty.

The managers of opera houses make no hesitation in giving performances of parts of the Nibelungen tetralogy with no reference to the other parts. "Die Walküre" proceeds along its solitary path with no conceivable explanation of Fricka's hold over Wotan or Sieglinde's elation on hearing the prophecy of Brünnhilde, of which the fulfillment is indefinitely postponed. The Volsung blood does not bloom; the twilight does not fall on the erring gods.

The concert halls echo with "selections" from the works of Wagner, just as they do with airs by

Handel, Mozart, and Verdi. The "Waldweben," the journey of Siegfried down the Rhine, and the great funeral hymn of Brünnhilde are delivered into the ears of people not yet acquainted with the opera in which the hero makes his first appearance nor that in which his death flames sweep away the sin stained Wahalla and light the path to a new world.

It might be argued and with no little force that these separate performances of dramas of the "Ring" cycle and excerpts from various scores indicate that in the final analysis Wagner's system failed and the royal prerogative of music to express the entire emotional content of a lyric drama exercises itself. Without doubt the music is the chief element in the union of the arts contemplated by Wagner. It is predominant, furthermore, because in spite of Wagner's ability as a writer of dramatic texts, he was before all things also a composer and it was in the music that his works made the furthest, most triumphant, and most generally recognized departure from all that had been possessed by the operatic stage before his time.

We may grant this without endangering the position already taken. There is plentiful evidence that the lofty artistic ideals of Wagner, his admirable adaptations of old legends, his exalted view of the conflict of human passions in the drama and of the saving grace of the woman soul and his ambition to lift the theatre out of the mire of commercial speculation are passing to-day unconsidered by audiences which wait eagerly to hear Elsa's "Dream" and Wotan's "Farewell." For these reasons what the operatic artists call a "restudy" of the whole work may not be ill-timed. The author of this book would rejoice to secure for Wagner a new trial at the bar of public opinion in order that his case might be properly presented.

This volume, written in 1900–01 and published on Nov. 23 of the latter year, must not be regarded as an expression of the author's opinions of Wagner and his works. It was asserted in the preface to the original edition that the book was intended to be expository, not critical. The author aimed to put before the reader a clear view of the man, his art theories and his application of them to the famous music dramas. In preparing this new edition some alterations have been made to bring the story of Wagner's life into conformity with the latest information, including that found in the extensive autobiography.

In other parts of the volume emendations have been made where demanded by newly acquired facts or the conclusions of recent scholarship on such items, for example, as the connection of Saemund the Wise with the Eddas. The appendix dealing with Wagner's conception of the ballet has been rewritten because since the publication of the book the ballet itself has undergone a radical reformation.

The reception of this volume was gratifying to its writer. That it has endured for twenty-one years is naturally still more gratifying. With its coming of age it appears in new garb, and, let us hope, with its younger imperfections eradicated.

PREFACE

THE purpose of this book is to supply Wagner lovers with a single work which shall meet all their needs. The author has told the story of Wagner's life, explained his artistic aims, given the history of each of his great works, examined its literary sources, shown how Wagner utilised them, surveyed the musical plan of each drama, and set forth the meaning and purpose of its principal ideas. The work is not intended to be critical, but is designed to be expository. It aims to help the Wagner lover to a thorough knowledge and understanding of the man and his works.

The author has consulted all the leading biographies, and for guidance in the direction of absolute trustworthiness he is directly indebted to Mme. Cosima Wagner, whose suggestions have been carefully observed. He is also under a large, but not heavy, burden of obligation to Mr. Henry Edward Krehbiel, musical critic of *The New York Tribune,* who carefully read the manuscript of this work and pointed out its errors. The value of Mr. Krehbiel's revision and his hints cannot be over-estimated. Thanks are also due to Mr. Emil Paur, conductor of the Philharmonic Society, of New York, for certain inquiries made in Europe.

The records of first performances have been prepared with great care and with no little labour. For the dates of those at most of the European cities the author is indebted to an elaborate article by E. Kastner, published in the *Allgemeine Musik. Zeitung,* of Berlin, for July and August, 1896. The original casts have been secured, as far as possible, from the programmes. For that of the " Flying Dutchman " at Dresden—incorrectly given in many books on Wagner—the author is indebted to Hofkapellmeister Ernst von Schuch, who obtained it from the records of the Hoftheater. The name of the singer of the Herald in the first cast of "Lohengrin," missing in all the published histories, was supplied by Hermann Wolff, of Berlin, from the records of Weimar. The casts of first performances in this country are not quite complete, simply because the journalists of twenty-five years ago did not realise their obligations to posterity. The casts were not published in full. The records have disappeared. The theatres in some cases—as in that of the Stadt—have long ago gone out of existence and nothing can be done. As far as given the casts are, the author believes, perfectly correct.

CONTENTS

PART I—THE LIFE OF WAGNER

PART II—THE ARTISTIC AIMS OF WAGNER

Contents

PART I

THE LIFE OF WAGNER

RICHARD WAGNER

CHAPTER I

THE BOYHOOD OF A GENIUS

"O kindischer Held ! O herrlicher Knabe."—SIEGFRIED.

THE ancestry of Richard Wagner need not be traced beyond his grandfather. This good man was Gottlob Friedrich Wagner, a custom house official, whose life-work it was to see that nothing was smuggled into Leipsic through the city gates. Gottlob Friedrich had a son to whom was given the second name of his father. Friedrich Wagner was a clerk of police. He had a considerable acquaintance with languages, and spoke French so well that when the French army under Napoleon occupied the city, he was appointed by Marshal Davoust to organise the police. Wagner's father was born in 1770, and his life was short. It is known that he had a taste for the theatre and for verse. After the battles of October 18 and 19, 1813, at the gates of Leipsic, when Napoleon's power was broken in Germany, the accumulation of dead around the city caused an epidemic fever, and among its victims was the police clerk Wagner. He passed away on November 22, 1813, leaving among other children a male babe of six months, destined to immortalise his name.   This child was Wilhelm Richard Wagner, born May 22, 1813, in " The House of the Red and White Lion," No. 88 Hause Brühl.

Wagner's mother, whom his father married in 1798, was Johanna Rosina Bertz, who died in 1848.   Richard was the youngest of nine children, the others being Albert, Carl Gustav, Johanna Rosalie, Carl Julius, Luise Constanze, Clara Wilhelmine, Maria Theresia, and Wilhelmine Ottilie.   Of these Albert became an actor and singer of considerable importance and finally stage manager in Berlin.   He married Elise Gollmann, a singer with a remarkably extensive voice, who is said to have sung " Tancredi " and " The Queen of the Night " equally well.   She bore him a daughter, Johanna, who became one of the most eminent sopranos of her time, and was the original Elizabeth in " Tannhäuser " at the age of seventeen.   Wagner's sister Johanna Rosalie was an actress and Clara was a singer.

When the epidemic had carried off the police clerk, the widow was in straitened circumstances.   Her oldest son was only fourteen years old and not competent to contribute to the support of the large family. The governmental pension was small and she had no fortune of her own.   At this trying period Ludwig Geyer, an old friend of her husband, asked her to be his wife, and although only nine months had elapsed since Friedrich Wagner's death, she, like a sensible woman, accepted the offer.   Geyer was a man of talent and well fitted to be the parental guide of the young Richard.   He was an actor, a singer, an author, and a portrait painter. As a singer he once appeared in "Joseph in Egypt," when that opera was produced by Weber on his assumption of the conductor's bâton at the Dresden opera. His gift for portrait painting is said almost to have reached genius. He was the writer of several comedies, and one of his plays, "The Slaughter of the Innocents," is still well known in Germany. To celebrate the sixtieth birthday of Richard Wagner his family at Bayreuth surprised him with a performance of this play, and he was much touched by it, for he always cherished a deep affection for his stepfather.

Owing to the employment of Geyer in a Dresden theatre, the whole family removed to that city. Here the education of the future composer began in earnest. The home influences were the example of Geyer and the sweet, gentle affection of the mother, to whom her children were the first of all considerations. The outside influence was found in the Dresden Kreuzschule, where the boy was entered under the name of Richard Geyer. This schooling, however, was not begun till after the death of the stepfather. In the beginning Geyer thought that Richard would make a good painter, but, the composer tells us in his ample autobiography, "I showed a very poor talent for drawing." Geyer died on September 30, 1821, still cherishing the belief that there was some sort of promise in the boy. "Shortly before his death," continues the autobiography, "I had learnt to play 'Ueb' immer Treu und Redlichkeit' and the then newly published 'Jungfernkranz' upon the pianoforte ; the day before his death I was bid to play him both these pieces in the adjoining room ; I heard him then

with feeble voice say to my mother : ' Has he perchance a talent for music ? ' On the early morrow,
as he lay dead, my mother came into the children's
sleeping room and said to each of us some loving
word. To me she said : ' He hoped to make *something* of thee.' I remember, too, that for a long time
I imagined that something indeed would come of
me."

Wagner was eight years old when his stepfather
died, and in order that the mother's cares might be
lightened, he was sent for a year to live with a
brother of Geyer at Eisleben, where he attended a
private school. It was in December, 1822, that he
began to go to the Kreuzschule in Dresden. If ever
there was a childhood in which the future man was
foreshadowed it was that of Wagner. His biographers have with one accord set down the statement that the boy showed no promise in his early
years. Look at them and see for yourself. At the
Kreuzschule he conceived a profound love for the
classicism of Homer, and to the delight of his teacher,
Herr Silig, translated the first twelve books of the
Odyssey out of school hours. He revelled in the
fascinations of mythology, and his fancy was so
stimulated that when commemorative verses on the
death of one of the boys were asked for, Wagner's,
having been pruned of some extravagances, were
crowned with the halo of type.

Thereupon this child of eleven resolved to become
a poet. He projected vast tragedies on the plan of
Apel's " Polyeidos " and " Die Aetolier." He plunged
into the deeps of Shakespeare and translated a speech
of Romeo into metrical German. Finally he began a

grand tragedy, which proved to be compounded of elements from "Hamlet" and "King Lear." He laboured on this for two years. "The plan," he says, "was gigantic in the extreme ; two-and-forty human beings died in the course of this piece, and I saw myself compelled in its working out to call the greater number back as ghosts, since otherwise I should have been short of characters for my last acts."

Huge poetic projects already throbbing in the young brain, music, too, seized him for her own. He would not stay away from the piano, and so the tutor who was guiding him through the mazes of Cornelius Nepos engaged to teach him the technic of the instrument. But the wayward Wagner would not practice. The moment that the tutor's back was turned he began to strum the music of "Der Freischütz" by ear, and he learned to perform the overture with "fearful fingering." The teacher overheard him and said that nothing would come of his piano studies. And so it proved, for Wagner never learned to play the piano. Yet was there nothing in all this to show the bent of the young mind ? Was it not a childhood meet for him who was one day to project tragedies before undreamed of on the lyric stage, and to cut loose from all the traditions of operatic music ? And was it not a good omen when at last there fell across his childhood the shadow of his artistic progenitor, Weber ? "When Weber passed our house on his way to the theatre," writes Wagner, "I used to watch him with something akin to religious awe ! " Indeed, Weber used to enter the house to talk to the sweet Frau Geyer, who was well liked among artists, and so perhaps the little Richard looked into the luminous depths of the eyes of the composer of "Der Freischütz."

Weber became the idol of his boyhood, and no doubt the worship of this real genius had some influence on the bent of Wagner's musical thought. It is narrated of him that, when he was not permitted to go to the theatre to hear "Der Freischütz," he used to stand in the corner of a room at home and count the minutes, specifying just what was going on at each particular instant and finally weeping, so that his mother would yield and send him happy off to the performance. However, in 1827 the family returned to Leipsic and that was the end of young Richard's close observation of Weber. A still more serious influence now entered into his life, for at the concerts of the Leipsic Gewandhaus he first heard the works of Beethoven. The overture to "Egmont" fired him with a desire to preface his own drama with such a piece of music. So he borrowed a copy of Logier's treatise on harmony and counterpoint and tried to learn its contents in a week. This was the crucial test of his genius. If he had not been born to be a composer, the difficulties which he encountered in his solitary struggle with the science of music would have turned him aside from the study forever. But it was not so. He says in his autobiography : "Its difficulties both provoked and fascinated me ; I resolved to become a musician." And thus we find Wagner, whose childhood has been pronounced insignificant, at the age of fifteen already a dramatist and eager to be a composer. To be sure, he was not a prodigy, but the future of the man was marked out plainly by the child ; and we shall see that from this time he moved steadily toward the goal of his ambition.

The progress was not accomplished without a struggle. As he himself tells us in his autobiography, his family now unearthed his great tragedy, and he was severely admonished that in the future it would be well for him to give less attention to Melpomene and more to his text-books. But he was not to be turned aside from his purpose. " Under such circumstances," he says, "I breathed no word of my secret discovery of a calling for music ; but nevertheless I composed, in silence, a sonata, a quartet, and an aria. When I felt myself sufficiently matured in my private musical studies, I ventured forth at last with their announcement. Naturally, I now had many a hard battle to wage, for my relatives could only consider my penchant for music as a fleeting passion—all the more as it was unsupported by any proofs or preliminary study, and especially by any already won dexterity in handling a musical instrument." We laugh, perhaps, at this awkward boy in his lumbering struggles, but there was something large in it all. He aimed at the top, and from the outset, pathetically enough, as it afterward proved, tried to hitch his "waggon to a star."

The family so far humoured his new ambition as to engage a music teacher for him, Gottlieb Müller, afterward organist at Altenburg. But a sorry time this honest man had with his eccentric young pupil. The boy was at this time head over ears in the romanticism of Ernst Theodor Hoffmann, then recently dead and still in the height of his fame in Germany. The astounding fecundity of this writer's invention of marvellous incidents inflamed the boy's mind, and threw him into a state of continual nervous excitement. He says himself that he had day-dreams in which the keynote, third and dominant, seemed to take form and to reveal to him their mighty meanings. But he would not study systematically, and his family apparently had ground for believing that music would soon be abandoned for some other fancy. Instead of treading patiently the rocky path of counterpoint, the impatient boy endeavoured at one leap to reach the top of the musical mountain, and wrote overtures for orchestra. One of them was actually performed in a theatre in Leipsic under the direction of Heinrich Dorn. It was, as Wagner confessed, the culminating point of his folly. The parts of the string instruments in score were written in red ink, those of the wood in green, and those of the brass in black. "Beethoven's Ninth Symphony," he says, "was a mere Pleyel sonata by the side of this marvellously concocted overture." At every fourth measure the tympani player had a note to be played forte, and when the audience had recovered from its astonishment at this wonderful effect, it burst into laughter.

But all these strivings were not in vain. As Adolphe Jullien notes in his "Richard Wagner," the influence of the Hoffmann stories was not lost ; "for the 'Brothers of Serapion ' contained an account of the poetical tourney at Wartburg, and some germs of 'The Meistersinger' are found in another story by Hoffmann, 'Master Martin, the Cooper of Nuremberg.'" Dorn, the conductor, became interested in young Wagner, and afterwards proved to be a valuable friend. The boy modestly and sincerely thanked him for producing the overture, and Dorn replied that he had at once perceived the boy's talent and that furthermore the orchestration had not needed extensive revision. Wagner now seemed to feel his own need of some sort of regular study, for he matriculated at the University of Leipsic, chiefly in order that he might attend the lectures on æsthetics and philosophy. Here again his want of application made itself apparent, and he entered into the dissipations of student life with avidity. But he soon wearied of them and once more settled down to the study of music, this time under Theodor Weinlig, who sat in the honoured seat of Bach as the cantor of the Thomas School.

In less than half a year Weinlig had taught the boy to solve the hardest problems of counterpoint, and said to him, "What you have made your own by this dry study, we call self-dependence." At this time, too, Wagner became acquainted with the music of Mozart and its influence upon his mind was very healthful. He laboured to rid himself of bombast and to attain a nobler simplicity. He wrote a piano sonata in which he strove for a "natural, unforced style in composition." This sonata was published by Breitkopf and Härtel, and was, so far as the records show, Wagner's real Opus 1. It shows no trace of inspiration, and can rank only as a conservatory exercise.

It was followed by a polonaise in D for four hands, Opus 2, and this was also printed by Breitkopf and Härtel. It is nothing more than school work, like its predecessor. The third work was a fantasia in F sharp minor for piano. The restraining power of the teacher is less apparent in this composition, which remains unpublished. In his article on Wagner in Grove's "Dictionary of Music," Mr. Edward Dannreuther quotes at some length from a personal conversation with the composer, who described Weinlig's method of teaching. It was a plain and practical method, in which example and precept were judiciously combined. Wagner said to Mr. Dannreuther, "The true lesson consisted in his patient and careful inspection of what had been written." It was fortunate for Wagner that he had such a mentor, and that he was in the beginning of his career as a composer compelled to learn and practice the old forms in which the fundamental laws of music found their perfect exemplification. His readiness to depart from the straight and narrow path would have led him into insuperable difficulties, and perhaps to hopeless discouragement, had he not possessed so kind and trustworthy a guide.

Young Wagner now launched upon musical activities of no small magnitude for one so youthful. In the year 1830 he made a pianoforte transcription of Beethoven's Ninth Symphony, and in a letter dated Oct. 6 he offered it to the Messrs. Schott, of Mayence. The offer was not accepted. He also wrote to the Peters Bureau de Musique, offering to make piano arrangements at less than the usual rates. In 1831 he composed two overtures, one a "Concert Ouvertüre mit Fuge" in C, and the other in D minor. This one is dated Sept. 26, with emendations dated Nov. 4. It was performed at one of the Gewandhaus concerts on Dec. 25, 1831. The *Allgemeine Musikalische Zeitung* said of it : "Much pleasure was given us by a new overture by a composer still very young, Herr Richard Wagner. The piece was thoroughly appreciated, and, indeed, the young man promises much : the composition not only sounds well, but it has ideas and it is written with care and skill, with an evident striving after the noblest." *

In 1832, when he was 19 years old, he wrote a symphony in C major.† The biographers of Wagner have agreed to disagree about this symphony, even the usually accurate Mr. Finck calling it a work in C minor. It is, however, plainly enough in C major. The history of this composition was peculiar. When he had finished it Wagner put it in his trunk and started for Vienna, " for no other purpose than to get a glimpse of this famed musical centre. What I heard and saw there was not to my edification ; wherever I went I heard 'Zampa' or Strauss's potpourris on 'Zampa'—two things that were an abomination to me, especially at that time." On the homeward journey he tarried a while in Prague, where he made the acquaintance of Dionys Weber, director of the Conservatory. This gentleman's pupils rehearsed the symphony. The score was next submitted to the directors of the Gewandhaus concerts at Leipsic.

The managing director was Rochlitz, editor of the *Allgemeine Musikalische Zeitung,* an authority on music, and he invited Wagner to call on him. "When I presented myself, the stately old gentleman raised his spectacles, saying, ' You are a young man indeed ! I expected an older and more experienced

---

* Quoted from " Wagner and his Works," by Henry T. Finck. 2 vols., New York, 1893.   † See Appendix *A.*

composer.'" The symphony was tried, and on Jan.
10, 1833, it was produced at a Gewandhaus concert.
In the season of 1834–5 Wagner, who was in Leipsic,
forced his score on the attention of Mendelssohn,
then the conductor of the Gewandhaus concerts, in
the hope of getting another performance. Mendelssohn put the manuscript away, and, though he often
saw Wagner, never spoke of the work. Wagner
was too modest to ask him about it, and so the score
was lost. In 1872 the orchestral parts were found in
an old trunk left by Wagner in Dresden in the course
of the revolutionary disturbances of 1849.

With the composition of this symphony, Wagner's
apprenticeship in instrumental music may be said to
have ended. His next venture was across that magic
border which separates the orchestra from the stage.
His period of juvenility was not quite ended, but he
may be said to have finished the preparatory stage of
his career and to be about to enter on the first years
of serious struggle toward his real goal. His boyhood was fairly indicative of his nature. Restless,
dissatisfied, eager to reach the topmost heights, and
not suited with the means at hand, we yet find him
experimenting with the methods of those who preceded him, analysing and assimilating the musical
past, and learning to conquer musical forms. In the
juvenile symphony he showed that he had honestly
solved the problems of construction, that he had
mastered the formal materials of his art. The wise
Schumann said, "Mastery of form leads talent to
ever increasing freedom." At nineteen years of age,
with the methods of Beethoven and Mozart firmly
fixed in his mind, the young Wagner had produced

a symphonic composition, which, while imitative in both themes and treatment, showed astonishing musical vigour and an enterprising spirit. The boy was on the verge of manhood, artistically as well as physically.

CHAPTER II

THE FIRST OPERAS

"You are a young man indeed!"—ROCHLITZ TO WAGNER

IN the year 1832, while he was in Prague, Wagner began his career as a composer of operas, and in his first attempt, as in all later ones, wrote his own libretto. His friend Heinrich Laube * had offered him a libretto on the subject of Kosciuszko, but he refused it, saying that he was engaged wholly on instrumental music. But his genius was for the stage, and his boyhood had been surrounded by the immediate influences of the theatre. It is, therefore, not surprising to find him at work on an opera. He says in his autobiography : "In that city [Prague] I also composed an opera book of tragic contents, 'Die Hochzeit.' I know not whence I had come by the mediæval subject matter :—a frantic lover climbs to the window of the sleeping-chamber of his friend's bride, wherein she is awaiting the advent of the bridegroom ; the bride struggles with the madman and hurls him into the courtyard below, where his

* Laube wrote in the *Journal du Monde Elégant,* of Leipsic, after the private performance of the symphony, the first public criticism of Wagner's work. It was favourable, and helped the young composer to gain a public performance.

14

mangled body gives up the ghost. During the funeral ceremony the bride, uttering one cry, sinks lifeless on the corpse. Returning to Leipsic, I set to work at once on the composition of this opera's first number, which contained a grand sextet that much pleased Weinlig. The text-book found no favour with my sister ; I destroyed its every trace."

We are indebted to the good Rosalie for her objections to this stupid and unpoetic book. Wagner's memory in regard to this juvenile work was not perfect. He presented an autograph of the numbers composed to the Würzburg Musikverein. They are an introduction, a chorus, and a septet, not a sextet as he said. This autograph copy is still extant. Franz Muncker, in his "Life of Wagner," says that the young librettist found his subject in Immermann's "Cardenio und Celinde" (1826), and that he arranged the conclusion of his story after that of the "Bride of Messina." The whole matter, however, may be dismissed as unimportant.

Wagner now went to Würzburg, and at the age of twenty sought employment as a musician through the influence of his brother Albert, then engaged in the Würzburg Theatre as actor, singer, and stage manager. Albert succeeded in securing for him a position as chorus master at ten florins a month. As an evidence of his gratitude he composed for Albert an aria of 142 measures to substitute for a shorter one in Marschner's "Der Vampyr." A phototype reproduction of this aria may be found in Wilhelm Tappert's "R. Wagner ; Sein Leben und Seine Werke." It has no especial interest except for collectors of Wagneriana.

In the year 1833 the young composer set to work on another opera. This was entitled "Die Feen," and although it was completed, its fate was not unlike that of its predecessor. It came to nothing in the composer's life, and though finished on Dec. 7, 1833, received its first performance in Munich on Jan. 29, 1888. Perhaps the best short account of this work that can be given is that of Wagner himself in his "Communication to my Friends." * He says :

"On the model of one of Gozzi's fairy tales ['La donna serpente'] I wrote for myself an opera text in verse, 'Die Feen,' [The Fairies] ; the then predominant romantic opera of Weber, and also of Marschner—who about this time made his first appearance on the scene, and that at my place of sojourn, Leipsic —determined me to follow in their footsteps. What I turned out for myself was nothing more than barely what I wanted, an opera text ; this I set to music according to the impressions made upon me by Weber, Beethoven, and Marschner. However, what took my fancy in the tale of Gozzi was not merely its adaptability for an opera text, but the fascination of the 'stuff' itself. A fairy, who renounces immortality for the sake of a human lover, can only become a mortal through the fulfilment of certain hard conditions, the non-compliance wherewith on the part of her earthly swain threatens her with the direst penalties ; her lover fails in the test, which consists in this, that however evil and repulsive she

* Published in the summer of 1851. It will be found in Vol. I. of W. Ashton Ellis's translation of Wagner's Prose Works. It is Wagner's most important paper in regard to his own artistic development.

may appear to him (in an obligatory metamorphosis) he shall not reject her in his unbelief. In Gozzi's tale the fairy is now changed into a snake ; the remorseful lover frees her from the spell by kissing the snake : thus he wins her for his wife. I altered this denouement by changing the fairy into a stone and then releasing her from the spell by her lover's passionate song ; while the lover—instead of being allowed to carry the bride off to his own country— is himself admitted by the Fairy King to the immortal bliss of Fairyland, together with his fairy wife."

This opera was offered to the director of the theatre at Leipsic, whither Wagner returned early in 1834, and it is evident that a production was promised, for Laube announced in his journal that immediately after "Le Bal Masqué" by Auber there would be brought forward the first opera of a young composer named Richard Wagner. But when Auber's work had completed its run, the director announced Bellini's "I Capuletti ed i Montecchi," and that was the end of "Die Feen" till 1888. Some of the commentators have found the germs of important features of Wagner's later works in this opera, but there is really no evidence that any direct connection exists. It is true that the story is mythical, but Wagner departed from the myth in his next opera. It is, perhaps, more significant that already the young writer showed some skill in the management of pictorial stage effects. The music was wholly imitative of Beethoven, Weber, and Marschner, with some minor borrowings from Mozart. Here and there can be found musical ideas which recur in later works and which are characteristic of Wagner. The score was constructed on the Italian opera model and contains the regular series of arias, scenas, cavatinas, etc. It has even a "mad scene." Furthermore it is a strikingly melodious score, and very light in touch. But the work has now only a historical interest, and its occasional performances in Munich, about the time that the foreign pilgrims to Bayreuth are in the land, are purely speculative enterprises.

Now came another change in the inner life of this budding genius. In the performance of Bellini's opera, he heard for the first time the great artist Wilhelmina Schroeder-Devrient, and the impression which she made upon him was lasting. As late as 1872 he said, "Whenever I conceived a character, I saw her." The imposing effect which her dramatic sincerity and her consummate command of style enabled her to make with the shallow music of Bellini caused Wagner to become doubtful as to the right method of attaining success. He was powerfully impressed with the importance of the dramatic element in operatic performance. The Leipsic Theatre next produced Auber's "La Muette de Portici," and again Wagner was astonished. Here he saw an opera in which rapid action, fiery impulse, and the manifestations of a revolutionary spirit achieved as strong an effect upon an audience as had the potent acting and singing of Schroeder-Devrient.

The light, spontaneous melody of Bellini seemed to him to express more directly the spirit of young life than the heavy music of the Germans ; the plan of Auber's work impressed him as well fitted for combination with the style and character of the Italian music. A union of the two, he thought, would lead toward a true embodiment of the spirit of the time, and so reach swiftly the public heart. The joy of life now became his battle cry. He steeped his soul in the physical literature of the time. He read with avidity the works of Wilhelm Heinse, "the apostle of the highest artistic and lowest sensual pleasures, amongst all the authors of the last century the one endowed with the warmest enthusiasm and finest comprehension for music." * "I was then twenty-one years of age," wrote Wagner, "inclined to take life and the world on their pleasant side. 'Ardinghello' (Heinse) and 'Das junge Europa' (Laube) tingled through every limb, while Germany appeared in my eyes a very tiny portion of the earth." Ludwig Börne, Carl Gutzgow, Gustav König, and last of all, Heinrich Heine, became influences in his daily life and thought. The utmost freedom in politics, morals, and literature, the most passionate physical enjoyment of the fleeting moment, were taught by these authors, to whom the reactionary movement in France against all moral and artistic law seemed most attractive. Mysticism ceased to charm Wagner, and he turned to revolutionary freedom in thought as the highest possible good.

With these ideas seething in his mind in the summer of 1834, while spending his holiday at Teplitz, he sketched the plot of his next opera, "Das Liebesverbot [Prohibition of Love] or the Novice of Palermo." In the fall he was obliged to accept a position as conductor in a small operatic theatre in Magdeburg. There he found in the ease with which public success was

* "Richard Wagner, a Sketch of his Life and Works," by Franz Muncker. Bamberg, 1891.

attained by trivial works further encouragement for the
revolt in his soul. He discharged his duties as conduct-
or with the greatest pleasure, and took much trouble
to give an impressive performance of Auber's "Les-
tocq." He had his "Feen" overture played, and
also an overture of his own to Apel's drama, "Christo-
pher Columbus." He made a New Year's piece out
of the andante of his symphony and some songs taken
from a musical farce. But meanwhile he worked
assiduously at the score of his new opera, with Auber
as his model and Schroeder-Devrient as his hope.

The foundation of the story was taken from Shakespeare's "Measure for Measure," but Wagner altered
the plot so as to introduce the revolutionary element
which at that time played so conspicuous a part in his
fancies. In a "Communication to My Friends"
Wagner many years afterward thus described his
opera: "It was Isabella that inspired me; she who
leaves her novitiate in the cloister to plead with a
hard-hearted Stateholder for mercy for her brother,
who in pursuance of a draconic edict has been condemned to death for entering on a forbidden, yet
Nature-hallowed, love-bond with a maiden. Isabella's
chaste soul urges on the stony judge such cogent reasons for pardoning the offence, her agitation helps her
to paint these reasons in such entrancing warmth of
colour that the stern protector of morals is himself
seized with passionate love for the superb woman.
This sudden, flaming passion proclaims itself by his
promising the pardon of the brother as the price of the
lovely sister's favours. Aghast at this proposal, Isabella takes refuge in artifice to unmask the hypocrite
and save her brother. The Stateholder, whom she

has vouchsafed a fictitious indulgence, still thinks to
withhold the stipulated pardon so as not to sacrifice his
stern judicial conscience to a passing lapse from virtue. Shakespeare disentangles the resulting situation
by means of the public return of the Duke, who had
hitherto observed events from under a disguise; his
decision is an earnest one, and grounded on the
judge's maxim, 'measure for measure.' I, on the
other hand, unloosed the knot without the Prince's
aid by means of a revolution. The scene of action I
transferred to the capital of Sicily, in order to bring in
the Southern heat of blood to help me with my
scheme; I also made the Stateholder, a Puritanical
German, forbid a projected carnival; while a madcap
youngster, in love with Isabella, incites the populace
to mask and keep their weapons ready: 'Who will
not dance at our behest, your steel shall pierce him
through the breast!' The Stateholder, himself induced by Isabella to come disguised to their rendez-
vous, is discovered, unmasked, and hooted; the brother
in the nick of time is freed by force from the execu-
tioner's hands; Isabella renounces her novitiate and
gives her hand to the young leader of the carnival. In
full procession the maskers go forth to meet their
home-returning Prince, assured that he will at least not
govern them so crookedly as had his deputy."

One has no difficulty in tracing in this arrangement
of the story the ideas that lay uppermost in Wagner's
mind at the time. The heavy, hypocritical governor
was a hit at his own countrymen, and the free life of
the Sicilians was his embodiment of the sensuousness
which he had learned from his recent readings to
admire. Auber's "Muette de Portici" no doubt

suggested the theatrical value of the revolution, and as he himself says in his account of the writing and production of this opera: "Recollections of the 'Sicilian Vespers' may have had something to do with it; and when I think finally that the gentle Sicilian Bellini may also be counted among the factors of this composition, I positively have to laugh at the amazing quid-pro-quo into which these extraordinary conceptions shaped themselves." *

The score of the opera was finished in the winter of 1835–36. The composer, who was entitled to a benefit as conductor toward the close of the season, naturally hoped to bring forward his work on that occasion. Unfortunately the manager was in arrears of salary to many of the company, and some of the principal artists gave notice of their intended departure before the end of March. Wagner, who was liked by all of them, succeeded in persuading them to stay a few days longer and to endeavour hastily to prepare his opera. Ten days were available for rehearsals. By dint of shouting, gesticulating, and singing with the singers, Wagner persuaded himself and them into thinking that the opera was in shape for production. There was a good advance sale of seats, but the manager stepped in and claimed the first performance of the work for himself, and so Wagner was perforce content to wait for the second for his benefit.

* Wagner wrote a long account of the conception, composition, and production of this juvenile work. It may be found in his collected prose writings, translated by W. Ashton Ellis. The translation from which these words are taken is in "Art, Life, and Theories of Richard Wagner," by E. L. Burlingame. In speaking of the "Sicilian Vespers," Wagner refers to history, not to Verdi's opera, which was not produced till 1855.

The first performance on March 29, 1836, was, according to Wagner's own account of it, absolutely incomprehensible. There were no libretti, and the singers were so uncertain of both text and music that no one could learn the story of the work from them. This was probably well for Wagner in one way, for the censor had passed the book on Wagner's assurance that the subject was from Shakespeare, and as the audience did not know what it was all about, no unfavourable comment was made on the licentious story. At the second performance, owing to the apparent incomprehensibility of the work when first heard, there were three persons in the auditorium, two of whom were the composer's landlord and landlady. Before the curtain went up, the husband of the prima donna, jealous of the tenor, set upon that singer and beat him so that he had to be carried from the theatré. The prima donna tried to interfere and she was also assaulted by her husband. A general fight seemed imminent, and the manager went before the curtain to tell the audience of three that " owing to various adverse circumstances which had arisen the opera could not be given." Wagner subsequently offered this opera to managers in Leipsic and Berlin, but it was not accepted. Later in Paris he contemplated a performance at the Théâtre de la Renaissance, and a translation of the text was begun. But, as Wagner tells us, " Everything promised well, when the Théâtre de la Renaissance became bankrupt! All trouble, all hopes had therefore been in vain. I now gave up my ' Liebesverbot ' entirely ; I felt that I could not respect myself any longer as its composer."

Mr. Finck recounts an interesting conversation he

had with Heinrich Vogl, the eminent Wagnerian
tenor, in 1891. Vogl said that after the success of
"Die Feen" at Munich it was thought that "Das
Liebesverbot" might also be given, and a rehearsal
was held. The "ludicrous and undisguised imitation
of Donizetti and other popular composers of that time"
caused general laughter,* but it was really the licentious character of the libretto that brought about an abandonment of the plan to perform the work. But the
composer had not yet found himself, and this was one
of his attempts to reach success as others had reached
it, without any realisation of the vital fact that he was
not artistically constituted as they were.

The failure of the Magdeburg Theatre once more
threw Wagner on his own resources. He had borrowed money recklessly, hoping to pay it from the
proceeds of the performance of his opera. Poor
Wagner! All his life he was ahead of his income,
and no amount of experience could teach him to man-

---

* Nevertheless there are passages which suggest the future Wagner.
Note this curious resemblance between a part of the chorus of nuns in
"Das Liebesverbot" and the so-called "feast of grace" theme in
"Tannhäuser."

LIEBESVERBOT.

Sal - ve re - gi - na coe - li! Sal - - ve!

TANNHAUSER.

age his finances. He went to Berlin to offer the "Liebesverbot" to the opera, but without success, and then he heard that there was an opening as musical director at the Königsberg Theatre. To that city, therefore, he went in the hope of securing the post. His Magdeburg friends, Frau Pollert, the prima donna, and Wilhelmina Planer, the actress, had found employment there, and the young composer was drawn after the second of these women by ties soon to become closer. He wrote to his friend Dorn to ask his aid, but it seems that the good Heinrich was unable to do anything for him. Nevertheless the Königsberg post was given to him and he began his duties in January, 1837, after nine months of idleness. Before taking this position Wagner had done two things which must now be recorded. He had written his first prose essay, and he had married. The essay contained some unwise comments on the "Euryanthe" of Weber, whom Wagner as a boy had venerated. He subsequently experienced a second change of heart in regard to this composer. He had a change of heart, too, in regard to his wife, also partly on artistic grounds. Glasenapp says of this hasty and ill-fated union :

"The link was now forged that bound his future to a helpmate with whom he had the smallest possible community of inner feeling. Beyond doubt, he brought her that genuine affection which survived the hardest trials it ever was put to; beyond doubt, the pretty, young, and popular actress meant well by the ardent young conductor when she joined her hand with his at a time of so little outward prospect; beyond doubt she expected much from his abilities. . . .

Any profounder sense of the enormous artistic significance of her husband never dawned upon her, either
in this cloudy period or at a later date ; and though
she made him loving sacrifices, she neither had the
blissful satisfaction of knowing to whom they were
offered, nor of affording the struggling artist a sympathetic ear in which to pour his deeper woes. Wagner
never forgot how she bore the trials of the next few
changeful years without a murmur; nevertheless, this
precipitate marriage of two natures so immiscible
dragged after it an almost endless chain of sorrows
and internal conflicts."

CHAPTER III

KÖNIGSBERG AND RIGA

" To extricate myself from the petty commerce of the German stage."
WAGNER

MINNA PLANER, as she was called, was the daughter of a spindle-maker, and according to Praeger,* who knew her well, went on the stage not because she was endowed with histrionic talent, but because it was necessary for her to contribute to the support of her father's family.   Wagner had become engaged to her while at Magdeburg, and he married her on Nov. 24, 1836, at Königsberg.   He was twenty-three years old and the wisdom of his marriage was what might have been expected of a boy.   From all the testimony it appears that the first wife of Richard Wagner was a good, gentle, loving woman, devoted to him in a mild, unimpassioned manner, and utterly incapable of understanding him.   At the outset of their married life, she was almost as improvident as he, and the burden of debt which he had accumulated at Magdeburg grew larger at Königsberg.   Later at Riga these two poor children lived in a house in the outskirts of a town and had to take a cab whenever they went to the theatre !

* " Wagner as I Knew Him," by Ferdinand Praeger, New York, 1892.

In later years Minna learned the meaning of economy, and she struggled bravely to make both ends meet, when there was nothing but ends. But never did she perceive the genius of her husband, and for that reason she was always impatient with his dreams of great achievements, when money could have been earned by prosaic labour at the expense of hazy aspirations. A woman of tender eye and sweet speech, she commanded the sympathy of Wagner's friends, and it was indeed a fatal misfortune for this gentle dove that she was mismated with an eagle. Certainly she suffered much and bore with patience, not only the privations of domestic life in straitened circumstances, but also the waywardness and eccentricities of a mind beyond her comprehension. Praeger says:

"As years rolled by and the genius of Wagner assumed more definite shape and grew in strength, she was less able to comprehend the might of his intellect. To have written the 'Novice of Palermo' at twenty-three and to have been received so cordially was to her unambitious heart the zenith of success. More than that she could not understand, nor did she ever realise the extent of the wondrous gifts of her husband. After twenty years of wedded life it was much the same. We were sitting at lunch in the trimly kept Swiss châlet at Zurich in the summer of 1856, waiting for the composer of the then completed 'Rienzi,' 'Dutchman,' 'Tannhäuser' and 'Lohengrin' to come down from his scoring of the 'Nibelungen,' when in full innocence she asked me, 'Now, honestly, is Richard such a great genius?' On another occasion, when he was bitterly animadverting on his treatment by the public, she said, 'Well, Richard, why don't you write something for the gallery?'"

That there was another side to the story is certain. From the beginning, though tender and considerate of his wife when at her side, and fully awake to her excellencies, Wagner was a victim of those irregularities of temperament which seem inseparable from genius, especially musical genius. He was inconstant as the wind, a rover, a faithless husband. His misdoings amounted to more than peccadilloes. He was guilty of many liaisons and the Sybaritic character of his self-indulgences increased as the years went by. It is not possible to give the details of these secrets of Wagner's life; but it must suffice to say that while Minna was unsuited to him through her inability to understand him, she was more sinned against than sinning. She was a faithful and devoted wife, patient in adversity and modest in prosperity. It is impossible to say the same of him as a husband. For twenty-five years they struggled along together, and the history of their existence makes one sympathise deeply with this sweet little woman. Enduring the most bitter privations, she saw a husband, who could have earned a good living by writing for the popular taste, deliberately refusing to do so and following the promptings of what must have seemed to her the wildest dreams. This same husband was also luxurious in habit, and was always deeply in debt. The wolf was continually at the Wagner door, even when the master had what to a less fastidious person would have seemed abundance. Wagner, on the other hand, must have hungered and thirsted for a companion who would understand his ideals and his purposes, and be willing to wait with him for the triumph that was sure to come. That these two ill-mated persons would separate was almost inevitable. It may be briefly recorded at this point that they did separate in August, 1861. Minna went to live in Dresden, where she died on Jan. 25, 1866.

The grip of poverty in Königsberg seems to have strangled the voice of Wagner's muse. He says in the Autobiography: "The year which I spent in Königsberg was completely lost to my art by reason of the pressure of petty cares. I wrote one solitary overture: 'Rule Britannia.'" He wrote also about this time an overture entitled "Polonia." The former is lost, but the Wagner family has the manuscript of the latter. The state of the composer's mind, and the actions to which it led are now best told in the "Communication to My Friends":

"One strong desire then arose in me, and developed into an all-consuming passion : to force my way out from the paltry squalor of my situation. This desire, however, was busied only in the second line with actual life ; its front rank made towards a brilliant course as artist. To extricate myself from the petty commerce of the German stage, and straightway try my luck in Paris : this, in a word, was the goal I set before me. A romance by H. König, ' Die Hohe Braut,' had fallen into my hands ; everything which I read had only an interest for me when viewed in the light of its adaptability for an operatic subject: in my mood of that time, the reading of this novel attracted me the more, as it soon conjured up in my eyes the vision of a grand opera in five acts for Paris. I drafted a complete sketch and sent it direct to Scribe in Paris with the prayer that he would work it up for the Grand Opéra there and get me appointed for its composition. Naturally this project ended in smoke."

The history of Wagner's first attempt to reach the goal of the opera composer of his day, the stage of the Grand Opéra in Paris, is worthy of particular note. He

despatched the manuscript and a letter for Scribe to
his brother-in-law, Friedrich Brockhaus, to send to
Paris. Hearing nothing, he wrote again six months
later, and sent to Scribe a copy of the score of "Das
Liebesverbot" as a specimen of his work. Scribe
answered this letter courteously and expressed interest
in Wagner and his music. The composer again sent
him a copy of the scenario of "Die Hohe Braut," but
put it into the post without any stamps and so never
heard of it again, nor received an answer from Scribe.
These facts were recorded in an old note book in which
Wagner made first draughts of his letters. The letter
giving this information was addressed to one Lewald,
a Leipsic journalist who had lived in Paris, and, after
reciting the facts, Wagner asked him to find out
whether Scribe had received the second letter and
whether he was still favourably inclined. If so, Wagner
said, he had another operatic plan in his mind, the
book of "Rienzi," which was just the thing for Paris.
This letter was published in the *Frankfurter Zeitung*,
and will be found quoted in Mr. Finck's "Wagner."
Nothing came of this correspondence, and Wagner
was fated not to enter Paris till some time later, and
then to find it a city of continual disappointment.

In the spring the Königsberg Theatre failed and
again Wagner was out of employment. Like many
other theatrical folk, the moment his salary stopped
he was in straits. So once more he called upon Dorn
for help. This critic had written of the "Rule Britannia" overture that it was a medley of Bach, Beethoven, and Bellini, but he still had faith in the genius
of Wagner. So through his influence Wagner was
appointed director of music in the theatre at Riga, on

the Russian side of the Baltic, under Karl von Holtei as manager. Wagner's wife and her sister, Theresa Planer, were also engaged for the comedy performances. Riga was a more prosperous town than either Magdeburg or Königsberg and at first Wagner, delighted with the higher salary, set to work with evident pleasure. The material in the company was good, and the composer was sufficiently interested in the singers to write several airs for them. He also conducted ten orchestral concerts, at which his overtures, "Rule Britannia" and "Columbus," were performed. He began to write a comic opera entitled "Die Glückliche Bärenfamilie" ("The Happy Bear Family") for which he found the material in a story in the "Arabian Nights." "I had only composed two numbers for this," he says, "when I was disgusted to find that I was again on the high road to music-making à la Adam. My spirit, my deeper feelings, were wounded by this discovery, and I laid aside the work in horror. The daily studying and conducting of Auber's, Adam's, and Bellini's music contributed its share to a speedy undoing of my frivolous delight in such an enterprise."

That inexpressible dissatisfaction with the extant state of the theatre, which finally made Wagner the reformer of the lyric drama, was already at work. The purely commercial spirit of the play-house was rapidly becoming intolerably antagonistic to him. He held himself aloof from the actors. He lived far away from the theatre. He shut himself up within himself, and he began to cherish dreams of breaking the sordid bondage of the German stage and reaching out into a broader and more vigorous artistic atmosphere. He laboured assiduously at Riga for good performances. The manager begged him not to overwork the singers, but the singers liked his enthusiasm and seconded his efforts. At this time, in his unsettled state of mind, he worshipped Bellini, and exalted the Italian song above all other forms of operatic music. He had "Norma" performed for his benefit on Dec. 11, 1837. He wrote articles praising Bellini, and his enemies delighted to quote these forty years later as evidence of Wagner's inconsistency. This undeveloped youth of twenty-four was groping for the path toward which his genius impelled him. That he could not find it at once was not remarkable. He needed the discipline of a larger experience and a closer contact with the great world. As yet he had been but playing in the nursery. His first pointed lessons were about to be received.

In the spring of 1839 his contract with Holtei expired. He could not find employment. He even wrote to the director of the theatre offering to return as assistant director or copyist, in fact, to do anything except, as he ironically said, black boots or carry water. Nothing came of all this, and debts began to press heavily on this most improvident of men. He had a grand opera partly written. It was made on the Meyerbeerian last, and that was fashionable in Paris. Thither he determined to go. But when he endeavoured to leave Riga, he could not get a passport because of his debts. So with his wife and his dog, he stole away like a thief in the night. Minna went across the border into Germany disguised as the wife of a lumberman. Wagner himself was aided by a Königsberg friend, Abraham Möller, who hid him in an empty sentry box till he could slip past the pickets on the boundary line. This same Möller went with him to the port of Pillau, where he, his wife, and his dog embarked on a sailing vessel for London, thence to descend upon Paris.* Paris was to be assailed with one opera completed and another half done. This second work was "Rienzi." During the years of struggle at Magdeburg, Königsberg, and Riga, while searching for material for a grand opera book, he had read Bulwer's novel, "Rienzi," and the subject seemed to him to be promising. The grandeur of the plan and the opportunities for operatic effects fired his mind, and in the summer of 1838 he began the libretto. At Riga, when he was holding himself aloof from the surroundings of the theatre, he was at work composing the music, and in the spring of 1839 the first two acts were finished. He had aimed to make this an imposing work, too grand in plan for production at a provincial German theatre. So it was with this uncompleted score that he put to sea, a sea far vaster than he at the time imagined it to be. For before leaving Riga he had fallen upon Heine's version of the legend of the "Flying Dutchman," and this sea voyage was to make the story vital in his mind and inspire him with the music for the first work in which the Wagner of the immortal dramas was revealed. He says in the autobiography:

"This voyage I never shall forget as long as I live; it lasted three and a half weeks and was rich in mishaps. Thrice did we endure the most violent of storms, and once the captain found himself compelled

* Mr. Finck, who relates these facts, obtained them from articles in the *Frankfurter Zeitung* and from some of Dorn's writings.

to put into a Norwegian haven. The passage among the crags of Norway made a wonderful impression on my fancy; the legends of the Flying Dutchman, as I heard them from the seamen's mouths, were clothed for me in a distinct and individual colour, borrowed from the adventures of the ocean through which I was then passing."

But at length London was reached, and Wagner, Minna, and the great Newfoundland dog were set down at a comfortless little hotel in Old Compton Street, Soho, a dozen doors from Wardour Street, with the purlieus of Seven Dials on one side of them and Oxford and Regent Streets within a few minutes' walk.* His first experience in the capital of Great Britain was the loss of his magnificent Newfoundland dog, to which he was much attached. Fortunately the intelligent beast found its master. Wagner was not far away from the house in which Weber had lived when he was in London, and "to that shrine he made his first pilgrimage." He visited the Naval Hospital at Greenwich and was duly impressed by the sight of the shipping on the Thames. He went over the hospital ship *Dreadnaught*, one of Nelson's old fleet, and he visited Westminster Abbey, where he paid special attention to the Poets' Corner. Standing before the statue of Shakespeare, he was carried away into a long reverie on the manner in which this master had triumphed by throwing aside all the rules of the old classic writers, and Praeger sees in this one of the germs of Wagner's daring reforms. The reverie ended when the patient Minna plucked him by the

* Praeger is the only authority for the incidents of Wagner's **first** visit to London.

sleeve and said, "Come, dear Richard, you have been standing here for twenty minutes like one of these statues and not uttering a word." And that was about the substance of Wagner's first experience in London. He says in his autobiography that nothing interested him so much as the city itself and the Houses of Parliament. He did not visit a single theatre.

He now set out for Paris by way of Boulogne, and at the latter place he tarried four weeks, because the most influential man in the operatic world of France, Giacomo Meyerbeer, was there enjoying his summer rest. It was of vital importance to Wagner to make the acquaintance of this great personage, and he did not think that the expense of a month's stay was too much to pay for the advantage. Meyerbeer, who was not averse to playing the dictator, received the poor German kindly, and after reading the libretto of "Rienzi," praised it highly. He was also flattering in his commendation of the two acts of the music which Wagner had finished. He was dubious as to the future of this young man, who had nothing on which to live while he lingered about the gates of the mighty in Paris, but he promised to do what he could for him. He said that letters of introduction were well enough in their way, but that persistence was the most valuable lever to success. With this advice he gave Wagner letters to Anténor Jolly, director of the Théâtre Renaissance, which produced musical works as well as plays; to Léon Pillet, director of the Grand Opéra; to Schlesinger, the publisher, and to Habeneck, the famous conductor.

Armed with these letters, and with that naïve trust

in the future which deserted him only in his equally naïve periods of utter despondency, Wagner set out for Paris, where he arrived in September, 1839. Only twenty-six years old, he had already produced two operas, partly written a third, and conceived the germ of a fourth, which was to make him famous. His experiences in Paris were to be of the bitterest kind, but of the most vital importance to his future career. He remained in the French capital till April 7, 1842, and in the intervening time disclosed himself as an artist, although as a man he nearly starved. Out of trials and tribulations are great spirits moulded. It was necessary for Wagner to despair of pecuniary success before he found the true path to immortal fame.

CHAPTER IV

"I, poor artist, swore eternal fidelity to my fatherland."—WAGNER

ON arriving in Paris Wagner took a furnished apartment in the Rue de la Tonnelerie. This was in an
unfrequented quarter, but the house was said to have
been occupied once by Molière. The apartment was
cheap, a matter of much moment to Wagner. The
young man at once started out with his letters from
Meyerbeer. They not only secured him an offer for
the immediate performance of one of his operas, but
they also opened many doors to him and insured him
a pleasant welcome. It is quite true, as Jullien* notes,
that he owed all he ever accomplished in Paris to
Meyerbeer and the men to whom he had Meyerbeer's
letters. In the beginning everything was most promising. The director of the Renaissance agreed to accept "Das Liebesverbot," and Dumersan, a maker of
vaudevilles, was set to work translating it. Schlesinger, the publisher, induced Habeneck, the conductor
of the Conservatoire concerts, to promise to try a new
overture, which Wagner had just completed. This

* "Richard Wagner, His Life and Works," by Adolphe Jullien;
translated by Florence Percival Hall. 2 vols. Boston, the J. B.
Millet Co.

was the work afterward known as "Eine Faust Ouvertüre." Wagner, delighted with his prospects, moved to No. 25, Rue du Helder, in the "heart of elegant and artistic Paris."

But suddenly the horizon became overclouded. The Conservatory orchestra did, indeed, try the overture, and Schlesinger inserted in his paper, the *Gazette Musicale*, a paragraph saying, "An overture by a young German composer of very remarkable talent, M. Wagner, has just been rehearsed by the orchestra of the Conservatoire, and has won unanimous applause. We hope to hear it immediately and we will render an account of it." As a matter of fact, the Conservatory orchestra had not been able to make head or tail of the overture, and the Théâtre de la Renaissance, instead of producing the "Liebesverbot," suddenly failed and the manager closed its doors. Quite disheartened by these reverses Wagner laid aside the "Faust" music, which he had intended to make the first movement of a "Faust" symphony. In 1855, when he was living at Zurich, he altered this familiar and admired overture to its present form.

Adolphe Jullien in his life of Wagner says that "If we have only an overture instead of a complete score of 'Faust,' we are indebted for this loss to the gold-laced musicians of the Conservatoire in 1840." Jullien appears to have supposed that Wagner contemplated an opera, but this is certainly an error. On Jan. 1, 1855, Franz Liszt wrote to Wagner and told of the completion of his "Faust" symphony. In his reply to this letter Wagner said :

"It is an absurd coincidence that just at this time I have been taken with a desire to remodel my old

'Faust' overture. I have made an entirely new score, have rewritten the instrumentation throughout, have made many changes, and have given more expansion and importance to the middle portion (second motive). I shall give it in a few days at a concert here under the title of ' A Faust Overture.' The motto will be:

> ' Der Gott, der mir im Busen wohnt,
> Kann tief mein Innerstes erregen ;
> Der über allen meinen Kräften thront,
> Er kann nach aussen nichts bewegen ;
> Und so ist mir das Dasein eine Last,
> Der Tod erwünscht, das Leben mir verhasst ! ' *

But I shall not publish it in any case."

In December of the same year, nevertheless, he wrote to Liszt confessing that the fiasco of the work was "a purifying and wholesome punishment" for having published it in spite of his better judgment.

Another failure of the unfortunate Paris period was in connection with a grand entertainment which Parisians were organising in aid of the Poles. The entertainment was to consist of the performance of an opera, on the subject of the Duc de Guise, the libretto written by "a noble amateur and set to music by the young Flotow." Wagner took the score of his overture, "Polonia," to M. Duvinage, the director of the orchestra, but this gentleman had no time to

---

* The God that in my breast is owned
Can deeply stir the inner sources ;
The God above my powers enthroned,
He cannot change external forces,
So, by the burden of my days oppressed,
Death is desired, and Life a thing unblest !

Goethe's "Faust," Act I, Scene 4.

Bayard Taylor's translation.

examine it. It may as well be recorded here that this overture was lost for forty years, and after passing through various hands came to rest in 1881 in the possession of M. Pasdeloup, the famous Parisian conductor, from whom Wagner recovered it. He had it played in that year to celebrate his wife's birthday.

Wagner was now in dire distress. He had expended all his resources, and he could not pay for the furniture of his apartment, which he had bought on credit. Schlesinger came to his aid once more, and took from him several articles for the *Gazette Musicale*. The first of these, "On German Music," appeared on July 12 and 26, 1840. A translation of it will be found in Vol. VII. of W. Ashton Ellis's edition of Wagner's prose works. Schlesinger had also at this time bought the score of Donizetti's "La Favorita," and Wagner was set to work making a piano arrangement of the music. Through the help of M. Dumersan, who had begun the abandoned translation of "Das Liebesverbot" into French, he obtained a commission to write music to a vaudeville, entitled "La Déscente de la Courtille," which Dumersan and Dupeuty had written. Gasparini * says that the bouffe singers of that time were incapable of singing anything more difficult than the music of "La Belle Hélène" and they quickly decided that the score "of the young German was quite impossible of execution." Gasparini also notes that there was one chanson, "Allons à la Courtille," which had "its hour of celebrity." M. Jullien is probably right in saying that this song was not the work of Wagner, and Mr. Edward Dannreuther in his excellent article in Grove's

* R. Wagner, par A. de Gasparini, Paris, 1866.

"Dictionary of Music" says that it has not been traced. He next endeavoured to earn a few francs by writing songs. He made a setting of a translation of Heinrich Heine's "Two Grenadiers," but it was not so good as that made by Schumann in the previous year, and singers did not take to it kindly. He composed also at this time "L'Attente" by Victor Hugo, "Mignonne" by Ronsard, and "Dors, mon enfant." Much as we like these songs now, at the time of their composition Wagner could not get them sung or published. "Mignonne" was printed in the *Gazette Musicale,* and with two others was afterward reprinted in Lewald's *Europa.* Wagner wrote the editor a letter begging that he might be paid for them at once. They brought him in from $2 to $3.75 each.

It was in the midst of these trials that Wagner wrote his famous story entitled "A Pilgrimage to Beethoven," which attracted the attention of Hector Berlioz. In a review of a concert organised by the *Gazette Musicale* the distinguished Frenchman spoke of the articles in that paper, and said : "For a long time to come will be read one by M. Wagner, entitled 'A Pilgrimage to Beethoven.'" As M. Jullien says, "Little did Berlioz know how truly he spoke." In the intervals of his labours at breadwinning Wagner worked at his "Rienzi." But he sank deeper and deeper into the mire of poverty. His few friends, Laube, Heine, and Schlesinger, could do little to cheer him, though the last named furnished him with the means of life. Berlioz, whom he had met, was not sympathetic to him, though he always cherished a high regard for the Frenchman's talent.

Schlesinger again came to the rescue and decided to

produce at one of the *Gazette Musicale* concerts a composition by Wagner. The "Columbus" overture was accordingly thus performed on Feb. 4, 1841. Schumann made a note of the performance in his paper, and Wagner, encouraged by this remembrance of him in Germany, sent the score to London to Jullien. But the manuscript, postage unpaid, came home to its maker, and he was too poor to take it from the postman. Accordingly that official put it back into his bag and walked off with it. And that was the last that was seen of this overture. Wagner's cup of misery seemed now to be brimming over. He abandoned all hope of success in the volatile French capital. He fled from his accustomed haunts, shunned the society of musicians, all mercenary and insincere as they seemed, and sought that of scholars and literary men, who at least had artistic ideals. He gave up all hope of having "Rienzi" produced at the Grand Opéra, and turned his weary eyes toward Dresden. There was an opera with an inspiring history ; a theatre with a long established routine ; and a company which included such artists as Tichatschek and Schroeder-Devrient.

Meyerbeer was master of the operatic world in Paris, and Wagner, who found him amiable as a man, could not sympathise with the blatant theatricalism of his "Les Huguenots" and "Robert le Diable." Halévy, he felt, had suffered his pristine enthusiasm to fade before the easy temptation of monetary success. Auber, whom he had once loved for his "Muette," he now despised for his unblushing search after popular approval. Only Berlioz pleased him, and he not fully. "He differs by the whole breadth of heaven," he says in the autobiography, "from his Parisian colleagues, for he makes no music for gold. But he cannot write for the sake of purest art ; he lacks all sense of beauty. He stands completely isolated upon his own position ; by his side he has nothing but a troupe of devotees, who, shallow, and without the smallest spark of judgment, greet in him the creator of a brand new musical system and completely turn his head;—the rest of the world avoids him as a madman. " In Paris he met Liszt, who was afterward his best friend, but at first was not pleasing to him. He heard him play a fantasia on airs from "Robert le Diable" at a concert in honour of Beethoven, and his sincere German heart was outraged at such desecration. He felt that the virtuoso was dependent on the public fancy and shallowness, and he compared his own independence with this state in an article entitled "Du Métier de Virtuose et de l' Indépendence des Compositeurs: Fantasie Esthétique d'un Musicien," which he published in the *Gazette Musicale* of Oct. 18, 1840.

On Nov. 19 of the same year the score of "Rienzi" was completed, and on Dec. 4 he sent it to Von Lüttichau, the director of the opera at Dresden, accompanied by two letters, one to the director himself and the other to Friedrich August II, King of Saxony. Neither of these letters seems to have effected anything, and Wagner then applied to Meyerbeer, who on returning to Paris in the summer of 1840 had found his young friend in dire distress. Meyerbeer wrote to the intendant, Von Lüttichau. "Herr Richard Wagner of Leipsic," he said, "is a young composer who has not only a thorough musical education, but who possesses much imagination, as well as general literary culture, and whose predicament certainly merits in every way sympathy in his native land." Three months after the writing of this letter Wagner received word that his opera had been accepted at Dresden, but it was sixteen months later when it was produced. Although he knew that in Fischer, the chorusmaster, Reissiger, the conductor, and Tichatschek, the tenor, who saw golden opportunities in the title rôle, he had friends at court, yet he suffered intense anxiety during the period between the acceptance and the production of the work. The correspondence with Fischer and Heine well shows the extent of this.*

Meanwhile Meyerbeer, wishing to do something to give immediate help to the unfortunate young man, placed him in communication with Léon Pillet, the director of the Grand Opéra. "I had already," says Wagner in the autobiography, "provided myself for this emergency with an outline plot. The 'Flying Dutchman,' whose acquaintance I had made upon the ocean, had never ceased to fascinate my phantasy ; I had also made the acquaintance of H. Heine's remarkable version of this legend in a number of his 'Salon'; and it was especially his treatment of the redemption of this Ahasuerus of the seas—borrowed from a Dutch play under the same title—that placed within my hands all the material for turning the legend into an opera subject." Wagner rushed to Pillet with this sketch for the book of the "Flying Dutchman," and the suggestion that a French text-book be prepared for him to set to music.

* R. Wagner : Letters to Uhlig, Fischer, and Heine. London, 1890.

Pillet accepted the sketch and there was much talk about the choice of a person to make a suitable French arrangement. Suddenly Meyerbeer left Paris again, and no sooner was his back turned than Pillet told the young German that he liked "Le Vaisseau-Fantôme" so well that he would be glad to sell it to a composer to whom he had long ago promised a libretto. Wagner naturally declined to accede to such a proposition and asked for the return of his manuscript. But Pillet was unwilling to part with it. Wagner left the manuscript in his hands, hoping that Meyerbeer would return and straighten out the affair. Pursued by creditors and harassed by want, he now left Paris and went to reside in the suburb of Meudon. Here he heard by chance that his sketches for "Der Fliegende Holländer" had been placed in the hands of M. Paul Foucher for arrangement, and that he was in a fair way to be cheated out of his book. So in the end he accepted $100 for it, and was thankful to get that.

"Le Vaisseau-Fantôme," libretto by Foucher and Revoil, music by Pierre Louis Phillipe Dietsch, chorusmaster and afterward conductor at the opera, was produced Nov. 9, 1842. It was a distinguished failure and was speedily consigned to oblivion. Meanwhile Wagner, who was not forbidden by the terms of his agreement with Pillet to write a German book of his own after his sketches, sat down to pen the text of "Der Fliegende Holländer," which still lives. In seven weeks he had written the whole work except the overture, and then his $100 were gone, and he had to revert to hack work to earn bread. He returned to Paris and lived most humbly at No. 10 Rue Jacob, where he made piano scores of Halévy's "Guitarréro" and "La Reine de Chypre."

It was at this time, too, in the beginning of the year 1841, that he wrote his pathetic sketch, "The End of a Musician in Paris," in which he delineated his own hopes and disappointments, and made the poor man die with the words, "I believe in God, Mozart, and Beethoven." When the score of the "Dutchman" was completed, he hastened to send it to his fatherland, but from Munich and Leipsic came the answer that it was not suitable to Germany. "Fool that I was!" he says; "I had fancied it was fitted for Germany alone, since it is struck on chords that can only vibrate in the German breast." Once more he turned for help to the musical dictator, Meyerbeer, who was in Berlin. He sent the new work to him with a request that he get it taken up by the opera in that city. The opera was accepted speedily, but there was no prospect of immediate production. Nor did Wagner see any prospects of any kind, except starvation, in Paris.

All through the winter of 1841–42 he hoarded his money in the hope of going to Germany for the production of his "Rienzi." In the same winter began the voluminous correspondence with his Dresden friends, Wilhelm Fischer and Ferdinand Heine. The former was addressed ceremoniously in the first letters as a new acquaintance. The latter was an old friend of the Wagner family. In his letters to these two men the poet-composer poured out the tortured anxiety of his soul over the promised production of "Rienzi." He gave invaluable suggestions as to the cast and the performance. He besought first one and then the other of the friends to let him know how and when the work would at length be given. He wrote to the artists, Tichatschek and Schroeder-Devrient. They paid no attention to him. Who was he, this unknown young composer, to trouble the darlings of the public? He grovelled before them and they spurned him. Reissiger's "Adèle de Foix" must be given before "Rienzi," for Reissiger was the conductor at Dresden. Then came Halévy's "Guitarréro," which Wagner knew well indeed. And finally when "Rienzi" seemed likely to get a hearing, Mme. Schroeder-Devrient decided that she needed a revival of Gluck's "Armida." Poor Wagner! He wrote of Schroeder-Devrient to Heine:

"I believe I have already written her a dozen letters : that she has not sent me a single word in reply does not surprise me very much, because I know how some people detest letter-writing ; but that she has never sent me indirectly a word or a hint disquiets me greatly. Great Heavens ! so very much depends upon her ; it would be truly humane on her part if she would only send me this message—perhaps by her chambermaid—'Calm yourself ! I am interested in your cause !'"

At length patience became impossible. He was eager to be on the spot and to exert his personal influence. Furthermore he wished his wife to take the baths at Teplitz. So on April 7, 1842, he was able to turn his face from Paris, the scene of so much achievement, so much disappointment, and move toward his native land. "For the first time," he says at the end of the autobiographic sketch, "I saw the Rhine. With hot tears in my eyes, I, poor artist, swore eternal fidelity to my German fatherland." But a little later the poor artist's name was on every tongue, in every print ; and the great Wagner war broke over Germany. For genius always arouses opposition, and there are few who can follow the seven league strides of a creative mind.

CHAPTER V

BEGINNING OF FAME AND HOSTILITY

" Before the world of modern art I now could hope no more for life."
WAGNER

THE excursion to Teplitz in the early summer of
1842 for his wife's health was of great importance in
the development of Richard Wagner, for it was there
and then that he completed the outline of the book of
" Tannhäuser." When he had finished " Der Fliegende Holländer," he searched for a new subject.
That he had not yet discovered in what direction his
genius called him is demonstrated by the fact that he
was attracted by the story of the conquest of Apulia
and Sicily by Manfred, the son of the Emperor Friedrich II. He made a plan for a book to be called " Die
Sarazener." In this Mme. Schroeder-Devrient was to
have the rôle of a half-sister of Manfred, a prophetess,
who led the Saracens to victory and secured Manfred's
coronation. The plot was shown to Mme. Schroeder-
Devrient some years later, but it did not please her,
and the work was dropped. And now there fell into
Wagner's hands a version of the " Tannhäuser "
legend, and his mind went flying back to Hoffmann's
" Sängerkrieg," which he had read in his youth. He
started to run down the different versions of the story,

and in so doing came upon the legends of "Parzival" and "Lohengrin." But it was the "Tannhäuser" legend which first absorbed him, and at once he began the plan which he completed at Teplitz.

The general rehearsals for "Rienzi" began in Dresden in July, for in spite of the anxiety of Wagner and his lack of information, the preparations for the production of his work had been going on very well. The summer past, the rehearsals were again pushed forward, and the composer found valuable allies in Tichatschek, who was enamoured of the title rôle, and Fischer, who saw the power and splendour of the glowing score. For though "Rienzi" is a work entirely opposed to the true Wagnerian methods and style, it is one of the greatest creations of the real French school, to which it strictly belongs. So on Oct. 20, 1842, the first of the Wagnerian works which still hold the stage, was produced at the Dresden opera and Wagner awoke the next morning to find himself famous. The performance was an almost startling success. Singers, orchestra, public, and critics were alike amazed and overwhelmed by the enormous breadth of style, mastery of technic, and maturity of methods shown in the work. Although the performance occupied six hours, the enthusiasm of the audience was not abated. The next morning Wagner went to the theatre to indicate the cuts which should be made in the over-long work, and was met with a storm of protests by the singers. Tichatschek declared that he would not spare a measure. "It is heavenly!" he exclaimed. A second and a third performance were given with growing receipts. At the third Reissiger resigned the conductor's baton to the young composer, and the public went wild with approval. All the wretchedness of Paris was gone and forgotten. The star of genius was in the ascendant ; the Rhine had been Wagner's Rubicon.

In subsequent performances the work was divided into two parts, the first and second acts being given on one evening, and the other three on another. It was five years, however, before the opera travelled as far as the stage of the opera at Berlin. Thence it went out into all the world. But it was the end of what may be called Wagner's first artistic period. The work was planned and executed on the conventional lines of the Meyerbeerian grand opera, and the music was a compound of French and Italian styles, with here and there a burst of the real Wagner of the future. The artistic convictions which were to develop into a complete theory of the music drama in the mind of Wagner had come to him in the composition of the "Flying Dutchman," and this work became the starting point of what is commonly called his second period, in which he produced it, together with "Tannhäuser" and "Lohengrin."

The winter at Dresden passed happily, for the young composer was enjoying the first fruits of success. Heinrich Laube, the old friend of Wagner and editor of the *Journal for the Polite World,* asked the composer to furnish material for an autobiographic sketch, and this Wagner wrote. This sketch will be found in the first volume of the collected prose writings of the master. It ends with the start from Paris for Dresden. The music of "Rienzi" began to be heard on the concert stage, and the name of Wagner, to be noised about as that of a man of high promise. It would have been extremely easy for him to achieve pecuniary success by writing more works on the popular lines of "Rienzi," but it was not in the man to sacrifice his artistic conscience to public favour.   Already the ideas which were to make him famous in time, but which were first to throw musical Europe into a ferment of dispute, had taken firm possession of his mind.   In March, 1843, August Roeckel, second music director at Dresden, and a life-long friend of Wagner, wrote to Ferdinand Praeger in London :

"Henceforth I drop myself into a well, because I am going to speak of the man whose greatness overshadows that of all other men I have ever met, either in France or England—our friend Richard Wagner.   I say advisedly, our friend, for he knows you from my description as well as I do.   You cannot imagine how the daily intercourse with him develops my admiration for his genius.   His earnestness in art is religious ; he looks upon the drama as a pulpit from which the people should be taught, and his views on a combination of the different arts for that purpose open up an exciting theory, as new as it is ideal."

This theory of a combination in one organic whole, of all the arts tributary to the drama, each part to be as important, as essential as the other, was the theory which Wagner now began to practice, which he first attempted to illustrate in his "Flying Dutchman," and which he subsequently preached in his principal prose writings.   It was the theory which met with active and obstinate opposition from those who either would not or could not climb to Wagner's artistic altitude, and who preferred to see in the opera nothing but a field for the display of pretty vocal pieces and voices trained to sing them.   Wagner's theory made the music and the singing subordinate to the dramatic design, transformed them from ultimate objects into means of expression ; and this was to his contemporaries a revolutionary idea for which they were not prepared.

"Der Fliegende Holländer" was produced at the Dresden opera on January 2, 1843, with Mme. Schroeder-Devrient as Senta, and Wagner in the conductor's chair. The work proved to be a disappointment to the public, which had looked for another "Rienzi" with glittering processions, splendid scenery, and groupings, and imposing action coupled with brilliant music. The simple story and action of the "Dutchman," interpreted largely by music of a purely emotional character, was too serious for the Dresden audience, and at that period for audiences elsewhere. To us of the present day this work is the essence of simplicity, and much of its music seems trivially light. But to the Germans of 1843 it was a most sombre tragedy.

"My friends," Wagner says, "were dismayed at the result ; they seemed anxious to obliterate this impression on them and the public by an enthusiastic resumption of 'Rienzi.' I was myself in sufficiently ill humour to remain silent and leave the 'Flying Dutchman' undefended." The critics of the day were nonplussed by the total departure from the recognised conventions of the contemporaneous stage, and they talked a deal of nonsense about the lack of melody in the work, a sort of nonsense which some old-fashioned persons have not done talking even yet. But we must remember that this new work was an artistic revelation ; and the general public never likes these. It desires only to be amused in the theatre, and only after much struggling yields to the power of genius, and renders homage to true works of art. Wagner himself realised that the general public could not be looked to for support in his radical departure from the easy path of tuneful dalliance, in which it was accustomed to travel. In his "Communication to My Friends" he says :

"From Berlin, where I was entirely unknown, I received from two utter strangers, who had been attracted towards me by the impression which 'The Flying Dutchman' had produced upon them, the first complete satisfaction which I had been permitted to enjoy, with the invitation to continue in the particular direction I had marked out. From this moment I lost more and more from sight the veritable public. The opinion of a few intelligent men took the place in my mind of the opinion of the masses, which can never be wholly apprehended, although it had been the object of my labour in my first attempts, when my eyes were not yet open to the light."

On May 22 the opera was given at Riga, and on June 5 at Cassel under direction of the famous composer, violinist, and conductor, Ludwig Spohr. The poem had been submitted to him and he had spoken of it as a little masterpiece. He had sent for the music, and at once decided to produce the work. It seems strange that Spohr, a composer of tendencies so different from Wagner's and so old a man (he was sixty-nine), should have been one of the first to perceive the power of the new genius. But in a letter to his friend Lüders he wrote :

"This work, though it comes near the boundary of the new romantic school _à la_ Berlioz, and is giving me unheard-of trouble with its immense difficulties, yet interests me in the highest degree since it is obviously the product of pure inspiration, and does not, like so much of our modern operatic music, betray in every bar the striving to make a sensation or to please. There is much creative imagination in it, its invention is thoroughly noble, and it is well written for the voices, while the orchestral part, though enormously difficult, and somewhat overladen, is rich in new effects and will certainly, in our large theatre, be perfectly clear and intelligible." *

* Spohr quotes this letter in his " Autobiography."

The completeness of the popular failure of the "Flying Dutchman" may be estimated from the fact that after the first performances in Dresden it disappeared from the *répertoire* of that opera for twenty years. It was produced in Berlin in 1844, and it was ten years after that when it was heard again anywhere. Wagner himself did not realise either the fulness or the significance of the failure of this work. He had only begun to experiment with his reformatory ideas, and that the public was not ready to accept them with acclaim could not have amazed him, though it doubtless brought him from the rosy heights of sanguinity down to the shadier levels of dull fact. To awaken from a hopeful dream, however illusive, is painful ; and Wagner was momentarily shocked and hurt. But as he had not yet grasped all the details of his own theories, so he failed to perceive the utterness of the public inability to comprehend his dawning purposes. It was not till after the production of his " Tannhäuser," which some of his most ardent admirers still regard as poetically his noblest tragedy, that he realised the solitariness of his genius, the shallowness of a public trained up to be lightly pleased.

Meanwhile he was appointed to a very important professional post. The deaths of Kapellmeister Morlacchi in 1841 and " Musik-director " Rastrelli in 1842 had made two vacancies in the Dresden Theatre. Wagner was one of those who applied for the secondary position at a salary of 1200 thalers (about $900) a year. Von Lüttichau, the Intendant (manager) excited by the success of " Rienzi," thought he had found a rare jewel, and supported Wagner, with the result that the composer was appointed Hofkapellmeister at 1500 thalers (about $1125).   The position of Hofkapellmeister also carried with it life incumbency, and a pension on retirement.   On January 10, 1843, he conducted Weber's "Euryanthe," this being the customary public "trial" representation.   He then made an unsuccessful trip to Berlin to try to push his "Rienzi."   Before the close of the month his appointment was formally made, and his first duty was to assist Hector Berlioz, who arrived in Dresden on February 1, in the rehearsals for his concerts.*

He served seven years as conductor at Dresden and

---

* In his letters from Germany Berlioz wrote of Wagner thus : "As for the young Kapellmeister, Richard Wagner, who lived for a long while in Paris without succeeding in making himself known otherwise than as the author of some articles published in the *Gazette Musicale*, he exercised his authority for the first time in helping me in my rehearsals, which he did with zeal and a very good will.   The ceremony of his presentation to the orchestra and taking the oath took place the day after my arrival, and I found him in all the intoxication of a very natural joy.   After having undergone in France a thousand privations and all the trials to which obscurity is exposed, Richard Wagner, on coming back to Saxony, his native country, had the daring to undertake and the happiness to achieve the composition of the text and music of an opera in five acts (' Rienzi ').   This work had a brilliant success in Dresden.   It was soon followed by ' The Flying Dutchman,' an opera in three acts, of which also he wrote both text and music. Whatever opinion one may hold of these works, it must be acknowledged that men capable of accomplishing this double literary and musical task twice with success are not common, and that M. Wagner has given enough proof of his capacity to excite interest and to rivet the attention of the world upon himself.   This was very well understood by the King of Saxony ; and the day that he gave his first kapellmeister Richard Wagner for a colleague, thus assuring the latter's subsistence, all friends of art must have said to His Majesty what Jean Bart answered Louis XIV. when he made him a commander of a squadron :   ' Sire, you have done well.' "

in that time rehearsed and conducted works by Weber, Spohr, Spontini, Mendelssohn, Mozart, Beethoven, Marschner, Gluck, and others, gaining an immense amount of valuable experience. The arrangement of Gluck's "Iphigenie in Aulis," which he made for the performance of February 22, 1847, is published and approved by critical authorities.

Concerts were given by the court orchestra, and in these he conducted the leading orchestral works, making a special study of the Beethoven symphonies. To this labour he applied all the results of his early studies of Beethoven, and his own ideas about conducting, together with some thoughts formed in listening to the Conservatoire concerts in Paris. The results of these studies and experiences he subsequently embodied in a book called "Ueber das Dirigen." (On Conducting). Among his other duties a certain amount of attention had to be given to the music of the Hofkirche. The choir consisted of fourteen men and twelve boys, and there was a full orchestra of fifty, including trumpets and trombones. Wagner said to Mr. Edward Dannreuther, "The echoes and reverberations in the building were deafening. I wanted to relieve the hard-working members of the orchestra and female voices, and introduce true Catholic church music *a cappella*. As a specimen I prepared Palestrina's 'Stabat Mater,' and suggested other pieces, but my efforts failed." Wagner was as true an artist in the matter of church music as he was in that of the stage, and he returned with joy to the glorious treasure-house of Roman art ; but he found his public just as unfit for that as for his new dispensations in the drama.

Wagner was made conductor of the Liedertafel, a chorus of men organised in 1839, and also of the Saengerfest of 1843. It took place in July of that year and the composer wrote for it " Das Liebesmahl der Apostel," a biblical scene. The story of this celebration of the Lord's Supper by the Apostles was this : The disciples being assembled for the feast, the Apostles arrive with the information that the penalty of death has been prescribed for teaching the Christian faith. Alarm fills every breast and the assembly prays to the Father to send them the Holy Spirit. Heavenly voices sound from above, telling the supplicants that their prayer has been granted. Then follows a convulsion of nature, caused by the descent of the Spirit, and the Apostles and Disciples go forth to preach the Gospel. A chorus of forty men represented the Disciples, and the heavenly voices were consigned to an invisible choir singing in the dome of the building. This bit of stage management, repeated in " Parsifal," was the only feature of the work that attracted special attention.* The correspondent of the Paris *Gazette Musicale*, Schlesinger's paper, wrote, " This last work, the conception of which is most daring, has produced an extraordinary effect, and one which it is impossible to describe. The King after the concert was over summoned the young author to him, and testified his satisfaction in the most affectionate terms." But the *Gazette Musicale's* Dresden correspondent trusted much to the effect of distance in magnifying the size of a popular demonstration. Wagner himself thought well

* In reality the most striking feature of this work is the complete silence of the orchestra till the descent of the Holy Ghost. The composition, however, is weak.

of this work, and lamented in a letter to Liszt in 1852 that choral societies did not perform it. But the truth is that the most noticeable qualities of the composition are purely theatrical, showing that Wagner's genius was entirely for the stage and not for the concert platform.

Spontini, the aged composer of "La Vestale," visited Dresden when his work was produced under Wagner's direction, and was treated by the young conductor with great veneration in spite of his troublesome demands for adherence to his old manner of performing the work. Wagner also entered heart and soul into a project which the Liedertafel had long cherished, namely, to carry the remains of Weber from London to Germany and inter them in the family vault at Dresden. The Liedertafel had raised some money by concerts, and now after Wagner had overcome the opposition of both the King and the Intendant, an operatic performance was given for the aid of the plan. The receipts, added to the funds already secured and augmented by the proceeds of a benefit given in Berlin by Meyerbeer, enabled the Liedertafel to send Weber's oldest son to London for the remains. He returned in December, and on the fourteenth of that month the ceremony of reinterment took place. The funeral music was arranged by Wagner from two passages in "Euryanthe," and he delivered the funeral oration, which was pronounced a masterly effort. It may be read in his collected prose writings. Taken all in all, the work of Wagner outside of the field of operatic composition was important while he was in Dresden. He certainly amazed the Germans themselves by his puissant revelations of the possibilities of the

Beethoven symphonies, and his interpretations of the works of other composers were so striking and so far out of the conventional ruts into which the easy-going kapellmeisters of the country had fallen that a coterie of bitter opponents to him arose. Among them he was known as Wagner, the iconoclast, and this deceptive appellation, applied to him because he was not satisfied with indolent mediocrity and slothful error, clung to him for many years, an empty formula which its users could not justify.

It was at this time that, smarting under the failure of his public to understand him, and half inclined to return to the easy path of popular success indicated by the triumph of "Rienzi," he showed to Mme. Schroeder-Devrient the sketch of "Manfred." She, however, was not pleased with the story and dissuaded him from attempting to develop it. That his own artistic conscience was at work, too, is shown by the words written by him in the "Communication to My Friends."

" Through the happy change in the aspect of my outward lot ; through the hopes I cherished of its even still more favourable development in the future ; and finally through my personal, and in a sense, intoxicating contact with a new and well-inclined surrounding, a passion for enjoyment had sprung up within me, that led my inner nature, formed among the struggles and impressions of a painful past, astray from its own peculiar path. A general instinct that urges every man to take life as he finds it now pointed me, in my particular relations as artist, to a path which, on the other hand, must soon and bitterly disgust me. This instinct could only have been appeased in life on condition of my seeking as artist to wrest myself renown and pleasure by a complete subordination of my true nature to the demands of the public taste in art. I should have had to submit myself to the mode, and to speculation on its weaknesses ; and here, on this point at least, my feeling showed me clearly that, with an actual entry on that path, I must inevitably be engulfed in my own loathing. Thus the pleasures of life presented themselves to my feeling in the shape alone of what our modern world can offer to the senses ; and this again appeared attainable by me as artist solely along the direction which I had already learnt to recognise as the exploitation of our public art-morass. In actual life I was at like time confronted — in the person of a woman for whom I had a sincere admiration — with the phenomenon that a longing akin to my own could only imagine itself contented with the paltriest return of trivial love ; a delusion so completely threadbare that it could never really mask its nature from the inner need.

"If at last I turned impatiently away and owed the strength of my repugnance to the independence already developed in my nature both as artist and as man, so did that double revolt of man and artist inevitably take on the form of a yearning for appeasement in a higher, nobler element; an element which, in its contrast to the only pleasures that the material present reads in modern life and modern art, could but appear to me in the guise of a pure, chaste, virginal, unseizable and unapproachable ideal of love. What in fine could this love-yearning, the noblest thing my heart could feel, what other could it be than a longing for release from the present, for absorption into an element of endless love, a love denied to earth, and reachable through the gates of death alone ? And what again at bottom could such a longing be but the yearning of love ; aye, of a real love, seeded in the soil of fullest sentience—yet a love that could never come to fruitage on the loathsome soil of modern sentience ? The above is an exact account of the mood in which I was when the unlaid ghost of ' Tännhauser ' returned again and urged me to complete his poem."

In these sentences one can easily find the mind of the Wagner who wrote "Tristan und Isolde," and this statement of the mood of the time explains why "Tannhäuser" stands more closely related to "Tristan" than any other of the master's works. Urged now by his artistic soul and dissuaded by the intuition of Mme. Schroeder-Devrient from yielding to a dangerous impulse, he turned once more to "Tannhäuser" and completed the work in April, 1844. "With this work I penned my death warrant," he says ; "before the world of modern art I now could hope no more for life. This I felt ; but as yet I knew it not with full distinctness :—that knowledge I was not to gain till later."

Every work that Wagner wrote was, at least in so far as it was related to his own life, epoch-making ; and the birth of "Tannhäuser" marks a departure so wide that it must receive special consideration. The great Wagner war began with the production of this drama, and in it the composer's opponents first discovered those "unmusical" traits which they celebrated for half a century, till the applause of the civilised world drowned out their noise. The hint at the dissatisfaction of the man with the "paltriest return of trivial love" shows us that the inability of the good Minna to enter into the lofty aspirations of her husband and her inevitable sympathy with the false impulses urging toward swift pecuniary success had already set at work in the mind of Wagner those dangerous longings which were eventually to lead to their separation.

CHAPTER VI

"LOHENGRIN" AND "DIE MEISTERSINGER"

"How curious I am to hear Liszt about it."—WAGNER

WHEN "Tannhäuser" had been completed Wagner went to Marienbad to spend the summer. While there he made the first drafts of his "Meistersinger" and "Lohengrin." He says : "As with the Athenians a merry satyr-play followed the tragedy, so, during that excursion, I suddenly conceived the idea of a comic play which might follow my minstrel's contest in the Wartburg as a significant satyr-play. This was the Mastersingers of Nuremberg with Hans Sachs at their head. Scarcely had I finished the sketch of this plot when the plan of 'Lohengrin' began to engage my attention, and left me no rest until I had worked it out in detail." Returning to Dresden he devoted himself to the preparations for the production of "Tannhäuser." For, in spite of the failure of "Der Fliegende Holländer," the Intendant had not wholly lost faith in the young man. August Roeckel, who was now always at Wagner's side, urged so eloquently the need of new scenery for this drama that painters were brought from Paris. The best singers available were placed at Wagner's disposal, and they vied with one another in studying this, to them, almost incomprehensible work. Tichatschek had to have the music of "Tannhäuser" lowered for him. Johanna Wagner, the daughter of the composer's brother Albert, was specially engaged for Elizabeth, and Schroeder-Devrient took Venus, while Mitter-würzer was the Wolfram. Wagner wrote an explanation of his poem, and placed it at the head of the libretto, which was sold at the door. On Oct. 19, 1845, the work was performed for the first time. The opening scene went for nothing. Schroeder-Devrient, who did not like the music of Venus, sang it badly, and the audience lost the entire significance of the episode. The ensuing scene went well and the popular septet at the end of the act gained the composer a recall. The march in the second act pleased, but the contest in the hall of song dragged listlessly. The evening star song was liked, but then came the true Wagner, the Wagner of the uncompromising music drama. The return of Tannhäuser and his despairing narrative were wholly lost on the audience. The public was unable to understand the aims of a man who, having a heroic tenor on the stage in a grand situation, would not write a pealing aria for him, but persisted in making him tell a story in a long declamatory recitative. The master's intent to put the dramatic situation before them was not discerned. All that was seen was that he would not write a pretty song when he might have done so. "Tannhäuser" reached its fourth performance on Nov. 2. The following day Wagner wrote to his friend Carl Galliard in Berlin, sending him a copy of the score:

"I have gained a big action with my 'Tannhäuser.' Let me give you a very short account of a few of the facts. Owing to the hoarseness of some of the singers, the second performance was played a week after the first ; this was very bad, for in the long interval ignorance and erroneous and absurd views, fostered by my enemies, who exerted themselves vigorously, had full scope for swaggering about ; and when the moment of the second performance at length arrived, my opera was on the point of failing ; the house was not well filled ; opposition ! prejudice ! Luckily, however, all the singers were as enthusiastic as ever ; intelligence made a way for itself, and the third act, somewhat shortened, was especially successful ; after the singers had been called out, there was a tumultuous cry for me. I have now formed a nucleus among the public ; at the third performance there was a well-filled house and an enthusiastic reception of the work. After every act the singers and the author were tumultuously applauded ; in the third act at the words, ' Heinrich, du bist erlöst,' the house resounded with an outbreak of enthusiasm. Yesterday at length the fourth performance took place before a house crammed to suffocation ; after every act the singers were called out, and after them on each occasion the author ; after the second act there was a regular tumult. Whenever I show myself people greet me enthusiastically. My dear Galliard, this is indeed a rare success, and under the circumstances one for which I scarcely hoped."

But in a short time Wagner realised that all the applause was for the popular numbers in his work, and for the stage pictures and ensembles. The drama as a whole had missed fire. The public did not know whatWagner designed. The ethical meaning of his play was hidden from the people. Its artistic purport was undiscerned. The public still went to the theatre to see the pretty pictures and hear the pretty tunes. Of the conception of an opera as the highest form of poetic drama they were as ignorant as they had ever been. A few years later Wagner, in recalling this, wrote in the "Communication to My Friends" :

" The public had shown me plainly by its enthusiastic reception of ' Rienzi' and by the colder treatment of the ' Dutchman,' what I must offer it to win approval. Its expectations I disappointed utterly. Confused and dissatisfied it left the first performance of 'Tannhäuser.' I was overwhelmed by a feeling of complete isolation. The few friends who heartily sympathised with me were themselves so depressed by my painful position that the perception of this sympathetic ill-humour was the only friendly sign about me."

From this time it is possible to trace two features in the career of Wagner. The first was a ceaseless effort to spread by polemical writings the meaning of his doctrines, and the second was a somewhat reckless determination to abide by them, come what might. Wagner has been charged with grave neglect of the practical affairs of life. He was interminably in debt. He borrowed money right and left, and seemed to entertain an idea that the world ought to support such a genius as he while he was pursuing his vast projects. This was not exactly the vein of Wagner's thought, though his reckless methods of expression might easily justify the belief that it was. The man was aflame with the fire of his own genius. He knew what it was in him to produce, and he rebelled bitterly against the constant pressure of his daily needs to turn him aside, to force him to write pot-boilers and abandon his vast conceptions. That a man with such an artistic conscience as Wagner's could not compromise we can easily understand ; and the struggle of the ensuing years began with the decision to bring the public to him, and not to descend to the flowery level on which it reposed.

Criticism of Wagner's writings at this time was of the most discouraging sort. In Dresden, for instance, the leading commentator was one Schladebach. This gentleman was, perhaps, a perfectly honest critic, but he was incompetent to discern the importance of a departure from the beaten path. He constituted himself the champion of classicism, for which poor conventionality is so often and so easily mistaken. When a number of famous masters have laid down the plan of opera, it is extremely confusing to a poor critic to have a stranger appear and propose a wholly different method of treating the form. Schladebach was incapable of understanding the theories and aims of Wagner ; so he praised whatever was good according to the old models, and condemned what departed from them. He was the correspondent of the leading papers of many German cities, and consequently the belief was spread abroad that, while this man Wagner had some talent, he was unpractical and hopelessly eccentric. The managers paid no attention to him, in many cases they did not even look at the scores which he sent them.

Robert Schumann, who went to live in Dresden in the fall of 1844, wrote to Dorn in 1846, "I wish you could see 'Tannhäuser' ; it contains deeper, more original, and altogether an hundredfold better things than his previous operas — at the same time a good deal that is musically trivial. On the whole, Wagner may become of great importance and significance to the stage, and I am sure he is possessed of the needful courage." Unfortunately the pressure of the general opinion of the time proved to be too strong even for Schumann, and a few years later he wrote that Wagner was "not a good musician." Spohr, who produced "Tannhäuser" in 1853, wrote, "The opera contains much that is new and beautiful, also several ugly attacks on one's ears." In another place he complains of the "absence of definite rhythm and the frequent lack of rounded periods." In none of the contemporaneous criticism, except that written by Wagner's intimates, can one find anything to show that the writers had discerned the artistic purpose of the composer. It is not strange that he felt that he stood alone.

Nor is it, on the whole, strange that he was misunderstood. As for the critics, they had formed their standards of opera on the masterpieces of Meyerbeer, Spontini, and Rossini. Even in Mozart they were unable to find justification for Wagner's ideas, for it was his novelty in form that confused them. The public had long placed opera in the category of "amusements." It went to the opera house to hear arias, duos, quartets, sung by great singers, while the story, told chiefly in recitatives, was regarded merely as an excuse for the presentation of certain poetic points of emotion to be set to music. When Wagner came, demanding that the music should be only one means of expression of the whole emotional content of a consistent drama, and that it should not be simply a string of pretty tunes, we can easily understand that he was far beyond the public of his day, and we can picture to ourselves the unhappy Intendant, asking him why it was necessary to be so distressing, and why Tannhäuser could not marry Elizabeth.

In the year 1847 Wagner's musical activity was confined almost wholly to work upon his "Lohengrin." He lived in retirement as much as possible, and gave himself up to the realisation of those artistic projects with which he felt that his entire surroundings were unsympathetic. In the winter of 1845 he had conceived and noted the principal themes. In the fall of 1846 he lived in a villa at Grosgraufen, near Pilnitz, and there he began the music. In the summer of 1847 he secluded himself wholly, and on August 28 he finished the introduction, which for more than half a century has thrilled hearers all over the world. The scoring of the entire opera was completed in the early spring. While Wagner must have realised the artistic value of this new work, he must also have seen how much further he had removed himself from the possibility of public comprehension than he had in his "Tannhäuser." He even doubted the practicability of opera as an art form. The Intendant of the Dresden opera did not feel any sympathy with the composer's experimental mood, and only the finale of the third act of "Lohengrin," performed on September 22, 1848, at the anniversary celebration of the orchestra, was heard in Dresden.

Meanwhile although "Tannhäuser" had been refused a hearing at Berlin, preparations had been made for the production of "Rienzi," and the birthday of the King of Prussia, Oct. 5, 1847, had been chosen as the date for the performance. Wagner went to Berlin to superintend the rehearsals. There he found that anti-Wagnerism was in full bloom. The newspapers began the attack before the work was made known, and every possible rumour that envy and jealousy could invent found ready acceptance. The fate of "Rienzi" was sealed in advance. The manager of the opera discovered that the text of the work breathed a revolutionary spirit quite out of keeping with the temper of a royal fête, and accordingly the production was postponed till Oct. 26. On that evening "Rienzi" was given, but the King was not present, the court did not attend, and Meyerbeer, who was the general director of music, was suddenly called out of town. There was an audience of good size and the applause was of a liberal character ; but there was no hope of permanent success in Berlin without the smiles of royalty and the favourable comment of the press. So Wagner saw his dreams of pecuniary aid from this early work fade away, and leave him to struggle with the constantly growing problem of how to live.

The eventful year 1848 was now at hand, a year which was big with incidents in the personal and artistic life of Wagner. It was in this year that the political troubles which harassed the kingdom of Saxony, and Germany in general, made themselves felt in the opera house and afterward in the career of the composer. The work of the opera house was affected by the general unrest. Nothing serious was undertaken. The list of the season was made up chiefly of works of the calibre of Flotow's "Martha," then in the height of its popularity. The orchestra gave three subscription concerts, and at one of these Wagner conducted Bach's eight-part motet, "Singt dem Herrn ein neues Lied." In March he finished the instrumentation of "Lohengrin" and then his mind began to busy itself with a new subject. The first which attracted him was "Jesus of Nazareth." The impulse which led him to the contemplation of this subject was so plainly identical with that which afterward led to the creation of "Parsifal" that it is worth while to note how far he went in its embodiment. He collected a large quantity of material for this projected work, and published it afterward in a volume of a hundred pages.*

At this period, too, he seriously contemplated the employment of the story of Barbarossa, or Friedrich Rothbart, as material for a lyric drama. His study of this subject was of inestimable value to him in shaping clearly in his mind the conviction that a mythical subject was more suitable than one historical for the purpose of musical treatment. He discovered that he could not give to the splendid personality of Barbarossa the necessary historical back-ground without overloading his opera with a host of minor details too inflexible for musical treatment. On the other hand to endeavour to sacrifice historical accuracy to dramatic requirements would materially change the true character of his subject. He became convinced that only a mythical subject, in which elementary world-thoughts and emotions were typified, would admit of free musical treatment. His serious study of this whole matter resulted in an essay entitled, "Die Wibelungen.—Weltgeschichte aus der Sage" ("The Wibelungs : world-history from the Saga"). The essay treats of the history of the world according to tradition, showing the agreement of history and mythology in certain elementary facts. It was written in 1848 and was published at Leipsic in 1850. It will be found in Vol. VII. of Mr. Ellis's translation of the prose works.

* "Jesus von Nazareth, von R. Wagner." Leipsic, 1887. Translation in 8th Vol. of Mr. Ellis's edition of the prose works.

CHAPTER VII

"ART AND REVOLUTION"

"Behold Mercury, and his docile handmaid, Modern Art!"

WAGNER

THE period of Wagner's life which we have now reached was one of much complication and of important results. With the decision to abandon the subject of Barbarossa he made another, namely that the story of the Nibelungen Lied and its original material as found in the Volsunga Saga would provide excellent material for a music drama. His conception was first formulated in an article entitled "The Nibelung Myth as Sketch for a Drama" (Ellis's translation, Vol. VII.). This was followed by the first form of the text of the drama, "Siegfried's Tod," a translation of which will be found in Mr. Ellis's eighth volume. Wagner's first thought was to tell the entire story of the death of Siegfried and the causes leading to it in one opera, but he was not long in discovering that this was impossible. In June, 1849, he wrote to Franz Liszt, with whom he had begun a correspondence * in 1841 (though it did not become continuous till 1845) in these words : "Meanwhile I shall employ my

* "Correspondence of Wagner and Liszt," edited by Francis Hueffer, 2 Vols., London, 1888.

time in setting to music my latest German drama,
'The Death of Siegfried.' Within half a year I shall
send you the opera completed." In 1851 in a long
letter to Liszt he explained how he had found it impossible to condense the whole story into one drama,
and afterward even into two, and thus how the work
had stretched itself into four separate dramas.

At the time of the writing of the original form of
the book Wagner also conceived some of the germs
of the music, and in this, too, lay the seed of a new
and wonderful development of his genius. His
" Lohengrin " marked a wide departure from the style
of his " Tannhäuser," but in the dramas based on the
Siegfried legend he went much further. He felt in the
beginning that he would be forced to do so, and in
the fall of 1850 he wrote to Liszt : " Between the
musical execution of my ' Lohengrin ' and that of my
'Siegfried' there lies for me a stormy, but I feel convinced, a fruitful world." The correspondence between Wagner and Liszt had grown into warmth
when the latter undertook the preparation of " Tannhäuser " for production at Weimar, where he was the
ruling power in music. No one who desires to be
intimately acquainted with the life of Wagner should
omit reading this correspondence, which throws more
light on the artistic and personal character of the two
men than anything else in existence. It is highly
creditable to Liszt that he early recognised the full
force of the genius of Wagner and bowed to him as a
superior. On the other hand Wagner, who was
hopelessly improvident and always in the depths of
monetary difficulties, came to lean on Liszt as a friend
in all needs.

It is possible that through the influence of Liszt Wagner might have gained wide recognition throughout Germany much sooner than he did, but his own sympathy with the revolutionary ideas of the time led him into direct conflict with authority in Saxony and drove him into exile. The story of Wagner's connection with the revolutionary movements of 1848 and 1849 has had several versions, and it has been the subject of acrid dispute between Wagner's devotees and those who are only candid friends. The story of the Saxon uprising need not be repeated here in detail. Suffice it to say that the impetus of the French revolution of 1848 moved the people of Saxony to demand of their king a constitution, a free press, trial by jury, national armies, and representation. The king refused to accede to the demands. A second time through a deputation Leipsic people demanded what they regarded as their rights and threatened to attack Dresden, if these were not conceded. The king adopted conciliatory measures, which served to allay the excitement for a time, but the people soon saw that under the surface oppression was gaining headway.

Wagner and his friend and assistant, August Roeckel, the latter an enthusiastic republican, became members of a society known as the "Fatherland Union," an organisation devoted to the furtherance of reform measures, but not in favour of direct disloyalty to the king. Before this society on June 16 Wagner read a paper entitled "What is the Relation of our Efforts to the Monarchy?" Wagner had previously drawn up for the government a plan for the reorganisation of the Dresden Theatre. In that paper he proposed that the changes in the existing arrangements be made so that the theatre would be brought into closer relations with the higher artistic life of the people. It was at this period, too, that he wrote "Art and Revolution," in which he still further demonstrated that he saw a connection between political and artistic reform, or rather that he believed the latter impossible under the restrictions of extant governmental control. He aimed at a sort of republican representation in art, a plan by which the literary and artistic elements of the community might have voices in the direction of the theatre. He saw no way of bringing this about except by a change in the nature of the government.

Therefore in this paper read before the Vaterlands-verein he demanded general suffrage, abolition of the standing army and the aristocracy, and the conversion of Saxony into a republic. His loyalty to the king was shown by his proposal that he should himself proclaim the republic and remain in office at its head. This speech was published and it caused a good deal of unfavourable comment. Yet it was not taken very seriously, for Wagner was warned that a Court Conductor should not indulge in such talk ; he wrote a long letter of extenuation to Lüttichau, the Intendant ; asked for a brief leave of absence, and obtained it. And that would have been the end of the matter in all probability, had not open insurrection broken out.

It was in regard to the acts of Wagner in the days of turmoil in May, 1849, that the acrid dispute before mentioned raged in 1892. This dispute was caused chiefly by the statements of Ferdinand Praeger in "Wagner as I Knew Him." Among other things Praeger said, "During the first few of his eleven

years of exile his talk was incessantly about the outbreak, and the active aid he rendered at the time, and
of his services to the cause by speech and by pen
prior to the 1849 May days ; and yet in after life, in his
talk with me, who held documentary evidence, under
his own hand, of his participation, he in petulant
tones sought either to minimise the part he played or
to explain it away altogether.   This change of front I
first noticed about 1864 at Munich."   With this as his
text Praeger set out to show that Wagner was a red-
handed revolutionary, and that he fought on the barricades in the streets of Dresden.

It was my fortune to read these assertions of
Praeger's before they were published.   The manuscript of his book was placed in my hands by his
publishers in 1892 to be prepared for the press.   The
author was dead and no changes could be made in his
work.   It seemed to me at the time that Praeger had
written incautiously of this whole matter, and that at
any rate he might fairly have represented Wagner as
desirous in after years to bury the memories of an unwise exhibition of his republican tendencies.   But of
Praeger's honesty I never had a doubt, nor had I any
reason to suppose that he was not well informed
(through his intimate friendship with Roeckel) of
Wagner's actions in the May days of 1849.   Pohl,
Glasenapp, and Tappert had said but little in regard to
the matter, and, as I was not editing, but merely
supervising the printing of the book, it would not
have been open to me to write so much as a foot-note
of warning to the reader to take Praeger's statements
with a grain of salt, even if I had been fully informed
of the real facts in the case.

But Wagner was not without a champion. Mr. W. Ashton Ellis, editor of "The Meister," and translator of the prose works, published in 1892 a complete answer to Praeger under the title of "1849 : a Vindication." In this he showed that Praeger had formed a theory as to Wagner's part in the revolution and had wrested the facts to make them appear as evidence. He also proved that some of the acts attributed to Wagner were those of a young journeyman baker of the same name. The real facts of the case, as I have sifted them from the conflicting testimony, appear to be these :

Wagner's mind was filled with a conviction that freedom and the honesty of art went hand in hand. His reformatory ideas embraced not only the stage, but its relations to governmental control, through which its artistic character must be touched and guided. The stage could never be brought to represent the spirit of the people till the government was. All around him he saw the relics of feudalism, and the innate hostility of these to that freedom of art and public to which he looked forward made him a republican at heart. His paper read before the Fatherland Union was, as we have seen, a plea for free government and representation by the people, but it was filled with a spirit of loyalty to the reigning king.

When the revolutionary movement took shape Wagner, as Mr. Ellis notes, did not hesitate between the dictates of his conscience and the preservation of court favour. He became, as he afterward confessed in a letter to Liszt, openly active in the movement. But the stories of his firing a musket from the barricades and setting fire to public buildings are pure fabrications. Praeger's narrative of his revolutionary activity is misleading, and Mr. Ellis's pamphlet has quite demolished it. Wagner assisted in getting men and stores into Dresden, and he probably carried a musket while engaged in this work. At the Town Hall he publicly embraced one of the revolutionary leaders after the latter had made a speech. On May 1, 1849, the king dissolved the Saxon diet, and the people went to arms. The insurgents were victorious in the beginning, but Prussian troops arrived 36 hours later, and the revolutionaries were put to flight. Wagner escaped from Dresden and hurried to Weimar, where he took refuge under the wing of Liszt, then actively preparing "Tannhäuser" for performance.

Mr. Praeger says : "Future biographers can no longer ignobly treat the patriotism of Wagner by striving to whitewash or gloss over the part he played during these sad days." It is the hope of the present biographer that he will not be accused of any attempt to conceal the truth in regard to this matter, especially as he has not been able to discover in it anything discreditable to Wagner. His action was injudicious, it was impulsive, it was shortsighted; but it was honest. If in after years Wagner saw that the regeneration of the theatre might be accomplished without the overthrow of extant forms of government, and if at the same time he wished ardently to return to his native land, it was not at all surprising that he expressed sorrow for his actions. It was quite natural indeed that in April, 1856, he wrote to Liszt:

" In regard to that riot and its sequels, I am willing to confess that I now consider myself to have been in the wrong at that time, and carried away by my passions, although I am conscious of not having committed any crime that would properly come before the courts, so that it would be difficult for me to confess to any such."

Disheartened as Wagner was at the inartistic conditions surrounding the theatre at Dresden, it was not astonishing that he rejoiced in the excuse for flight, and that he hastened to Weimar with a jubilant spirit. That Liszt was glad to receive him thus unexpectedly goes without saying. It was this meeting which perfected the understanding between these two remarkable men, and which cemented indissolubly the friendship hitherto dependent on their letters for its support. They came to know one another intimately, and from that time onward Liszt was the main prop of Wagner. As Mr. Finck well summarises it in his life of Wagner: "A few letters had passed between the two, and they had met several times, but it was not until this occasion that their hearts were really opened towards each other, and the beginning was made of a friendship unequalled in cordiality and importance in the history of art, and without the existence of which the world would in all probability have never seen the better half of Wagner's music dramas. It was Liszt who helped him with funds when he would otherwise have been compelled to stop composing and earn his bread like the commonest day labourer; Liszt who sustained him with his approval when all the critical world was against him; Liszt who brought out his operas when all other conductors ignored them; Liszt who wrote letters, private and journalistic, about his friend's works and aims, besides three long and enthusiastic essays on 'Tannhäuser,' 'Lohengrin,' and the 'Dutchman,' which were printed in German and French, and with the Weimar performances of these operas, gave the first impulse to 'the Wagner movement.'"

Of the greatest importance to Wagner was Liszt's understanding of his artistic aims. Wagner said that when he saw Liszt conduct a rehearsal of "Tannhäuser," he recognised a second self in the achievement. Discouraged as he had been on leaving Dresden, his spirits now rose again, and he would undoubtedly have settled down in Weimar to pursue his artistic labours under the protection of Liszt, had not news come that he was wanted by the police. A warrant was issued for him as a politically dangerous person and his description was published. As soon as this news was received, Wagner, acting on Liszt's advice, fled.

So hasty was his departure that, as we learn from a letter of Liszt to Carl Reinecke, he left Weimar on the very day of a performance of "Tannhäuser," which he, therefore, did not witness. This was in the latter part of May. He went directly to Zurich, where he remained a few days and obtained a passport for France. He wrote from Zurich to a Weimar friend, O. L. B. Wolff, that Liszt would soon receive a bundle of scores from Minna, his wife.

"The score of my 'Lohengrin,'" he wrote, "I beg him to examine leisurely. It is my latest, ripest work. No artist has seen it yet, and of none have I therefore been able to ascertain what impression it may produce. Now I am anxious to hear what Liszt has to say about it."

From this same letter we learn that Minna had been left in the city from which Wagner had fled. He says:

"That wonderful man must also look after my poor wife. I am
6

particularly anxious to get her out of Saxony, and especially out of that d——d Dresden."

It is necessary only to say that while Liszt at first had doubts of the public success of "Lohengrin," owing to what he called its "superideal character," he immediately recognised its artistic greatness, and was the first to bring it before the public.

In Zurich Wagner contemplated the stern necessity of doing something toward the support of himself and wife, and he saw in the production of an opera in Paris his only hope. Accordingly he set out for the French capital. Liszt had already written to Belloni, an influential person in the musical circles of Paris:

"In the first place, we want to create a success for a grand, heroic, enchanting musical work, the score of which was completed a year ago. Perhaps this could be done in London. Chorley, for instance, might be very helpful to him in this undertaking. If Wagner next winter could go to Paris backed up by this success, the doors of the Opéra would stand open to him, no matter with what he might knock."

Wagner had a consultation with Belloni in Paris, and was convinced that nothing could be done with his extant works. He decided that he must spend a year and a half in the preparation of a new work, and for that purpose he must live in seclusion with his wife. He tells Liszt in a long letter that he has decided on Zurich, and begs Liszt to make arrangements for an income for him from his works so that he can live to write more. He says that he is fit for nothing but to write operas; he must create some genuine art work or perish. He has arranged to send from Zurich to Belloni a sketch of a work for Paris, and Belloni is to get a French version made. Meanwhile Wagner will be working on the "Death of Siegfried." And so, after this brief and futile visit to Paris in June, 1849, we find him back at Zurich early in July. And now it became his fixed idea to get his wife out of Dresden and settled down in some sort of a home in Zurich. But he had no means. Once more, then, he appealed to the unfailing friend Liszt. He tells the great pianist that he has no further resources, and says:

"You, therefore, I implore by all that is dear to you to raise and collect as much as you possibly can, and send it, not to me, but to my wife, so that she may have enough to get away and join me with the assurance of being able to live with me free from care for some time at least. Dearest friend, you care for my welfare, my soul, my art. Once more restore to me my art! I do not cling to a home, but I cling to this poor, good, faithful woman, to whom as yet I have caused nothing but grief, who is of a careful, serious disposition, without enthusiasm, and who feels herself chained forever to such a reckless devil as myself."

These words go far toward revealing the true nature of the relations of Wagner and Minna. They also do credit to his justice, but at the same time show how completely unsettled he was at this period. Liszt hastened to reply in a letter beginning : "In answer to your letter I have remitted one hundred thalers to your wife at Dresden. This sum has been handed to me by an admirer of 'Tannhäuser,' whom you do not know and who has especially asked me not to name him to you." *

In due time Minna arrived in Zurich only to begin

* In his residence at Zurich, Wagner was also pecuniarily aided by Wilhelm Baumgartner, a music teacher, Jacob Sulzer, a local office holder, Mme. Laussot, and Frau Julie Ritter, whose son Carl was associated with Wagner's musical activities in the Swiss city. Frau Ritter placed a permanent fund to Wagner's credit. Others who aided him will be incidentally mentioned.

to combat her husband's artistic inclinations. He was eager to write "The Death of Siegfried." She urged him to abandon his unprofitable ideals, and to write for Paris the sort of opera that Paris would like. For Minna was ashamed of living on the charity of friends, and for that we cannot blame her. Nor can we even yet bring ourselves quite into agreement with Wagner in the belief that the world ought to take care of him while he was creating his immortal works. Yet there was something large and genial in the conception. The man felt the power that was in him, and he refused to stifle it in order that he might discharge the simple duties of a plain citizen and support himself and his family at the sacrifice of his future, and the future of his art.

It was to this struggle between himself and his own desires on the one hand and his wife and Liszt on the other that his inactivity in musical production for a long period was due. His whole mind was in a state of unrest. Yet the period of his exile proved in the end to be the most fruitful of his life, and in Zurich the name of Wagner was made immortal.

CHAPTER VIII

"Doch ich bin so allein."—SIEGFRIED

THE first years of Wagner's residence at Zurich were occupied with the writing of works designed to propagate the reformatory ideas which he aimed at introducing into the composition and performance of opera. It has been noted that after the first performances of "Tannhäuser" he felt that the public would have to be educated up to his conception of art, and he now set to work to produce the necessary doctrinary essays. Through the kindness of Otto Wesendonck, a music-lover and admirer of his work, he was able to rent at a low price a pretty châlet overlooking the lake, and there he lived and laboured in retirement. He was too profoundly discouraged at first to undertake composition, and for five years he brought forth no music. The problem of how to live stared him in the face in all its frightful nakedness. He wrote to Liszt in the fall of 1849 :

"How and whence shall I get enough to live ? Is my finished work ' Lohengrin ' worth nothing ? Is the opera which I am longing to complete worth nothing ? It is true that to the present generation and to publicity as it is these must appear as a useless luxury. But how about the few who love these works ? Should not they be allowed

to offer to the poor suffering creator—not a remuneration, but the bare
possibility of continuing to create ? . . . Tell me; advise me !
Hitherto my wife and I have kept ourselves alive by the help of a
friend here. By the end of this month of October our last florins will
be gone, and a wide, beautiful world lies before me, in which I have
nothing to eat, nothing to warm myself with. Think of what you
can do for me, dear, princely friend. Let some one buy my ' Lohengrin,' skin and bones ; let some one commission my ' Siegfried.' "

And so he went on, begging Liszt to save him and
his wife from absolute want. He had not even an
overcoat. The score of "Lohengrin" was eventually
sold to Breitkopf and Härtel for a few hundred thalers,
but the means of subsistence were provided for Wagner by Liszt and other friends. Yet even in this
lamentable state of affairs he could not drive himself
to compose. He could only write his literary works.
In these he embodied what has come to be known as
the Wagnerian theory of the music drama, the theory
which finds its only full and satisfying illustration in
the works of this master, though its elementary principals were recognised and obeyed by earlier writers.
He says himself in "The Music of the Future," "My
mental state resembled a struggle. I tried to express
theoretically that which under the incongruity of
my artistic aims as contrasted with the tendencies
of public art, especially of the opera, I could not
properly put forward by means of direct artistic
production."

The principal works written by him in this state of
mind were "Art and Revolution," 1849, "The Art-
work of the Future," "Art and Climate," "Judaism
in Music," 1850, "Recollections of Spontini," 1851,
" On the Performance of ' Tannhäuser,'" and "Opera
and Drama," 1852. Of these the last is the most im-

portant to the student of Wagner's theories, but at the time of publication it was the article on "Judaism in Music" which raised the largest disturbance. The criticisms of Meyerbeer contained in it have been used by Wagner's enemies down to the present day as evidence that he was an ungrateful man. The fact that these censures were wholly for Meyerbeer, the composer, should, however, be borne in mind ; for in Wagner the artist always governed the man, and the timely aid given to him by Meyerbeer in the dark days in Paris was bound to take a place in his estimation second to the popular composer's palpable seeking after the applause of the inartistic masses.

The article on "Judaism in Music" was printed in Brendel's *Neue Zeitschrift für Musik* for Sept. 3 and 6, 1850. Eleven masters at the Leipsic conservatory, where Brendel lectured on the history of music, wrote to him asking him to resign or reveal the name of the author. He refused to do either, thereby leaving the eleven irate masters in a ludicrous position. But the hostility of the press to Wagner was aroused by the article, for his authorship was speedily suspected. In 1869 he issued a revised and enlarged edition of this article and then a host of replies appeared. None of them, however, dealt candidly with the artistic questions. Most of them rested with accusing Wagner of assailing rival composers because they were Jews. The chief points made in Wagner's article were that the Jews were not an artistic people, that they could not be so because they were not sincere, because they had no nation, no home, no language, but lived to please the people of the country in which they chanced to be and whose language they spoke. Mendelssohn and Meyerbeer were quoted as examples.

In "Opera and Drama" Wagner set forth the principles which, according to him, should govern the creation of art work for the stage. These principles we shall have opportunity to examine in detail when we come to the study of the Wagnerian theories. Let it suffice here to quote Muncker's admirable summary of the essay :

"Systematically he examined in what manner all the arts, plastic, mimic, phonetic and oral, had in the antique tragedy combined to the highest mutual purposes, and how thereafter, released from this close and life-like union, the single arts had in their individual development either stagnated or degenerated. He refused to acknowledge the objections that only the mild atmosphere of Greece had been able to ripen the artistic power of intuition and formation, out of which the Attic tragedy had grown. Only the historical man, the man independent of nature, has awakened art to life ; and only he, noble and strong, who through the highest power of love has attained true liberty, can newly create the vanished dramatic work of art, just as he alone, his life and death, is its subject ; for this reason there can be only one principal consideration for art, and that is the true nature of the human race. Strictly Wagner weighed the unsuccessful attempts of the last century externally to combine the sister arts (without any of them giving up their egotistic purposes) in the oratorio and particularly in the opera, the trysting place of their most selfish endeavours. He contrasted with these inorganic species the loving union of the single arts in the work of art of the future, in the true drama, that, like the Attic tragedy, employed the same artistic means, only on a greater scale and with a higher technical perfection, in the same manner and for the same purposes. Like the Attic tragedy, it is to be represented by the people, or rather the totality of different artists is to represent it for the people ; just, however, as the single arts can here for the first time freely and naturally unfold their innermost nature, so the individuality of the single artist can, just in that community with the whole, significantly develop itself."

In this essay he ruthlessly exposed the musical shallowness of Rossini and Meyerbeer. He saw at the time that his criticism of the latter would expose him to the charge of ingratitude, but the artist in him prevailed, and he spoke his mind freely. It should be added that he praised certain passages in Meyerbeer's works, especially the great duet in the fourth act of "Les Huguenots."

In the early years of his exile he undertook once more the task of writing an opera for Paris. He went so far as to make a prose sketch of a libretto entitled "Wieland the Smith." In after years he offered the book to Liszt, saying that it reminded him of a period of pain. The labour of writing this work was distasteful to him, and he began it only at the earnest solicitation of his wife and Liszt. The sketch, which is an elaborated scenario, is included in Mr. Ellis's translation of the prose works.

The only musical work which Wagner did in the early years at Zurich was the conducting of some orchestral concerts, and the superintending of performances at the city theatre. It was at this time

that Wagner's acquaintance with the afterward famous pianist and conductor, Hans von Bülow, began.
Von Bülow had abandoned the career planned for him
by his father and gone to Zurich literally to throw
himself at the feet of Wagner. The master secured
him the post of assistant conductor at the opera,
where he supported his protégé against the intriguing
of the singers and the orchestra. After six months of
experience there Von Bülow was sent with a letter
of introduction from Wagner to Liszt, whose pupil
he became, and whose daughter Cosima he married.
Little did either he or Wagner think at the time that
he would be conductor of Wagner's greatest works,
and that his wife would become the second spouse of
the famous composer.

The year 1850 was made a memorable one in Wagner's life by the first performance of "Lohengrin,"
which had slept in silence for three years. In the
"Communication to My Friends" Wagner wrote of
the movement toward the production thus :

" At the end of my latest stay in Paris, as I lay ill and wretched,
gazing brooding into space, my eye fell on the score of my already
almost quite forgotten ' Lohengrin.' It filled me with a sudden grief to
think that these notes should never ring from off the death-wan paper.
Two words I wrote to Liszt. His answer was none other than an
announcement of preparations the most sumptuous — for the modest
means of Weimar — for ' Lohengrin's ' production."

Even at this distance the words of that letter of
April 21, 1850, are pathetic :

" DEAR FRIEND : I have just been looking through the score of my
' Lohengrin.' I very seldom read my own works. An immense desire has sprung up in me to have this work performed. I address this
wish to your heart : Perform my ' Lohengrin ' ! You are the only one

to whom I could address this prayer ; to none but you should I entrust the creation of this opera ; to you I give it with perfect and joyous confidence."

How faithfully Liszt fulfilled the trust imposed upon him may be seen from one of his letters to Wagner in the course of the preparations for the opera's production.

" Your ' Lohengrin ' will be given under exceptional conditions, which are most favourable to its success. The management for this occasion spends about 2,000 thalers, a thing that has not been done in Weimar within the memory of man. The press will not be forgotten, and suitable and seriously conceived articles will appear successively in several papers. All the personnel will be put on its mettle. The number of violins will be slightly increased (from 16 to 18) and a bass clarinet has been purchased. Nothing essential will be wanting in the musical material or design. I undertake all the rehearsals with pianoforte, chorus, strings and orchestra. Genast will follow your indications for the mise-en-scène with zeal and energy. It is understood that we shall not cut a note, not an iota, of your work, and that we shall give it in its absolute beauty, as far as is in our power."

The date chosen for the production was Aug. 28, the birthday of Goethe, when a large number of visitors would be in Weimar to attend the unveiling of a monument to Herder. Wagner was anxious to be present at the performance, but the risk of arrest, if he set foot on German soil, prevented him from going. Liszt was profoundly moved by the work, but he was not satisfied with the performance nor the reception by the public. The singers did not know how to deliver Wagner's music, and the general public found this, the most popular of all Wagner's creations, quite beyond its comprehension. The performance lasted five hours, owing to the singers' treating all the arioso passages as recitatives, and Wagner accordingly wrote to Liszt explaining how this music should be sung. The whole series of letters on the manner of performing "Lohengrin" is full of instruction as to Wagner's dramatic ideas and the proper method of singing his music. Liszt and Genast, the stage manager, however, saw no way out of the difficulty except by making cuts, and these were accordingly made, but under protest from the composer, who authorised only one in the latter part of Lohengrin's narrative.

The production of the most popular of all operas now before the public was accomplished in the absence of its composer. Indeed, it was not until May 15, 1861, in Vienna, that poor Wagner heard this beautiful and touching work. While it was in course of preparation at Weimar he was labouring at Zurich, as we have seen, and was fighting ill-health, too. His low spirits brought on an attack of dyspepsia, and with this came another lifelong enemy, erysipelas. The cheerfulness and devotion of the unhappy Minna helped him through this trying period, and he further solaced himself by long walks into the forest, accompanied by his dog Peps. He declaimed aloud against the density of the public and the machine-made music of some of his contemporaries, and when Peps answered his master's voice with a lively bark, Wagner would pat his head and say, "Thou hast more sense, Peps, than some of these contrapuntists." Liszt continued to push the fortunes of "Tannhäuser" and "Lohengrin" at Weimar, and although it was three years before the latter was performed elsewhere, it became the fashion to visit Weimar to hear it.

Wagner closed the literary work of this period by writing the "Communication to My Friends," which.

with the autobiography, forms the most satisfactory material for the study of his long career. This communication is rather a story of his artistic development than of the incidents of his life, but it is a fascinating piece of self-examination, and throws more light than anything else upon the motives which led to the composition of the most famous of Wagner's dramas.

It was at this time that he entered upon the task of writing his long-cherished "Death of Siegfried," which he had shaped into a drama in three acts and a prologue in the autumn of 1848. It was in June, 1849, that he wrote to Liszt that he would have the drama completed in half a year. In the spring of 1851 Liszt learned that there was to be a prefatory drama called "Young Siegfried," and on June 29 Wagner wrote to him that the poem was finished. On Nov. 20 of the same year Wagner wrote a long letter, in which he set forth the development of the entire plan. He had found that his story was too long and complex to tell in two dramas, and that he would have to make three, with a prologue.

Thus he had finally developed the plan of what was to be his most imposing, if not his greatest, work, a work rivalling in the immensity of its conception and its dramatic seriousness the ancient trilogies of the Greeks. It was altogether fitting that this *magnum opus* should have acquired its full and definite shape in his mind at a time when his invention was refreshed by abstinence from musical production, and when the appetite for composition was springing up anew. Early in 1853 the poem in its new form was completed, and on Feb. 11 he sent a copy to Liszt.

The latter wrote: "You are truly a wonderful man, and your 'Nibelung' poem is surely the most incredible thing which you have ever done." In a letter written in 1871, to Arrigo Boito, the famous Italian composer and librettist, he said: "During a sleepless night at an inn at Spezzia the music to 'Das Rheingold' occurred to me. Straightway I turned homeward and set to work." He finished the full score of "Das Rheingold" in May, 1854, and in the following month he began that of "Die Walküre." The score of this work was finished in 1856, and part of "Siegfried" was written in the next year.

The sleepless night at the Spezzia inn occurred in the course of a journey into Italy made in 1853. It was a journey made in the vain hope of cheering the drooping spirits of Wagner, who was always fond of travel. His life in Zurich had its pleasant side. He had made friends, some of whom, notably Wille, a former journalist of Hamburg, and his wife, a clever novelist, understood and adored him. But he suffered from dyspepsia, insomnia, and erysipelas, the latter returning with wearing persistency; and he writhed under the restraints of an exile which for artistic reasons he could not but desire to terminate. In some of the cities of Germany his works were performed without understanding and in a way to make him shiver with anguish, yet he was helpless. On all sides he was critically assailed for faults that were not his, and would instantly have disappeared if his operas had been properly interpreted. In Berlin, where he might have reaped at least a decent pecuniary profit from performances, jealousy, intrigue, and Philistinism prevented his works from reaching the stage.

And the demon poverty pursued him to the verge of madness. He suffered from the agonising fear that at length he would be forced to abandon all the splendid imaginations that were burning within him and divert his whole life into the sordid channels of bread-and-butter drudgery. He cried to Liszt and other friends to save him. For this he has been called a beggar; but if we obey Charles Reade's injunction, "Put yourself in his place," the thing wears a different aspect. Wagner was profoundly convinced of the greatness that was within him, and it maddened him to think that he might have to stifle it. He wrote to Liszt: "I am in a miserable condition, and have great difficulty in persuading myself that it must go on like this, and that it would not really be more moral to put an end to this disgraceful kind of life."

In these circumstances, it was perhaps the best thing that could have happened to him that in that sleepless night at Spezzia he was haunted by the thought that the music of "Rheingold" must be written, and went home to chain himself again to the pathetic task of heaping one silent score upon another. The time came when he did not believe that he would live to finish the mighty tetralogy which is now the glory of the lyric stage. But even in the face of despair he could not repress the impulses within him, and back to Zurich he went, and the wonderful measures of the prologue of the "Nibelung" drama sprang into being. Even as he had out of despair forged the links of his first success, "Rienzi," so again the fires of anguish lit the forges of the "Schwarzalben" and the "Wonniges Kind."

CHAPTER IX

A STRANGER IN A STRANGE LAND

" This red republican of music is to preside over the Old Philharmonic of London, the most classical, orthodox, and exclusive society on this globe."—Letter of Ferdinand Praeger to the New York *Musical Gazette*.

THE musical activities of this period were about to be interrupted by a voyage so strange that we can hardly conceive it as possible. That Richard Wagner, the reformer, should go to England to conduct the then most stagnant musical organisation in the world, the London Philharmonic, before the most conservative musical public on earth, seems little short of humorous. Yet this thing actually happened. And the musicians of the London orchestra, to their credit, recognised the greatness of their new conductor and played as they had never played before. But this is anticipating. In Zurich he was already known as a conductor before he had set foot on Swiss soil. So it is natural that the musical authorities of the place should have sought his services as soon as he was settled. We have already noted that he conducted some concerts and supervised the operatic performances at the theatre where Von Bülow and Carl Ritter conducted. But the good Swiss were not satisfied with this. They desired the excitement of the production of one of Wagner's works under his own direction. Accordingly, in May, 1852, "The Flying Dutchman" was given, but because the singers treated the work as an old-fashioned opera, it did not make a deep impression. Nevertheless, in February, 1855, "Tannhäuser" was produced in Zurich. It was at this period, too, that Wagner took up the old "Faust" overture and revised it, making changes which drew expressions of delight from Liszt.

At this time the warfare of two musical societies in London was to have an unexpected influence on the movements of Wagner. The London Philharmonic Society had suffered a split, caused by dissensions which need not be discussed here, and a New Philharmonic had been formed. The insurgent forces proceeded to formulate a plan of campaign which threatened disaster to the older army. As a master stroke, they secured as conductor no less a personage than Hector Berlioz, the famous French composer. It now became necessary for the older body to deal a counterblow. But where to turn for a conductor whose name would excite public interest in such a manner as that of Berlioz they knew not. In the midst of their confusion arose Ferdinand Praeger, the London friend and admirer of Wagner, of whom he had first heard through August Roeckel. Praeger knew that there would be opposition to Wagner, but he knew, too, that the name of the composer of the music of the future would arouse public curiosity and that audiences could be got for his concerts. And audiences were what the staid and languishing Old Philharmonic most needed. On the other hand, there was something to be done in London in the way of correcting false impressions of Wagner's works. As Liszt wrote to him on learning that he was to make the visit:

"The London Philharmonic comes in very aptly, and I am delighted. As lately as six months ago people used to shake their heads, and some of them even hissed, at the performance of the ' Tannhäuser' overture, conducted by Costa. Klindworth and Remeny were almost the only ones who had the courage to applaud and to beard the Philistines who had made their nests of old in the Philharmonic. Well, it will now assume a different tone, and you will revivify old England with the Old Philharmonic."

Liszt as usual wrote in an encouraging strain, but it is likely that he really believed that Wagner would profit by some personal contact with the public. For the history of this incident we must turn to the pages of Praeger, who acted as Wagner's private agent in making the engagement, and who first suggested it to Prosper Sainton, the eminent violinist and a director of the Philharmonic. It was an ill-advised visit, but it was made by Wagner chiefly because he hoped through this introduction to the English public to bring out his operas in London. On Jan. 21, 1855, he wrote to Fischer in Dresden:

"At the end of February I go for two months to London, to conduct the concerts of the Philharmonic Society, for which they expressly sent one of their directors here to persuade me. As a rule, that kind of thing does not suit me; and as I am not to get much pay for it, I would scarcely have consented, had I not therein seen a chance of next year bringing together in London—under the protection of the Court—a first-rate German opera company, with which I could give my operas, and at last my ' Lohengrin.'"

Mr. Anderson, conductor of the Queen's private band,

and an acting director of the Philharmonic, was sent
to Zurich to negotiate with Wagner. Some correspondence had already taken place, and the composer
had demanded conditions which were waived after
conversation with Mr. Anderson. The question of
terms was speedily disposed of, the irresponsible
Wagner saying that he was too busy to think about
them. After Mr. Anderson had returned to London
Wagner wrote to Praeger and suggested giving a concert of his own works, but this alarmed the conservative Philharmonic people, and a compromise was
effected by the promise of the performance of selections. It was arranged that the composer should stay
at Praeger's house, 31 Milton Street, till a quiet and
secluded lodging, where he could go on with the scoring of the trilogy, could be found for him. He arrived
in London on Sunday, March 5, 1855. The lodging
was found at 22 Portland Terrace, Regent's Park.
Much of the work of scoring the "Nibelung" dramas
was done at this place.

The first meeting between Wagner and Mr. Anderson in London was not encouraging. The Philharmonic director suggested the performance of a prize
symphony by Lachner, whereupon Wagner rose ex-
citedly from his chair and exclaimed : "Have I, therefore, left my quiet seclusion in Switzerland to cross
the sea to conduct a prize symphony by Lachner ?
No, never ! If that be a condition of the bargain I at
once reject it, and will return." *

The matter was smoothed over, but it was only one
of several similar outbreaks on the part of the impatient
artist. Fortunately, as Praeger notes, Wagner had a

* Praeger, "Wagner as I Knew Him," p. 231.

keen sense of humour, and when there was a ludicrous aspect in the scenes of misunderstanding it sufficed to put him in a pleasant mood once more.

Wagner made only one visit of ceremony in London, and that was a call on Sir Michael Costa. He flatly refused to call on the musical critics of the London papers, and Praeger says that this was to his injury. This state of affairs is not easy to understand in the United States, where visits to critics are looked upon with suspicion, and are discouraged by the critics themselves. Praeger records that Mr. Davison, the editor of *The Musical World*, then an influential paper, declared that as long as he held the sceptre of musical criticism, Wagner should not acquire any hold in London. In these circumstances it is not at all astonishing that the new conductor received not a little censure. It is only right to mention, however, that some of the London papers viewed his work without prejudice and praised what appeared to them to be its excellences. That Wagner was an uncommonly fine conductor cannot be doubted, and the musicians of the Philharmonic, as soon as they had recovered from the surprise caused by Wagner's spirited and truthful readings of the works under rehearsal and his emphatic insistence on the correct treatment of every passage, together with vigour of style, applauded him and obeyed him with delight.

The first concert took place on March 12. The programme, like that of all the other concerts, was absurdly long, and this was one of the things against which Wagner vainly fought. The list comprised a symphony by Haydn, an operatic trio, a Spohr violin concerto, the Weber aria, "Ocean, thou mighty mon-

44943

ster," Mendelssohn's "Fingal's Cave," overture, Beethoven's "Eroica" symphony, a duet by Marschner,
and the overture to "Die Zauberflöte." Wagner
amazed the Londoners by giving readings of the orchestral works instead of permitting the orchestra to glide
through them in the conventional slovenly way. He
even restored the true tempi in the "Eroica," in which
London conductors had been playing the first movement slowly and the funeral march quickly. He astonished the great body of Mendelssohnians, which
infested London then as it has ever since, by reading
the overture with beautiful colour and intelligence.
Several of the papers abused him roundly, but *The
Morning Post* discovered in him the ideal conductor.

At the second concert on March 26, Wagner conducted the overture to "Der Freischütz," Beethoven's
ninth symphony, and the prelude to "Lohengrin."
The Weber overture had to be repeated, which goes
to show that the audience was not insensible to Wagner's enthusiastic sympathy with the music of his
great predecessor. The dates of the other concerts
conducted by Wagner were April 16 and 30, May 14
and 28, and June 11 and 25. In addition to the Beethoven symphonies already mentioned he directed the
fourth, fifth, sixth, seventh and eighth; also the
"Leonora" overture, No. 3, and the violin concerto,
Mozart's symphonies in B flat and C, Mendelssohn's
Scotch and Italian symphonies, Spohr's C minor symphony, Cipriani Potter's symphony in G minor, and
some minor works. The overture to "Tannhäuser"
was produced at the fifth concert, and was received
with acclamations by the audience and derision by
the critics. It was repeated at the seventh concert by

royal command. The Queen and the Prince Consort attended this concert and had Wagner before them in the salon. There the Prince Consort suggested the desirability of translating some of Wagner's operas into Italian that they might be presented in London, and the Queen said, "I am most happy to make your acquaintance. Your composition has charmed me."

Wagner left London the day after his last concert, and he was heartily glad to shake the dust of the British capital off his feet. Musical criticism in London was stilted, timorous, afraid of new thoughts, unable to grasp any departure from the conventionalities with which it was acquainted, and desperately opposed to musical progress along lines not laid down by Mendelssohn and Handel. It was to be expected that the commentors would oppose the entire Wagner system, but the vituperative strain in the criticisms suggests the probability that the writers felt and writhed under the power of the man. It must be understood that similar criticism was written in Germany, and that the "music of the future," as it was derisively called, was not peacefully permitted to become the music of the day. The younger generation of opera-goers cannot realise the state of mind into which their forerunners were thrown when they were asked to accept the opera as a play, and not as a mere string of pretty vocal pieces, loosely connected by the pretence of a plot. In London, where the opera was the amusement of fashionable society, the music of Wagner was bound at first to meet with opposition. For fashionable society always has been and still is opposed to all that is dignified, serious, or uplifting in life or art.

Aside from some scoring of the Nibelung dramas,

Wagner did little productive work in the uncongenial atmosphere of London. Praeger introduced to him Karl Klindworth, who was engaged to make piano scores of the first dramas of the trilogy. This was, perhaps, the most serious musical achievement of the London visit. It should be said, however, that the friends whom Wagner found in London were the nucleus of a substantial support for him in that capital, and when the movement to build the Bayreuth Theatre took shape, the English Wagnerites were among the sturdiest upholders of the plan.

Wagner went home to Zurich by way of Paris, and soon after his arrival took his wife for a short visit to Seelisberg, near the Alps. Just before starting his dog Peps died, and the letter in which he communicates this fact to Praeger is so full of warm feeling that it is a revelation of the richness of the heart of this singular and erratic being. He said in part :

"The day of our departure for Seelisberg was already fixed, where, as I wrote to you, I was going with my wife, my dog and bird.* Suddenly dangerous symptoms showed themselves in Peps, in consequence of which we put off our journey for two days so as to nurse the poor dying dog. Up to the last moment Peps showed me a love so touching as to be almost heartrending ; kept his eyes fixed on me and though I chanced to move but a few steps from him, continued to follow me with his eyes. He died in my arms on the night of the ninth or tenth of this month, passing away without a sound, quietly and peacefully. On the morrow, midday, we buried him in the garden beside the house. I cried incessantly, and since then have felt bitter pain and sorrow for the dear friend of the past thirteen years who ever worked and walked with me. It has clearly taught me that the world exists only in our hearts and conception."

*A parrot which he had humorously taught to say frequently : "Richard Wagner, you are a great man."

At this period he received an offer to visit America. He mentions it in one of his letters to Praeger and also in other correspondence, especially that with Liszt. He had been told while in London that he would receive this invitation, and he wrote to Liszt : "While here I chew a beggar's crust, I hear from Boston that 'Wagner nights' are given there. Everyone persuades me to come over ; they are occupying themselves with me with increasing interest ; I might make much money there by concert performances, etc. 'Make much money!' Heavens! I don't want to make money if I can go the way shown me by my longing." Indeed Wagner thought of money only as the means which would enable him to carry out his plans for the production of the Nibelung dramas. He was sorely tempted for a time by the possibility of earning enough in the United States to do as he pleased, but he finally wrote to Liszt, with more than usual penetration, that he was not the kind of man to be successful with a money-making speculation, and that he had decided not to be turned aside from his artistic purposes. And thus ended the attempt to induce Wagner to visit a country, which in its state at that time would have been quite as uncongenial to him as London.

CHAPTER X

A SECOND END IN PARIS

"People treat this unfortunate Wagner as a scamp, an impostor, an idiot."—HECTOR BERLIOZ

THE composer now set to work right gladly on his "Walküre." He was eager to finish it and begin the writing of what was still called "Jung Siegfried." For a time he was impeded by the illness of his wife and afterwards his own, but on October 3, 1855, he was able to send to Liszt the first two acts of "Die Walküre." Liszt and his beloved Countess Wittgenstein went over them together and both wrote to Wagner of the marvellous effect which this music made upon them. The last act was finished in April, 1856, and was also despatched to Liszt. In October of this year Liszt, the Countess Wittgenstein, and her daughter went to Zurich to visit Wagner. Of course the score of "Die Walküre" occupied their attention, and Liszt, Wagner, and the wife of Kapell-meister Heim gave a rehearsal of the work at the Hotel Bauer before a number of personal friends. The rehearsal moved the hearers greatly and, as Mr. Finck notes, they "would have been no doubt greatly surprised had any one foretold that twenty years would elapse before this drama would have its first adequate performance."

Together, too, Liszt and Wagner gave an orchestral
concert at St. Gall, on November 3, 1856, when Wagner conducted the "Eroica" symphony and Liszt his
"Orphée" and "Les Préludes." But perhaps the
greatest concert of the Zurich series was that given by
Wagner in May, 1853, when he assembled an orchestra
of 72 men from different parts of Germany, and gave
selections from "Lohengrin" as they were never
given before and have probably not often been given
since. Of his visit Liszt wrote in several of his
numerous letters. He said to his friend Dr. Adolf
Stern, of Dresden, where the name of Wagner was
certainly familiar.

"In spite of my illness I am spending glorious days with Wagner,
and am satiating myself with his ' Nibelungen ' world, of which our
business musicians and chaff-threshing critics have as yet no suspicion.
It is to be hoped that this tremendous work may succeed in being performed in the year 1859, and I, on my side, will not neglect anything
to forward this performance as soon as possible—a performance which
certainly implies many difficulties and exertions. Wagner requires for
this purpose a special theatre built for himself, and a not ordinary
acting and orchestral staff. It goes without saying that the work
can only appear before the world under his own conducting ; and if,
as is much to be wished, this should take place in Germany, his pardon must be obtained before everything."

These remarks of Liszt admirably sum up the situation in regard to the "Nibelung" dramas. It was
long after the date named when they saw the light of
publicity, and in the meantime many events of significance were to take place. Not the least of these
was to be the temporary abandonment of the beloved
Siegfried subject for another work. This was the
great "Tristan und Isolde," which many of Wagner's
admirers regard as his most inspired creation. This

work, like the "Flying Dutchman," the first in which the real Wagner was disclosed, was the fruit of discouragement. Although, through the liberality of Liszt and a few others, including the devoted Mathilde Wesendonck (who is still — August, 1900 — living in Berlin), the Wagners were able to live in comfort, and Minna could afford to make Richard a present of silk dressing-gowns and even silk trousers for house wear on his return from London, the composer saw no way to convince the world that he was not a mere bundle of eccentricities, but a master with living embodiments of the true theory of the lyric drama. He was sore at heart, weary of writing a majestic four-night drama which might never see the light of the stage.

In 1854, while he was at work on "Die Walküre," the stories of "Tristan" and "Parsifal" had come to his attention, and the plan of the former work was sketched. In the winter of 1854–55 he wrote to Liszt: "As I have never in life felt the real bliss of love, I must erect a monument to the most beautiful of all my dreams, in which, from beginning to end, that love shall be thoroughly satiated. I have in my head 'Tristan und Isolde,' the simplest, but most full-blooded musical conception. With the black flag which floats at the end of it I shall cover myself to die." In the midst of a letter of January, 1855, Liszt interrupted the discussion of other matters to exclaim: "Stop! One thing I forgot to write to you: Your 'Tristan' is a splendid idea. It may become a glorious work. Do not abandon it." In the summer of 1856 Wagner wrote again: "I have again two splendid subjects which I must execute. 'Tristan und

Isolde' you know, and after that the 'Victory,' the most sacred, the most perfect salvation."

This "Victory"* was a Buddhistic subject, which Wagner had in mind for a short time, but which he abandoned for the superior attractions of "Parsifal." The leading theme, that of the renunciation of sexual love by the hero, and the assent to it by the heroine, who had at first passionately loved the unmoved hero, bore a close resemblance to the personal purity of Parsifal and to the negation of the desire to live, pictured in "Tristan" as the highest issue of real love. These thoughts appealed to Wagner, whose mind at this time was deeply under the influence of the philosophy of Schopenhauer. The Buddhistic quietism which prevailed in Schopenhauer's philosophy seemed to offer a solution to the life-problems confronting Wagner, and it was natural that he should seek to embody the emotional essence of this philosophy in his music dramas. In 1854 he sent a copy of the poem of the Nibelung dramas to Schopenhauer as a mark of his esteem.

With all these thoughts active in his mind, the poem of Gottfried von Strassburg on "Tristan und Isolde" offered him an opportunity to embody his ideas in what he called the "simplest and most full-blooded musical conception." He was eager to begin a work

* A sketch of this drama, under the title of "The Victors," was found among Wagner's papers, dated May 16, 1856. The hero, Ananda, an absolutely pure man, renounces sexual love. He is passionately beloved by Prakriti, the beautiful daughter of King Tchandala. The heroine, after vainly suffering the torments of unrequited passion, renounces love, and is received into the order of Buddha by Ananda. The idea of salvation through negation is found in Wagner's "Tristan" and again in his "Parsifal."

which might possibly be produced, and all at once came the needed final incentive. Dom Pedro, the Emperor of Brazil, had become interested in the Wagner movement, and he sent an agent to the composer to ask him if he would write an opera for the Italian company in Rio Janeiro. He might name his own terms, provided he would promise to go to Brazil and conduct the work. Wagner was at first touched by this munificent offer, but he soon saw the hopelessness of trying to get Italian opera singers to perform such a music drama as he was about to write. But the Emperor's offer shaped his resolution, and in the latter part of June, 1857, he wrote to Liszt: "I have determined finally to give up my headstrong design of completing the 'Nibelungen.' I have led my young Siegfried to a beautiful forest solitude and there have left him under a linden tree, and taken leave of him with heartfelt tears." And later, in the same letter, he told Liszt that he had decided to write "Tristan und Isolde" and have it performed at Strassburg with Niemann and Mme. Meyer.

On the last day of 1857 the first act of "Tristan" was finished. Wagner now made a trip to Paris, on money borrowed from Liszt, in the hope of being able to arrange a performance of "Rienzi," but nothing came of the journey, except that a waiter in the house in which he lived stole a large part of the advance royalties which Breitkopf and Härtel had paid him on the completion of the first act of the new work. He returned to Zurich and there Liszt sent to him Carl Tausig, the pianist, who became one of his firmest friends and supporters, and who subsequently made the piano arrangement of "Die Meistersinger."

Tausig, with all his genius, was only a boy of seventeen at this time, and he could not satisfy the craving of Wagner for sympathetic intellectual companionship. Unfortunately the composer had in previous years sought this in the society of Mrs. Wesendonck, before mentioned, and aroused the jealousy of poor Minna. This jealousy led in 1856 to an open outbreak, for Wagner wrote to Praeger, who was on his way back to London after a visit to the composer, "The devil is loose. I shall leave Zurich at once and come to you in Paris." But a little later he wrote that the matter had been smoothed over. This, however, was one of the evidences that this unhappily assorted union was slowly nearing its dissolution.

In June, 1858, Wagner sketched the second act of "Tristan und Isolde," and then a desire for quiet and the luxurious atmosphere of Italy took possession of him. Venice, not having any German alliance, and there being consequently no danger of his arrest there, seemed to be the desired place, and thither he went. He wrote the music of the second act of the opera in Venice. Then came news that a projected production of "Rienzi" in Munich had been abandoned, and that a new Intendant, who had no artistic feeling, had gone to reign in Weimar and make Liszt powerless. On the heels of these misfortunes came an attempt of the Saxon government to drive him out of Venice. Disheartened, embarrassed, and in debt, he went to Switzerland and secluded himself on the shores of the Lake of Lucerne. There in the summer of 1859 he completed, after four months' work, the third act of "Tristan." The completed score was placed in the hands of Breitkopf and Härtel, and then Wagner set to work to find an opening for its production. Various difficulties arose. In some places where he could have had singers he dared not set foot. In other places he could get no competent performers.

Wagner's final departure from Zurich was undoubtedly due to the action of Mr. Wesendonck. The nature of the attachment between Mrs. Wesendonck and the composer could no longer be concealed. Wagner had dedicated to her a sonata and the prelude to "Die Walküre." He had set words of hers to music. She was his friend, his confidante. According to M. Belart, in whose "Richard Wagner in Zurich," published in Leipsic in 1900, this whole matter was discussed, Wagner left Zurich finally and suddenly on Aug. 17, 1859. Mr. Wesendonck, when questioned about the matter in after years, said flatly that he compelled Wagner to go. He went to Jacob Sulzer, previously mentioned, borrowed some money, and started for Geneva. Minna Wagner went to Dresden. This was the beginning of the end between them. There is some discrepancy in the dates. There is no doubt that Wagner went to Lucerne when he returned from Venice, but he must have gone again to Zurich in the course of the summer. At any rate when he went to Geneva, he was en route for Paris, and the Wesendonck entanglement was at an end. In 1865 Wagner wrote to the injured husband:

"The incident that separated me from you about six years ago should be evaded; it has upset me and my life enough that you recognise me no longer, and that I esteem myself less and less. All this suffering should have earned your forgiveness, and it would have been beautiful, noble, to have forgiven me; but it is useless to demand the impossible, and I was in the wrong."

It was in September, 1859, that Wagner arrived in the French capital. He settled in the Rue Newton, near the Arc de Triomphe, and there he and Minna, who had rejoined him, received their friends every Wednesday. Among the frequenters of their home were Émile Ollivier, the French statesman and husband of Liszt's daughter Blandine; Frédéric Villot, keeper of the imperial museums; Edmond Roche, afterward the translator of "Tannhäuser"; Hector Berlioz, Carvalho, director of the Théâtre Lyrique; Gustave Doré, Jules Ferry, Charles Baudelaire, and A. de Gasparini, afterward one of the biographers of Wagner.

Later, when the composer had taken a new residence at No. 3, Rue d'Aumale, there was added to this number Cosima, a younger daughter of Liszt, married two years previously to Hans von Bülow. By arrangement with M. Carvalho, Wagner gave three concerts in the Théâtre des Italiens on Jan. 25, and Feb. 1 and 8, 1860. The overture to "Tannhäuser" and the prelude to "Tristan und Isolde" were given at these entertainments. These concerts were pecuniarily disastrous, and so also were two given in Brussels in March. Both press and public were nonplused by Wagner's music, and it remained for Hector Berlioz to lead, by an article published in the *Gazette Musicale,* in the subsequent general attack. Meanwhile Wagner was striving to induce M. Carvalho to produce "Tannhäuser" at the Théâtre Lyrique, when suddenly an unexpected power intervened.

According to Wagner's account given to Praeger, the Emperor Napoleon III., in conversation with the

Princess Metternich, asked her if she had heard the latest opera of Prince Poniatowski. She answered that she had, and that she did not care for such music. "But is it not good?" asked the Emperor. "No," she responded. "But where is better music to be got, then?" "Why, your Majesty, you have at the present moment the greatest composer that ever lived in your capital." "Who is he?" "Richard Wagner." "Then why do they not give his operas?" "Because he is in earnest, and would require all kinds of concessions and much money." "Very well; he shall have carte blanche." The Emperor accordingly gave orders that "Tannhäuser" should be mounted at the Grand Opéra. This stroke of fortune came like lightning out of a clear sky, yet Wagner was not altogether blind to the difficulties in the way of a satisfactory performance.

With the scenic preparations, which now began, he was delighted, for the resources and skill of the leading opera house of Europe were at his disposal. But the lack of singers trained in the theory of the lyric drama hampered him. He stipulated that Albert Niemann should be engaged for the title rôle, and that he should have time to learn the French text. He asked for Faure to create the rôle of Wolfram for the Parisians, but that new and rising star demanded too large a salary, and Morelli was engaged for the part. With this singer, and Mme. Tedesco, the Venus, Wagner had no end of trouble, as they were Italians and utterly without comprehension of his ideas. Marie Saxe, who had a lovely voice, was wooden in her acting, and Wagner had to drive her to movement and life. Edmond Roche's translation of the text proved to be

8

too rough for use, and finally Charles Nuitter, who translated Bellini's "Roméo et Juliette" for the Opéra, was employed to finish the work.

In his anxiety to make himself and his purposes known to the Parisians Wagner published four of his dramatic poems, prefaced by a letter on music,* in which he endeavoured to set forth his ideas. M. Adolphe Jullien says of this letter: "As Wagner had in 1860 already written 'Tristan und Isolde,' and as that poem figured in his book, he instinctively carried the history of his life and of the development of his ideas beyond the point of 'Tristan,' without reflecting that he was thereby exceeding his aim, it being simply a question of preparing people to hear 'Tannhäuser.'" There is no doubt that this letter did much to confuse those Frenchmen who read it and to deepen the spirit of opposition to Wagner's reformatory theories.

But despite all these things the production of "Tannhäuser" might have come to a successful issue but for one difficulty. The gentlemen of the Jockey Club, who were among the most important of the subscribers to the Opéra, and who, of course, did not at any time desire to take the entertainment seriously, were in the habit of arriving after their dinners in time for the ballet. In the original version of "Tannhäuser" there was no attempt at a ballet, and Alphonse Royer, the director of the Grand Opéra, besought Wagner to introduce one in the hall of song, in the second act. This the composer peremptorily refused to do, because it would interfere with the dramatic integrity of the scene. He would consent only to a

* "The Music of the Future," W. Ashton Ellis's translation of Wagner's Prose Works, Vol. III.

rearrangement of the first scene, where, in the revels in the Venusberg, a ballet with some significance might be introduced. He therefore rewrote this scene, cutting out the stirring finale of the overture and raising the curtain on the second appearance of the bacchanalian music, which was now extended and elaborated so that a pantomimic ballet might be danced. He also elaborated the scene between Tannhäuser and Venus, after this ballet, according to his later conceptions of music drama. The music of this new scene was written in the style of " Tristan und Isolde," and, at every performance of the Parisian version of " Tannhäuser," obstinately refuses to amalgamate in style with the rest of the score. This whole new scene was beyond the comprehension of the Parisian public of 1861, but might have been tolerated had it not been a direct affront to the subscribers. A further element of danger lay in the fact that the conductor was no other than Dietsch, the musician who had failed with " The Phantom Ship" after Wagner had sold that text to Léon Pillet.

The first performance took place on Wednesday, March 13, 1861. After the first act the gentlemen of the Jockey Club went out and bought all the hunting whistles they could get, and as soon as the second act began they set up a din which gradually drowned out the performance except in the forte passages. In the third act pandemonium reigned, and the thrilling narrative of Tannhäuser was unheard in the chorus of yells from the auditorium. Wagner's friends applauded, and the Emperor on several occasions led the favourable demonstrations, but Wagner was taught that in Paris the coryphée ranked above high art.

Before the second performance, March 18, Royer succeeded in inducing Wagner to cut out some of the most familiar parts of the work, a portion of the Venus scene, the plaintive melody of the shepherd's pipe, the hunting horns and the appearance of the dogs at the end of the first act, and other similar things, all now known to every lover of Wagner's work. The gentlemen of the Jockey Club again drowned the latter half of the opera with their whistles, despite the plain protest of a large part of the audience led by the Emperor. The third performance was given on a Sunday in order that the subscribers might not be present. That the general public was interested in the opera is proved by the receipts : First performance, 7,491 francs; second, 8,415; third, 10,764.

Wagner now refused to allow the performances to continue, and as he had borne much of their expense he left Paris burdened with debts. But the shrieks of the Jockey Club whistles had resounded across the Rhine and stirred up a Teutonic indignation, which was eventually to be of much benefit to him. The French public was not unjust to Wagner; he knew that and testified to it; but, as Charles Baudelaire exclaimed in his pamphlet on the episode, "'Tannhäuser' was not even heard."

CHAPTER XI

A MONARCH TO THE RESCUE

"My King, thou rarest shield of this my living."—WAGNER

WAGNER went from Paris to Vienna, where he hoped that a production of "Tristan und Isolde" might be arranged. The manager of the opera house, when he learned that the composer was about to visit the city, prepared a special performance of "Lohengrin." This took place on May 15, 1861, and for the first time Wagner himself heard the work which has touched the hearts of so many thousands of his fellow-creatures. At the end of each act the audience forced him to acknowledge its applause, and at the conclusion of the performance he was called before the curtain three times and compelled to make a brief speech. Many times afterward did he refer to the intoxication of that wondrous May night. Think of it! Thirteen years after it was written, and eleven years after its first performance, the writer of the most popular opera in the world heard it for the first time. And even then this master, who had already written "Rienzi," "The Flying Dutchman," "Tannhäuser," "Lohengrin," "Das Rheingold," "Die Walküre," part of "Siegfried," and "Tristan und Isolde," was a wanderer on the face of the earth, an outcast, and could not make a living from his music.

His early works were now beginning to find their way to the stage, but the royalties paid in the German theatres were too small and the performances too infrequent to bring him in a satisfactory income. His first effort, therefore, was to get "Tristan und Isolde ' produced, and to his great joy the manager of the Vienna opera accepted the score. Preparations were at once made for the production. But, alas! that was still far away. The rehearsals began in the fall, but the tenor, Ander, was taken sick, and the whole winter was lost. When the work was resumed, it dragged along at a snail's pace, and finally, after fifty-four rehearsals, the drama was abandoned as impossible. Ander, the Tristan, told Dr. Hanslick that as fast as he learned one act he forgot another. Wagner, on the contrary, asserted in after years that all the singers went through the whole work with him at the piano. However, it is not difficult to conceive that the artists of that day may have found "Tristan und Isolde" impracticable, seeing that the work never was really *sung* until within the last half-dozen years, when the greatest vocal artists of the world appeared in it.

While the Viennese were floundering, Wagner found it necessary to do something toward earning money, and so he undertook a concert tour. In Carlsruhe, Prague, and Weimar negotiations for the production of Tristan fell through, but in the last-named place Wagner was royally received in the summer by Liszt and the other musicians. The general amnesty which had been granted some years before to the rebels of 1848 made it possible for him to go openly to Germany, except the kingdom of Saxony, and even

that was soon opened to him. He planned a tour,
and reluctantly prepared to produce excerpts from his
own works, as the only means of advertising them.
He confesses that dire necessity forced him to this
step so inconsistent with his theories, and his enemies
did not hesitate to taunt him with the inconsistency.
He was alone in his travels, for the winter of 1861 in
Paris had been the last straw on the back of the patient Minna. She could no longer endure her life with
this "monster of genius," who would not be a faithful husband, who wrote works ridiculed by the world,
and could not earn bread and butter. She left him and
went back to Leipsic to live with her relatives. She
and her husband never came together again, though
they occasionally referred to one another with tolerance
in their letters to third persons. Minna died in 1866.

The concert tour began in the winter of 1862, and
Wagner travelled in Germany and even into Russia.
In the latter country alone did his entertainments
bring him in any substantial pecuniary returns. He
was in Moscow when he learned that the rehearsals
of "Tristan und Isolde" had been abandoned at
Vienna. He had become indifferent on the subject.
He was almost convinced that he ought to give up his
attempt to be a composer. Mr. Finck notes that at
one time he seriously thought of going to India as a
tutor in an English family. Let it be borne in mind
that in 1863, while he was still wandering about, giving these concerts, he was fifty years old, and that,
with a surging consciousness within him that he had
created immortal works, he was stared at by people
wherever he went as a freak and a madman, and was
caricatured and ridiculed by almost the whole press of

Europe. And all this because he had dared to say that an opera was a poetic drama, and should be so written, so performed, and so received by the public.

Yet in these years of hardship, sorrow, and discouragement he wrote the text of his most humorous work. He took up and completed the book of "Die Meistersinger," of which he had made a sketch in 1845, just after the production of "Tannhäuser." This work was done in the course of a temporary residence in Paris in the winter of 1861–62. The text was published, or rather printed for circulation among his friends, in 1862. The version now known to all music lovers shows many changes. The copyright of the drama was sold to Messrs. Schott, of Mainz, and accordingly Wagner went to Biebrich, a little town opposite Mainz, to compose the music. He subsequently continued his labours at Penzing, near Vienna, and there also he published the text of "Der Ring des Nibelungen" as a piece of literature. He declared that he did not expect to finish the music, and that he had no hope of living to see the work performed. It was at this time that Wagner's affairs sank into such a state that he was overwhelmed. He decided to go to Russia and remain there the rest of his life. But first he must finish the score of "Die Meistersinger." So he wrote to his old friend, Mme. Wille, at Zurich, and asked her to receive him for a short time. Like the familiar man in the play, he arrived on the heels of his letter, and Frau Wille had to exert herself to make all ready for the great man. But she realised that all Wagner's doings and sayings would have historical importance, and she made notes from which she afterward published a valuable article.

From this we learn that the great musician while in her home was the prey of conflicting emotions, but was most frequently plunged in despair. He had a deep, a passionate conviction of his own powers. He was inspired with an absolute prevision of the world-wide glorification that would come to his name when once his works were adequately made known. And because of this he suffered agonies of mind and heart while the scores lay silent in his desk. He cried out against the niggardliness of a world which refused him a few luxuries when he was preparing joy for so many thousands. He felt that the time would come when the world would be ready to heap all kinds of honours on his head, but he feared that it would come too late.

Yet in this state of mind the genius of production would not sleep within him. He worked unceasingly at the score of "Die Meistersinger," and, according to Mme. Wille's own account, with a perfect satisfaction as to its greatness. Wagner had what has frequently been called the vanity of men of genius. He spoke with childish naïveté of his works. He spoke of himself without hesitation as a great man, and he had not even the slightest consciousness that a difference of opinion was possible. But such vanity is pardonable in a man who so thoroughly justifies it. Cicero, Napoleon, and Beethoven had a similar sort of vanity. The world has learned to smile indulgently upon it. And whereas in Wagner's lifetime his vanity and love of luxury made him perhaps not an altogether agreeable companion, they detract in no way from his claims to recognition as one of the most remarkable men ever born.

One day, while at the Willes', Wagner received

word that his Viennese creditors were on his track, and he resolved to go away. He was at his wits' end, for everywhere "Tristan" was pronounced impossible, and "Die Meistersinger" was refused before the score was seen. He went to Stuttgart with the vain hope that he could arrange for the performance of some of his operas there and thus earn enough to stave off misfortune for a time. And even while he had fled, his fortune was pursuing him. At last to this weary wanderer, this "Flying Dutchman" of musical history, were to come rest and peace and a perfect love. At last one dream of all his years of insatiable longing was to be realised. At last his scores would sound "from off the death-wan paper," and the world would learn the true might of Richard Wagner.

In the preface to the poem of the "Nibelung's Ring," Wagner had described the means and manner of performance — had, in a word, laid down the plan of Bayreuth. But he felt that only a monarch could afford to give the financial support to such a scheme, and he wrote, "Will that king be found?" Now there was a young prince who fed his soul on Wagner's works and who worshipped the master in secret. At fifteen he had heard "Lohengrin," and, like all whose operatic experience began with Wagner, he had become an ardent Wagnerite. He had watched his idol's career of misfortune in helpless pity. And then suddenly the King of Bavaria went to join his fathers and this generous youth seated himself upon the throne. One of his first acts was to send a messenger to bid Wagner come to his capital and complete the majestic labours of his life in peace.

Herr Sauer, the appointed messenger, searched high and low. He delved in Wagner's old haunts at Vienna, but the very memory of the mad composer seemed to have gone. So he went down to Switzerland and hunted in Zurich and Lucerne. But there was no Wagner. Then Baron Hornstein, a minor composer, met him out in a boat on Lake Lucerne and told him that Wagner was in Stuttgart. At any rate this is the story told to Mr. Finck by Heinrich Vogl, the tenor, who said that Wagner confirmed it. Sauer took Wagner to Munich, and there on May 4, 1864, he wrote to Frau Wille that it all seemed like a dream.

"He wants me to be with him always, to work, to rest, to produce my works; he will give me everything I need; I am to finish my Nibelungen and he will have them performed as I wish. I am to be my own unrestricted master; not Kapellmeister — nothing but myself and his friend. All troubles are to be taken from me; I shall have whatever I need, if only I stay with him."

This enthusiastic youth of eighteen, with a royal treasury at his disposal, and the splendid musical traditions of Munich reaching away behind him to the era of Orlando Lasso, was to be the saviour of Wagner's work. He was already a worshipper of the art of the master, and he speedily proved himself to be attached to him by a deep personal affection. On Lake Starnberg, no great distance from Munich, the King gave Wagner a pretty villa, and there he spent the summer of 1864. The King's summer palace was only a mile or two away, and the monarch and composer were much in one another's company. The young King's friendship was of a passionate kind, such as only romantic youths entertain, and, unfortunately, of the sort that was sure in the course of time to lead to scandalous comment in the polite society of a court.

In honour of his new patron Wagner wrote in that summer the "Huldigungs Marsch," which has the romantic character implanted in all Wagner's concert pieces. Here, too, at the wish of his young patron, Wagner wrote his essay on "State and Religion" (Mr. Ellis's translation, Vol. IV.). As in all the other writings of Wagner bearing upon the conduct of a State, in this essay art is held up as the panacea for all ills. He saw the ideal of the State embodied in the person of the King, who by the nature of his position must take life most seriously, and in whose inability to attain ideal justice and humanity there is something tragic. But for these ideals the King is bound to strive and so must lead a life of misery if he does not seek the only solace, namely, religion. Then follows a long definition of religion. How shall the King endure? By refreshing his mind with the pleasing distractions of art. The essay easily convinces the reader that Wagner was not, as he often wished be, a philosopher, but simply an artist whose reasoning flexibly followed the flow of his ruling instincts.

So passed the first summer under the royal protection, pleasantly, almost idyllically. But now serious work was to begin. In the autumn the two friends returned to Munich. A residence in a quiet part of the city was set apart for the use of Wagner, and he prepared to resume the production of his masterpieces. Hans von Bülow, his former pupil, was summoned with a view to his becoming the conductor of "Tristan und Isolde." This beginning was effected in the summer, for Mme. von Bülow, little dreaming whither she was going, arrived in Munich with her two daughters in June, and Von Bülow followed the next month. The influence of Cosima von Bülow upon Wagner began at once. He had been lonely and depressed ever since his separation from his wife, and the advent of this woman of artistic temperament and commanding intellect, the fruit of the illicit union of Franz Liszt and the brilliant Countess d'Agoult (the "Daniel Stern" of French literature), aroused in him new conceptions of the "eternal woman-soul."

Peter Cornelius, the pupil of Liszt and composer of the admirable "Barber of Bagdad," was also summoned, and not far away lived the young Hans Richter, afterward to be one of the principal conductors of Wagner's music. The ardent young King was all eagerness to begin the work of performance, but Wagner was hampered by the want of singers capable of singing such new music as that of "Tristan und Isolde." In Ludwig Schnorr von Carolsfeld and his wife were found representatives of the hero and heroine, but Wagner foresaw that the method of singing the music drama of the future would need wide study, and so he wrote a long paper on a plan for a school of music in Munich. This paper gave a detailed outline of the operation of a conservatory, and set forth as its purpose the artistic interpretation of the works of the older German masters, and leading thence to the treatment of the modern music drama. The old Munich Conservatory was closed by the King's order in the early summer of 1865. But the plan to reopen it on the lines laid down by Wagner failed through the hostility of the local musicians. It was reopened in 1867 under Hans von Bülow, who was able to carry out Wagner's ideas only to a limited extent.

In October the King decided that "Der Ring des Nibelungen" should be produced, and the date was set for it three years thence. On December 4 "Der Fliegende Holländer" was performed, and on December 11, January 1, and February 1 Wagner conducted concerts. In January Gottfried Semper, the architect, was called to Munich to be consulted about plans for the new theatre for the Nibelung dramas. And meanwhile the preparations for the production of "Tristan" went forward. Wagner's star was at last in the ascendant.

CHAPTER XII

SOME IDEALS REALISED

"Lausch', Kind ! Das ist ein Meisterlied."—DIE MEISTERSINGER

AND now, under the guidance of a monarch to whom Wagner's art was almost the inspiration of life, Munich, which in 1858 had rejected "Der Fliegende Holländer" as unsuitable to the German stage, was about to produce "Tristan und Isolde," the supreme essence of Wagner's matured genius. In April, 1865, the composer wrote a general letter inviting his friends everywhere to go to Munich and attend this first of all Wagner festivals, three performances of a work already eight years old, set down for May 15, 18, and 22. But postponements took place, and the work was not produced until June 10. It was repeated on June 13 and 19 and July 1. Each performance was attended by a large audience, and the applause was of the most vigorous kind. Much of the success was due to the superb conducting of Von Bülow, whom Wagner called his second self, and the inspired interpretation of Tristan by Ludwig Schnorr. Wagner declared that his ideal was fully realised by this great artist, and he bemoaned Schnorr's subsequent untimely death as the greatest possible loss to him and his work.* The

* A gentleman, who in his youth heard Schnorr sing Tristan, has

composer's essay on this singer is a most eloquent tribute from a creative to an interpretative artist, and throw invaluable light on Wagner's theories of performance in general and the presentation of "Tristan und Isolde" in particular.

It may easily be understood that this was a period of unalloyed happiness for Wagner. His highest dreams were being realised, and he was working out his artistic purposes with a free hand. But such an Elysium could not last. His enemies were striving against him with might and main. The newspapers were used unscrupulously to spread all kinds of damaging reports. It was said that he was endeavouring to substitute art for religion in the State, that he was leading the young King into reckless extravagances which threatened the stability of the national treasury. The King was, indeed, considering the plan to build a special theatre for the production of the Nibelung dramas. Such a theatre was subsequently built at Bayreuth, and Munich might have had the honour and the profit which have since accrued to that little city, had it not been for the determined opposition of narrow-minded intriguers.*

The story was published that the new theatre was

assured me that he was not the typical German representative of the part, but that he approached in his singing the manner of Jean de Reszke. Schnorr's voice, my informant says, was a beautiful, sweet, lyric tenor, and his style was one in which a fluent and touching cantabile was the most conspicuous feature. This statement, in conjunction with Wagner's declaration that Schnorr fulfilled his ideal, should contribute something toward a destruction of the foolish notion that Wagner's music ought not to be beautifully sung.

* The Prinz Regenten Theatre, opened in the summer of 1901, stands almost on the spot on which King Ludwig's was to stand.

to cost millions. Other equally wild assertions were made. The people became aroused, and finally police and court officials represented to the King that Wagner's life was in danger. The composer had already answered in a calm and dignified letter the various newspaper calumnies, but that availed him nothing. The King besought him to leave Munich, in order that public confidence might be restored. And accordingly, after a stay of a year and a half in the city, he departed in December, 1865, to his favourite refuge, Switzerland. He made a short stay at Vevey and Geneva, and then in February, 1866, settled at Triebschen, near Lucerne, where he remained, with little interruption, till he removed to Bayreuth in 1872. Most of the frantic opposition to the royal support of Wagner appeared to have arisen from the project of bringing to ideal production the Nibelung cycle, and so this was for the time abandoned. As Wagner himself tells us, in his "Final Report" on the preparation of these dramas (Ellis's translation, Vol. V., p. 310):

"Now that I and my usual project had been placed in broad daylight, it really appeared as if all the ill will that had lurked before in ambush was determined to make an open attack in full force. Indeed, it seemed as though no single interest, of all those represented by our press and our society, was not stung to the quick by the composition and plan of production of my work. To stay the disgraceful direction taken by this feud in every circle of society, which recklessly assailed alike protector and protected, I could but decide to strip the scheme of that majestic character which my patron had accorded it, and turn it into a channel less provocative of universal wrath. Indeed, I even tried to divert public attention from the whole affair by spending a little hard-won rest on the completion of the score of my 'Meistersinger,' a work with which I should not appear to be quitting the customary groove of performances at the theatre."

o

It may not be out of place to add here that calumny pursued him after his retirement from Munich, and one of the most interesting stories was that he had left his wife to starve. To this falsehood the unhappy Minna replied with great dignity and a touch of pathos in a statement published in January, 1866, a fortnight before her death. She said:

"The malicious reports which certain Vienna and Munich papers have been publishing for some time concerning my husband compel me to declare that I have received from him up to date a pension which amply suffices for my support. I seize this opportunity with so much the more pleasure since it enables me to destroy at least one of the many calumnies which people are pleased to launch against my husband."

This statement is indisputable evidence that there was no harsh feeling in the heart of the wife who had parted from him.

Mme. von Bülow with her children joined Wagner at Triebschen, while Hans was obliged to go to Basle to teach. In his place he left Hans Richter, who thus became intimately associated with the creative work of Wagner. The separation between Von Bülow and his wife proved to be final, and the daughter of Liszt imitated her illustrious father by recognising the supremacy of the claims of love over all other obligations. In 1866 the public feeling against Wagner had somewhat declined, and the King decided to have model performances of "Tannhäuser" and "Lohengrin" at Munich. Von Bülow was made Kapellmeister and devoted himself, heart and soul, to the preparations for these performances. In March, 1867, Wagner went to Munich to supervise some of the rehearsals, and again he visited the capital in May for

the same purpose.   A general rehearsal took place on
June 11th, and everything went to the satisfaction of
the master.

To his intense surprise, the next day the King sent
away Tichatschek and Mme. Bertram-Mayer, who had
been especially engaged, and announced that their
places would be taken by Heinrich Vogl and Therese
Thoma, afterward his wife.   This was the result of a
new intrigue against Wagner, and he, despairing of a
perfect performance in these conditions, at once left
the city.   The first of these "model" performances
took place on June 16 and was successful in spite of
the sudden changes.   But it was not what Wagner
would have called an ideal performance, and some of
the customary cuts were made.   Despite the continued opposition to Wagner the King retained his
love for the "music of the future," and he determined
that "Die Meistersinger" should be produced in the
year 1868.   Public feeling against Wagner still further
diminished, and he was able to visit Munich frequently
to superintend the rehearsals, which were under the
direction of Von Bülow as conductor and Richter as
chorus master.   The best obtainable artists in Germany were secured, and no pains were spared in the
preparation of the troublesome but essential details of
nuance and stage business.   On June 21, 1868, the
opera was produced, and its success was most decided.

And now Wagner returned to his magnum opus,
"Der Ring des Nibelungen."   But the King could not
wait.   He was eager to hear at least a part of it, and
so he gave orders that "Das Rheingold" should be
prepared.   Again there were troubles of all kinds.

The composer's directions were so inadequately followed that the machinery for the first scene was
almost worthless. Richter, who had succeeded Von
Bülow as Kapellmeister, was so displeased with the
preparations that he refused to conduct, and finally
Franz Wüllner was secured in his place. After several postponements the work was produced in a
bungling style on Sept. 22, 1869. Wagner made a
feeble effort to save the performance from disaster,
but the result was practically a fiasco. The King,
however, was bound to hear more of the trilogy, and
accordingly, on June 26, 1870, "Die Walküre" was
performed, the Vogls appearing as the lovers. The
audience was somewhat better pleased with this work
than with the "Rheingold," but the production could
not be called a success. These performances were
premature, and they may be said to have flashed in
the pan.

It was at this period that an event occurred which
Wagner's friends had for some time expected. The
marriage of Cosima Liszt and Hans von Bülow had
not been happy, and the estrangement between them
was accelerated by the woman's quick conception of
a passion for Wagner. When Von Bülow went to
Basle to teach, the beginning of the end had come,
and it was not long after that when the relations between Wagner and Mme. von Bülow could no longer
be kept secret. "If it were only someone whom I
could kill," said Von Bülow, "he would have been
dead before this." The great conductor could not
think of slaying the great master. In the autumn of
1869 the Von Bülows were divorced. In July, 1870,
Wagner wrote to Praeger:

" My dear Ferdinand, you will no doubt be angry with me when you hear that I am soon to marry Bülow's wife, who has become a convert in order to be divorced."

A little later Praeger received the wedding cards announcing that they had been married on Aug. 25 at the Protestant Church of Lucerne. The attitude of Liszt toward this union may be understood from Wagner's statement that he was more annoyed by his daughter's change of religion than by her divorce. That the divorce and the marriage had to come about, however, may be inferred from the fact that in the summer of 1869 Mme. von Bülow had borne to Wagner a son.* The existence of this child was first definitely mentioned by Wagner in a letter to the Zurich friend, Mme. Wille, dated June 25, 1870, accepting an invitation to visit her, but deferring the date till he and Mme. von Bülow could go as man and wife.   In November of the same year Wagner wrote to Praeger, and closed the letter with these words:

" Often do I now think of you because of your love for children. My house, too, is full of children, the children of my wife, but beside there blooms for me a splendid son, strong and beautiful, whom I dare call Siegfried Richard Wagner. Now think what I must feel that this at last has fallen to my share.   I am fifty-seven years old."

Cosima Wagner was twenty-nine years old at the time of her marriage to the composer.   Many foolish

* The date of Siegfried Wagner's birth has never been made known by the Wagner family.   In his chronological table of the incidents of Wagner's life, Houston Stewart Chamberlain notes, in the year 1869, "Siegfried Wagner born on June 6 of the marriage with Cosima Liszt."   In spite of the direct and the indirect falsehoods contained in this note, I have reason to believe that the date is correct.

stories have been told of her coming between him and his first wife. The reader of this volume can see for himself that there is not the slightest foundation for these tales. The facts of the divorce and marriage may be permitted to stand without comment. But it should be said that Cosima Wagner gave to her husband a loyalty, a devotion, and a sympathetic comprehension which made him a wholly happy man in his domestic life. In 1871 Wagner composed, in honour of the child and to celebrate his wife's birthday, the popular "Siegfried Idyll." Richter gathered the necessary musicians at Lucerne and rehearsed the piece, and at the proper time performed it on the stairs of the villa at Triebschen, to the surprise and joy of Mme. Wagner. The leading themes of the composition are taken from "Siegfried" and are combined with an old German cradle-song.

In 1870 Wagner published two important prose works, "On Conducting" and "Beethoven." The former arraigns the mechanical Kapellmeisters of Germany in good round terms, and sets forth Wagner's ideas as to the proper manner of directing the performance of the classic orchestral works. It is an eloquent and instructive little book, and should be read by all music-lovers. The study of Beethoven is less clear in style and dips into metaphysical discussion, but it contains artistic views of high dignity. In 1871 the composer wrote the familiar "Kaisermarsch," intending it as a musical celebration of Germany's triumph in the conflict with France. It may be noted that the Emperor accorded to this attention the very scantest courtesy. We have now reached the period when Wagner left Munich for Bayreuth. The time was approaching when the great Nibelung drama must be launched in its entirety. The plan to build a theatre for it in Munich had, as we have seen, fallen through. A new site had to be found and new plans to be adopted for bringing to a successful issue the most formidable theatrical project of the century.

CHAPTER XIII

FINIS CORONAT OPUS

" Vollendet das ewige Werk:
Auf Berges Gipfel
Die Götter-Burg,
Prunkvoll prahlt
Der prangende Bau ! "

RHEINGOLD

IT was in April, 1872, that Wagner went to Bayreuth
to live. He at first occupied rooms in the small hotel
belonging to the Castle Fantaisie, in the village of
Donndorf, an hour's ride from Bayreuth. Subsequently
he moved into hired apartments in the town. Meanwhile a new home for him was in process of erection,
and in 1874 he and his family took possession of the
Villa Wahnfried, where his widow and children still
live. This house was built in accordance with Wagner's own ideas, and in it at last he found that domestic peace and comfort for which he had longed through
so many years of struggle. But the theatre and the
performance of the Nibelung drama were still at a distance. Work on the "Festspielhaus," as it is called,
was in progress, but the difficulties in the way of its
completion seemed wellnigh insuperable. Money,
money, was still the cry. The history of the inception and progress of the Bayreuth project might well

be told at great length, but it must be narrated as briefly as possible.

Why had Wagner selected Bayreuth as the scene of the crowning labour of his career ? Other cities in Germany had offered him inducements, but they were precisely the sort of inducements that a man of Wagner's artistic ideas could not appreciate. He could have gone to cities in which he would have had ready-made publics in the shape of summer tourists in large numbers, but such publics he did not desire. He wished to bring to the performance of his magnum opus an assembly gathered for no other object. He desired the representations to take place where they alone would be the moving thought in the public mind. People must go to Bayreuth solely to attend the Wagner performances, and thus the audience would come into the theatre in the right mood. Again, Bayreuth was in Bavaria, and Wagner wished to carry out in the dominion of his royal friend the great project of his life.

But how was the necessary money to be raised ? Performances of the older works brought in but little, and concerts were expensive. At this juncture Carl Tausig, the young pianist, conceived a plan, which he elaborated with the aid of the Baroness Marie von Schleinitz. It was estimated that the entire expense of preparing and performing "Der Ring des Nibelungen" would amount to about 300,000 thalers, or $225,000. The plan was to sell 1000 certificates of membership among the supporters of Wagner's ideas. The holder of one certificate was to be entitled to a seat at each of the three series of performances. Any person could buy several certificates, and three might unite in the purchase of one, each of the three thus attending one series. Tausig had other ideas in his head for the assistance of Wagner, but he was suddenly carried away by typhoid fever at the age of thirty.

Meanwhile Emil Heckel, a music publisher of Mannheim, had proposed the formation of Wagner societies, and had organised one in Mannheim, in June, 1871. Heckel's scheme was a sort of lottery, each member paying five florins and being entitled to one chance in a patron's certificate, one of which was bought for each thirty-five members. The society was also to give concerts and to use the proceeds in the purchase of certificates. The Wagner society plan spread, and organisations of this kind were formed in leading cities in Europe and America. Wagner busied himself conducting concerts and pushing the production of his works, but the raising of the funds proceeded very slowly. Nevertheless, on May 22, 1872, Wagner's fifty-ninth birthday, the corner-stone of the new theatre was laid with appropriate ceremonies. Burgomaster Muncker, from whose son's book quotations have been made, and Frederick Feustel, a banker, had, as the heads of a committee of the citizens, presented to Wagner a site for the edifice. Niemann, Betz, Fräulein Lehmann, and Frau Jachmann (née Wagner) had volunteered to sing. Vocal societies from Leipsic and Berlin, and orchestral players from Vienna, Leipsic, Weimar, and other cities had offered their services. And so Wagner was able to prepare one of those ideal performances of Beethoven's Ninth Symphony in which he delighted. The concert took place in the old opera house of Bayreuth, and was followed by the laying of the corner-stone. The band played the "Huldigungsmarsch," while Wagner struck the stone three times with a hammer, and said, "Bless this stone! May it stand long and hold firmly." King Ludwig telegraphed his congratulations. Rain fell, and the assembly returned to the old theatre to complete the ceremony. Musicians and singers, the Wagner family, the composer, the burgomaster, and others were grouped on the stage. The burgomaster delivered an address of welcome, and then Wagner read a fervent speech. At the close of it he raised his hands and the chorus burst into the chorale from the last scene of "Die Meistersinger."

The air was full of hope, yet in January, 1874, Wagner had to tell Heckel that he was about to announce to the public the complete collapse of the Bayreuth scheme. The money could not be raised. Once more King Ludwig came to the rescue, with a contribution of 200,000 marks. The Viceroy of Egypt gave $2,500, and 404 patron's certificates had been sold by July, 1875. So Wagner, although he foresaw a heavy deficit, announced that the performances would take place in the summer of 1876.

Meanwhile he travelled about, giving concerts and supervising performances of his older works, and adding here a little and there a little to the sum needed for carrying out his plans. Through Theodore Thomas he at this time received $5000 for the composition of the "Centennial March," written for the opening of the Centennial Exposition at Philadelphia. This is Wagner's poorest music, but he must have been very glad to get the money, and we Americans can revel in the trilogy and forget the march.

At length, in August of 1876, the long-awaited event took place, and the little town of Bayreuth awoke one morning, Byron-like, to find itself famous. The Emperors of Germany and Brazil, the King of Bavaria, the Grand Dukes of Weimar, Baden, and Mecklenburg, Prince Vladimir of Russia, and the Prince of Hesse; eminent musicians headed by Franz Liszt, Camille Saint-Säens, and Edward Grieg; critics from all countries, and supporters of Wagner from all over Europe and even from America, crowded into the town to hear this new thing in operatic art, this "music of the future." The enemy, too, was well represented, and the glitter of the critical axe was seen among the flaunting banners. The German Emperor arrived on August 12th, and was received with due ceremony. He stayed for only two of the first series of performances, but Mr. Finck has clearly proved that he went to Bayreuth with that intention, and was not driven away by the music as some of Wagner's opponents have asserted.

The first performance took place on August 13. It was to begin at 5 P. M., but was postponed till 7, because the Emperor of Brazil could not reach the city in time for the earlier hour. An audience of wonderful composition assembled in the theatre, after the trumpeters had blown a motive from the last scene to announce that the performance was about to begin. The first impression of wonder was created by the darkening of the auditorium, it being part of Wagner's plan that the attention of the audience should thus be centred on the stage. Then came the surprising effect of the concealed orchestra, playing down in its pit between the stage and the audience, the pit fancifully christened the "Mystic Gulf." Such a rich, homogeneous instrumental tone was new to all the hearers. The curtain rose, and the depths of the Rhine were revealed. The audience entered a new world of operatic experience. The performance moved smoothly, except that some of the stage mechanism was defective. Indeed, the hitch in the passage from Scene I. to Scene II. drove Wagner out of the theatre. After the performance there were tumultuous calls for Wagner and the artists, but no one responded.

On the following night "Die Walküre" was given, but owing to the indisposition of Unger, the leading tenor, "Siegfried" had to be postponed till August 16. "Götterdämmerung" was performed on August 17. The third and fourth works of the series were on these dates heard in public for the first time. After "Götterdämmerung" the audience again called for the composer and the performers, and now Wagner appeared and made a brief speech of thanks and promise for the future. The curtains were drawn aside and all the artists were seen. When the three series of performances had been completed there was a banquet, at which Wagner further explained his hopes for the coming years, and at which he paid a warm tribute of gratitude to his first friend and helper, Liszt.

Thus was finally brought to representation the great tetralogy, on which Wagner had worked more than a quarter of a century, and which was, without doubt, the chief labour of his life. From 1848 his mind had been filled with the story of "Siegfried." He had laid it aside from time to time to produce other works, but it had been the chief aim of his existence. Early in his labours on it he had discovered that the narration would require the building of a tetralogy, and he had also foreseen that a special theatre must be built. No playwright or composer had ever before entertained such a project, and now at last it was accomplished. The critics departed in a state of confusion, as well they might, having been called upon to face an art utterly unknown, and brought before them in a condition of complete development. That their comments showed an almost total failure to understand what Wagner had attempted was natural. If they had understood him, they would have been men of genius themselves. Some men of genius did understand him, and that was his highest reward. The musical world was rent asunder with arguments for and against the new art, but Wagner had at least lived to see one dream of his life realised.

Some description of the Festspielhaus must be included at this point. The theatre occupies an isolated position on a slight eminence about fifteen minutes' walk from the town. The portion containing the auditorium is small, and about half as high as that containing the stage. Two stages, one above the other, are used, so that while one scene is before the audience the other is preparing in the cellar. This device was made known to New Yorkers in the Madison Square Theatre, where the famous double stage of Steele Mackaye was for a time the talk of the town. Wagner's plan was older than Mr. Mackaye's. The Festspielhaus proscenium is extremely plain, and is so contrived that it creates an illusion as to the distance between the audience and the stage. No prompter's box and no footlights are visible to the spectators. In front of the stage and running partly under it is the pit for the orchestra, so arranged that the musicians are wholly unseen by the audience, and the conductor is visible only to the singers.

The auditorium itself is small and rigorously plain. The parquet seats 1300 persons. Above the last row of seats, and extending all the way across the rear of the auditorium, is a gallery, containing nine boxes for the use of titled visitors. Above this gallery is a second one containing 200 seats. The seating capacity of the entire theatre is about 1500 The parquet seats are arranged in easy curves, so that every person faces the stage and has a perfect view. There are no side seats and no proscenium boxes. The sides of the auditorium are finished with Renaissance columns; and sixteen wide passages, eight on each side, give easy egress from the house. There are no chandeliers. The lighting outfit of the auditorium is just sufficient to enable the audience to find its way about. While the performance is going on, all lights in front of the stage are extinguished. The entire aim of the plan of this house is to remove everything which can suggest the conventional theatre, and to concentrate the attention of the audience on the stage.

Wagner's principal assistant in the building of this theatre was Karl Brandt, of Darmstadt, with whom he consulted in regard to everything. The architect, engaged on Brandt's advice, was Otto Bruckwald, of Leipsic. The scenery for the Ring dramas was designed by Prof. Joseph Hoffmann, of Vienna, and painted by the Brothers Brückner, of Coburg. These are the men to whom Wagner expressed himself as especially indebted for aid in carrying out his ideas. Of the performers engaged in this remarkable undertaking mention will be made in the study of the dramas, which will form a separate part of this work.

The first Bayreuth festival resulted in a deficit of $37,000. And so Wagner, with the artistic dream of his life realised, found himself once more the victim of monetary embarrassments. He went into Italy for a little rest, and was received with distinction in several cities. The violinist Wilhelmj, who had been concertmeister of the festival orchestra, suggested that a series of concerts in London would go far toward raising the money needed to meet the deficit. Several of the Bayreuth singers were secured, and the concerts were announced for May 7 to 19, 1877. Wagner conducted one half of each concert and Richter the other half. This was the beginning of Richter's great vogue as a conductor in London. The concerts were a failure, and two supplementary entertainments at popular prices were given in order to help the situation. But Wagner left London with his affairs still in a bad condition. The London visit was notable for the fact that on May 17 he read the poem of his new drama, "Parsifal," to a circle of friends at the house of Edward Dannreuther. He read the same work to German friends at Heidelberg on July 8, while on his way back to Bayreuth.

The financial difficulties were finally solved by the disposal to Munich of the rights of performance of the "Ring." Wagner had said that the work really belonged to the King, who had agreed to pay him a pension on condition that he should complete and produce the work. The Intendant of the Munich Opera House saw in the deficit at Bayreuth his opportunity to acquire the right to perform the work. He agreed to pay the deficit provided the royal right to "Der Ring" be enforced for the benefit of the Munich theatre. Wagner was obliged to accept this solution of his difficulties, and thus Bayreuth lost the sole right to the tetralogy. The dramas of the "Ring" now began to be played separately, much to Wagner's displeasure, but they grew in popularity, and the royalties were good to have. Angelo Neumann organised his travelling Nibelung Theatre, with several of the Bayreuth artists and Anton Seidl as conductor, and gave complete performances, except for cuts authorised by Wagner, in many cities of Germany and Italy. Meanwhile Wagner was engaged in completing what was to be his last work. He had conceived it in 1865, but had found no opportunity to do more than write the book. His health was not of the best, and he was eager to retire to the seclusion of Wahnfried and finish his drama. The settlement of the pecuniary troubles arising from the first festival enabled him to carry out his project. He was to write one more work, filled with ecstatic piety, and then go to his rest.

10

CHAPTER XIV

THE LAST DRAMA

" Alles wird mir nun frei."—GÖTTERDÄMMERUNG

In the fall of 1877 Wagner's mind was occupied with a plan to found at Bayreuth a music school similar in plan to that which he had once hoped to have in Munich. Delagates from the Wagner societies were invited to the city to consider the project, but they, alarmed by the large deficit remaining from the festival of 1876, declined to further the scheme. At this gathering of delegates the various societies were reorganised into one general association, having its headquarters at Bayreuth; and that the members and the other sympathisers with his aims might have some definite object before them, Wagner announced that subscriptions would apply to the production of his new work, "Parsifal." It was at this time his purpose to produce this drama in 1880, but various causes, including poor health, combined to prevent the fulfilment of this intention. Naturally the lack of funds was a prime cause for the postponement. Wagner announced the change of date in a communication to his subscribers, dated Bayreuth, July 15, 1879.

Meanwhile a new medium of making known his

plans and ideas had been found. In January, 1878, appeared the first number of a monthly periodical called the *Bayreuther Blätter,* edited by Hans von Wolzogen, who is now known to all students of Wagner's scores as the author of handbooks explaining the leading motives of the music. Wagner himself was an active contributor to this journal, and wrote some of his most interesting papers for it. Meanwhile he worked assiduously at the music of " Parsifal." That he did not finish it till the beginning of 1882 was due to a variety of causes, among which was a fresh outbreak of his old enemy, erysipelas. This sent him, in the last days of 1879, into southern Italy in search of relief. He was not in a sanguine temper at this time, and he wrote for the opening of 1880 a querulous article, showing that he still felt the hostility of criticism and the inability of the public to comprehend his artistic purposes. He said :

" Nothing, in fact, seems farther from our public situation of the day than the founding of an artistic institution whose use, nay, whose whole meaning, is understood of the veriest minority. Indeed I believe I have done my best to state both things distinctly : but who has yet heeded ? An influential member of the Reichstag assured me that neither he nor any of his colleagues had the faintest notion of what I want. And yet, to further my ideas I can think only of such as know absolutely nothing of our art, but devote themselves to politics, trade, or business ; for here a ray may sometimes strike an open mind, whereas among those interested in our present art I fancy I might seek such a mind in vain. There reigns the obstinate belief that art is but a métier, its object to feed its practitioner ; the highest-placed Court theatre Intendant never gets beyond that, and consequently it does not occur to the State to mix itself in things that rank with the regulation of commerce. There one swears by Fra Diavolo's ' Long live art ; above all, the lady artists,' and sends for Patti."

To the casual observer Wagner at this period probably seemed to have reason to be well pleased with his
life. He was rid of the burden of the deficit remaining after the "Ring" performances, he had a beautiful
home, a devoted wife, and was surrounded by friends
who gave him that ceaseless praise for which his
heart ever hungered. But Wagner could not forgive
the world for not taking him at his own valuation.
He resented Germany's reluctance to accept the new
gospel of art which he preached. Nevertheless he
laboured away at the score of "Parsifal," drifting off
into that religious mysticism which has affected so
many composers in their old age, and at the same
time believing that now at last he was writing something which would not be practicable outside of
the secluded auditorium of Bayreuth. Fragments of
the work were scored from time to time, and at the
Wahnfried Christmas festival of 1878 the prelude was
performed by the Meiningen Court Orchestra. But it
was not till after the trip to Italy that he was ready to
begin active preparations for the performance of the
drama. The piano rehearsals were begun in August,
1881. But in the winter of 1881–82 bad health again
sent Wagner south, and he completed his score in
January in Palermo.

He returned to Bayreuth in May. The subscriptions
for the "Parsifal" production arrived very slowly, and
at the close of 1881 the amount subscribed was still
lamentably small, but once more King Ludwig came
to the rescue. He offered Wagner the use of the
forces of the Munich Opera House, in return for which
that theatre acquired the exclusive right to the performance of "Die Feen." Nevertheless in the end

Wagner was compelled, in order to meet all expenses, to abandon his plan of giving the performances for his subscribers alone. The first two performances were exclusive, but the general public was admitted to the others with the happiest results.

The final rehearsals began with July, 1882, and the first performance was given on July 26. Fifteen other performances were given, the last on Aug. 29. The production engaged the services of a number of the best singers in Germany, many distinguished principals consenting to take small parts. The scenery and stage effects again commanded high praise, and Wagner's skill as a designer of stage pictures was conceded even by those who refused to allow him genius as a dramatist. Again, too, there was an unfortunate hitch in the mechanical devices. The panorama in the first act, showing the country through which Gurnemanz and Parsifal pass on their way to the castle of Monsalvat, was mistakenly constructed to move half as fast as it should have moved, and as there was not time after the discovery of the error to rectify it, Wagner had to have the music of the scene played through twice. But the solemn drama created a profound impression, and many of the critics who had found little to please them in the "Ring" admitted that "Parsifal" exercised a potent spell on their minds.

The exertions necessary for the production of "Parsifal" had told severely on Wagner. It is said that at one rehearsal he fainted, and, on recovering, exclaimed, "Once more I have beaten Death." Dr. Standthartner, one of his firm Viennese friends, examined him in the course of the summer, and found that a heart affection, from which the composer had long been suffering, had made dangerous progress. Wagner was not told of his exact condition, but he was warned that immediate rest and relief from care was absolutely essential. He was a man of sixty-nine and he had done an enormous amount of work. Furthermore he had taxed the resources of his system by indulgence in passionate moods, which were naturally followed by periods of intense depression.

After the "Parsifal" performance he went with his family to Venice, where he took up his residence in the Vendramin Palace on the Grand Canal. The household consisted of Wagner, his wife, Siegfried, the Count Gravina and his wife (daughter of Von Bülow), her sisters, Liszt, and the Russian painter Joukowsky, who had designed the scenery of "Parsifal." Perl* gives a most interesting account of the domestic life of the family in the last days of the master's life. He lived in the greatest seclusion, receiving no visitors and making almost no calls. He arose early and occupied himself with writing, no one being allowed to disturb him while so engaged. The products of his pen were chiefly articles for the *Bayreuther Blätter*. About noon his wife joined him and gave him the substance of the morning's mail, sedulously concealing anything which might excite him. In the afternoon, after a nap, he went out with his family, if the weather was pleasant, in a gondola, and frequently made excursions of some length. In the evening the old palace (it was built in 1481) was brilliantly lighted up, and Wagner listened to one of his family reading aloud.

*" Richard Wagner in Venice," by Henry Perl. Augsburg, 1883.

Liszt arrived in the middle of November, and Wagner began to be reminiscent. He suddenly remembered his juvenile symphony, and decided that on Christmas, 1882, it should be performed, not as a Christmas festivity, but in honour of his wife, whose birthday was Dec. 25. The concert-room and orchestra of the Liceo Benedetto Marcello were lent to him for the purpose, and he rehearsed the composition himself with the greatest ardour. Wagner afterward wrote a report on the performance of this youthful work, which he said went extremely well, owing to the natural disposition of the Italian musicians for tone and phrasing, and also owing to the large number of rehearsals which he was able to have. The symphony, too, "really seemed to please," and some Italian critics spoke well of it. Wagner himself did not overrate his boyish composition, but its revival was a pleasant occasion. At the end of the performance Wagner laid down the baton and declared that he would never conduct again. He had felt the strain of the physical effort. But his words, read in the light of subsequent events, acquired that appearance of prophecy which men's latest utterances so often gain from their propinquity to the end.

Dyspepsia had tortured him for years, and the irregularities of digestion had finally developed the heart affection, before mentioned, to a serious condition. Wagner was attended in Venice by Friedrich Keppler, but he disobeyed the physician's directions constantly. He was especially careless about exertion, and was not wholly observant of the necessary caution in the matter of eating. He fell faint several times in the course of the winter, but always strove to conceal

the fact from his family.   After Liszt's departure on
Jan. 13 he became even more careless, and entered
with great avidity into the preparations for the Bayreuth festival of the following summer.   On Feb. 13,
1883, he rested till late.   At noon he called the maid,
who sat outside his room, and ordered a light luncheon.   It was his intention to go out in his gondola at
four.   Soon after the luncheon had been brought the
maid heard Wagner call for her in a faint voice, and
running into the room found him in agony.   "Call
my wife and the doctor," he said.   The wife reached
his side in time to witness his last struggle.   When
the doctor arrived he was dead.

King Ludwig sent Adolf Gross, a Bayreuth banker,
who had long been an ardent supporter of Wagner,
to Venice as his representative.   Venice offered a
public funeral, but the widow declined it.   Silently
through the canals on Feb. 16 went a draped gondola
with the body.   A special mourning car carried the
remains to Bayreuth.   That city had indeed been
stricken in the loss of him who had made it famous.
At the railway station on the arrival of the funeral
train a public ceremony took place.   After Siegfried's
funeral march had been played Burgomaster Muncker
and Banker Feustel spoke.   The Bayreuth Liederkranz
sang the chorus arranged by Wagner for the burial of
Weber in Dresden.   The funeral procession then
moved to Wahnfried, where the remains of the poet-
composer were interred.

Feustel had said in his speech at the station that
Bayreuth's most dignified tribute to the memory of
the dead master would be the "Parsifal" performances
in the coming summer.   These were given, but with-

out the presence of the widow. She secluded herself even from Liszt, her father. But the following year she took up the task of continuing the festivals, which have lately reflected her ideas as to the proper method of interpreting her husband's masterpieces.

What embryonic works Wagner left is not known. He had written an extensive autobiography, but his family did not yet see fit to publish it. It was finally brought out in 1911. There is an excellent translation into English (Dodd, Mead & Co.). The rumour that Wagner left sketches for a drama on a Buddhistic subject rests on slight foundation. The materials for this drama, "The Victors," were absorbed in the plan of "Parsifal." He left some minor prose writings which are included in the ten volumes of his works and which may be found by the reader of English in the last volume of Mr. Ellis's translation. Gross, the Bayreuth banker, guaranteed the "Parsifal" performances of 1883, and superintended the settlement of the dead man's financial affairs. The consolidation of all the Wagner societies continued the work of supporting the festivals till their aid was no longer needed. In later years the receipts from the festivals and the royalties from the numerous performances of Wagner's works have enabled his family to live in luxury. Siegfried Wagner has become a musician and a composer. He shows no evidence of inheriting his father's genius, but he works assiduously and with effect in preparing performances at Bayreuth, which, in spite of many changes, continues to be the Mecca of all worshippers of Wagner's genius.

CHAPTER XV

THE CHARACTER OF THE MAN

"Close up his eyes and draw the curtains close,
And let us all to meditation." HENRY VI.

"THE noble and kindly man as his friends knew him, and the aggressive critic and reformer addressing the public, were as two distinct individuals." These words of Edward Dannreuther are the explanation of the many contradictory reports as to the personality of Wagner. Those to whom he opened his inner self, to whom he addressed his feelings and his hopes, who, in a word, understood him as both man and artist, were united in praise of his personality. Liszt, Praeger, Uhlig, Roeckel, Fischer, Von Bülow, Judith Gautier, Baudelaire, Frau Wille—all the company of Wagner's friends and helpers loved his nature and found in him none of that arrogance, that intolerance, that insufferable conceit, which the unsympathetic outer world condemned. With his friends, who understood the purpose of his life and the aims of his ambition, he was generally in a state of spiritual relaxation, and was simply himself. With those who failed to understand him, and with all those whom he recognised as enemies of his artistic ideas, he never relaxed the spirit of determined opposition to indolent and slothful conceptions of life and art ; and with them he was consequently always in a mood of hostility.   To such he was rude, discourteous, and intolerant.   His nature was irritable, and even his friends had to endure curt and hasty speech at times.   To his enemies he was never polite, except occasionally in written communication.   He was not a politic man, for he was too nervous in habit and too impulsive in utterance.   He possessed the gentle art of making enemies as few other men could, yet he was highly successful in gaining friends, and those whom he got he kept.   His early Dresden friends were always his friends.   The Zurich coterie adored him to the end. Those who were intimately associated with him in Bayreuth loved and reverenced him.   Muncker, the Munich professor, whose book was translated into curious English by another German,* could write thus of him:

" With passionate warmth he was beloved by numerous friends who for a lengthy space of time could not grasp the idea of his death.   In a full measure he deserved this love.   He was a man as good as he was great.   In his nature height of mind, depth of feeling, and childlike amiability were blended.   The energetic strength of his will was paired with heartfelt mildness ; the susceptibility of his mood, attributable to his many adversities and to his heart trouble, with an unfailing and sincere desire for reconciliation ; the seriousness of his mind, which in social intercourse involuntarily mastered all, with an inexhaustible love for jest and humour.   He loved and was mindful for every creature, man or animal, that needed help or sympathy.   Courageous truthfulness was the foundation of his character.   Therefore he was simple and natural in his demeanour and an outspoken enemy of all bombast.   He was proud, but modest in spite of his consciousness of what he desired, knew, and accomplished.   As his memory retained

* I have taken the liberty of changing the wording of the translation in two places where the meaning was obscure.

alive what long already was past, so he thankfully never forgot the good that others had done him, and faithfully clung to his friends, even if time and space separated them from him.   Himself clear in his thoughts and intentions, he demanded the same clearness in those who wished to associate with him."

The testimony of others who knew Wagner longer and more intimately than Muncker is in a similar vein. It is difficult in the face of such evidence to accept the assertions of those contemporaries who saw in him only the narrowest and most selfish egotism.   That he had serious faults and many foibles goes without saying.   That he was an agreeable companion to any one not absorbed in his artistic ideas cannot be believed.   Geniuses, self-centred as they must be, devoured day and night by passionate yearning for the attainment of ideal ends, are not often pleasant acquaintances.   Wagner did not differ from other great men.   People who were uncongenial to him have said that he was invariably rude and overbearing. Edward Dannreuther, who was his friend, says: "He had no pronounced manners in the sense of anything that can be taught or acquired by imitation.   Always unconventional, his demeanour showed great refinement.   His habits in private life are best described as those of a gentleman.   He liked domestic comforts, had an artist's fondess for rich color, harmonious decoration, out-of-the-way furniture, well-bound books and music, etc."

And here we come upon one of the traits of this singular man, which has properly given rise to the largest amount of derogatory comment.   He certainly had luxurious tastes, and he never resisted the temptation to gratify them even when he could not afford to do so. He loved fine surroundings. He was fond of rich garments, especially for indoor wear during his working hours. In later years, when his worldly position had improved somewhat, he employed an expensive Viennese dressmaker to make the silken robes which he wore in the house. He sent her the most elaborate designs for his dressing-gowns, which he seems to have planned with fastidious care. He paid her absurd prices for his robes. This was only one form of Wagner's extravagance. He wore silk underwear at all times, and Praeger endeavours to show that he was forced to do this in order to diminish as far as possible the irritability of his skin caused by the erysipelas, of which he was a lifelong victim. Wagner himself realised that his habits were luxurious, but he held that luxury was a necessity to him. He knew that he would be blamed for taking this position, and in a letter of 1854 to Liszt he wrote:

" How can I expect a Philistine to comprehend the transcendent part of my nature, which in the conditions of my life impelled me to satisfy an immense inner desire by such external means as must to him appear dangerous and certainly unsympathetic ? No one knows the needs of people like us. I am myself frequently surprised at considering so many 'useless' things indispensable." Later in the same year he wrote a letter in which he shows plainly how his craving for luxurious surroundings as an aid to work affected his financial affairs. He said:

" I cannot live like a dog. I cannot sleep on straw and drink bad whiskey. I must be coaxed in one way or another if my mind is to accomplish the terribly difficult task of creating a non-existent world. Well, when I resumed the plan of the ' Nibelungen ' and its actual execution, many things had to co-operate in order to produce in me the necessary, luxurious art mood. I had to adopt a better style of life than before. The success of ' Tannhäuser,' which I had surrendered solely in this hope, was to assist me. I made my domestic arrangements on a new scale. I wasted (good Lord, wasted!) money on one or the other requirement of luxury. Your visit in the summer, your example, everything, tempted me to a forcibly cheerful deception, or rather desire of deception, as to my circumstances. My income seemed to me an infallible thing. But after my return from Paris my situation again became precarious. The expected orders for my operas, and especially for ' Lohengrin,' did not come in ; and as the year approaches its close I realise that I shall want much, very much, money in order to live in my nest a little longer."

That there is a plaintive and unmanly weakness in all this is not to be denied. But we have to bear in mind that if Wagner had not received the assistance of his friends and been enabled to live as he wished to live and to work according to his fancies, we should not require biographies of him, and his great dramas would not have been the delight of two continents. That there was still further weakness in the metal of this man is shown by the extremities of depression into which he sank. Suicidal thoughts were no strangers to him and restlessness and discouragement were much too common. In a letter of March 30, 1853, he says to Liszt:

"What can help me ? My nights are mostly sleepless, weary, and miserable. I rise from my bed to see a day before me which will bring me not one joy. Intercourse with people who torture me and from whom I withdraw to torture myself ! I feel disgust at whatever I undertake. This cannot go on. I cannot bear life much longer."

Yet in spite of these pitiable feelings the artistic

impulse was all potent within him.   In the beginning
of 1859 he wrote to his fidus Achates: "Believe me
implicitly when I tell you that the only reason for my
continuing to live is the irresistible impulse of creating
a number of works of art which have their vital force
in me. I recognise beyond all doubt that this act of
creating and completing alone satisfies me and fills me
with a desire of life, which otherwise I should not understand."   And yoked with these ideas always went
his conviction that the world owed him a gratuitous
living that he might accomplish the creative functions
of his genius. In October, 1855, he wrote to the
amiable Franz:

"America is a terrible nightmare. If the New York people should
ever make up their minds to offer me a considerable sum, I should be
in the most awful dilemma. If I refused, I would have to conceal it
from all men, for everyone would charge me in my position with
recklessness. Ten years ago I might have undertaken such a thing,
but to have to walk in such by-ways now in order to live would be
too hard—now when I am fit only to do and to devote myself to that
which is strictly my business. I should never finish the 'Nibelungen'
in my life. Good gracious! such sums as I might earn in America
people ought to give me without asking anything in return beyond
what I am actually doing, and which is the best that I can do."

And then he adds pathetically that he is better fitted
to spend money than to earn it.

In such a man as Wagner the artistic traits are
dominant. They rule the personality. The conviction of this man that he had in him the conception of
epoch-making works, and his recognition of the fact
that the world was his artistic enemy, were the moving forces of his life. Without constantly keeping
this in mind, it is quite impossible to comprehend the

character of Wagner. It explains at once its weakness and its strength. It accounts even for his domestic history, while it does not justify it. His first wife was a good woman, and in a way he loved her. But she was never able to become an essential part of his life, because she could not enter into his artistic thoughts and purposes. Hence she was unable to control his impulses to wander. Cosima von Bülow understood him before she went to live under the immediate influence of his mind. That they should have been drawn to one another was inevitable. He who in letters to Liszt had cried out in anguish of his need of a home and woman's care was very ready to accept them at her hands at no matter what sacrifice, and she in the same spirit was ready to give them. To her Wagner was constant in spite of the fact that temperamentally he was an inconstant man. She controlled his desires, and they needed control.

The artistic aspirations which governed his entire career made it a disappointment. Wagner died a disappointed man. That he was gratified by the production of the "Ring" at Bayreuth there need be no denial. That he enjoyed to the fullest the praises of those who seemed to comprehend his ideals is beyond doubt. But, nevertheless, he realised that he had not penetrated the public mind. He saw plainly that the applause for his works was not for their revelation of a new standpoint in operatic art, but for their purely theatrical effectiveness. The public never saw beneath the surface. He felt that he was wholly misunderstood. In a letter of 1859 to Liszt he said :

"I never had much pleasure in the performance of one of my operas, and shall have much less in the future. My ideal demands have increased, compared with former times, and my sensitiveness has become much more acute during the last ten years while I lived in absolute separation from artistic public life. I fear that even you do not quite understand me in this respect, and you should believe my word all the more implicitly."

Again and again he spoke in no doubtful terms of his knowledge that the public did not understand his aims. He was delighted by every evidence of sympathy, but he suffered untold agonies of mind from the fact that "Tannhäuser," "Lohengrin," and "Die Meistersinger" were treated by the world as mere operas, and that there was no evidence that the operatic public understood his departure from the old and insincere methods of the commercial theatre. The disappointment which Wagner experienced from the failure of the world to grasp his ideals would have continued, had he lived longer. Even now only a few ardent lovers of the loftiest things in art have entered fully into the spirit of his conceptions. One has only to attend a performance of "Siegfried" before an ordinary audience of professed Wagnerites to see how far short of a complete understanding of Wagner his friends still are. Thousands of well-meaning persons regard themselves as disciples of this unique master when they have learned the contents of Hans von Wolzogen's handbooks and can identify every leading motive in each score when it is heard in the orchestra. The praise of all such people was vinegar and gall to Wagner. He felt that he was utterly misunderstood, and that was torture to his sensitive spirit.

He was unhappy, too, because he could not get his works properly performed. Perhaps he never experienced deep delight at any representation except the

first of " Tristan und Isolde," in which the splendid
work of Schnorr filled him with joy.   But his " Lohengrin " and his " Tannhäuser " were never given to his
satisfaction, for there were absolutely no singers who
united the ability to declaim the recitative and to deliver the plentiful cantilena also.   Not only was there
a lack of singers, but there were no stage managers
who understood him, and so all over Germany his
works were performed in a spirit foreign to their
poetic content, and the master was misrepresented to
a public which would have found it almost impossible
to comprehend him in the most favourable conditions.
Mr. Dannreuther says : " The composer of ' Tristan'
confronted by the Intendant of some Hoftheater, fresh
from a performance of Herr von Flotow's ' Martha' !
A comic picture, but unfortunately a typical one, im-
plying untold suffering on Wagner's part."

Wagner was under medium size, but had the appearance of being somewhat taller than he really was.
In 1849 the police description of him ran thus :
"Wagner is 37 to 38 years old, of middle height, has
brown hair, wears glasses ; open forehead ; eyebrows
brown ; eyes grey-blue ; nose and mouth well pro-
portioned ; chin round.   Particulars: in speaking and
moving he is hasty."   Animation marked all his ways,
and at times he revelled in the wildest spirits.   Periods of deep depression occurred to him, but his
nervous energy seldom deserted him.

The study of his personality will always bring one
back to the same point.   He was entirely dominated
by his artistic nature and ambition.   His life can be
understood only by an analysis of his motives based
on this premise.   Wagner, the man, was the creature

of Wagner, the dreamer of "Siegfried." There has never been a clearer instance of the mastery of genius. He was unceasingly driven by it from boyhood to the grave. It made him selfish, intolerant, dogmatic, dictatorial. But it achieved its ends. The grave at Wahnfried contains only ashes. All that was vital in Richard Wagner lives still in the dramas and the prose works. The forces which were in the man are just as active now as they were when he laughed and stormed in the villa at Bayreuth.

The Character of the Man

PART II

THE ARTISTIC AIMS OF WAGNER

"Every bar of dramatic music is justified only by the fact that it explains something in the action or in the character of the actor."— WAGNER TO LISZT, SEPTEMBER, 1850.

CHAPTER I

THE LYRIC DRAMA AS HE FOUND IT

WHAT was this man Wagner trying to do?
Broadly stated, the purpose of his life was to reform
the lyric drama, to restore to it the artistic nature with
which it was born, and to bring it into direct relation
to the life of the German people. His ideal was the
highest form of the drama, with music as the chief
expository medium ; and his most earnest desire, to
make that drama national, both in its expression of
the loftiest artistic impulses of the Teutonic people
and in their recognition of that fact. The whole controversy about the works of Wagner arose from the
determined opposition of those who were unwilling
to see the existing order of things operatic changed.
The opera, as it was when Wagner hurled his new
ideas and works into the theatrical arena, was a vastly
different thing from the music-drama, and the confusion in the public and critical mind, resulting from
the fact that Wagner used the outward and visible
signs of opera, brought about a bitter conflict. This
conflict cannot end till the whole public realises that
although it goes on Monday night to hear " Lucia di
Lammermoor " and on Wednesday to hear " Tristan
und Isolde," both employing song instead of speech,

and both outwardly built on theatrical lines, it is nevertheless confronted by two radically different forms of art, working for diametrically opposite results.

That we may the better understand the matter we must shortly rehearse the story of the birth and development of the lyric drama. The opera was born at the end of the sixteenth century of an effort to reconstruct the extinct Greek drama. The projectors of the movement knew that the Greeks delivered the lines of their tragedies in an artificial manner closely resembling chanting. In their endeavours to provide something similar to this, they invented dramatic recitative. At first this recitative was employed only in the construction of monologues, but as the explorers in new musical territory gained confidence, they made wider reaches. At the close of the century "Eurydice," a drama in music, by Rinuccini and Peri, was publicly performed. The new form of play gained immediate popularity, and the progress of the lyric drama was begun.

The inventors of the new form had just ideas. Peri believed it to be the office of dramatic music to embody, intensify, and convey to the hearer the emotional content of the text. His method of accomplishing this was to imitate in music the nuances of the voice in speaking. In agitated passages he used a faster movement and irregular rhythm. In unimpassioned speech he wrote his music more smoothly. His ideas were undeniably correct, but they could not be adequately carried out with the resources of vocal music in his day. The art of solo writing was in its infancy, and the melodic and harmonic expression of dramatic emotion had just begun. Consequently Peri's music was monotonous. There was no wide difference between his delineation of sadness and his embodiment of despair. Furthermore his attempted fidelity to the inner nature of speech led him away from definite musical phraseology. His music was totally deficient in form, and it was the discernment of this weakness and the attempts of his successors to provide the remedy that led the opera out of the path of dramatic sincerity.

Monteverde, the most gifted of the early composers of opera, made remarkable essays at combining musical clearness and symmetry with dramatic expression, but his works show us that the materials of the art were as yet so embryonic as to prohibit complete success. But the instantaneous popularity of opera made it a veritable gold-field for composers, and it speedily became the California of all the adventurous spirits of music in the beginning of the seventeenth century. These writers naturally sought the shortest and easiest path to popularity, and this was soon proved to be in the provision of vocal airs of simple, clearly defined form and pretty melody. The operatic aria was thus developed and became the central sun of the operatic system.

But as solo arias could not make up the entire scheme of the opera, duets, trios, and quartettes were introduced, care being taken to conserve in them the principles of the air. It was soon found that a sharp demarcation had to be made between these set pieces and the ordinary dialogue by means of which the stories of the operas were told. So gradually an opera came to be a symmetrically arranged series of solos, duets, trios, quartettes, and other set pieces, joined by a chain of recitative. In all this development purely musical requirements had been considered. The librettist, therefore, was merely the servant of the composer, and it was his business to arrange his book with a view to a pleasing succession of pieces in the aria form, or some form very similar to it. His story had to be so constructed that it could be told in the dialogue between the set pieces, and by means of this dialogue it should lead up to situations at which the arias could be effectively, if not quite appropriately, introduced.

This was the condition of the opera in the middle of the eighteenth century at the advent of Mozart and Gluck. It should be noted that occasionally composers arose who had some sense of their obligations to dramatic art and who endeavoured to improve the æsthetic nature of the opera. Lully and Rameau in France did much along this line and established traditions which have been of lasting benefit to the lyric art of their country. But neither they nor their immediate successors discovered the radical evil of the system upon which they were working. The ground-plan of the opera was still musical. There was still no thought of first writing a dramatic poem and then setting it to music. The demands of the score formulated the plan for the libretto.

Mozart had not a drop of the reformer's blood in his veins. The incongruity of the extant form of the opera seems never to have occurred to his mind. He accepted the plan of the lyric drama as it was handed down to him by his forerunners without question, and by the sheer force of his incomparable genius succeeded in writing immortal apologies for its existence. In his hands the aria took a new meaning, and the recitative became a flexible and responsive instrument. His treatment of the carefully built ensembles, which had come to be a feature of opera, was that of a genius of the first order. So great, indeed, was this man that to-day the works of all his successors who wrote operas on the old plan become as farthing rushlights before the splendour of his glowing masterpieces. Antiquated as the style of Mozart's music is, his operas speak the accents of inspiration and come before us with the gesture of authority.

Gluck, on the other hand, without the musical genius of Mozart, had the insight of a cosmopolitan coupled with the impulses of a progressist. The external defects of the opera were patent to his sane consideration, and he sought at once for the corrective. He was a sincere, conscientious reformer; and he did not a little to cut away the growth of underbrush which had sprung up around the trunk of operatic art. But he did not discern that the twig had been bent, the tree inclined; and that the trunk itself needed to be hewn down and the growth started again from the root. He saw that there was too much difference between the recitative and the aria, and that the latter was an impediment to the progress of the drama. He perceived that the composers had catered too much to the vanity of singers and had permitted a richly ornamental style of song, antagonistic to broad dramatic expression, to become the type of operatic music. He refused to write with a constant view to helping the singer to display his voice and technic. He insisted that the business of the music was to voice the content of the text, or as he himself expressed it, "I endeavoured to reduce music to its proper function, that of seconding poetry by enforcing the expression of the sentiment and the interest of the situations without interrupting the action or weakening it by superfluous ornament." He strove to curtail the empty parade of musical devices and to restore that intimacy between text and song which had been the chief charm and the most potent argument for the existence of the "Drama per Musica" in its original form.

But Gluck failed to achieve his purpose because he retained the set musical forms which dictated the shape of the text and demanded the old-fashioned arrangement of the scenario. He did not reach that level of enlightenment from which he might have seen that the radical error of opera lay in regarding music as an end and not as a means. The stumbling-block of the lyric drama had been the aria, and to this fact Gluck was strangely blind. It may not be amiss to conjecture that, even if he had perceived the nature of this fault, he would not have known how to correct it ; for the development of musical design had not advanced far enough to offer the suggestion of a better plan. Gluck saw the evil effect of the empty repetitions in the aria and expressly forbade them ; but he was too wise to believe that he could proceed wholly without musical design. To have done so would have thrown him back to the era of Peri and would have resulted in chaos and a confusion of the public mind. Therefore, retaining the aria in a slightly modified form, he strove with the deepest earnestness and with admirable skill to infuse into the music of his works a genuine dramatic expressiveness. He made his arias delineative of the situations and he paid the homage of an artist to the text, instead of writing pretty tunes for their own sake. He tried to arrange the ballets, which his French public demanded, so that they should constitute part of the action of the drama and not be an interruption to it. And he made a special study of the resources of instrumental expression.

His public at first fought him with stubborn determination, but he conquered it in the end. Yet his influence on the operatic stage was not permanently felt outside of France. The impetus given to Italian opera by the easily attained popularity of the aria writers and the bent imparted to it by their style remained. The applause of the unthinking, who constitute the vast majority of theatre-goers in all countries, is much more readily obtained by the agile delivery of a brilliant air with a simple dance rhythm as its basis than by a seriously conceived dramatic piece, which demands that the auditor shall bring both intelligence and sensibility into the presence of the singer. The Italian writers sought for this easy applause, and the famous Rossini, Donizetti, and Bellini, who were the princes of the Italian stage when Wagner was born, wrote wholly for the pleasure of the ear. The Italian opera was in its entirety a musical product, making but the shallowest pretence at representation of the thought of the text, and scorning real dramatic sincerity. The old forms prevailed and the librettist was but a purveyor to the composer.

In France some outward pretence of adhering to the long-established dramatic principles of the French lyric drama remained, but here the musical dictator of

the day was Meyerbeer, a man who sought popula\
applause as ardently as any Italian, but who adopted
a slightly different plan of gaining it. Whereas the
Italian appealed to his public chiefly by musical sweet-
meats, Meyerbeer deftly aimed at a combination of
showy musical effects with all the resources of theatricalism. He brought to its perfection the ground-plan
of the French grand opera, in which a striking succession of scenes is one of the most potent elements of
attractiveness. Here the librettist must not only provide for the usual alternation of solos with duets, trios
or quartettes, and ensembles, but must also plan the
story of his book so that a simple cottage or moonlight
love scene shall be followed by a grand pageant or a
glittering ballet. One has only to recall the progress
of the scenes in "L'Africaine" or "Les Huguenots"
to see how the Meyerbeerian plan is worked out, and
to realise how it has dominated the modern opera in
such creations as Gounod's "Faust" and Verdi's
"Aida."

The theatricalism of the ground-plan infused itself
into the music with Meyerbeer. He was always
planning for the immediate theatrical effect, never
thinking of the deep dramatic truthfulness which
might be imparted to music. For this reason his music is hollow and the bones of it rattle. Occasionally
he is carried away by a really noble dramatic situation
and writes greatly, as in the final duet of "Les Huguenots." But the problem of Meyerbeer was precisely
the same as that of Rossini, namely, how best to tickle
quickly the fancy of the great unthinking masses and
to fill the theatre. Thus Wagner found the opera established on a purely commercial basis, with art de-

graded to the dust. It was this which filled him with disgust, and against which he fought throughout his life. It is not to be denied that in the beginning he tried to reach the public by the same means as Meyerbeer. He tried to serve both art and Mammon, but he speedily discovered that real success could not be thus gained. He learned in writing "Rienzi" that he was following the wrong path. In entering upon this path, however, he was certainly led astray partly by the victories of Weber.

This master had in his "Der Freischütz" produced in 1821 a work which not only was essentially German, but which abandoned much of the outward appearance of opera. He announced his position by the definition of opera as "an art work complete in itself, in which all the parts and contributions of the related and utilised arts meet and disappear in each other, and, in a manner, form a new world by their own destruction." It was his belief that a libretto should not be made simply as a framework for the old-fashioned sequence of tunes, but should have an organic union with the music, and he said, "It is the first and most sacred duty of song to be truthful with the utmost fidelity possible in declamation." He had no respect for the established forms, but held that the form of the music should be prescribed by the poem. Nevertheless one finds that in its outward aspects the Weber opera, by reason of its employment of the German folksong style, treads a path not remote from that of the aria. For Weber did not discover any principle of musical design which would enable him to free himself from some restraint by the cyclical song form. Spoken dialogue takes the place of recitative in his works, but the vocal numbers, introduced in much the same way as in the older works, are of the song family, and in spite of an immensely widened and deepened expression, the dominance of a purely musical pattern is not escaped.

Such was the condition of operatic art and such the natural attitude of the public toward it when Richard Wagner began to look beyond the narrow boundaries of his small estate and dream of fame as an artist. The burning desire of the Königsberg and Riga period was, as he has expressed it in the "Communication to My Friends," "to extricate myself from the petty commerce of the German stage, and straightway try my luck in Paris." But it was only the puny huckstering of the little theatres which offended him. He had yet to learn that the commercial element was just as conspicuously present in more pretentious undertakings. He fell in love with Bulwer's "Rienzi," and at once saw in it material for an opera.

"This Rienzi with great thoughts in his head, great feelings in his heart, amid an entourage of coarseness and vulgarity, set all my nerves a-quivering with sympathy and love ; yet my plan for an art work based thereon sprang first from a perception of the purely lyric element in the hero's atmosphere. The Messengers of Peace, the Church's summons to awake, the battle hymns—these were what impelled me to make an *opera* : ' Rienzi.' "

In trying to make this opera he learned that the impulse of a true art work must come not from without, but from within ; that an opera which might be truly called a lyric drama could not be created out of the desire of some one to set the tempting portions of a lyric book to tuneful music, but only out of the demand of a great drama for the musical form of speech.

In writing the book of "Rienzi" he thought only of producing an effective opera libretto, and to this end he followed the Meyerbeerian ground-plan. His goal was the Paris Grand Opéra, and a grand opera was what he wrote. The materials of the story he saw "in no other light than that of a five-act opera, with five brilliant finales, and filled with hymns, processions, and the musical clash of arms." But even while fashioning this material for purely theatrical effect, he sought to make contributions toward real art, and it was the impossibility of combining the Meyerbeerian make-believe with the fruit of his artistic nature that showed him how far he was astray from the path leading to substantial and permanent success. Nevertheless he would no doubt have struggled on to force himself to travel the highway toward the Grand Opéra, had he not found the gates locked against him. It was in his despair that he at last resolved to write that which was in him and take no thought of external success. And it was of this first travail of freed genius that were brought to birth the fundamental tenets of his dramatic creed, previously cherished only in the secret womb of his mind.

12

CHAPTER II

THE REFORMS OF WAGNER

WE may now approach the study in detail of Wagner's artistic aims. I have already said that his purpose was to restore artistic truth, dramatic sincerity, to the opera, and to bring it into some relation to the life of the German people. Recapitulated with more particulars, then, the reforms at which he aimed were these :—

(1)—The music had come to be the end instead of a means of expression, and consequently musical forms dominated. Wagner strove to confine music to its proper function of expression. He desired to prevent its being regarded as the object of the lyric drama, but wished it to take its legitimate place as one of the factors in the composition of such a play. His labour in this direction included the disuse of the set musical forms.

(2)—He sought to make a complete organic union of the elements of the drama employed in opera, a union in which each part should be essential and all should work together for a common end, namely the embodiment of the poet's thought.

(3)—He endeavoured to make the " libretto " a consistent drama, but always suitable to the emotional expressiveness of music.

(4)—He aimed to bring the lyric drama out of the slough of mere commercialism, and give it a direct relation to and influence upon the intellectual and æsthetic life of the people.

We have seen that when he set out to free himself from the petty commercialism of the German theatre, Wagner fondly dreamed that with a " grand opera " produced on the stage of the Grand Opéra of Paris, he would emancipate himself. But in writing that work and labouring for its production, he learned two vital facts, namely, that artistic success could not be attained on the lines of the typical grand opera and that from petty commercialism he had only approached that of a larger field. He saw on every hand the theatre in the hands of mere speculators, who sought not art, but money, and who were ready to sink all artistic principles in order that they might appeal to the debased tastes of "the stolid German Philistine or the bored Parisian roué." When he turned his eyes backward along the path of history, he saw that it had been thus for centuries. In the end he came to the conclusion that only in the relation of the Greek drama to the Greek people could he find that Arcadian perfection for which he sought. And so he asked himself whether it was not possible to rise once again to the lofty level of the Greek tragedy and thus bring the theatre into relation to the heart and mind of the people. In his conception of the lyric drama he believed that he saw the means of doing this.

The student of his artistic work will find his ideas set forth in three of his literary compositions, " Art and Revolution," " The Art Work of the Future," and

"Opera and Drama." In "Art and Revolution" he studied the theatre of Æschylus and Sophocles and examined the reasons for its decline. In the devotion of Greek religion to the ideals of beauty Wagner found the explanation of the Grecian fidelity to the true principles of all art and of the final union of the arts of poetry, music, and mimetics in the Greek drama. He saw the highest period of this drama coincident with the supremacy of Athens. With the decline of the Athenian state came the decline of the Greek drama, and "the mad laughter of Aristophanes." The spirit of community, he says, split into a thousand lines of egotism, and the union of the arts which made the drama also was dissolved.

Then came the era of philosophy, which was inimical to art, and the dawn of Christianity was still less favourable to it. The old Greek freedom in the contemplation of nature and untrammelled worship of beauty for its own sake could not live under the reign of Christian teaching. With the changes in public thought resultant on the new teachings of Christianity and philosophy, art assumed a new relation to the national life, and in Wagner's opinion a social revolution alone would be the instrument to restore it to its pristine standing. With his social views we need not now concern ourselves. The point for us to bear in mind is that, like the founders of opera, he went back to the Greek drama for his first principles and in it found a union of the arts of poetry, music, and action. This union suggested to him, as it had to Peri and his friends, the laws on which must stand the modern play in music.

From this point he starts in his "Art Work of the

Future." He finds that after the dissolution of the old union of the arts, each sought its own development on independent lines and that each had at times sunk to the level of a mere amusement. Various unsuccessful attempts had been made to reunite these arts, but their independence had increased constantly till in Wagner's day each had touched the uttermost limits of its development and could not possibly go further. It was necessary, therefore, that each should sacrifice some measure of its independence in order to unite with the others in an artistic entity. This in Wagner's mind was a musical drama, in which poetry, painting, music, and acting should unite in an organic whole.

Having in this essay laid down the fundamental demands for his ideal lyric drama, he made in "Opera and Drama" an exhaustive study of this form of art. The first part of the work is devoted to a critical sketch of the development of opera. The text is that which we have already noted, that the means of expression, music, had been taken for the end, while the real object, the drama, had been made subsidiary to the production of pretty music in set forms. With this as his theme, Wagner examined the works of the various operatic masters and adduced evidence to establish his position. It was this part of his book which caused the bitterest comment at the time of publication.

The second part of the work is given to a study of the spoken drama, and it shows that Wagner was a close student of the works of the leading English, French, and German dramatists. It is in this survey that he indicates the special nature of the difficulties placed in the way of dramatic treatment by historical subjects, which he himself found impracticable for operas. He notes how Schiller laboured unsuccessfully to give clearness and form to the mass of historical details which he introduced into his "Wallenstein," while Shakespeare rested upon the firm ground of the auditor's imagination and painted in broad lines. Here the author propounds his own theory that for an ideal drama a mythical subject is the best, because it admits of a centralisation of the poet's thought upon the characters and emotions of the personages and rids him of the limitations of historical colour, or conventions of time or place.

"In the drama," he says, " we must become knowers through the Feeling. The Understanding tells us ' So is it,' only when the Feeling has told us, ' So must it be.' Only through itself, however, does this Feeling become intelligible to itself ; it understands no other language than its own. Things which can only be explained to us by the infinite accommodations of the Understanding embarrass and confound the Feeling. In Drama, therefore, an action can only be explained when it is completely vindicated by the Feeling ; and it thus is the dramatic poet's task, not to invent actions, but to make an action so intelligible through its emotional necessity, that we may altogether dispense with the intellect's assistance in its vindication. The poet, therefore, has to make its main scope the choice of the Action, —which he must so choose that, alike in its character as in its compass, it makes possible to him its entire vindication from out the Feeling ; for in this vindication alone resides the reaching of his aim."

This is the kernel of the second part of "Opera and Drama." In the third part he examines the materials of the poetic drama. He studies the technical resources of rhythm and rhyme and endeavours to show how far they can be utilised by the dramatist. From this he advances to an examination of the type of verse best suited to the purpose of the lyric drama, and here we are made acquainted with the theory of his own verse. He discourses on the functions of melody and harmony in the expression of the feelings of a drama and expounds his ideas as to the powers and uses of the orchestra. Finally he shows how he believes that the development of a drama should lead to periods of emotional exaltation, or, technically, emotional "situations," in which the expressiveness of melody would be employed with all its resources to enforce the poet's thought. The principal tenet of this part of the book is that the music must grow inevitably out of the emotional character of the scene, and that its technical potencies must be employed in proportion to their fitness for specific kinds of expression.

It is in his studies of the spoken historical drama and his expression of his ideas as to the proper materials for the lyric story that we must find the formation of Wagner's fundamental theory that the myth offered the best subject-matter for the musical dramatist. The details of movement and accessories required in a historical drama are in the way of the necessary process of focussing the music on the grand emotions of the play. The simplification of the story, so that its central situations are emotional and not merely theatric, is impossible when historic truth is preserved. But all mythology is the embodiment of primary world-thoughts. It is the poetry of peoples, and he who looks below the surface will find in it the whole heart of a nation. And thus the personages of mythologic story became world-types. They are embodiments of racial or national ideals. They are free, unconventional, elemental. Wagner came to discern in their qualities the requisites for heroes and heroines of the lyric drama. And from the philosophy of Schopenhauer, of which he was a student, he drew encouragement and support.

According to Schopenhauer it is the work of Art to represent for us the eternal essence of things by means of prototypes. The human mind should rise above the conditions of time and place, cause and tendency, and thus come to the contemplation of eternal ideas. This contemplation is the privilege and the duty of Art. Where, then, was Wagner to find eternal ideas suitable for dramatic treatment except in their personifications in mythology ? Certainly they were not to be found in librettos of the " Semiramide" or " Sonnambula " variety. Again turning his eyes to the Greek theatre, he found that Æschylus and Sophocles had used the great myths of their people, and that by doing so they had brought their theatre into direct relation with the national life and thought. Why, then, could not he, by using the myths of the Teutonic races, create genuine works of art and reknit the bond between the stage and the national heart ? This was the splendid vision which dwelt in his mind in the days of poverty and struggle. It was this which stayed his hand when easy offers of pecuniary success were almost within his grasp. It was this hope which led him forever away from the " pomp and circumstance " of the historical opera, and brought forth works whose kinship to " Rienzi " is so difficult to trace.

The myth, then, became the subject-matter on which he reared his poetic structure. As he has summarised his thoughts on this topic for us in "A Communication to My Friends" it may be well to quote his words :

"I turned for the selection of my material once for all from the domain of history to that of legend. . . . All the details necessary for the description and preservation of the conventionally historic, which a fixed and limited historical epoch demands in order to make the action clearly intelligible—and which are therefore carried out so circumstantially by the historical novelists and dramatists of to-day—could be here omitted. And by this means the poetry, and especially the music, were freed from the necessity of a method of treatment entirely foreign to them, and particularly impossible as far as music was concerned. The legend, in whatever age or nation it may be placed, has the advantage that it comprehends only the purely human portion of this age or nation, and presents this portion in a form peculiar to it, thoroughly concentrated, and therefore easily intelligible. . . . This legendary character gives a great advantage to the poetic arrangement of the subject for the reason already mentioned, that, while the simple process of the action—easily comprehensible as far as its outward relations are concerned—renders unnecessary any painstaking for the purpose of explanation of the course of the story, the greatest possible portion of the poem can be devoted to the portrayal of the inner motives of the action—those inmost motives of the soul, which, indeed, the action points out to us as necessary, through the fact that we ourselves feel in our hearts a sympathy with them."

With the idea of founding a national drama on the great mythological thoughts of his people, and keeping constantly in mind the conviction that his business was not the mere telling of a story in verse and music, but the presentation to the minds of his auditors of the underlying emotions of the drama,- he quickly realised that the set forms of the old opera were of no use to him. He could not construct a libretto with the regularly recurring duets, trios, and ensembles, if he meant to be true to dramatic art. To abandon these established patterns, however, meant to throw over both the poetic and musical fashions of the older lyric writers. If his people were not to sing arias and duets, but to speak a convincing dialogue, with speech raised to a higher power by the use of music instead of blank verse, as in the spoken drama, he must find new types, both poetic and musical. But with Wagner it must be constantly borne in mind that the dramatic speech is not text first and music afterward, but is both at once. His conception of the talk of his dramas was that of words made vocal in the musical sense by their own inner demand for emotional symbolism. In other words the music must be the direct and inevitable outgrowth of the poetry and the two must be joined in a perfect organic union.

It became necessary, therefore, that he should cast about for some new musical form for the foundation of his drama, for there cannot be music without form. The new pattern did not develop itself immediately in his mind. The first principle of it occurred to him when he was writing "Der Fliegende Holländer." This first principle was that the musical expression of a particular mood, having been found, should be retained. "When a mental mood returned," he says, "its thematic expression also, as a matter of course, was repeated, since it would have been arbitrary and capricious to have sought another motive so long as the object was an intelligible representation of the subject and not a conglomeration of operatic pieces." This at once disposed of the aria, which was a completed musical piece. Wagner conceived the music to be inseparable from the speech and therefore to be completed only at the end of the drama. The melody had thus to become endless, a melody made up of many thematic ideas, all worked up wholly for the purpose of mood painting, and built into a grand form dictated and justified solely by the emotional scheme of the play.   With this conviction he steered a happy course between mere formalism and chaotic formlessness.   He avoided the set patterns of the older school and escaped the dictation by the verse of the musical shape and figure, yet he also weathered the shoals of musical incoherency.   For the identification of the thematic ideas with the poetic thoughts enabled him to make on perfectly logical and natural grounds those melodic repetitions without which music is devoid of form.

Every student of music knows that a melody is constructed of certain phrases which have identifiable rhythmic and melodic shape.   The identity of any tune is established by the repetition of these phrases in a regular order.   When the repetitions are arranged on a plan similar to that of a verse of poetry, as in the case of such a tune as "Home, Sweet Home," the form of the music becomes that known as the song form, which lies at the basis of nearly every musical composition not strictly contrapuntal.   Any music in which certain melodic shapes, known as figures, are not preserved and repeated, in which each phrase once heard is not heard again, is absolutely chaotic and does not convey to the human mind the conception of design, and hence also not of melody. Wagner, in striving to avoid the musical domination of the older forms, had to see to it that he did not fall into this kind of chaos.   He had to devise a larger and less confining form, but he had to have a form nevertheless.

But as soon as he had conceived the idea of preserving throughout his drama the first thematic
expression of any mental mood or idea, he had the solution of his problem in his hands.   For now the musical repetitions were bound to become numerous and
to acquire from the text a direct and unmistakable
significance which they could not possibly have by
themselves. And the criticism to which this form
might be open, if it were used as a purely musical
one, at once falls to the ground when it is remembered that the object is not musical alone, but also
dramatic, or musico-textual. The organic union of
the word and the tone makes the assistance given by
the text in explaining the meaning (sometimes arbitrary) of the music entirely defensible, and indeed
thoroughly commendable.

CHAPTER III

THE MUSICAL SYSTEM

In its details this Wagnerian system of musico-textual speech divides itself into music constructed of leading motives, or themes with a specified meaning, and music of the picture, or purely scenic music, such as that of the sailors in the first scene of "Tristan und Isolde," or the "Waldweben" of "Siegfried." And again the sung parts of the score divide themselves into ordinary speech, or quasi-recitative, and the speech of the high emotional situation, which is either intensely declamatory or extraordinarily melodious, according to the nature of the mood which has been reached.* A further feature of the scheme, which must not be overlooked, is that the repetitions of the thematic ideas are given chiefly to the orchestra, which thus becomes not a mere accompaniment, but a most potent explicator of the drama. This treatment of the orchestra makes it the creator of a musical atmosphere which surrounds the actors in the drama. Even when one has no acquaintance whatever with the specified meanings of the "leading motive" ("leading" should read "guiding"), the

---

* Even the purely lyric style is sometimes employed in strong situations where a song might be used, as in the case of Siegmund's Love Song.

dramatic influence of the musical background is such that he is brought into a complete emotional accord with the action on the stage. Thus the orchestra becomes a most potent factor in demonstrating and making effective Wagner's tenet that "In the drama we must become knowers through the Feeling. The Understanding tells us 'So is it,' only when the Feeling has told us, 'So must it be.'" It was with thoughts of this in his mind that Wagner wrote on Sept. 9, 1850, to Herr Von Zigesar :

"An audience which assembles in a fair mood is satisfied as soon as it distinctly understands what is going forward, and it is a great mistake to think that a theatrical audience must have a special knowledge of music in order to receive the right impression of a musical drama. To this entirely erroneous opinion we have been brought by the fact that in opera music has wrongly been made the aim,—while the drama was merely a means for the display of the music. Music, on the contrary, should do no more than contribute its full share towards making the drama clearly and quickly comprehensible at every moment. While listening to a good—that is, a rational—opera, people should, so to speak, not think of the music at all, but only feel it in an unconscious manner, while their fullest sympathy should be wholly occupied by the action represented. Every audience which has an uncorrupted sense and a human heart is therefore welcome to me as long as I may be certain that the dramatic action is made more immediately comprehensible and moving by the music, instead of being hidden by it."

From the actual potency of Wagner's music in producing the proper emotional mood in the auditor and from his own words, such as the above, the present writer has frequently argued that an intimate acquaintance with the leitmotiv scheme is not necessary to an understanding of the Wagner dramas. To comprehend and appreciate the grandeur of such scenes as the "Todesverkündigung" in "Die Walküre," the death of Siegfried and the immolation of Brünnhilde it is not needful to be able to catalogue the guiding themes as they pass through the vistas of the glowing score. All that is essential is an open mind. The eloquence of the music will do the rest. And if the guiding motives fail to create the proper emotional investiture for the same, then they are valueless, even at Wagner's own rating, for he says that we must feel before we can understand a drama. And we ourselves can readily see how useless it is to tell us the specified meanings of sweet musical phrases if they do not, when heard, help to warm into a vitalising glow the significance of the text and action. If they fail to do this, the organic union so ardently sought by Wagner does not exist. If they succeed, it matters not at all whether we know their names.

But we are all Elsas to these Lohengrins and Wagner himself was one of the Ortruds, for he has tempted us to ask the question, which is, fortunately for us, not fatal to our happiness. It becomes natural and proper therefore for every student of this master's works to take cognisance of the leitmotiv system and to aim at a thorough comprehension of its nature and its purpose. These have been very often misrepresented, and, even by many devoted admirers of Wagner's works, are yet misunderstood.

It was out of his first conviction that the musical embodiment of a mood having once been found should not be changed that the leit motif system grew. This first conviction led him to adopt in "Der Fliegende Holländer" certain musical phrases as typical of principal ideas in the play. He made a theme for the Dutchman's personality, a melody for his longing, another for the personality of Senta, the redeeming potency in the drama. In making these themes he sought to render them expressive not only of their primary dramatic ideas, but of the beautiful symbolism which lay behind these ideas. As this symbolism appealed largely to the sensibility of the hearer, it was peculiarly fitting that he should summon the aid of the music to the work for which it was best suited, namely the awakening of the sensibilities and through them of the emotions.

Out of this first experimental use of leading themes, Wagner gradually advanced to a complete and elaborate system. The student will look in vain for the finished system in "Tannhäuser" and "Lohengrin." In the former of these two works the leit motif is not employed and there is rather a tendency to use what is called "music of the scene" as a reminder of the place of the occurrence of an action than to repeat music expressive of the emotion lying behind the action itself. In "Lohengrin," however, one finds the leading motive employed in a few instances in precisely the same manner as it is in "Siegfried" or "Tristan," but not with the same persistency. It was in the construction of the great trilogy and its prologue that he found the full value of his system of musical cross-references, for in the vast complexity of this story, the explanatory force of music to which a direct meaning had been given was afforded the widest possible field of action.

The student of the system will find that the leading motives, guiding themes, typical phrases, or whatever one pleases to call them, are of several kinds. Some are employed very arbitrarily, it must be admitted, but

the text always makes their meaning clear and thereafter one easily understands the composer's intent.
They may be divided as follows : motives of personalities, as the Donner, the Siegfried-Hero, the
Brünnhilde motive ; those of the moving forces of the
drama, as the contract, the need of the Gods, and
the curse ; those of the tribal or racial elements, as the
Volsung, or the Nibelung motive ; those of places,
objects, and occupations, as the smithy, the sword,
the Walhalla, and those of the scene, as the Rhine
music, the forging, and the fire music.   This is a rude
classification, but it will answer the present object,
which is an exposition of the nature and aims of the
system.   The music of the tribal or racial elements
and that of the scene, the student will find, is seldom
modified in the course of the drama, while that relating to personalities is often changed in conformity
with alterations in the characters of which it is typical.   In "Der Ring des Nibelungen" the motives of
the Tarnhelm, the gold, the Rhine, the sword, the
dragon, and similar musical devices retain their original form almost always, though occasionally the demands of harmony and figure call for more or less
altered suggestions of them.

But the personal themes are sometimes submitted
to the processes of thematic development employed
in symphonic composition, and this resource of music
is always used by Wagner with a direct intention to
depict some development of character.   The system
of alteration may be summarised in this rule : if the
object represented in the music is one subject to
change, its representative theme is liable to development, but otherwise it will keep its original form,

unless there is a musical necessity for slight change or the possibility of dramatic suggestion in it. Those familiar with the dramas will recall that in the last scene of "Götterdämmerung" the Rhine music undergoes a harmonic change eloquently expressive of the mood of the Rhine maidens after the refusal of Siegfried to return the ring. It will be found, too, that any scenic music which is designed for more than one hearing has a deeper purpose than mere pictorial description and is designed as an aid in the creation of a proper mood of receptivity in the auditor, and thus as an assistance to complete understanding.

In the earlier dramas the proportion of scenic music to what may be called expository music is large. One finds many pages of "Lohengrin," for example, which consist of purely scenic writing. The arrival of Lohengrin and the combat in the first act, the approach to the cathedral in the second, the bridal chorus—these, when examined, are found to be pure music of the scene. The motives which are repeated with specified significance are few, and they deal chiefly with the moving forces of the drama, the Grail and the fatal question, the hatred of Ortrud and the knightly power of Lohengrin.

But the early works of Wagner show his musical system in its embryonic state, and, while the study of the scores is from that point of view particularly interesting, for satisfactory illustrations of the method we must go to the later dramas. Here we are constantly confronted with evidence of Wagner's sincerity of purpose, his unflagging endeavour to achieve that organic union of text and music which was so dear to his heart. In "Das Rheingold," for instance, occurs for the first time a theme to be heard often in the subsequent dramas, the theme of the sword. The composer was not content to make a theme of any sort and arbitrarily call it the sword motive. He tried to produce something which should suggest the sword and the heroic uses to which it was to be put, and thus he composed this brilliant and martial theme, intoned by a trumpet :

Another artistically constructed motive, which may be quoted here, is that representative of the Tarnhelm, the mystic cap which Mime makes for Alberich and which renders the wearer invisible. In this motive Wagner creates the atmosphere of mystery by making the tonality of the music uncertain through the use of the empty "fifth." Some of the most effective

themes are those which are associated with personalities in their visible aspects, as the fire music, which represents Loge, and the "Ritt-Motiv," or galloping figure, of Kundry in "Parsifal." Motives of this kind Wagner devised with great musical skill, for they impress the mind of the hearer in two ways, bringing before it a part of the pictorial movement of the drama and also representing certain personal attributes, while

at the same time they are so made that they readily lend themselves to thematic variation without
losing their identity.

The attentive listener to these later dramas of Wagner, then, will find, in the fully developed musical
system, voice parts which consist of declamation occasionally rising into the sublimest kind of arioso, without once sacrificing the poetic spirit to any demand
of mere musical formalism, and an orchestral accompaniment which is not an accompaniment in the
sense of merely affording support to the singer's
voice, but is independent and expressive of much that
the actors do not utter. This expressiveness is gained
by the employment of themes to which a definite
meaning has been attached, no matter how arbitrarily, by their association with a picture, an action,
a personality, or a thought. This association is made
perfectly comprehensible to every listener who bears in
mind that the text is the explanation of this music,
and its only explanation. The music never exists for
its own sake, but is a vital part of the speech of the
drama. The orchestra is always an explicator, never
a mere support. And here and there we meet
with passages of merely descriptive or scenic music,
in which not even guiding themes of scenic nature
are used. The ultimate purpose of the entire
musical scheme is organic union with the text so
that the music shall give perfect expression to the
drama of emotions which is being enacted, and
place the hearer in the proper moods for the reception of it. While all the old musical forms employed
in opera are abandoned, Wagner avoids formlessness by the repetition of identified themes. In

summing up this important matter let me quote Wagner's own words from "A Communication to My Friends" :

" This opera form [the old form] was never of its very nature a form embracing the whole drama, but rather an arbitrary conglomerate of separate smaller forms of song, whose fortuitous concatenation of arias, duos, trios, etc., with choruses and so-called ensemble-pieces, made out the actual edifice of opera. In the poetic fashioning of my stuffs [materials] it was henceforth impossible for me to contemplate a filling of these ready-moulded forms, but solely a bringing of the drama's broader object to the cognisance of the feeling. In the whole course of the drama I saw no possibility of division or demarcation, other than the acts in which the place or time, or the scenes in which the *dramatis personæ* change. Moreover the plastic unity of the mythic stuff brought with it this advantage, that, in the arrangement of my scenes, all those minor details which the modern playwright finds so indispensable for the elucidation of involved historical occurrences were quite unnecessary, and the whole strength of the portrayal could be concentrated upon a few weighty and decisive moments of development. Upon the working out of these fewer scenes in each of which a decisive ' Stimmung' [mood] was to be given its full play, I might linger with an exhaustiveness already reckoned for in the original draft ; I was not compelled to make shift with mere suggestions, and — for the sake of economy — to hasten on from one suggestion to another ; but with needful repose I could display the simple object in the very last connections required to bring it home to the dramatic understanding. Through this natural attribute of the stuff I was not in the least coerced to strain the planning of my scenes into any preconceived conformity with given musical forms, since they dictated of themselves their mode of musical completion. In the ever surer feeling hereof it thus could no more occur to me to rack with wilful outward canons the musical form that sprang selfbidden from the very nature of these scenes, to break its natural mould by violent grafting-in of conventional slips of operatic song. Thus I by no means set out with the fixed purpose of a deliberate iconoclast [Formumänderer—lit., changer of forms], to destroy, forsooth, the prevailing operatic forms of aria, duet, etc., but the omission of these forms followed from the very nature of the stuff, with whose intelligible presentment to the feeling through an adequate vehicle I alone had to do. . . .

"Just as the joinery of my individual scenes excluded every alien and unnecessary detail, and led all interest to the dominant Chief-mood, so did the whole building of my drama join itself into one organic unity, whose easily surveyed members were made out by those fewer scenes and situations which set the passing mood: no mood could be permitted to be struck in any one of these scenes that did not stand in a weighty relation to the mood of all the other scenes, so that the development of the moods from out each other, and the constant obviousness of this development, should establish the unity of the drama in its very mode of expression. Each of these Chief-moods, in keeping with the nature of the stuff, must also gain a definite musical expression, which should display itself to the sense of hearing as a definite musical theme. Just as in the progress of the drama the intended climax of a decisory Chief-mood was only to be reached through a development, continuously present to the feeling, of the individual moods already roused, so must the musical expression, which directly influences the physical feeling, necessarily take a decisive share in this development to a climax ; and this was brought about quite of itself, in the shape of a characteristic issue of principal themes, that spread itself not over one scene only (as heretofore in separate operatic 'numbers'), but over the whole drama, and that in intimate connection with the poetic aim."

Where Gluck had sought to make music enforce the expression of the sentiment of the text, Wagner aimed to make it the very expression itself, and in following out this purpose he elaborated the system of musical presentation of the content of a drama which carried him entirely away from the beaten paths of opera. It was the radical departure of his system which aroused the opposition of a deep misunderstanding. His contemporaries saw what he had abolished from his works, but could not comprehend the substitute. And even to-day, when the Wagner drama is accepted the world over, there is still a general failure to understand that the leitmotiv system was conceived as the only preservation of necessary musical method in a drama which had banished from its scheme the use of the established operatic forms.

CHAPTER IV

THE SYSTEM AS COMPLETED

WAGNER, in striving for a complete and natural revelation of the emotional content of his dramas, discovered that the continual flow of music which he had adopted was not possible if fixed verse-figures were employed. The verse-figure prescribes and limits the musical figure. Nevertheless there must be some rhythmic principle in the verse. Wagner found that which was most suited to his needs in the ancient staff-rhyme, or alliterative verse. The fundamental basis of this verse is consonance of sounds, not confined to the final rhyme but employed in the body of the verse and thus made a part of its inner nature. Not a little excellent information as to the exact nature of the alliterative verse may be obtained from the introductory essay to the second volume of Percy's "Reliques." It should be mentioned that Percy was acquainted with Icelandic literature and first made it known in England when he translated Mallet's "Northern Antiquities." He tells us that the Icelandic language is of the same origin as the Anglo-Saxon, and that was the reason why both employed the staff-rhyme. The alliteration consisted in "a certain artful repetition of sounds in the middle of the verses. This was adjusted according to their rules of prosody, one of which was that every distich should contain at least three words beginning with the same letter or sound.   Two of these correspondent sounds might be placed either in the first or second line of the distich, and one in the other ; but all three were not regularly to be crowded into one line.   This will best be understood by the following examples " :

" Meire og Minne   Gab Ginunga
  Moga heimdaller.   Enn Gras huerge."

This verse was used by the old poets of the Saxons in Britain.   The epic of " Beowulf " is written in this style and so are the poems of Caedmon, the noted paraphraser of the scriptures.   An authoritative writer says :

" The poetry of the Anglo-Saxons was neither modulated according to foot-measure, like that of the Greeks and Romans, nor written with rhymes, like that of modern languages.   Its chief and universal characteristic was a very regular alliteration, so arranged that in every couplet there should be two principal words in the first line beginning with the same letter, which letter must also be the initial of the first word on which the stress of the voice falls in the second line.   The only approach to a metrical system yet discovered is that two risings and two fallings of the voice seem necessary to each perfect line."

A specimen of this alliterative verse from the works of Caedmon shows the peculiarity of the construction.

" Se him cwom to frofre.
  & to feorh-nere.
  Mid lufan & mid lisse.
  Se thone lig tosceaf.
  Halig and heofon-beohrt.
  Hatan fyres.
  Tosweop hine & toswende.

> Thurh tha swithan miht.
> Ligges leoma." *

The reader will note the alliteration of the l's in the third and fourth lines, and the h's in the next two. The change in vowel sounds following the consonants was deemed by Wagner as of especial value in music.

As the English language developed, this method of rhythmic construction remained in use, and we find that it is used in such old poems as "Piers Plowman's Vision" (about 1350).

> "In a Somer Season when hot was the Sunne,
> I Shope me into Shroubs as I a Shepe were ;
> Habite as an Harmet, unHoly of werkes,
> Went Wyde in thys world Wonders to heare."

Wagner, however, modelled his verse on that of the original writers of it, as their language was more closely affiliated with German than the early English was. He made an exhaustive study of the constitution of the staff-rhyme, and saw in its conservation of the elementary principles of poetic speech the factor necessary to the perfection of an organic union with music. For those who have studied the conventional formulas of musical expression—the major

---

* Who to them came for comfort,
And for their lives' salvation,
With love and with grace ;
Who the flames scattered
(Holy and heaven-bright)
Of the hot fire,
Swept at and dashed away,
Through his great might,
The beams of flame.
                    —Paraphrase of the Song of Azariah.
Thorpe's translation.

and minor modes, chromatic progressions, the declamatory style as opposed to the pure cantilena, the crescendo and diminuendo, the agitato—know that all these have been transferred from the natural employment of vocal tone and articulation in speech as influenced by the emotions which these musical symbols are intended to represent. And we know, too, that the reflex action of music in producing in the hearer the emotions which it aims to depict is due to its adoption of methods founded on man's oral expression of his feeling. Wagner saw in the staffrhyme the first attempt to systemise into poetry the elevated speech of emotion, and he discerned in it technical features admirably suited to his plan. In "Opera and Drama" he says :

"In Stabreim the kindred speech-roots are fitted to one another in such a way that, just as they sound alike to the physical ear, they also knit like objects into one collective image in which the Feeling may utter its conclusions about them. Their sensibly cognisable resemblance they win either from a kinship of the vowel sounds, especially when these stand open in front without any initial consonant (' Erb und eigen.' ' Immer und ewig '); or from the sameness of the initial consonant itself, which characterises the likeness as one belonging peculiarly to the object (' Ross und Reiter.' ' Froh und frei '); or again, from the sameness of the terminal consonant that closes up the root from behind (as an assonance), provided the individualising force of the word lies in that terminal (' Hand und Mund.' ' Recht und Pflicht ')."

The fruits of these philological considerations reveal themselves to the hearer of the works in a wonderfully delicate perfection of accentuation and cadence, which simulates that of the spoken line in a vivifying manner. One has only to read, as one would naturally speak, such words as " Winterstürme wichen dem

Wonnemond," and then sing them to the opening notes of " Siegmund's Love Song" to see how beautifully this staff-rhyme adapts itself to the needs of what Wagner called "Word-tone-speech," an expression which explains itself. Furthermore, these lines of staff-rhyme have no metrical domination over the music. A single reading of any familiar passage in the later works will show the reader that the lines of the verse do not set the limits for the phrases of the music as they do in the old song forms, but that the composer is entirely free in his phraseology, while he can never quite obliterate the rhythmic basis of the verse. This plasticity was of inestimable importance in the Wagnerian system, with its endless melody, its independent accompaniments, and its disuse of the old forms.

We have now made an examination of the artistic aims and methods of Wagner. The reader should now be able to grasp the basic truth that his mature works are not to be viewed as operas but as poetic dramas. The argument is frequently made that no serious criticism of opera is necessary because it is an absurdity throughout. People do not sing ; therefore all attempts at dramatic verity in the lyric drama are useless. And from this is drawn the conclusion that it makes no difference whether composers write pretty tunes merely for their own sake, and use the set forms and conventions of the old opera, or write an endless recitation with an orchestral background. The object should be to please, and since the entertainment is musical, let us have pretty tunes at all costs.

The same arguments, of course, apply in a way to all forms of the poetic drama. People do not speak blank verse, nor talk in metaphors. It is altogether improbable that Henry V. or Richard II. or Macbeth even rose to such heights of speech as Shakespeare's personages. The ground upon which the poetic drama rests is that of symbolism, and in the lyric play this, by reason of the flexibility of music, may reach its highest elevation. The symbolism of the Wagnerian drama is both poetic and musical. With the former I shall attempt to deal in the study of the individual plays ; but of the musical symbolism it may here be said that while technically the speech of the Wagnerian drama is but blank verse raised by song to its highest power, the representation of emotional moods by the musical symbols, vocal or orchestral, is cast in a mould far grander than that of the spoken drama, and its influence upon the auditor is immeasurably larger. If by the employment of these musical symbols the dramatist can cause the auditor to throb with the emotions of the personages in the drama, he has accomplished the ultimate aim of his art and justified his form.

To achieve this result requires perfect sincerity on the part of the dramatist and the most exquisite adaptation of the theatrical means to the end in view. The old opera had abandoned all but a shallow pretence of these, and had given itself to the easy business of tickling the ear. Wagner's work is an appeal to the intelligence through the feeling. His ambition was to give the lyric theatre vitality and an influence with the public. To do this he was forced to abandon all that he found ready to hand, and to build again from the foundations. In doing so he restored some of the outward semblance of the conventions. He wrote duets, as in the second act of "Tristan und

Isolde." But he did this with a perfect comprehension of the power of music to symbolise an emotional state shared by two lovers. On the other hand, he raised the orchestra to the position of an exponent of the dramatic thought, and this, again, was done with a masterly conception of the potency of absolute music in painting mood-pictures. Here he found an agency for symbolism in the poetic drama far beyond the loftiest dreams of the poet of the spoken play.

The motto of the attendant at Wagner performances, then, must be, "The play's the thing," and he must measure their value and estimate their influence upon him wholly from that point of view. A drama in music was the conception of the originators of what came to be called Opera ; but it had been, as we have seen, lost to sight in Wagner's youth by reason of the immense popularity of the easily made productions of Rossini, Donizetti, and Bellini, in which the music was the ultimate object and the libretto only a means toward its production. Wagner's ideal was a drama in which music should he a factor valuable wholly because of its power to embody and convey emotions. That such a form of drama departed from the more material realism of the spoken play was not a matter to trouble a profoundly æsthetic intellect. Wagner, like the greatest masters in all forms of art, was opposed to that kind of realism which bases its claims on its copying of mere objects or external phenomena. This is the cheap realism of the sensational drama, which puts fire engines and hansom cabs and professional burglars on the stage, and holds that it thus reproduces human life. It is, perhaps, a form of art, but it is a low one, because it has not the imaginative or symbolical elements which are essential to high art. It is the art which copies, not that which creates. The painter who reproduces on his canvas a group of flowers or a human form may be a master of the technics of painting, but the fervid imagination of Turner's "Slave Ship," with its ill-drawn figures, is worth a thousand copies of real things.

As art rises in the scale of nobility, it appeals more and more to the imagination, till it reaches that point at which, in Schumann's words, "only genius understands genius." Advancing along this path, art tends always toward the employment of symbolism. Poetry is in every nation the first and most convincing demonstration of the feeling of humanity for symbolical expression. Poetic forms are in themselves symbolic, and the figures of speech employed in them are word-symbols meant to awaken the imaginative powers of the reader. The drama in its earliest phases was purely artistic, coupling, as it did, the symbolism of a highly organised mythology with poetic speech. The blank-verse plays of Shakespeare are filled with the noblest symbolism of the spoken play, and those who decry them as unreal because of their poetic form and diction show an utter inability to understand artistic design.

In its inception the opera was, as we have seen, an attempt to revive the form of the antique drama of Greece. Its originators cherished an honest purpose, but their knowledge was not sufficient to carry it to a successful issue. Neither had they at their command a rich enough *materia musica,* for until their day composers had devoted themselves to the expression of contemplative religious feeling and the musical symbols of human passion were yet undeveloped. Unfortunately for the "Drama per musica," as the early masters called it, the first attempts at the construction of definite operatic forms led directly away from the honesty of dramatic art and turned opera into a series of tunes, each complete in itself, and strung upon a slender thread of recitative. Wagner, setting out as he did to build a national drama, had no reason whatever for following the methods of the Italian composers. His aim was to embody certain national thoughts, as projected in the great folk-legends of the Teutonic people, in artistic plays, and to use for that embodiment the most influential means at his command. Music was his vocal instrument instead of speech, not simply because he was a musician, but also because he was convinced that it would afford him the loftiest utterance for the emotional substance of his dramas.

For these were not to be dramas in which the mere telling of a story was the object in view. The drama was to be, not a series of incidents of pictorial efficiency, but a development of feelings and an exhibition of typical humanity, embracing those wonderful world-heroes and heroines into whose conception have been poured the concentrated imaginings of several races and centuries. For such a play as "Tristan und Isolde," in which the movement is entirely emotional and not incidental, the spoken form would have been prolix and wearisome. This play, given without music, would become a dreary stretch of talk. On the other hand, the simplicity of the action and the intensity of the emotions permit the composer to expend his entire force upon the musical expression of feeling, thereby confining himself strictly to the province of music and raising the symbolism of the drama to the highest power. Herein lies one of the principal differences between the spoken and the sung play. Yet in it also is to be seen a demonstration of the indisputable fact that the works of Wagner are dramas. So, then, we must view them ; and, so doing, we shall approach the contemplation of Wagner's art work from the point desired by him. We shall enter into his domain in the spirit of sympathetic understanding, and it will be to us not a valley of shadows, as it is to those who enter with closed eyes, but a sea of splendour and sunlight, where the spirit may

> " Burst all links of habit—there to wander far away
> On from island unto island at the gateways of the day."

14

PART III

THE GREAT MUSIC DRAMAS

INTRODUCTORY

IT is customary to divide the artistic career of Wagner into three periods, the first embracing the production of the early works and "Rienzi," the second that of "Der Fliegende Holländer," "Tannhäuser," and "Lohengrin," and the third that of the remaining works. It is the opinion of the present writer that the recognition of four periods would make the matter clearer to the lover of this master's creations. The early works, which are not heard except in one or two places, may be left out of consideration. We may then classify "Rienzi" as the production of the first period. "Der Fliegende Holländer" should stand in a period by itself, as representing the purely embryonic epoch of the true Wagner, while "Tannhäuser" and "Lohengrin" may properly be allotted to a third or transition period. The remaining works may be regarded as belonging to the period of the mature Wagner, though there would be no serious difficulty in subdividing this part of his artistic career. It seems to me, however, that no satisfactory end would be gained by doing so.

The reader of this book has already seen that in writing "Rienzi" Wagner was actuated by purposes entirely different from those which moved him in the creation of "Der Fliegende Holländer." The first of the lyric dramas presently to be examined was, as its maker said, a grand opera pure and simple. Then came the days of despair in Paris, when Wagner, hoping nothing for the future, gave free rein to his artistic impulses and produced the dramatic story of the unhappy Vanderdecken. In the creation of this drama nothing influenced Wagner's mind but the desire to write according to the dictates of his own artistic conscience. But he had not yet worked out a scheme of dramatic composition. He had only just come upon the fundamental ideas of his plan. Its details were still far away from his conception. "Embryonic," then, is the term to apply to this period of his productivity.

With "Tannhäuser" there entered into the field of his artistic vision those broader musical and ethical conceptions of the lyric drama which afterward developed themselves into a complex and influential system. With "Lohengrin" we see these ideas taking more definite shape. The literary and musical plan of the drama is more closely organised, and the musical style is more clearly defined. The diction becomes more akin to that of later works, and the methods show more certainty and more mastery. "Lohengrin" is a long advance beyond "Der Fliegende Holländer." It prepares us for such a work as "Die Meistersinger," though hardly in full for "Parsifal." It must be borne in mind that the original conception of "Die Meistersinger" belongs to the same period as "Lohengrin," and that although the music was not written till long afterward, the score must naturally have been coloured by the first thoughts of the work and so have come somewhat under the influence of the "Lohengrin" style.

In the early dramas we meet with Wagner's inclusion of ethical ideas in his designs. One seeks in vain among the old popular operas of the Rossini or Meyerbeer schools for a drama with a moral. But owing to Wagner's adoption of the myth as the material from which to erect his dramatic structures, the inclusion of an ethical lesson in each of his schemes followed almost inevitably. For mythology is essentially ethical. Wagner, however, humanised the teachings of the mythologies into which he delved by emphasising the beautiful idea of the saving grace of woman. He did not, perhaps, deliberately adopt as the motto of his works the line of Goethe, "The woman-soul leadeth us ever upward and on," but it may be inscribed upon them without violence to their intent. We may see by an examination of the original sources of the dramas how the importance of this thought in the works is due to the deliberate purpose of Wagner himself to bring it to the front. In some of the original stories it plays little or no part, but in the Wagner music drama the "Ewig-Weibliche" is always impressed upon the imagination of the auditor with all the skill of the dramatist and all the eloquence of the musician.

In "Lohengrin," as the reader can see for himself, the master made a special point of excluding the operation of this principle, because he desired to bring forward a study of a woman who had no love in her nature. With Wagner the woman-soul could be influential for good only when acting under the guidance of love. Ortrud acted under the dictates of hate, and her influence was therefore destructive, but ultimately futile. The reader will readily perceive the dramatic, poetic, and musical value of this thought. In all the

Wagnerian dramas we are confronted with studies of the warring of good and evil principles. When the good principle is identified or associated with the love of woman, and that love is made the saving grace of its object, the dramatic force of the story is splendidly intensified, the scope of the poetry and the music immeasurably widened. Especially is the music benefited by the possibility of identifying the highest ethical idea of the poem with the most beautiful and potent of its emotions ; for it is the peculiar privilege of the music to voice the emotional content of the drama, and when this becomes one with the ethical idea, the auditor is led by the music into the very shrine of the poet's imagination. The reader will note, too, that in those dramas in which the love of a woman does not figure as a saving influence, the tragic fate of the hero is accentuated, and the woman herself is made a more conspicuous embodiment of grief.

In most of the works of Wagner there is to be found a philosophical or metaphysical basis, and this is most easily discovered in the later dramas. The poet-composer was at different times deeply influenced by the writings of Feuerbach and Schopenhauer. From the former he obtained some of the vaguer conceptions of his philosophy, but the latter supplied him with definite ideas. It was in the early fifties that Wagner was a student of Feuerbach, and his mind eagerly caught at the thoughts contained indefinitely in such phrases as "highest being — the community of being," "death, the fulfilment of love," and such declarations as "only in love does the finite become the infinite." These ideas later took clearer shape in his mind when he gathered from Schopenhauer the sharply cut description of the negation of the will to live as the highest abstraction and elevation of thought.

With love figuring as a community of being, with death as its highest fulfilment, and with the absolute effacement of the desire of life as the loftiest aspiration of human passion, Wagner was equipped with a philosophical background for several of his most dramatic conceptions, notably for "Tristan und Isolde." Yet one has no difficulty in understanding his own assertion that the negation of the will to live and the community of being had entered his mind in an indefinite shape long before he read the works of the two philosophers, for they may be traced in the story of "Der Fliegende Holländer."

Some of Wagner's biographers, notably Houston Stewart Chamberlain, to whom this master was little short of a divinity, have devoted much space to the consideration of Wagner as a philosopher. The truth is that he was never a philosopher at all in the strict sense of that term. He was a groper after philosophies. He sought for a rational foundation for his artistic theories and endeavoured to found them upon metaphysical tenets borrowed from works which seemed to meet his needs. But there is no difficulty in perceiving that what always appealed to him in a philosophy was its poetic or dramatic material. That he was sometimes mistaken as to the real value of that material is not astonishing. The best text-books of Wagner's philosophy are his dramas. Therein one finds that the ethical side of a philosophy was what touched him most directly, and that it did so because of its close relation to the principles underlying the tragic in human experience. This is paying a higher compliment to Wagner than to call him a philosopher, for it is practically asserting that his dramatic nature was his guiding star.

It is easy to note that in "Der Fliegende Holländer" Wagner more nearly rid himself of those hampering historical details to which he objected than he did in "Tannhäuser," and more especially than in "Lohengrin." The legend of the "Flying Dutchman" was not one of the great world-thoughts, but it had the advantages of being founded on an incident which might be repeated at any time and in any place — namely, the periodical landing of the wanderer. In "Tannhäuser" and "Lohengrin," and in "Parsifal," Wagner used material found in the great cycle of tales belonging to the Christian mythology of Germany, England, and France. He found himself unable to avoid introducing some of the historical details contained in the original stories. Because of their sources and nature these three dramas have been classed as the Christian trilogy of Wagner in contradistinction to the Nibelung works, which are called the pagan trilogy. While this classification is justified by the nature of the works, it should be remembered that Wagner himself repudiated any intention to produce works charged with a religious purpose. Ethical ideas, indeed, he always cherished, but he denied that he taught Christianity. He recognised the assistance which art had given to religion, and he saw that in Greece the dramatisation of national religious beliefs had given to the stage a power unknown in modern times. But he himself was too wise to dream of making the lyric drama a mere corollary or illustration to the pulpit text. A passage in "A Communication to My Friends," quoted in the account of his resumption of work on "Tannhäuser," explains the mood which governed him in the composition of the score. He says that at the time he was yearning for a pure and unapproachable ideal of love. "What, in fine," he continues, "could this love-yearning, the noblest thing my heart could feel, what other could it be than a longing for release from the present, for absorption into an element of endless love, a love denied to earth and reachable through the gates of death alone ? . . . How absurd, then, must those critics seem to me, who, drawing all their wit from modern wantonness, insist on reading into my 'Tannhäuser' a specifically Christian and impotently pietistic drift !"

We may now proceed to the study of the great dramas which have for so many years been the joy of the artistic mind and the torture of the indolent. The last word of this author on the subject of studying these dramas is this: Learn the text. By the text the music must be measured. By the text the music must be understood. By the music the text is illuminated and made vital. But every measure of Wagner's music is explained by the poetry. It is useless to go to the performance of a Wagner drama with your mind charged with thoughts of the music. Think of the play and let the music do its own work. That is what Wagner himself asks you to do, and it is the only fair test to which to put him. If his music vitalises the drama for you, it matters not whether you know the leading motives or the harmonic scheme or the orchestration. The work of the music is accomplished. But that work cannot be accomplished if you are in the dark as to its purpose. And ¡n the dark you must always be unless you have a full knowledge of "what is going forward on the stage." To gain that you must know the entire text. Therefore the written word of the drama is your guide to its comprehension.

RIENZI

THE LAST OF THE TRIBUNES.

Grand Tragic Opera in Five Acts;

First performed at the Royal Saxon Court Theatre, Dresden, October 20, 1842.

Original Cast.

Cola Rienzi	Tichatschek.
Irene	Fräulein Wüst.
Steffano Colonna	Dettmer
Adriano . . .	Mme. Schroeder-Devrient.
Paolo Orsini	Wächter.
Raimondo	Vestri.
Baroncelli	Reinhold.
Cecco del Vecchio	Risse.
A Messenger of Peace . . .	Thiele.

Hamburg, 1844; Königsberg, 1845; Berlin, Oct. 26, 1847; Prague, 1859; Hanover, 1859; Weimar, Wiesbaden, and Darmstadt, 1860; Mayence, 1863; Stockholm, 1864; Bremen, Gratz, and Stettin, 1865; Würzburg, 1866; Schwerin, 1867; Rotterdam, 1868; Leipsic, 1869; Paris (in French translation by Charles Nuitter and J. Guillaume), April 6, 1869; Cassel, 1870; Augsburg, Carlsruhe, Vienna, and Munich, 1871; Mannheim and Magdeburg, 1872; Brunswick, 1873;

Venice, 1874; Strassburg and Breslau, 1875; Bologna and Madrid, 1876; Cologne and Florence, 1877; Riga, 1878; New York, in German by the Pappenheim-Adams Co., Mar. 4, 1878, and in English, Jan. 27, 1879; London, Italian and English, 1879; St. Petersburg, 1879; Rome, Innsprück, Freiburg, and Ghent, 1880; Frankfort-on-the-Main, 1881, and Basle, 1882.

First performance in New York, Academy of Music, March 4, 1878, by the Pappenheim-Adams Company.

Cast.

Adriano . . .	Mme. Eugenia Pappenheim.
Irene	Miss Alexandre Human.
Cola Rienzi	Charles Adams.
Paolo Orsini	A. Blum.
Steffano Colonna	H. Wiegand.
Raimondo	F. Adolphe.
A Messenger of Peace . . .	Miss Cooney.

Conductor, Max Maretzek.

The names of the singers of Baroncelli and Cecco del Vecchio were not advertised nor mentioned in the newspapers.

RIENZI

THE first of the series of great musical works by which the fame of Wagner was made does not call for extended discussion. Its source is familiar to every reader of English literature, and its method of construction and style of composition are those employed in the operas of the Meyerbeerian school. In the fact that Wagner wrote his own libretto, which awakened the interest even of Hector Berlioz, and in the immense vigour and wonderful colour of the score, lie the chief indications of the Wagner of the future. The reader has already learned how Wagner undertook this work with the deliberate purpose of making it a lever to pry open the doors of the Paris Grand Opéra. With that idea in mind it is not at all astonishing that he should have followed the model of Meyerbeer, who was in Wagner's early days the master spirit of the world of French music.

Wagner in subsequent years was extremely particular to keep before the minds of his friends the fact that it was not simply pecuniary success that he sought. He was eager to shine as an artist. That we must concede. He was, indeed, ambitious, and had a profound conviction of his own genius. But in these early days, when the inner artistic struggle found its companion piece in the outward fight for existence, Wagner had not reached the æsthetic convictions which afterward came to him. Therefore his conception of Bulwer's "Rienzi" was wholly as material for the libretto of a grand opera of the Meyerbeerian school. We have seen how his first attempt to enter Paris was with the scenario of "Die Hohe Braut," which was sent to Scribe, but lost in the mail for want of proper prepayment of the postal charges. We then find that Wagner wrote in 1837 to his Leipsic friend Lewald, who had some acquaintance in Paris, telling him that he had in his mind the book of "Rienzi."

"I intend," he said, "to compose it in the German language, to make an attempt whether there is a possibility of getting it performed in Berlin in the course of fifty years, if God grant me so long a life. Perhaps Scribe will like it, in which case Rienzi will learn to sing French in a moment; or else this might be a way to goad Berliners into accepting the opera if they were told that Paris was ready to bring it out, but that preference was for once to be given to Berlin; for a stage like that of Berlin or Paris is absolutely necessary to bring out such a work properly."

Nothing came of this correspondence, and Wagner's "Rienzi" was not permitted to astonish the Parisians. Nevertheless he began himself to write the libretto at Riga in the summer of 1838. In the spring of 1839 he had composed the music of the first two acts, and with this uncompleted score he set out from Riga on the voyage which ultimately landed him in Paris. Of his meeting with Meyerbeer at Boulogne, his exhibition of his manuscript to the great dictator, his completion of the work in the days of his hardship in Paris (in 1841), and the sending of the bulky score to Dresden the story has been told in the biographical part of this book. It need not now be repeated. Of the instantaneous success of the opera at Dresden there is plentiful evidence. It was in the style which the public of the time admired and it heaped up effects enough to dazzle the crowd. But it must be said for Wagner that he had some dim thought when he began this work of producing something really artistic He was simply mistaken as to the method. At this point I must ask the reader to accept Wagner's own words as a better exposition of himself and his purposes than anything which I can invent. In the "Autobiographic Sketch " he says :

"Since I was so completely bare of Paris prospects, I took up once more the composition of my ' Rienzi.' I now destined it for Dresden: in the first place, because I knew that this theatre possessed the very best material—Devrient, Tichatschek, etc.; secondly, because I could more reasonably hope for an entrée there, relying upon the support of my earliest acquaintances. My ' Liebesverbot ' I now gave up almost completely; I felt that I could no longer regard myself as its composer. With all the greater freedom I followed now my true artistic creed in the prosecution of the music to my ' Rienzi.' "

Further, let the reader note well these passages from " A Communication to My Friends ":

"My home troubles increased ; the desire to wrest myself from a humiliating plight now grew into an eager longing to begin something on a grand and inspiring scale, even though it should involve the temporary abandonment of any practical aim. This mood was fed and fostered by my reading Bulwer's ' Rienzi.' From the misery of modern private life, whence I could nowhere glean the scantiest stuff for artistic treatment, I was borne away by the picture of a great his-torico-political event, in lingering on which I needs must find a salutary distraction from the cares and conditions that appeared to me as nothing else than absolutely fatal to art. In accordance with my particular artistic bent, however, I still kept more or less to the purely

15

musical, or rather, operatic standpoint. This Rienzi with great thoughts in his head, great feelings in his heart, amid an entourage of coarseness and vulgarity, set all my nerves a-quivering with sympathy and love; yet my plan for an art-work based thereon sprang first from the perception of a purely lyric element in the hero's atmosphere. The 'Messengers of Peace,' the Church's summons to awake, the Battle hymns—these were what impelled me to an opera: 'Rienzi.'" . . .

"To write an opera for whose production only the most exceptional means should suffice—a work, therefore, which I should never feel tempted to bring before the public amid such cramping relations as those which then oppressed me, and the hope of whose eventual production should thus incite me to make every sacrifice in order to extricate myself from those relations,—this is what resolved me to resume and carry out with all my might my former plan for 'Rienzi.' In the preparation of this text also I took no thought for anything but the writing of an effective operatic libretto. The 'Grand Opéra' with all its scenic and musical display, its sensationalism and massive vehemence, loomed large before me; and not merely to copy it, but with reckless extravagance to outbid it in its every detail became the object of my artistic ambition. However, I should be unjust to myself did I represent this ambition as my only motive for the conception and execution of my 'Rienzi.' The stuff really aroused my enthusiasm, and I put nothing into my sketch which had not a direct bearing on the grounds of this enthusiasm. My chief concern was my Rienzi himself; and only when I felt quite contented with him did I give rein to the notion of a 'grand opera.' Nevertheless from a purely artistic point of view this 'grand opera' was the pair of spectacles through which I unconsciously regarded my Rienzi-stuff; nothing in that stuff did I find enthrall me but what could be looked at through these spectacles. True, that I always fixed my gaze upon the stuff itself, and did not keep one eye open for certain ready-made musical effects which I might wish to father on it by hook or crook; only, I saw it in no other light than that of a 'five-act-opera,' with five brilliant 'finales,' and filled with hymns, processions, and the musical clash of arms. Thus I bestowed no greater care upon the verse and diction than seemed needful for turning out a good and not trivial opera-text. I did not set out with the object of writing duets, trios, &c., but they found their own way in here and there because I looked upon my subject exclusively through the medium of 'Opera.' For instance, I by no means hunted about in my stuff for a pretext for a ballet ; but with the eyes of the opera-composer I perceived in it a self-evident festival that Rienzi must give to the People, and at which he would have to exhibit to them in dumb show a drastic scene from their ancient history : this scene being the story of Lucretia and the consequent expulsion of the Tarquins from Rome. Thus in every department of my plan I was certainly ruled by the stuff alone ; but, on the other hand, I ruled this stuff according to my only chosen pattern, the form of the Grand Opera. My artistic individuality, in its dealings with the impressions of life, was still entirely under the influence of purely artistic, or rather art-formalistic, mechanically operating impressions." *

The reader will now understand the artistic ideas which governed Wagner in the production of his only "grand opera." He was, as he himself declares, true to the artistic creed which he cherished at that time, but that creed was opposed to the one afterward formulated in his mind. His first artistic beliefs were founded on the theory that not the ground-plan, but the external treatment, of the grand opera was at fault. He fancied that he could preserve the element which he has called "art-formalistic" and yet reach dramatic verity. He aimed at a consistent embodiment of character in his hero ; he sought to give to all the factors of the opera, even such accessories as the ballet, a direct and powerful dramatic significance ; but it had not yet come to him that he must, in order to make a consistent drama in music, sacrifice form to content, and get rid of the whole mechanical apparatus of the spectacular opera. Here, then, let me quote the most significant passage of all, one from the "Autobiographic Sketch":

* Prose Works, Vol. I., W. A. Ellis's translation.

"When in the autumn [or 1838] I began the composition of my
'Rienzi,' I allowed naught to influence me except the single purpose
to answer to my subject. I set myself no model, but gave myself
entirely to the feeling which now consumed me, the feeling that I had
already so far progressed that I might claim something significant
from the development of my artistic powers, and expect some not insignificant result. The very notion of being consciously weak or
trivial—even in a single bar—was appalling to me."

The frequent iteration of such statements shows how
anxious Wagner was in subsequent years lest he should
be accused of deliberately pandering to that depraved
public taste which he decried. In his endeavour to
treat the grand-opera form honestly he accepted as his
musical models several of his predecessors. In "Die
Feen" he believed that he was following the lead of
Beethoven, Weber, and Marschner, and in "Das
Liebesverbot" he turned for help to Auber and
Bellini. In "Rienzi" he utilised elements from all of
these, and added to them the pomp of Spontini and
the external glare of Meyerbeer. The libretto, as he
says, is simply a good opera book. One looks in
vain through it for more than traces of the dramatic
power and real poetry to be found in the later works.
Similarly the music is just good opera music of the
most pretentious kind. It glitters, but seldom glows.
It astonishes, but seldom moves. The instrumentation shows many of the idiosyncrasies of the later
Wagner, but it is generally without inner strength.
The whole work is superficial, and calls for precisely
the same sort of criticism as the operas of Meyerbeer
do. And this result came in spite of the fact that
Wagner, according to his own account, was appalled
by the very thought of being consciously weak or
trivial for a moment. That he was weak and trivial

often will be patent to any hearer of the opera. Indeed, one need not go so far as that. The overture is played often in concert and a novice can easily detect the bombastic emptiness of its resounding finale, even at the same time as he notes the resemblance of the sequences of chords in the brass to some afterward heard in "Der Fliegende Holländer." But Wagner himself tells us that before he had completed "Rienzi" he became doubtful as to the possibility of bringing about any real success by the methods which he was employing. He began to foresee the future with its wide departure for him from the traditions of opera. He began to realise that he could not cater to the extant public taste, but must create for himself a new one. But it was not till despair made him withdraw himself from all relations to the outer world that he entered upon the development of the true Wagnerian music drama.

"Rienzi," then, must be viewed simply as a grand opera of the old-fashioned sort. We must regard its libretto as an exemplification of the clever ground-plan of Meyerbeer, its music as the artistic offspring of the "Jewish banker to whom it occurred to write music," of Spontini, Rossini, and other composers of the pseudo-grand style. The story of the opera is substantially that of Bulwer's novel, and needs no review here. In the making of this book Wagner was simply an adapter. He re-created nothing. In his other works we shall find that he added to the literary substance of every subject which he treated. But such was not the case with "Rienzi." The joints are plainly visible. The carpenter work is creditable, but it is not architecture. One might almost say the same thing about the music. It is in the main good, work-manlike music, with inspiration carefully fanned by the breaths of older composers. Occasionally the real Wagner peeps out and there are some passages of fine vigour and even expressiveness. But this is an opera in which one can go through the score and pick out the "good things," just as one could from the old scores of Donizetti and Bellini.

The reader of Bulwer, for instance, will miss from the opera the figure of Nina, the wife of Rienzi, but he will find that her place is well filled by the sister, Irene, of whom Wagner makes a conspicuously noble character. Furthermore Wagner in drawing the character of his hero went to the original historical sources and so made him a stronger personage than Bulwer did. "Un signor valoroso, accorto, e saggio" is this Rienzi, as Petrarch called him. He speaks in broad and commanding accents, as in his address to the nobles and in the prayer. And it is at such points that we find the best music. The prayer is set to one of the finest melodies in all opera. Again we see that in the chorus and solo of the messengers of peace Wagner found material for good writing of both verse and music. The prayer opens the fifth act, when Rienzi, feeling that the end is near, calls on the Lord to preserve the work which he has achieved.

> " Allmächt'ger Vater, blick' herab,
>   Hör' mich im Staube zu dir fleh'n !
> Die Macht, die mir dein Wunder gab,
>   Lass jetzt noch nicht zu Grunde geh'n ! "

> Almighty Father, look on me !
>   Hear thou my humble fervent prayer !

Let not the power I had from Thee
Pass from me in this dark despair.

With the second stanza comes the fine melody
heard in the overture:

he - - ben, was im staub ver - senkt. &c.

Thou gavest me of Thy all-wondrous might,
  High gifts, O Lord, didst Thou on me bestow,
To light up those who live in night,
  To raise up those who bend so low.

M. Schuré has said :

" ' Rienzi ' is a work of the composer's youth, unequal, but already full of force and strength, brilliant and full of fire. The reformatory ideas of the author are not yet apparent. The libretto is cut according to the rules of tradition—choruses, ensembles, resounding marches, grand airs, trios, septets, ballet—nothing is wanting. The music, without betraying any imitation in particular, has a strong Italian colouring, but the individuality of the composer is shown as well in the heroic grandeur of his broad melodies as in the warmth and riches of his instrumentation. In short, ' Rienzi ' is already the work of an independent master without being that of an innovator."

In the last sentence M. Schuré has nearly touched the truth, but I am inclined to think that he and Mr. Hueffer somewhat overrate the importance of this work. It is most probable that the melody of the prayer will come to be accepted as the one inspired thing in the whole score. Certainly the air of Adriano, so often sung on the concert stage, is but a weak and bombastic imitation of a Weber grand aria of the style of "Ocean, thou mighty monster," with leanings toward the manner employed in the monologue of Ortrud in Act II. of " Lohengrin."

We may therefore dismiss " Rienzi " as a mistake of Wagner's youth. He had not yet found himself. He might have achieved popularity and made money with this sort of writing, and knowing his great vanity and love of luxury we should not have been surprised if he had continued to produce works of this pattern if the first one had brought him immediate success. We ought, perhaps, to be very grateful to the years of privation in Paris which developed the real Wagner, though it is possible that his own ambition to stand alone would have had the desired result in the course of time, even had the years 1840 and 1841 been easier for him.

DER FLIEGENDE HOLLÄNDER

Romantic Opera in Three Acts

First performed at the Royal Saxon Court Theatre, Dresden, Jan. 2, 1843.

Original Cast

Senta	Mme. Schroeder-Devrient.
The Dutchman	Wächter.
Daland	Risse.
Erik	Reinhold.
Mary	Mme. Wächter.
Helmsman	Bielezizky.

Conductor, Richard Wagner.

Riga and Cassel, 1843 ; Berlin, 1844 ; Zurich, 1852 ; Schwerin, Weimar, and Breslau, 1853 ; Frankfort and Wiesbaden, 1854; Hanover, Carlsruhe, and Prague, 1857; Mayence and Vienna, 1860 ; Königsberg, 1861 ; Lucerne, 1862 ; Munich, 1864; Stuttgart, 1865 ; Olmütz, 1866 ; Rotterdam and Dessau, 1869 ; Hamburg, Darmstadt, Mannheim, Gratz, 1870 ; London (Italian), July 23, 1870 ; Vienna, Brunswick, and Brünn, 1871 ; Brussels and Stockholm, 1872 ; Budapesth, Stettin, Augsburg, Magdeburg, Sondershausen, and Baden, 1874 ; Strassburg, 1875 ; Lübeck, Freiburg, and Salzburg, 1876 ; Philadelphia, 1876 ; Dublin and Bologna,

1877 ; Würzburg, 1877 ; New York, Jan. 26, 1877 ;
Innsprück, 1880.

First performed in America as "Il Vascello Fantasma," in Philadelphia, Nov. 8, 1876, by the Pappenheim Company.

First performed in New York at the Academy of Music, Jan. 26, 1877, by the Kellogg English Opera Company.

Cast.

Senta	Clara Louise Kellogg.
The Dutchman	W. T. Carleton.
Daland	Mr. Conly.
Erik	Mr. Turner.

Conductor, S. Behrens.

First performed in New York in German at the Academy of Music, Mar. 12, 1877.

Cast.

Senta . . .	Mme. Eugenia Pappenheim.
The Dutchman	A. Blum.
Daland	Mr. Preusser.
Erik	Christian Fritsch.
Mary	Miss Cooney.
Steersman	Mr. Lenoir

Conductor, A. Neuendorff.

THE FLYING DUTCHMAN

"DER FLIEGENDE HOLLÄNDER" is the first of the works of Wagner which shadow forth the style, the system, and the mastery of lyrico-dramatic art found in his later works. All these elements of this master's art, however, are here found in an embryonic and experimental stage. Nothing is developed, and nothing is definite. Wagner himself did not realise the significance or possible extent of his movement. He was at this time wholly unconscious of the fact that he was laying the foundations of a new method of composition in musical drama. He was aiming only at writing an expressive score, in which the characters of his play, their emotions and their actions, should be drawn with all the powers of music.

The work was written at Meudon in the spring of 1841. All except the overture was completed in seven weeks. Of the fate of the first sketch of this lyric drama, of the hardships of the composer's life at the time of its execution, of the first performances, the reader has already been told. He has seen also how the stormy voyage to London impressed upon his mind the legend of the "Flying Dutchman" with which he had already made acquaintance. It now becomes our duty to examine the sources from which Wagner derived the poetic materials of this play and to ascertain how he treated them. In the "Flying

Dutchman" the poetic ability of the master was first exhibited. He ceased to be a mere libretto-writer and became a dramatic poet. His version of the famous old legend is a lovely one, and much of its increased beauty is the product of his own genius. It was, as he himself said in the oft-quoted "Communication," the "first folk-poem that forced its way into my heart, and called on me as man and artist to point its meaning, and mould it in a work of art."

It was while in Riga that he made his first acquaintance with the story. "Heine takes occasion to relate it," he says, "in speaking of the representation of a play founded thereon, which he had witnessed —as I believe—at Amsterdam. This subject fascinated me, and made an indelible impression upon my fancy ; still it did not as yet acquire the force needful for its rebirth within me." The story of Heine was in "The Memoirs of Herr Schnabelewopski." It is not certain whose play it was that Heine meant. Francis Hueffer, in his "Richard Wagner," * expresses the belief that the play was that of Fitzball, which was running at the Adelphi Theatre in 1827, when Heine visited London. Mr. Hueffer bases his argument largely on the fact that two features of Fitzball's play, both additions to the old legend, are mentioned by Heine as appearing in the drama which he saw. These are the pictures of the Dutchman on the wall of Daland's house, and the taking of a wife by the wandering seaman. Mr. Hueffer adds :

"Here, however, his indebtedness ends. Fitzball knows nothing of the beautiful idea of woman's redeeming love. According to him the Flying Dutchman is the ally of a monster of the deep, seeking for

* The Great Musicians Series, Charles Scribner's Sons.

victims. Wagner, further developing Heine's idea, has made the hero himself to symbolise that feeling of unrest and ceaseless struggle which finds its solution in death and forgetfulness alone. The gap in Heine's story he has filled up by an interview of Senta with Erik, her discarded lover, which the Dutchman mistakes for a breach of faith on the part of his wife, till Senta's voluntary death dispels his suspicion."

It should be noted that Mr. W. Ashton Ellis, whose translation of Wagner's prose works has been so often quoted, wrote a paper to disprove the theory of Mr. Hueffer as to the play having been Fitzball's. The matter, after all, is not one of great importance. Wagner got his materials from Heine's book, which contained a version of a very old legend, and in making the text of his lyric drama, he altered and improved that material as Mr. Hueffer has indicated.

The late Mr. John P. Jackson, formerly musical editor of *The New York World,* in the admirable introduction to his translation of the text of this opera, at one time used at the Metropolitan Opera House, says that the Fitzball play was founded on a version of the legend printed in *Blackwood's Magazine* in May, 1821. That version runs thus :

"She was an Amsterdam vessel and sailed from port seventy years ago. Her master's name was Van der Decken. He was a staunch seaman, and would have his own way in spite of the devil. For all that, never a sailor under him had reason to complain ; though how it is on board with them nobody knows. The story is this : that in doubling the Cape they were a long day trying to weather the Table Bay. However, the wind headed them, and went against them more and more, and Van der Decken walked the deck, swearing at the wind. Just after sunset a vessel spoke him, asking him if he did not mean to go into the bay that night. Van der Decken replied, ' May I be eternally damned if I do, though I should beat about here till the day of judgment.' And to be sure, he never did go into that bay, for it is believed that he continues to beat about in these seas still, and will do so long enough. This vessel is never seen but with foul weather along with her."

This is practically the original story of the "Flying Dutchman." It is no new tale, but, like nearly all myths, a development. In the literature of Greece we find the wanderer in the person of Ulysses, yearning for hearth and home and the joys of domestic love. In the early period of Christianity the myth entered and gave us the gloomy figure of the Wandering Jew, accursed and hopeless of all save the end in oblivion. With the Dutch the legend in the Middle Ages was easily transferred to their own favourite element, the sea, whereon at that time they were among the most daring and skilful. The struggle of the Dutchman against contending winds and waves typified their own battles with the powers of Old Ocean, and their determination to conquer at all hazards.

Later writers than those of the dark ages endeavoured to give this legend an end. In its original form it stands suspended with the Dutchman a creature without hope. Captain Marryatt, in his "Phantom Ship," releases the wanderer from his ceaseless journeyings by means of an amulet, or religious charm. Sir Walter Scott's version of the tale—wherever he found it—is a curiously poor one. According to him, the vessel was laden with precious metal. A murder was committed on board, and as a punishment for it a plague fell upon the crew. No port would permit the ship to enter, and it was doomed to float about aimlessly forever. There is no poetry and a total absence of the personal tragedy in that version. The idea of the salvation of the wanderer through the self-sacrificing love of woman, an idea to be found in literatures much older than this, was introduced into the story before Heine saw the play of which he wrote. It is quite possible that Heine never saw such a play, yet the fact remains that in the Fitzball drama the Dutchman did take a wife, only, however, to make an offering of her to a sea monster — a grotesque and utterly unpoetical idea.

Wagner got his beautiful ending from Heine. Mr. Hueffer has taken the trouble to retail the story as told in " The Memoirs of Herr von Schnabelewopski." The sentence of Van der Decken is that he shall wander till doomsday unless he shall be released by a woman faithful until death. The Devil does not believe in the existence of women of that sort, and therefore allows the wanderer to go ashore once every seven years to see if he can find such a one. (How was it that the Devil was so often mistaken about women ?) He meets with failure after failure, till finally he falls in with a Scotch merchant, whose daughter has already learned his story and formed a romantic attachment for him. She has his picture in her room, and when her father, having accepted the Dutchman's offer for her hand, brings him home, she at once recognises him and determines to sacrifice herself to save him. Just at this point Herr von Schnabelewopski is called away for a short time, and when he returns he sees the Dutchman about to sail away without his wife. He loves her and would save her from his fate. But she, true to her vow, ascends a high rock, whence she throws herself into the sea. The spell is broken and the united lovers enter eternal rest. The reader will now see that it was the void occasioned by the temporary absence of von Schnabelewopski which Wagner filled with the interview between Senta and Erik. Except for the introduction of this character, a tenor, necessary to afford both dramatic and musical contrast to the story, Wagner has followed Heine closely, as lovers of the dramatist's works will at once perceive.

Out of this material Wagner constructed a drama which at the time of its production was as novel as "Tristan und Isolde" was in later years. In it we first meet with this master's remarkable power of concentrating in each scene the emotional moods and pouring them out to us in the music, while in those portions of the score devoted to musical description, such as the sea music and the sailors' choruses, we may note his ability to make dramatic atmosphere. How these powers reveal themselves to us in the grand duo of the last scene of Siegfried and the Waldweben ! It is worth while hearing "Der Fliegende Holländer" occasionally, if only to study the embryonic Wagner. Now let us see how Wagner himself regarded the subject-matter of his story.

" The figure of the Flying Dutchman," he says, "is a mythical creation of the folk. A primal trait of human nature speaks out from it with a heart-enthralling force. This trait, in its most universal meaning, is the longing after rest from amid the storms of life." He traces the older forms of the legend as seen in the stories of Ulysses and the Wandering Jew, and then says :

" The sea in its turn became the soil of Life; yet no longer the land-locked sea of the Grecian world, but the great ocean that engirdles the earth. The fetters of the older world were broken; the longing of Ulysses, back to home and hearth and wedded wife, after feeding on the sufferings of the ' never-dying Jew ' until it became a yearning for

Death, had mounted to the craving for a new, an unknown home, invisible as yet, but dimly boded.   This vast-spread feature fronts us in the mythos of the 'Flying Dutchman,' that seaman's poem of the world-historical age of journeys of discovery.   Here we light upon a remarkable mixture, a blend, effected by the spirit of the Folk, of the character of Ulysses with that of the Wandering Jew.   The Hollandic mariner, in punishment for his temerity, is condemned by the Devil (here obviously the element of Flood and Storm) to do battle with the unresting waves to all eternity.   Like Ahasuerus, he yearns for his sufferings to be ended by Death; the Dutchman, however, may gain this redemption, denied to the undying Jew, at the hands of — a Woman who, of very love, shall sacrifice herself for him.   The yearning for death thus spurs him on to seek this Woman; but she is no longer the home-tending Penelope of Ulysses, as courted in the days of old, but the quintessence of Womankind; and yet the still unmanifest, the longed-for, the dreamt-of, the infinitely womanly Woman— let me out with it in one word: the *Woman of the Future*."

With this broad, poetic view of his subject-matter Wagner set out to write a text book which should be a real drama and not a mere libretto.   "From here," he says, "begins my career as poet, and my farewell to the mere concoctor of opera texts."   In this drama are embodied the fundamental ideas of the entire Wagnerian system.   Here they appear to us in their first stage of development, incomplete, unformed, and scarcely recognised by their own creator.   The value of the mythologic matter, however, already forced itself upon the mind, and the conviction of its suitability to musical embodiment, because freed from hampering accessories, came to him at this period of his career.   I have already quoted his words as to the employment of myths as subjects for music dramas. I may be pardoned for quoting here a passage from my introductory essay in the Schirmer vocal score of the drama :

" Wagner divined clearly the necessity of subordinating mere pictorial movement to the play of emotion, and it will easily be discerned that the three acts of ' The Flying Dutchman ' reduce themselves to a few broad emotional episodes. In the first our attention is centred upon the longing of the Dutchman, and in the second upon the love of Senta. In the third we have the inevitable and hopeless struggle of the passion of Erik against Senta's love. All music not designed to embody these broad emotional states is scenic, such as the storm music and choruses of the sailors and the women. Furthermore the student will do well to note that the chief personages of the story are types. Van der Decken is typical of the man struggling under the burden of his own follies, while Senta is the embodiment of the woman-soul, which, according to Goethe, ' leadeth us ever upward and on.' "

In the structure of this drama the reader will find that Wagner did not abandon the old operatic forms. He employed duets, solos, choruses, etc., as an opera composer would. He did not use the leitmotiv system, but only hit upon its fundamental idea. He did not use the staff-rhyme. In fact we find in this work only a perfectly sincere attempt to make a good play and to express its feelings in music. He says himself of this work :

" In it there is so much as yet inchoate, the joinery of the situations is for the most part so imperfect, the verse and diction so often bare of individual stamp, that our modern playwrights—who construct everything according to a prescribed formula, and, boastful of their formal aptitude, start out to glean that matter which shall best lend itself to handling in the lessened form—will be the first to count my denomination of this as a ' poem ' a piece of impudence that calls for strenuous castigation. My dread of such prospective punishment would weigh less with me than my own scruples as to the poetical form of the ' Dutchman,' were it my intention to pose therewith as a fixed and finished entity ; on the contrary I find a private relish in here showing my friends myself in the process of ' becoming.' The form of the ' Flying Dutchman,' however, as that of all my later poems, down even to the minutiæ of their musical setting, was dictated to me by the subject-matter alone, insomuch as that had become absorbed into a definite colouring of my life, and in so far as I had gained by practice and experience on my own adopted path any general aptitude for artistic construction."

In the " Autobiographic Sketch" he tells us how, after disposing of the first sketch to Pillet, he set to work to compose his own music.

"I had now to work post-haste to clothe my own subject with German verses. In order to set about its composition I required to hire a pianoforte ; for, after nine months' interruption of all musical production, I had to try to surround myself with the needful preliminary of a musical atmosphere. As soon as the piano had arrived, my heart beat fast for very fear ; I dreaded to discover that I had ceased to be a musician. I began first with the 'Sailors' Chorus' and the 'Spinning Song' ; everything sped along as though on wings, and I shouted for joy as I felt within me that I was still a musician."

This statement affords sufficient evidence that nothing revolutionary was in Wagner's mind when he sat down to compose "Der Fliegende Holländer." No vision of the polyphonic web of "Tristan und Isolde" rose in his brain ; no conception of an operatic score in which every melodic idea should have a direct message. He began with two purely lyric numbers, and it was not till he reached the ballad of Senta in the second act that the first principles of the leitmotiv system dawned upon him, and then only in such shape as they had occurred to others before him. The ballad as a whole is a purely lyric number, written in a plain song form ; but in it occur the two principal typical themes of the drama. The first is that designed to represent the Dutchman as a wanderer without rest :

The second theme, a broad, flowing, tender melody, is designed to typify the redeeming principle, the self-sacrificing love of the woman.

In the "Communication to My Friends" he says :

"In this piece I unconsciously laid the thematic germ of the whole music of the opera : it was the picture *in petto* of the whole drama such as it stood before my soul ; and when I was about to betitle the finished work, I felt strongly tempted to call it a 'dramatic ballad.' In the eventual composition of the music the thematic picture, thus evoked, spread itself quite instinctively over the whole drama as one continuous tissue ; I had only without further initiative to take the various thematic germs included in the ballad and develop them to their legitimate conclusions, and I had all the chief moods of this poem, quite of themselves, in definite shapes before me. I should have had stubbornly to follow the example of the self-willed opera-composer had I chosen to invent a fresh motive for each recurrence of one and the same mood in different scenes ; a course whereto I naturally did not feel the smallest inclination, since I had only in mind the most intelligible portrayal of the subject-matter and not a mere conglomerate of operatic numbers."

One other musical thought in this work must here be enumerated because of a special meaning which it had for its composer. In 1866 Ferdinand Praeger was dining with Wagner in Munich, when the conversation turned upon "the weary mariner, his yearning for land and love, and Wagner's own longing for his fatherland at the time he composed the 'Dutchman.'"

Wagner went to the piano, and said, "The pent-up
anguish, the homesickness that then held possession
of me, were poured out in this phrase":

"At the end of the phrase," continued Wagner,
"on the diminished seventh, in my mind I brooded
over the past, the repetitions, each higher, interpreting the increased intensity of my sufferings."

The "Flying Dutchman," then, is the product of
Wagner's genius in its embryonic stage. The grasp
of tradition and operatic convention upon his mind is
not yet shaken off. The chorus of sailors in the first
finale is in a popular, rhythmical, melodic vein and
might almost have been written by a Frenchman.
The opening of Act II. is constructed on wholly operatic lines, with its gay chorus followed by the dramatic ballad. Then follow two purely operatic scenes,
the duets of Senta and Erik and Senta and the Dutchman. In the last act the paucity of material forced
Wagner to spin his web very thin indeed. He con-
sumes as much time as possible with his theatrically
contrasting choruses of merry-making betrothal guests

and ghostly wanderers of the sea.   The machinery of
the stage creaks through the whole scene till the entrance of Senta and Erik brings us once more face to
face with human nature.   The scene is brief, and it is
not to be praised.   It would have been more beautiful
to make the Dutchman depart out of sheer love for
Senta and unwillingness to win salvation through her
sacrifice.   But the act ends effectively.   Perhaps the
most striking proof in all this curious score that Wagner had not yet found himself is in the duet of Daland
and the Dutchman in Act I.   The Dutchman asks if
Daland has a daughter and on receiving an affirmative
reply, says, " Let her be my wife."   Daland, "joyful
yet perplexed," exclaims :

> " Wie ? Hör ich recht ? Meine Tochter sein Weib ?
> Er selbst spricht aus den Gedanken ! "

And with this Wagner ushers in a very Italian duet :

On the other hand, there are not a few manifestations in "Der Fliegende Holländer" of the future Wagner. In the first place, the overture is a splendid exemplification of his musical style and his method of construction and it employs some of the materials of the opera in a masterly manner. Again the solo of the steersman, succeeded by the outburst of the storm and the appearance of the Dutchman's ship upon the raging deep, produces an effect similar to that of the song of the sailor followed by the passionate utterances of Isolde in the first scene of "Tristan und Isolde." The solo of the Dutchman in Act I., while more conventional in its melodic manner than Wagner's later music, gives a foretaste of the power exhibited in the second act of "Lohengrin" in expressing dark and bitter moods. In the musical and dramatic characterisation of Daland one may discern something of the facility which afterward made so much of Hans Sachs. Indeed in characterisation more than in anything else does this opera herald the coming master, for Van der Decken, Senta and Daland are clearly and completely drawn musically and dramatically. They are living figures in the gallery of Wagner portraits ; and while we may not deny that "Der Fliegende Holländer" is a comparatively weak production, we would not readily part with the dreamful, devoted, ill-fated Senta.

In the instrumentation, also, one finds evidences of the real Wagner. The high, shrieking brass chords of the diminished seventh, heard in the "Rienzi" overture, are here repeated; the rich use of divided strings is found ; and the beautiful employment of wide harmonies in the wood wind leads the mind forward toward the final exit of Elizabeth in "Tann-häuser" and the entrance of Elsa in "Lohengrin." But, view this work as we may, we cannot regard it as standing beside the two lyric dramas of the transition period. It is the work of an independent and gifted mind of 28, a work of radiant promise, but not of mature genius.

TANNHÄUSER UND DER SÄNGERKRIEG AUF WARTBURG

Grand Romantic Opera in Three Acts.

First performed at the Royal Saxon Court Theatre, Dresden, October 19, 1845.

Original Cast.

Hermann, Landgrave of Thuringia	Dettmer.
Tannhäuser	Tichatschek.
Wolfram von Eschenbach	Mitterwurzer.
Walther von der Vogelweide	Schloss.
Biterolf	Wächter.
Heinrich der Schreiber	Gurth.
Reimar von Zweter	Risse.
Elizabeth, Niece of the Landgrave,	Fräulein Johanna Wagner.
Venus	Mme. Schroeder-Devrient.
A Young Shepherd	Fräulein Thiele.

Weimar, 1849 ; Schwerin and Breslau, Freiburg and Weisbaden, 1852; Königsberg, Hamburg, Darmstadt, Elbing, Cassel, Frankfort, Posen, Leipsic, Riga, Barmen, Bremen, Bromberg, Cologne, Danzig, Düsseldorf, Prague, and Stralsund, 1853 ; Wolfendbüttel, Rostock, Reval, Neisse, Magdeburg, Glogau, Mayence, Gumbinnen, Gratz, Aix-la-Chapelle, Augsburg, and

Stettin, 1854; Strassburg, Lübeck, Coburg, Bamberg, Munich, Mannheim, Antwerp, Zürich, Würzburg, Carlsruhe, Hanover, 1855 ; Berlin, 1856 ; Vienna, Dessau, and Sondershausen, 1857 ; Stuttgart, 1859 ; New York, April 4, 1859 ; Rotterdam, 1860 ; Paris, 1861 ; Brunswick, 1861 ; Olmütz and Amsterdam, 1862; Munich, Paris version, 1867 : The Hague, 1870; Budapesth, 1871 ; Bologna, 1872 ; Brussels, 1873 ; Lucerne, 1874; Copenhagen, 1875; London (Italian), May 6, 1876; New York (Italian) and Moscow, 1877; Trieste, 1878; Innsprück and Salzburg, 1880 ; Ghent and London (English), 1881.

First performed in America at the Stadt-Theater, New York, April 4, 1859.

Cast.

Hermann	Graff.
Tannhäuser	Pickaneser.
Wolfram	Lehmann.
Walther	Lotti.
Biterolf	Urchs.
Heinrich der Schreiber . . .	Bolten.
Reimar von Zweter	Brandt.
Elizabeth	Mme. Siedenburg.
Venus	Mme. Pickaneser.
Shepherd	(Not given).

Conductor, Carl Bergmann.

TANNHÄUSER

WITH "Tannhäuser" we enter upon what may fairly be called the transition period of the genius of Wagner. While in certain passages this work is quite as much indebted to older opera as "Der Fliegende Holländer," and in others falls into a cheap and tawdry style of melody quite unworthy of its composer, it nevertheless contains parts which rise to heights never before attained except perhaps in Beethoven's "Fidelio." The book will especially repay study, for in it we find the first complete demonstration of Wagner's powers as a dramatist and a dramatic poet. His skilful weaving of the dramatic web out of materials scattered and apparently unrelated places him among the masters of theatrical writing. It will be our pleasure first to examine the sources of the drama and the manner in which Wagner employed them.

"Tannhäuser" was first conceived by Wagner in 1841, and the scenic sketches, with the provisional title "Venusberg, Romantic Opera," were made in 1842. The poem was finished on May 22, 1843. Owing to his being occupied with the preparations for the production of "Der Fliegende Holländer" and with other matters, Wagner did not complete the score till April 13, 1845. When the work was in preparation for performance at the Paris Grand Opéra ın 1861, Wagner rewrote some portion of the score. The reader will recall that the members of the Jockey Club demanded their usual terpsichorean titbit, but that Wagner would not consent to write an ordinary ballet and thrust it into his drama at a certain hour. He insisted that the ballet should take its proper place in the dramatic scheme and that it should have a meaning.

He accordingly wrote a new and careful elaboration of the scene in the Venusberg at the opening of Act I. In the first, or Dresden, version of the work the overture is a complete number, and as such is frequently heard on the concert platform. In the Parisian version the overture does not come to an end, but at the second appearance of the bacchanalian music the curtain rises and the ballet begins. It is descriptive of the revels of the realm of Venus—"a wild and yet seductive chaos of movements and groupings, of soft delight, of yearning and burning, carried to the most delicious pitch of frenzied riot." * He then extended the dialogue between Venus and Tannhäuser to a scene of considerable dimensions, its chief purpose being a further revelation of the character of Venus. Undoubtedly this Parisian version was nearer to Wagner's heart than his first one, but its music does not well bear critical examination, for the style of the added part is that of the "Tristan" period, while the old "Tannhäuser" music is of a much more primitive sort.

So much for the writing of the opera. It is a curious fact that Wagner has recorded as his sources

* Wagner, "On the Performing of Tannhäuser," Prose Works, Ellis, Vol. III.

of inspiration a book which cannot be found and a
condition which did not exist. He says that while
"Rienzi" was in preparation at Dresden, the German
"Volksbuch" of "Tannhäuser" fell into his hands.
Now no one has ever been able to find such a book,
and learned authorities declare that there never was
one. But Wagner further says that he had made the
acquaintance of Tannhäuser in Tieck's narrative,
which he now reread. He read also the "Tann-
häuserlied." He says: "What most irresistibly attracted me was the connection, however loose,
between Tannhäuser and the 'Singer's Tourney in the
Wartburg,' which I found established in that Folk's
book." With this second subject he had already
made some acquaintance in a tale of Hoffmann, and
he now decided to read the mediæval epic, "The
Sängerkrieg." There is no connection at all between
the incidents of the old Tannhäuser legend and "The
Sängerkrieg." This is a condition which Wagner
himself created, and his error in supposing that he had
discovered it in the legend is an amusing instance of
the occasional inability of genius to analyse its own
workings. What Wagner did was to accept Lucas's
identification of Tannhäuser with one of the personages in the epic, thus bringing the two stories together, as we shall presently see.

The legend of Tannhäuser is found in old folk
tales, mostly in the popular form of ballads. An
English translation of one of these, printed with the
original music in Böhme's "Altdeutsches Lieder-
buch," is reproduced in Jessie Weston's excellent
work, "Legends of the Wagner Drama." The story
contained in this is that Tannhäuser, a knight, has

spent much time in the cave of Venus, but has grown weary and would depart. Venus tells him that he has sworn a solemn oath with her "for aye to dwell." He denies that he has so sworn. She offers him her fairest maid as wife if he will stay, but he declines, saying,

> " Nay, an I took another wife,
>   I here bethink me well,
>   My lot for all eternity
>   Would be the flames of hell."

Venus still pleads with him and bids him think upon her charms and the joys of life in the Venusberg. He declares that his "life is waxen sick and faint," and again begs for leave to go. Finally he calls upon the Virgin to aid him. Then Venus tells him to go, but adds that wherever he goes he shall sing her praise. He departs, and determines to seek Pope Urban at Rome and ask absolution. The Pope, who holds in his hand a withered staff, says :

> "This staff shall bud and bloom again
>   Ere grace to thee be shown."

Tannhäuser in despair returns to the arms of Venus. On the third day after his departure from Rome the staff buds and blossoms. The Pope seeks for Tannhäuser, but it is too late ; he has returned to his sin, and for this Pope Urban's soul is to be counted lost on the Judgment Day.

There is absolutely nothing in that story to suggest any connection with the contest of minnesingers in the Castle of Wartburg in 1204 A.D., the year in which Wolfram von Eschenbach is known to have been the guest of Hermann, Landgrave of Thuringia. This contest is described in the poem, or collection of poems called the "Wartburgkrieg," which dates from the 13th century and gives us an interesting view of the Court of Hermann of Thuringia. It is not certain that all of this poem has come down to us, nor do we know who wrote it. Simrock, the German editor of the work, believed that its earliest part was written about 1233. Some verses, believed to have been by Walther von der Vogelweide, appear in the work. The latest part of it probably dates from 1287.

The poem contains no such contest in song as that which takes place in the second act of Wagner's drama, but it does describe a debate as to the glories of certain princes. Heinrich von Ofterdingen, Heinrich der Schreiber, Walther von der Vogelweide, Biterolf, and Reimar von Zweter take part in the discussion, while Wolfram von Eschenbach, the famous author of "Parzival," is the umpire. It was in reading this poem that Wagner's attention was called to Wolfram and his works, and thus he discovered the legendary world of "Lohengrin" and "Parsifal." The "Wartburgkrieg" contains other matter, but that just summarised is all that Wagner found for his "Tannhäuser." He got from the mediæval epic the atmosphere of Hermann's Court, for this potentate was famous in his day as a patron of poetry and an encourager of the art of the knightly minnesinger. He obtained also the idea of the contest of song — which in history was rather one of poetry — and the names of the historical minnesingers. In adopting this material to his dramatic purpose Wagner omitted Heinrich of Ofterdingen and substituted Tannhäuser for him. He furthermore changed the subject of the controversy.

Whence came the lovely character, one of the noblest of all Wagner's heroines, Elizabeth, the Landgrave's niece ? She is not to be found in the Tannhäuser legend nor in the "Wartburgkrieg." It is altogether certain that Wagner found the suggestion for this beautiful character in the story of Saint Elizabeth of Hungary, the daughter-in-law of Hermann of Thuringia. She was affianced in childhood to the Landgrave's eldest son Ludwig ; and when married the pair led a rigorously monastic life and devoted themselves to holiness. Ludwig died young and his brother Heinrich was harsh to Elizabeth. The pure and lofty stature of this saintly princess furnished Wagner with the personality which he needed as the element of opposition to the baneful influence of Venus.

We have now before us the sources from which Wagner drew the materials for this noble drama. Let us see how he utilised his matter. In the first scene we behold Tannhäuser in the arms of Venus, sick and weary of sensual delight and eager to return to the smell of the green grass and the song of birds, and still more to the rhythmic alternation of pain and pleasure which makes the song of human life. His senses are nauseated with their own ceaseless gratification. Who, then, is this Venus, and what is she doing in the subterranean world of the 12th century ? She is plainly the Venus of Roman mythology, the Aphrodite of the Greeks, the Astarte of the Phœnicians. The atmosphere which surrounds her is that of the classic Venus. She is further identified by the pictures of Leda and the Swan and Europa and the Bull, taken from classic fable and illustrating stratagems of the passion over which Venus presided. Before the Romans pushed their way into Germany, the old Teutonic mythology had its goddess Freya, the wife of Odin, queen and leader of the Valkyrs. But the Scandinavian myth made Frigg, or Fricka, the queen, and Freya the second in rank. She was the goddess of love and beauty. The South German races confounded the two and added qualities not known in the northern mythology. They made Freya coincident on one side with Hel, the goddess of the underworld and of the dead, and on the other with Holda, the goddess of the spring, of budding and fructification. Thus when the Romans carried their mythology into Germany it was not at all extraordinary that the attributes of Freya and Venus should have become mingled in the minds of the people.

These simple-minded people did not readily part with their poetic mythology when Christianity mastered their hearts. The old deities were supposed to have retired into caves or mountains, there to dwell till recalled to activity. Venus, according to various traditions, lived in more than one cave, but her favourite abode was the Hörselberg in Thuringia. The propinquity of this cave to the Castle of Wartburg naturally led Wagner to choose it as the scene of Tannhäuser's retirement. In the drama the knight's feelings and desires are precisely the same as those of the hero of the old legend. Wagner adds the beautiful poetic touches of his yearning to hear the song of birds and once more to suffer pain. Furthermore he makes it clear to us that the Venus of his imagination was not without womanly feeling, and that her passion for Tannhäuser was a very real one. She scornfully gives him leave to go, but it is finally his despairing cry to the Virgin for aid which acts as a charm to remove the spell of enchantment. He instantly finds himself in the valley before the Wartburg, and hears the tinkling of sheep-bells, while a young shepherd carols a lay to the May and to Holda, the representative of the beneficent side of the evil goddess just left. It is in such details of fancy as these that Wagner demonstrates his right to consider himself a poet.

With the disappearance of the red and glittering cave of Venus and the appearance of the cool, fresh greens of the landscape—a striking pictorial contrast, full of theatrical effectiveness, and showing Wagner's employment of the combined arts of poety, music, painting, and action in the new dramatic form — we enter the domain of the "Wartburgkrieg." The Tannhäuser of the old legend steps into the shoes of Heinrich of Ofterdingen. The adventure which has befallen him is not unsuited to his character, for the real Tannhäuser was a bit of a Don Juan and had many "affairs." It seems that he repented and became a wiser and a better man in later life. In the ballad Venus foretold that he would sing her praises wherever he went, but in the drama this prediction is made by Tannhäuser in the first scene. That Wagner had a purpose in the change is shown by Tannhäuser's outbreak in the hall of song. Efforts have been made to prove that Heinrich of Ofterdingen and Tannhäuser were one and the same person, for the existence of the former is problematical, and also to prove that

Tannhäuser did really visit the Court of Hermann. Neither has been established as a fact. The matter is of little importance to us. The personages in the song contest, except Tannhäuser, are historical, and Wagner has been faithful in his representation of their characters. He has chosen for dramatic purposes to accentuate the poetic side of Wolfram's character. Wolfram was celebrated as a champion of Christianity, and was an ardent advocate of nobility of heart in woman in preference to merely external beauty. In the very beginning of his "Parzival" he says :

" Many women are praised for beauty; if at heart they shall be untrue,
Then I praise them as I would praise it, the glass of a sapphire hue,
That in gold shall be set as a jewel ! Tho' I hold it an evil thing,
If a man take a costly ruby, with the virtue the stone doth bring,
And set it in a worthless setting: I would liken such a costly stone
To the heart of a faithful woman, who true womanhood doth own.
I would look not upon her colour, nor the heart's roof all can see ;
If the heart beateth true beneath it, true praise shall she win from
me." *

In the hall of song the contest is on a similar theme, and Wolfram was well chosen by Wagner to oppose the passionate ideas of the wandering Tannhäuser. Walther von der Vogelweide has little importance in Wagner's " Tannhäuser," but is mentioned again in "Die Meistersinger," when young Walther von Stolzing claims him as master. Vogelweide was a poet of renown in his day, a contemporary of Wolfram, a Tyrolean by birth and a lyric singer. He was a man of station and had an estate near Würzburg, where he was buried. Reimar was also a notable poet in his

* "Parzival," a knightly epic, by Wolfram von Eschenbach. Translation by Jessie L. Weston. London, David Nutt.

day, but of Biterolf little is known except that there
was such a man.

These are the personages who greet Tannhäuser
when Wagner's wonderful transformation scene has
closed, when the effect of the beautiful pictorial
change has died away, and the solemn strains of the
pilgrims' chorus, so gently beneficent after the passionate witcheries of the wild bacchanal, have melted
into the distance. And with the advent of these historic figures there begins the operation of the elevat-
ing principle of the drama, the influence of Elizabeth.
With their simple and yet aspiring spirits they furnish
a beautiful contrast to the carnal creatures whom we
have just left in the Hörselberg. The latter typified
the gratification of the senses, while these are an expression of the higher desires of man, presently to be
shown to us in their loftiest embodiment, the eternal
woman-soul, which "leadeth us ever upward and
on."

In the experience of Tannhäuser Wagner has set before us the struggle of the pure and the impure, the
lusts and the aspirations of man's nature. It is essentially the tragedy of the man. We may try as we
please to exalt the importance of Elizabeth as a dramatic character, but the truth is that she is merely the
embodiment of a force. Tannhäuser is typical of his
sex, beset on the one hand by the desire of the flesh,
which satiates and maddens, and courted on the other
by the undying loveliness of chaste and holy love. If
ever a sermon was preached as to the certainty with
which the sins of the flesh will find a man out it
is preached in the second act of this tremendous
tragedy, when the flame of old passions sears the front

of new happiness and drives the errant out of paradise.

Here Wagner has risen far above his material. In the pomp and circumstance of the mediæval contest of song he has displayed active fancy, for the scene as presented is his rather than history's. In the culmination of the catastrophe he has wrought with the craft of genius, for in the period of which he wrote the yielding of a man to sensual temptation would never have caused such a stir. Tannhäuser would have been damned rather for worshipping a heathen goddess, an enemy of the Christian Church, than for slumbering in the soft embraces of a wanton. Hence, though struck to the heart by more than mortal wound, Elizabeth thinks first of her lover's sin :

> ' Was liegt an mir ?   Doch er—sein Heil!
> Wollt Ihr sein ewig Heil ihm rauben ? "

"What matters it for me ?   But he—his salvation ! Would you rob him of his eternal salvation ? "   With this beautiful plea of the stricken Elizabeth Wagner shows how perfectly he understood the tragic elements of his story, for he makes the saving principle again, as in "Der Fliegende Holländer," one of self-effacement, a love faithful unto death.

In the final act Elizabeth, her last hope of the return of Tannhäuser gone, consecrates her soul to heaven, relinquishes the desire of life, and ascends to her last home.   Wolfram, who has loved her, and who thus becomes, in his self-sacrifice, a foil to the passionate and self-gratifying Tannhäuser, sits at the foot of the Hörselberg and philosophises to the evening star. Tannhäuser returns, cursed by Rome, and plunged in despair. His narrative is the climax of power in the opera, one of the most intensely tragic pieces of writing in all dramatic literature. His senses reel; the old world of lusts and passions opens the portals of its rosy dreamland, and the songs of its sirens again lure him back to the arms of Venus and bury the newly awakened soul in the depths of sensual debauchery. But no; the eternal feminine still strives to save. The sainted Elizabeth, dead, is yet the guardian angel of this poor wanderer, and as her funeral bier is laid before him he sinks beside it with the last unutterably pathetic supplication of a still repentant spirit:

> "Heilige Elizabeth, bitte für mich!"

"Holy Elizabeth, pray for me." And Wolfram pronounces the benediction in the words, "Er ist erlöst" ("he is redeemed"). The sprouting staff of the Pope, which has followed him from Rome, is laid upon his dead body, and the solemn chorus of the pilgrims chant the entrance of his purified spirit into its eternal rest. Thus did Wagner, out of the simple and unrelated materials of the old Tannhäuser myth and the "Wartburgkrieg," fashion the tragedy of a man's soul. Women never find in "Tannhäuser" all that a man finds there. The experience of the story lies beyond the pale of the feminine nature, but every man must bow his head in reverence to the genius which thus made quick the battle of passion against purity for the possession of the masculine soul. Wagner wrote no mightier tragedy than this.*

* It is worthy of note that in 1863 there was printed in Mobile, Ala.,

The music of "Tannhäuser" commands less admiration than the book. Some of it is worthy of the mature Wagner, but much is trivial and some is positively weak and puerile. Wagner had not yet grasped a new conception of the lyric drama; he had thus far only enlarged and extended the old one. He was not yet ready to set aside all the old formulæ; but he was striving to give them a new significance. Hence in "Tannhäuser" there are passages of a familiar operatic cut, such as the scene of Tannhäuser and the courtiers in the first act, ending with the finale of that act, the duet between Tannhäuser and Elizabeth in Act II., and Wolfram's address to the evening star in Act III. On the other hand, most of the score shows wide departures from the older operatic manner. There is a sincere attempt to make the musical forms follow the poem. There is an abundance of real dialogue, in which the setting of the text is constructed on the purest dramatic lines. This is especially true of the scene between Tannhäuser and Venus, the debate in the hall of song, and the narrative of Tannhäuser. But such admirable pieces of writing as the address of the Landgrave to the contestants and the pathetic prayer of Elizabeth have also a large dramatic value because of their perfect embodiment of the feeling of the scene.

a long blank-verse poem, entitled "Tannhäuser; or, The Battle of the Bards," by Neville Temple and Edward Trevor. This was a paraphrase —and in some places a translation—of Wagner's opera book. It was written by two young men in the English civil service in Germany and sent over to America by a friend. It transpired that "Edward Trevor" was no less a personage than Robert, Lord Lytton, better known as Owen Meredith, author of "Lucile."

The leitmotiv is not employed in "Tannhäuser." Arthur Smolian wrote a pamphlet on the music of this opera. It was prepared for the *Bayreuther Taschenbuch* of 1891 and translated into English by the indefatigable Ashton Ellis. It professes to name and catalogue the leading motives of "Tannhäuser," but what it really does is to prove that there are none. The author quotes Wagner: "The essential feature of Tannhäuser's character is his instant and complete saturation with the emotions called up by the passing incident, and the lively contrasts which the sudden changes of situation produce in his utterance of this fulness of feeling. Tannhäuser is never a 'little' anything, but each thing fully and completely." Mr. Smolian says : "With the foregoing words, in which Wagner defines the nature of his hero, we might also most fittingly describe the individuality of the 'Tannhäuser' music." Here, then, he should have stopped, for he had spoken the truth, and his thematic catalogue is misleading. The music of "Tannhäuser" is nearly all written freely for the investiture of the passing mood, and those portions which are accorded special meaning and are used for repetition may speedily be enumerated and dismissed.

These divide themselves naturally into two classes, representing respectively the good and the evil principle of the action. These themes, which have such significance that they are repeated in the exposition of the drama, are first heard and most easily identified in the magnificent overture. This opens with a serene statement of the theme typifying the holy thought, the religious mood of the good characters in the play.

This thought is employed as the melody of a chorus of pilgrims, and it reappears in a triumphant proclamation at the end of the drama when the good principle emerges victorious from the battle against the evil:

The intoning of this solemn melody is interrupted in the overture by the intrusion of the music of the bacchanalian orgies in the cave of Venus, which begins with this phrase, given out by the violas:

Tannhäuser's hymn in praise of Venus appears in the overture and is, of course, again heard in the first scene of the drama. It is repeated with immense significance, but not at all in the manner of a leitmotiv, in the scene of the hall of song.

Dir tö - ne Lob! Die Wunder sei'n ge - prie - sen.

Harp. *ff*

In the overture the listener will hear after one of the passages of turbulence this theme intoned by a clarinet.

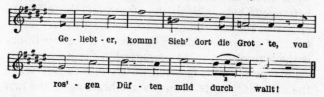

Ge - liebt - er, komm! Sieh' dort die Grot - te, von

ros' - gen Düf - ten mild durch wallt!

Later he will recognise its significance, when in the first scene he hears it sung by Venus with the words of pleading. The reader is now in possession of all the thematic ideas of the score of "Tannhäuser" which approach in their nature the musical phrases employed by Wagner in later works. And yet it is only an approach. In the second act, when Wolfram is preaching the beauties of ideal love, thoughts of the unbridled gratifications of the Hörselberg flash through Tannhäuser's mind and we are informed of it by the repetition of the bacchanale motive. And when at length, taunted into recklessness by the words of his opponents, Tannhäuser launches into the praise of sensual love, he naturally does so in the hymn to Venus from the first scene. And that is the extent of the repetition of primary material in the second act.

In the third act, when Tannhäuser in his despair calls upon Venus, we are informed of her appearance before his fancy by the return of the bacchanalian music. We also see her revealed in the rosy light of her cavern, but this is a complete concession to the public want of imagination. Wagner's original intention was to let the music tell the story of her nearness, but he came to the conclusion that he would not be understood, and so he placed Venus and her court before our eyes. With the return of the pilgrims' chorus at the end of the drama we meet the last repetition of a thematic idea. In none of these repetitions is the leitmotiv method employed. They are simply such repetitions as Gounod makes in "Faust" when the mad Marguerite imagines she hears again the first salutation of Faust, or in "Roméo et Juliette," when the dying Romeo's disordered mind carries him back to the chamber scene and "Non, ce n'est pas le jour."

The dramatic power of "Tannhäuser" is not to be sought in evidences of the development of the future Wagnerian system except in the fidelity of the music to the underlying thought, and of the masterful employment of operatic materials hitherto used wholly with a view to musical effectiveness. In characterisation, too, this score shows an advance over that of "Der Fliegende Holländer," which itself was far ahead of its contemporaries. Wagner himself lays stress upon the deep significance of passages of free composition. For example, he says that in the stanza which Tannhäuser sings in the finale of the second act ("Zum Heil den Sündigen zu Führen")—a stanza which is usually buried by the ensemble—"lies the whole significance of the catastrophe of Tannhäuser, and indeed the whole essence of Tannhäuser ; all that to me makes him a touching phenomenon is expressed here alone." And various remarks in his long and—for the theatre—important essay on the performing of "Tannhäuser" show how far from his mind in the preparation of this work was the fully developed Wagnerian system of "Tristan und Isolde." The union of the arts tributary to the drama in the "art work of the future" had already been conceived by him, and the greatness of "Tannhäuser," together with the causes of its radical difference from the typical opera of its time, must be sought in the evidences of Wagner's successful employment of this union. Neither verse nor music had yet disclosed the complete Wagner ; but here we find the master in his transitional stage. The puissant eloquence of the vital scenes of "Tannhäuser" will long keep it before the public in spite of its inherent weaknesses.

LOHENGRIN

Romantic Opera in Three Acts.

First performed at the Court Theatre, Weimar, August
28, 1850.

Original Cast.

Lohengrin	Beck.
Telramund	Milde.
King Henry	Höfer.
Herald	Pätsch.
Ortrud	Fräulein Fastlinger.
Elsa	Fräulein Agthe.

Wiesbaden, 1853; Stettin, Breslau, Frankfort,
Schwerin, Leipsic, 1854; Hanover, Darmstadt, Riga,
Prague, Hamburg, Cologne, 1855; Würzburg, May-
ence, Carlsruhe, 1856; Munich, Sondershausen,
Vienna, 1857; Dresden, Berlin, Mannheim, 1859;
Danzig, Königsberg, 1860; Rotterdam, 1862; Gratz,
1863; Budapesth, 1866; Dessau, 1867; Milan, Cassel,
Baden, St. Petersburg, 1868; Olmütz, Stuttgart,
Gotha, 1869; Brussels, Brunswick, Magdeburg, The
Hague, Copenhagen, 1870; Bologna, New York, 1871;
Nuremberg, Florence, 1872; Lübeck, 1873; Stockholm,
Strassburg, 1874; Boston, 1875; London, Covent Gar-
den, May 8, 1875; Dublin, 1875: Basle, Trieste, 1876;

San Francisco, Philadelphia, Chemnitz, Crefeld, Temesvar, Salzburg, Melbourne, Lemburg, 1877; Görlitz, Barmen, Regensburg, Rome, 1878; Altona, Liegnitz, 1879; London (English), Genoa, 1880; Liverpool, Antwerp, Venice, Nice, Naples, Moscow, Madrid, Münster, 1881; Innspruck, Barcelona, 1882.

First performed in America in German at the Stadt Theater, New York, April 3, 1871, under Adolf Neuendorff.

Cast.

Lohengrin	Theodore Habelmann.
Telramund	Herr Vierling.
King Henry	Herr Franosch.
Herald	W. Formes.
Ortrud	Mme. Frederici.
Elsa	Mme. Louise Lichtmay.

First performance in Italian, Academy of Music, March 23, 1874.

Cast.

Lohengrin	Italo Campanini.
Telramund	Giuseppe del Puente.
King Henry	Giovanni Nannetti.
Herald	A. Blum.
Ortrud	Annie Louise Cary.
Elsa	Christine Nilsson.

LOHENGRIN

I.—The Book

WHEN he was collecting the materials for "Tannhäuser," Wagner, as we have seen, read the "Parzival" of Wolfram von Eschenbach. The last one hundred lines of that poem contain one of the versions of the story of Lohengrin. It is an insufficient story, however, and would not in itself have provided the foundation of Wagner's most popular work. As I have said in my introduction to the Schirmer edition of the vocal score of " Lohengrin," "Wagner's method of literary composition was to gather all the versions of a national mythological legend, and select the incidents and characters which fitted into his plan." This plan, of course, grows out of his perception of the dramatic possibilities of the story. The sources of Wagner's poem, then, in addition to " Parzival," were " Der Jüngere Titurel," a poem by Albrecht von Scharffenberg, giving a full account of the Holy Grail and its guardians, and also recounting the life and death of Lohengrin after leaving Brabant ; *Der Schwanen-Ritter,* by Konrad von Würzburg, a poem dating from the latter half of the thirteenth century; " Lohengrin," a poem by an unknown Bavarian poet, and the popular form of the legend as given by the Grimm Brothers in the "Deutsche Sagen."

At Marienbad in the summer of 1845 he laid down the outlines of his plan, and in the winter ensuing he wrote the book and invented some of the melodic ideas. He began the actual composition of the opera with the narrative of Lohengrin in the final scene, because, like the ballad of Senta, that monologue contained the most significant musical germs in the whole score. While living at Grossgraufen, near Pilnitz, he wrote the music of the third act between September 9, 1846, and March 5, 1847. The first act was composed between May 12 and June 8, 1847, and the second act between June 18th and August 2d of the same year. The prelude was finished on August 28, 1847, and the instrumentation was made during the following winter and spring. The score of the opera was not published for several years, because Meser, who had printed the previous works of the composer, had lost money by the ventures. Breitkopf & Härtel subsequently secured the score at a small price, not because they were niggardly in offering, but because Wagner's works had no large market value at the time, and he was anxious to sell, being in his chronic condition of financial embarrassment.

The Lohengrin poem gives the story thus : Elsa, daughter of the Duke of Brabant, is left in care of Frederic of Telramund. He aspires to her hand, but she refuses him. He then accuses her before the Emperor of having promised to be his wife and having broken the promise. The Emperor declares that the case must be tried by the ordeal of battle. A passing falcon falls at Elsa's feet with a bell tied to its leg. In her agitation she rings the bell. The sound reaches Monsalvat, where it acts as a summons to Lohengrin,

the son of Parzival.   A swan appears on the river and
Lohengrin knows that he is ordered to go with it.
On arriving at Antwerp, five days later, Lohengrin is
received with honour, and with Elsa sets out for the
court of the Emperor at Mayence.   There the combat
is fought and Telramund defeated.   Lohengrin marries Elsa, having extracted from her the promise not
to ask his name or country.   They live together two
years.   Then in a joust Lohengrin conquers the Duke
of Cleves and breaks his arm.   The Duchess of Cleves
sneers at Lohengrin because no one knows who he is.
This preys on the mind of Elsa till she asks the fatal
question.   Then Lohengrin, in the presence of the
Emperor and the Court, tells his story, steps into the
swan-boat and vanishes.

The story of the "Chevalier au Cygne," as found in
the Grimm version also, is evidently a combination of
two legends.   The first deals entirely with the transformation of human beings into swans, and the second with the Swan-Knight.   The mother-in-law of a
queen, out of hatred, endeavours to make away with
her seven children, each of whom was born with a
silver chain about its neck, and to throw suspicion on
the queen.   She gives them to a knight to slay, but
he contents himself with leaving them in a wood,
where they are found and cared for by a hermit.   The
king's mother subsequently learns that the children
are still alive, and sends a servant to kill them and
bring the chains as evidence.   He finds six children,
one having gone on a short journey with the hermit,
and when he takes the chains off their necks they
turn into swans and fly away.   The king's mother
now brings the false accusation against the queen,

and the king declares that, unless a champion can be found to establish her innocence, she must die.   An angel goes to Helyas, the son who was not found by the servant, and tells him who he is and of his mother's danger.   Helyas goes to Court, declares himself, fights for his mother, and conquers.   The chains are brought forth, the six swans fly in, Helyas puts the chains around their necks, and they resume their human forms.

Subsequently Helyas sees a swan appear, drawing a boat, and knows that he is summoned.   At Nimwegen he finds that before the Emperor Otto the Duchess of Bouillon has been accused by her brother-in-law of poisoning her husband.   The Emperor has ordered the settlement of the case by the ordeal of combat.   Helyas defends the Duchess, overthrows her accuser, marries her daughter, and becomes the father of Godfrey of Bouillon.   After seven years the Duchess asks the fatal question, and Helyas, without answering it, goes away forever in his swan-boat.   The reader will easily discover in the latter part of this story how the Lohengrin legend has been used to manufacture a supernatural father for Godfrey of Bouillon.   It was not at all uncommon for the poets of the mediæval period thus to celebrate the mighty.

We have now before us the chief materials out of which Wagner made his beautiful dramatic poem, for the story of Wolfram's "Parzival" served principally to set him on the track, and to make suggestions as to the character of Elsa.   That story tells simply that the Duchess of Brabant refused to be the wife of any man save him whom God should send her, and so Lohengrin came and the marriage took place, with the stipulation that he should not be asked his name or race. After some years she asked the fatal question and he returned to Monsalvat.

The Elsa of Wolfram was evidently inclined to become a nun, but in two lines of the "Parzival" Wagner found a suggestion as to her nature of which he made eloquent use in his first act :

" In God was her trust, whatever men might in their anger speak,
   And, guiltless, she bare the vengeance her folks on her head would
   wreak."

The absolute confidence of Wagner's Elsa in the readiness of Providence to send her the knight of whom she had dreamed and her unresisting attitude in the presence of her accuser and her king were certainly drawn from these lines of Wolfram's.

From the story of the Swan-Knight he gathered the idea of the transformation of a human being into a swan by a malignant woman, and his tremendously dramatic development of this idea is seen in the plot of his opera. The accusation of Telramund is increased by the assertion that Elsa has murdered her brother, a suggestion drawn, of course, from the accusation against the queen in the "Chevalier au Cygne." He has in reality been transformed into a swan by Ortrud, the wife of Telramund, a character wholly invented by Wagner. It is she who performs the office attributed in the old story to the Duchess of Cleves, that of inspiring distrust and questionings in the mind of Elsa. The character of Telramund is the merest sketch in the sources of the drama and its individuality is entirely the result of Wagner's dramatic skill.

The scene is laid at Antwerp, as it is in the Bavarian poet's version, but is retained there instead of being shifted to Mayence. The heroine is the Duchess of Brabant. The monarch, however, is not Otto, but Henry I., who reigned from 918 to 936. In his treatment of this character Wagner adheres to historic truth. Henry was a progressive and an aggressive monarch, and he not only led his people in successful wars against the Huns, but brought order out of political chaos at home. It is to these historical matters that the King refers in the speeches of the opening scene of the opera.

In the old stories the Knight has several days in which to reach the woman in distress and fight for her. Wagner has made this episode far more dramatic by requiring the immediate presence of the champion, by the ingenious plan of having the first call unanswered, and by making the fight for Elsa's life and honour take place at once. The arrival of Lohengrin is one of the most theatrically effective scenes in all opera, and the sweet and gentle farewell to the swan, following the hubbub of excitement, affords one of those splendid musical contrasts which are to be found in all Wagner's works and which are, as in this case, entirely his own. The first act of the opera leans heavily on the sources of the story, but the reader can have no difficulty in seeing how ingeniously Wagner has utilised his materials. At the end of the combat it has in recent years been the custom to employ a piece of stage business, authorised by the Bayreuth management, which is destructive of much of the effect of the scene, and obviously contrary to Wagner's original conception. Lohengrin does not fell Telramund "with one mighty stroke," as the stage direction in the score says he should, but holds his sword on high, while Frederic, without being struck at all, falls, overcome by the mysterious power which emanates from it. Of course this belittles the knightly character of Lohengrin, who conquers not by his prowess, but by the intervention of supernatural power, and furthermore it is opposed to the text. The Herald in his address to the combatants just before the King's prayer says :

> " Durch bösen Zaubers List und Trug
> Stört nicht des Urtheils Eigenschaft."

"By evil magic's cunning and deceit distort not the nature of the judgment." The meaning of that speech is certainly a prohibition of the exercise of supernatural power by Lohengrin. And in the old stories it is always related that he defeated his opponent in equal combat. The supernatural element is sufficiently to the fore in this first scene in the appearance of the Swan-Knight in answer to the prayer and in reward of the faith of the innocent maiden under accusation. The love of Lohengrin for Elsa is in accordance with the old stories, and so is Elsa's offer of her crown, her domain, and herself. To the fall of the curtain at the end of Act I. Wagner followed the sources of his story closely, the changes being such as I have pointed out, and chiefly of a kind demanded by the technics of dramatic construction.

But with the second act we enter a chapter more fully the product of Wagner's genius. The original sources give only suggestions of it. The scene between Telramund and Ortrud at the beginning of this act, so much disliked by those to whom only the saccharine melodies of love and mystic knighthood are pleasing, is one of the most important in the drama. Telramund, robbed of sword and fame, reproaches Ortrud for inducing him to make the accusation against Elsa. He recognises the sacred character of Lohengrin, but Ortrud scoffs at it. She calls her husband's attention to the condition imposed upon Elsa by Lohengrin, that she must ask neither his name nor the place whence he came. Ortrud reveals the fact that if he is forced to answer this question his power is at an end. But Ortrud further counsels her husband to proclaim that the victory was won by magic, thus breaking the law of the sacred ordeal. Still further she says that, if Lohengrin can only be wounded in the slightest way, his power will vanish. To Telramund she entrusts this part of the task, while for herself she reserves the business of inspiring distrust in the mind of Elsa.

She addresses the maiden on her balcony in the accents of despair. Elsa in pity descends to lead her into the house. Then Wagner makes use of the mediæval belief that the old pagan gods had not ceased to exist, but were temporarily in retirement from the assaults of Christianity. Ortrud, who is a pagan at heart, calls on the old Norse gods to aid her in overthrowing these Christian enemies of theirs. When Elsa appears, this dark woman at once expresses her fear that a knight who appeared by magic may disappear. Elsa's trust is not yet to be shaken, and Ortrud follows her into the house. When Elsa and her train are moving toward the church, Ortrud claims the right of precedence and, like the Duchess of Cleves in the old tale, flings the taunt of Lohengrin's namelessness at Elsa. Again the maiden defends her spouse elect. Lohengrin and the King appear. Telramund, carrying out his part of the task, comes forward and declares that Lohengrin conquered him by the aid of magic. The King and the nobles, with full faith in the nature of the judgment, refuse to listen to him. He then whispers to Elsa that if she will admit him to the chamber that night he will clear all doubt. Lohengrin orders him away and leads Elsa into the minster.

Throughout this act the immense dramatic skill of Wagner is manifested. With only a few meagre suggestions from the old legends,—basic ideas, indeed, but undeveloped,—he built up an act of extraordinary dramatic power and musical fecundity. In its construction this act equals anything in the entire range of opera. The effective series of pictures, ranging from the dismal pair on the cathedral steps in the gloom, through that of Elsa apostrophising her lover on the moonlit balcony, the entrance into the house of the two women in the glimmer of the torches, the break of day, and the growing glitter of the festal morning with its pageant, up to the splendid climax of the scene in the denouncement of Frederic and the final entry into the church, are as ingeniously arranged as anything in the Meyerbeerian operas ; but these scenes succeed one another in a perfectly natural and poetical sequence, and without forcing theatrical craft upon our attention. And in this act Wagner develops with transcendent power the characters of Ortrud and Telramund. Of the malignant pagan sorceress his own words are the best description. In one of the letters to Liszt he says :

" Ortrud is a woman who does not know love. By this everything most terrible is expressed. Politics are her essence. A political man is repulsive, but a political woman is horrible. This horror I had to represent. There is a kind of love in this woman, the love of the past, of dead generations, the terribly insane love of ancestral pride which finds its expression in the hatred of everything living and actually existing. In man this love is ludicrous, but in woman it is terrible, because a woman, with her strong natural desire for love, must love something ; and ancestral pride, the longing after the past, turns in consequence to murderous fanaticism. In history there are no more cruel phenomena than political women. It is not therefore jealousy of Elsa, perhaps for the sake of Frederic, which inspires Ortrud, but her whole passion is revealed only in the scene of the second act, where, after Elsa's disappearance from the balcony, she rises from the steps of the minster and invokes her old, long-forgotten gods. She is a reactionary person, who thinks only of the old and hates everything new in the most ferocious meaning of the word ; she would exterminate the world and nature to give new life to her decayed gods. But this is not merely an obstinate, morbid mood in Ortrud ; her passion holds her with the full weight of a misguided, undeveloped, objectless feminine desire for love ; for that reason she is terribly grand."

This Ortrud of Wagner's touches hands with the Lady Macbeth of Shakespeare. The same ambition, the same political, unsexed womanhood, the same desperate daring, and the same brazen resolve appear in both. Both seek a throne by foul means. Both are labouring for their husbands, and both fear the weakness of the spouse. Ortrud might fairly take from the lips of Lady Macbeth her invocation :

> " Come, you spirits
> That tend on mortal thoughts, unsex me here ;
> And fill me, from the crown to the toe, top-full
> Of direst cruelty ! Make my thick blood,
> Stop up th' access and passage to remorse ;
> That no compunctious visitings of nature
> Shake my purpose, nor keep peace between
> Th' affect and it ! "

Telramund, "infirm of purpose," like Macbeth, is swayed and mastered by the superior force of his wife's indomitable will and insatiable ambition. Fate follows his footsteps as relentlessly as it does those of the Thane of Cawdor, and when he falls a victim to vaulting ambition, which overleaps itself, he falls a victim of Nemesis.

The last act places before us several salient features of the original material. Elsa, not after years of married bliss, but on the bridal night, asks the fatal question. Here Wagner shows a deep appreciation of the poetic possibilities of the theme, undoubtedly suggested to him by the resemblance of the situation to that of Zeus and Semele in classic fable. Elsa never could have grasped the essential nature of this sacred messenger, and so Wagner cuts the knot by ending the marriage at its very outset, before the final surrender of the heroine's womanhood. Lohengrin was never hers ; she was never his. Frederic's last attempt follows the utterance of the question, and then before the assembled court, on the river bank where first he appeared, Lohengrin tells the marvellous, thrilling tale of Monsalvat, the Holy Grail and his origin, opening to us for a few moments the cathedral vistas of Wagner's "Te Deum,"—"Parsifal." Ortrud prematurely triumphs and announces that the swan is the missing brother : she herself placed the chain about his neck. Lohengrin calls upon God, and the spell is broken. The rightful heir of Brabant is restored to his sister's arms, and the Swan-Knight floats away in his shallop, this time drawn by a dove, the messenger of heaven. The reader will have no difficulty now in recognising the sources of these incidents, except, perhaps, in the death of Telramund, which was suggested to Wagner, as was the idea of robbing Lohengrin of his saintly power by wounding him, by passages in "Der jüngere Titurel." The narrative of Lohengrin is suggested by Wolfram's "Parzival."

One more note must be made before we pass to a brief examination of the music of Wagner's most popular work. There is a strange resemblance between some of the fundamental features of the story of "Lohengrin" and those of "Der Fliegende Holländer." Senta and Elsa are both dream-haunted maidens. Both dream of lovers. About each of the lovers there is something mystic or supernatural. Each of the lovers is to come to the maiden from the water. In each case the maiden is called upon to submit to a certain ordeal, and her failure is to result in the return of the lover to the element from which he came. And in one element of the story the fact is similar, but the relations of the personages changed. In one a maiden is to save the lover ; in the other, the lover comes as a champion and saviour. Is it not possible that the origin of the two legends is the same, the story of Skeaf, the mysterious king of the Angles, who drifted to their shores in a rudderless shallop when a babe, and grew to be a good and great monarch ? When he died, they laid his body in the shallop and the little vessel floated away into the unknown, whence it came.

II.—The Music

And now let us look at the music of this opera, music which is usually listened to with complacent admiration for its mellifluous melody, but too seldom considered in respect of its dramatic significance. "Lohengrin" is musically far in advance of "Tannhäuser." True, there is not in this opera any piece of writing so puissant in its revelation of a human heart as the narrative of the returned pilgrim, but the score in its entirety is more closely knit, more coherent in style, more certain in its characterisations, more dramatic in its development of emotional climaxes and its explication of the scenes. In "Lohengrin" we find the grasp of his material much firmer in Wagner's hands. The organism is higher ; the unity of word, action, and tone nearer to that for which the author constantly sought.

"Tannhäuser" is a hybrid. Old forms jostle the new ; thin melodic strophes in conventional song-patterns lower the potency of some scenes to the level of Italian opera. But in "Lohengrin" the song form disappears forever from the Wagnerian scheme. The music is the utterance of speech ; the melody, the spontaneous embodiment of feeling. There is no longer any recitative. There is only musical dialogue. And the leitmotiv, temporarily laid aside in the composition of "Tannhäuser," returns with wider and deeper and more varied meaning. We are at the culmination of the transition period of Wagner's genius, standing at the outer gates of "Tristan" and "Die Meistersinger."

Wagner himself recognised the nature and the limits of the advance made in this opera. He declares in the "Communication" that he was here seeking to free himself from the tyranny of the final cadence — that which tells the ear of the completion of a melodic form — and to make the music the outgrowth of the speech.

But he saw in later years that he was still under the domination of melodic fashion in "Lohengrin"; and it is precisely his subservience to this fashion, with which the easy-going public from long use has become familiar, that makes "Lohengrin" the favourite of opera-goers the world over. We find the most potent evidences of the domination of the closing cadence in Elsa's narrative, in the duet of Ortrud and Telramund in the second act, and in the passages of the duet in the chamber scene. On the other hand, there is a close approach in the score of "Lohengrin" to the endless melody of the later dramas, and we are not surprised by the recollection that the Nibelungen trilogy was the next work to which Wagner turned.

The prelude to "Lohengrin" may be described as an instrumental representation of the vision of the Holy Grail. The motive on which it is built is that which throughout the opera typifies the sacredness of Lohengrin and his identity as a messenger of the Grail.

THE GRAIL.

This theme is heard at the begininng of the prelude in its first form. It is heard again when Lohengrin prepares to bid farewell to the swan which is to return to Monsalvat, the palace of the Grail, thus announcing the idenity of the knight as a messenger of the Grail. It is not heard again till the third act, except for a passing moment in Act II., where the

Herald's delivery of Lohengrin's message to the nobles is preceded by the Grail motive, the first half intoned by the trumpets on the stage and the second half by the orchestra. It then disappears till the final scene of the opera, when it sounds forth as the warp and woof of that marvellously lovely piece of writing, the narrative of Lohengrin's origin. Next to the Grail motive stands that which is indicative of the knightly nature of Lohengrin. This motive immediately follows the

LOHEGRIN THE KNIGHT.

first appearance of the Grail motive in the first act and becomes the instrumental background to Elsa's "In lichter Waffen Scheine ein Ritter nahte da" ("I saw in splendour shining a knight of glorious mien"). It is heard again when Lohengrin appears in the distance coming down the Scheldt in answer to Elsa's prayer, and at the end of the first act, when the triumph is complete, it peals forth fortissimo. It announces Lohengrin's entrance in Act II. and again in the final scene of the opera. At the end of all Wagner shows us that the knightly character of Lohengrin is intimately associated with his position as guardian of Brabant, for the knighthood motive is transferred in all its splendour to the rescued Gottfried, while, as Lohengrin disappears in the distance, it is heard for the first time in the minor mode. Another motive, which is a companion of Lohengrin's, is the swan motive. This is heard as the accompaniment to the

THE SWAN.

closing words of Lohengrin's farewell to the swan in Act I.; again in Act III., when the half-hysterical Elsa fancies she sees the swan coming to take Lohengrin away, and finally when the Knight is about to address the swan preparatory to his departure in the last scene. A part of the melody which accompanies the entrance of Elsa in the first act is also evidently designed to act as a leading motive. This may be called the motive of Elsa's faith. It is repeated immediately

ELSA'S FAITH.

after the entrance of the maid, when the King asks her if she will be judged by him, and the stage direction bids her make a gesture expressive of her

complete trust.   In the last scene, when Elsa enters
dejected after having broken her vow, the King asks
her the cause of her sadness, and she tries to look him
in the face but cannot.   Then we hear the broken
faith motive:

ELSA'S FAITH BROKEN.

Two themes are employed to signify the evil elements
of the drama.   The first of these is the prohibition
motive:

THE PROHIBITION.

The ban of secrecy imposed by Lohengrin becomes a
potent weapon for evil in the hands of Ortrud.   It is
heard ominously in the introductory measures of the
second act, and with portentous meaning when Or
trud begins to unfold her plan to Frederic.   When
Ortrud in the scene with Elsa says, " May he never
leave thee who was by magic hither brought," the

prohibition motive is given out adagio by the wind;
and at the end of act, as Ortrud expresses by face
and gesture her triumph over Elsa entering the cathedral, this motive is pealed forth at full power by the
trumpets and trombones.   It recurs in most mournful
instrumental colour at the end of the chamber scene in
Act III., when Elsa has asked the fatal question.   The
other theme significant of evil is the motive of Ortrud's
influence:

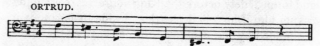

ORTRUD.

This is first heard in the introduction to Act II.   It reappears when Ortrud begins to reveal her ideas to
Frederic, and accompanies each of her suggestions for
the overthrow of Lohengrin and destruction of Elsa.
It is heard again in the accompaniment to the short
ensemble which succeeds Lohengrin's appeal to Elsa
in the finale of Act II., when to his dismay he sees
that she is wavering.   Again it sounds when Frederic
whispers to Elsa in the same scene, and when the
maid declares her doubts in the chamber scene it is
repeated to show that she is acting under the influence of Ortrud.   This is a very close approach to the
fully developed employment of the leitmotiv, for in
the later dramas we find these themes frequently used
to connect the passing action with the influences
which have led to it or to associate it with an absent
personality.

A less important motive, but one whose treatment
foreshadows Wagner's later musical method, is that
of the ordeal:

19

THE ORDEAL.

This makes its appearance in Act I. after the nobles
shout "Zum Gottesgericht!" ("to judgment of God!"),
and immediately before the King addresses Telramund
asking him if he will do battle. In the major mode it
is sounded by the trumpets on the stage as the summons to Elsa's champion to appear, and its fundamental rhythm becomes that of the music to which the
six nobles pace off the measurement of the ground.
In the fight itself this motive is worked out orches-
trally as an accompaniment to the action. It belongs
strictly to the music of the scene, yet it is treated
thematically and developed as far as needed.

These are all the leading motives of "Lohengrin."
The rest of the music is freely composed, but
the attentive hearer will note that while ethereal
string harmonies intone the Grail motive, Lohengrin's
knighthood is announced by the brass, and to
the wood wind choir is allotted Elsa's music. For
the rest the lover of this opera must seek his intellectual enjoyment in the general fidelity of the
score to the thought of the text, to the increasing
freedom from the shackles of formularies, and to the
flexible, changeful, constantly significant harmonic
plan.

The enormous variety of the rhythmic effects is obtained without frequent changes of time. The first

act, for example, is all in common time up to the beginning of the King's prayer, which is in three-fourths measure. At the beginning of the combat the common time returns and is continued till the end of the act. The entire second act is in common time. In the third act two-fourths time is used for the "Bridal Chorus" and then the composer returns to common time and retains it to the end. These facts are alone sufficient to show the wide gulf which separates the Wagner score from that of the old-fashioned Italian opera, wherein the elementary dance rhythms are all used with as much variety as possible. Wagner attains an infinitely greater variety of styles and expression with only two interruptions of his original time signature.

Yet the one thing which Wagner felt most keenly in the composition of this opera was his subserviency to rhythm — not musical, but poetical. He admits that he had not yet freed himself from old melodic ideas and that the dominance of the cadence was still felt in his work, but his real difficulty was the inflexibility of verse written in modern metre, which makes such rigorous demands for imitation in the form of the musical setting. He was in later works to find the solution of that problem and enter the kingdom of perfect freedom from textual rule. The music of "Lohengrin," then, must be regarded as standing midway between the style of "Der Fliegende Holländer" and that of "Die Meistersinger." Its extraordinary popularity is due to the external and sensuous charms of its melody, which make their appeal to the aural palate of those incapable of comprehending a dramatic scheme such as Wagner's.

This outward attractiveness of the music Wagner himself would have been the first to blame, and he always felt that his own beautiful conception of the character of Lohengrin was not revealed to the public.

TRISTAN UND ISOLDE

Action in Three Acts.

First performed at the Royal Court Theatre, Munich,
June 10, 1865.

Original Cast.

Tristan	. .	Ludwig Schnorr von Carolsfeld.
Kurvenal	. . . . .	Mitterwurzer.
Melot	. . . . . .	Heinrich.
Marke	. . . . . .	Zottmayer.
Isolde	. .	Mme. Schnorr von Carolsfeld.
Brangäne	. . . . . .	Mlle. Deinet.

Weimar, 1874; Berlin, 1876; Königsberg, Leipsic,
1881; Hamburg, 1882; London, June 20, 1882.

First performed in America at the Metropolitan
Opera House, New York, on December 1, 1886.

Cast.

Tristan	. . . . .	Albert Niemann.
Kurvenal	. . . . .	Adolph Robinson.
Melot	. . . .	Rudolph von Milde.
Marke	. . . . .	Emil Fischer.
Isolde	. . . . .	Lilli Lehmann.
Brangäne	. . . . .	Marianne Brandt.
Ein Hirt	. . . . .	Otto Kemlitz.
Steuermann	. . . .	Emil Saenger.
Seemann	. . . . .	Max Alvary.

Conductor, Anton Seidl.

TRISTAN UND ISOLDE

I.—Sources of the Story

FROM the dramatic and musical style of "Lohengrin" to that of "Tristan und Isolde" is a far cry, and the reader must brace his intellectual forces to assault a new world. It would be easier for some reasons to take up the consideration of this work after that of the "Meistersinger" and "Der Ring," but such a proceeding would lead to a confusion of historical facts in the mind of the reader, and therefore we shall take it up in the order of its production. We must bear in mind that before writing the score of this work Wagner wrote those of "Das Rheingold" and "Die Walküre," and that therefore he had entered into his fully developed style. Further than that we shall see that he went beyond his own conceptions of his theories, and that in this work he gave us the fullest, freest, and most potent demonstration of the vitality and justice of his methods and his style.

In an undated letter to Liszt, written in the latter part of 1854, Wagner says: "I have in my head 'Tristan und Isolde,' the simplest but most full-blooded musical conception: with the 'black flag' which floats at the end of it I shall cover myself to die." But in the meantime, as we have seen, he was working on the first parts of the "Ring" series.

When he had about half written "Siegfried" there came upon him a period of depression. He felt that he was writing works which he would not live to see produced. He hungered for a closer, an active connection with the stage, and he needed money, and so he regretfully laid aside the "Ring" scores and set to work on the poem of "Tristan und Isolde." This was written at Zurich in 1857. The music was begun in the same year, and the score of the first act was finished at Zurich on December 31st. The second act was finished at Venice in March, 1859, and the third at Lucerne in August of the same year.

Many persons labour under the delusion that "Tristan und Isolde" is a new fancy of Wagner's ; they do not know that the tale is one of the famous old legends of the Arthurian cycle and that it ranks as one of the great epics of mediæval Europe. First of all, however, this story belonged to the great English cycle of legends, which have supplied material to so many poets down to Tennyson and Swinburne. The latter wrote a version of this very tale under the title of "Tristram of Lyonnesse," which is only a modern adaptation of the earliest known title, "Tristam de Leonois," a poem dating from 1190.

The story is of Celtic origin, yet we find that it first took definite poetic shape in France. The Arthurian cycle consists of the "Romance of the Holy Grail," "Merlin," "Launcelot," "The Quest of the Saint Graal," and "The Mort Artus." From the last was drawn the beautiful "Morte d'Arthur" of Sir Thomas Mallory, a story of which about one-third is devoted to the life and adventures of Tristram, not properly told in this version. How was it that the French

romantic poets were engaged in celebrating the doings
of English heroes? In the heart of the Midi the forerunners of the Troubadours sang the deeds of Arthur
and Launcelot and Merlin, just as Tennyson did in the
latter half of the nineteenth century. As far as we
can ascertain at this time, the exploits of Arthur, which
had been narrated in scattered song and story for many
a long year through all the vales of England, were
compiled by Geoffrey of Monmouth. He died in 1154,
the year in which Henry II. ascended the throne of
England. Henry was of the house of Anjou, and
united the crowns of England and Normandy under his
sceptre. At about the same period, according to Professor Morley, Walter Map, an Archdeacon of Oxford
(1154–89), is believed to have introduced the Holy
Grail into the romances which existed before his time.

The conditions were now precisely right for the introduction of the Arthurian legends and the Grail into
the romantic literature of France. The Norman Court
took great delight in the English tales. The French
poets were only too glad to find new material which
was sure of favour in high places. And their own
blood was not averse to the nature of the poetry. The
French of the Middle Ages were a wonderfully cosmopolitan people. Near Tours, far to the north of the
sunny land of the Troubadour, Charles Martel crushed
and scattered the army of the Prophet, and for centuries after that the Saracen trod the valleys of the Midi.
Long before that the Greeks had sent settlers into the
region, and the old nature-loving Hellenic spirit found
its expression and its means of preservation in the folk
songs and dances of the people. But the inhabitants
of the Midi were, nevertheless, Celts. Matthew

Arnold says : "Gaul was Latinised in language, manners, and laws, and yet her people remained essentially Celtic." And so we need not be astonished at finding the Celtic Arthurian legends taking root in the literature of mediæval France. Robert de Borron, a Trouvere, born near Meaux, wrote about 1170 or 1180 the Provençal version of the Grail legend. Chrétien de Troyes, another of the French romanticists, wrote a version of the Grail legend about the same time as Borron.

Of the oldest French versions of the Tristram tale, two are known. M. Gaston Paris and Dr. Golther have put forth in their books on the Tristram legend studies of what is called the minstrel version of the story. The first was made by Beroul in England out of the scattered traditions relating to Tristan. It dates from 1150 and only a fragment of it remains. There was also a very early German version by Eilhart von Oberge, and from this indirectly originated the unsatisfactory version given by Mallory. The other old French one was that of Thomas of Brittany, an Anglo-Norman. This poem was the previously mentioned "Tristam de Leonois," and from it, about 1210, Gottfried of Strassburg, a German, drew the great mediæval Teutonic form of the tale, the direct source of Wagner's work.

The story as told by Gottfried is briefly as follows : Morold, an Irish warrior, brother of Ireland's Queen, holds Cornwall in fear, and demands a tribute to his King and master. Tristan, nephew of King Mark of Cornwall, challenges him to mortal combat. Morold wounds Tristan, and declares that, as his sword was poisoned, only his sister, Queen Isolt of Ireland, can heal the wound. Tristan smites Morold's head off, but a piece of the sword remains in the skull. **Tristan's** wound will not heal, so in company with his servitor Kurvenal and several other attendants he sails for Ireland to seek aid of Queen Isolt. Morold's body and head are taken back to Ireland. Tristan appears before the Queen disguised as a harper, calling himself Tantris. The Queen, pleased with his music, agrees to heal him if he will teach music to her daughter, also named Isolt. He consents, is healed, and returns to Cornwall. There he sings the praises of the Queen's daughter, the younger Isolt, and offers to return to Ireland and ask for her hand for his uncle, King Mark. He goes, and, on his arrival, finding the land devastated by a dragon, slays the monster and cuts out its tongue. Being overcome by the creature's foul breath, he sinks unconscious, and the Queen's steward, who has heard the sound of the conflict, comes and cuts off the dragon's head to show as evidence that he slew the beast. The steward claims the hand of the Princess, which has been promised to the slayer of the dragon, but the Queen Mother by her magic discovers that another did the deed, and going forth at dawn finds the unconscious Tristan.

It is now decided that the question between Tristan and the steward shall be settled by combat, and the Princess orders Tristan's armour to be made ready. In looking at the sword she discovers the nick in the blade, and finds that the splinter from Morold's head, which has been preserved, fits it. It also dawns upon her that " Tantris " is " Tristan " reversed. She would slay Tristan, but the Queen desires to know what matter of great import brought him again to Ireland. He makes known his mission, and as the Queen professes herself ready to forgive Tristan for killing Morold, her brother, the compact is made. Princess Isolt goes with Tristan. As they depart for Cornwall, the Queen confides to Brangäne, the Princess's kinswoman and companion, a love potion, to be given to King Mark and the Princess on the marriage night that they may ever afterward love each other. The Princess is loath to leave her own people, and she hates Tristan for having slain her Uncle Morold.

On the way to Cornwall a serving-maid, who is asked for a drink for Tristan and Isolt, ignorantly gives them the love potion, and they love one another. The poem narrates many incidents in the course of deceit pursued by the lovers, but they need not be recapitulated here. The King's steward, Majordo, aided by the dwarf, Melot, watches the lovers and informs the King of their infidelity. But with the help of Brangäene's cunning, they several times avoid detection. The King even banishes them from Court, but, finding them asleep in a forest retreat with a naked sword between them, takes them back, though he orders them to remain apart. Finally he surprises them in the garden, and then Tristan is forced to flee from Cornwall. He finds a refuge in Arundel, the land of Duke Jovelin, whose daughter, Isolt of the White Hand, falls in love with him. As he is always singing of his lost Isolt, she thinks that he loves her. He, hearing nothing from the old Isolt, deems himself forgotten, and concludes that it would be as well to marry Isolt of the White Hand.

Gottfried's poem ends here. In the other versions, however, the tale is completed. Tristan does marry the second Isolt. He receives a poisoned wound while aiding a friend to meet clandestinely another man's wife. Knowing that none save his first Isolt can heal the wound, he sends Kurvenal to bring her, telling him that if he succeeds in getting her he must hoist a white sail when entering port on his return, but if he fails he is to hoist a black one. Isolt of the White Hand hears this, and when the ship is sighted bearing a white sail, she tells her husband that it is black, whereupon he turns his face to the wall and dies. Tristan's Isolt arrives to find him dead. She lays herself on the bier beside him and expires. King Mark, having learned the story of the love potion, has the two buried in the same chapel, on opposite sides. A rose tree grows from Tristan's tomb and a vine from Isolt's, and the branches reach across the chapel and intertwine.

II.—Wagner's Dramatic Poem

The falsehood of the second Isolt has greatly annoyed some of the modern writers. Bayard Taylor simply declined to believe that such a thing happened. Matthew Arnold made the second Isolt faithful to her love. She nursed her dying husband tenderly even while waiting for the first Isolt to arrive. But Wagner wisely ignored this part of the legend. We hear nothing of any second Isolt. As is invariably the case, his treatment of the story draws together all the beauties of the original material and moulds them into a compact, consistent whole, instinct with dramatic force and poetic beauty. In attempting to set forth the Wagnerian arrangement of the materials, I find it difficult to proceed coolly and systematically. There is a witchery in this marvellous drama of fatal love that masters my mind. If the reader finds me wanting in the calm of judicial equipoise, let him forgive me, for I am dealing with that which lies next to my heart. As Louis Ehlert says :

" When in the second act Isolde is awaiting her lover, when the orchestra throbs with a thousand pulses and every nerve becomes a sounding tone, I am no longer the man I am through the rest of the year, nor am I artistically and morally a responsible being : I am a Wagnerian."

For the perfect understanding of the story the first act of the drama is the most important. It is also that which the fewest persons closely study. Edward Schuré, in " Le Drame Musicale," says :

" The fundamental idea of the legend is that of the love-philtre, fatal, irresistible, overpowering and uniting two human beings ; of love vanquishing everything, honour, family, society, life and death, but which is itself ennobled by its very grandeur and fidelity. For it bears within itself its own punishment as well as its justification, its religion and its world, its hell and its heaven, supreme sorrow and supreme consolation."

While this may be a correct view of the old legend, it is not true of Wagner's drama. In the latter the philtre performs the office of Fate in the ancient Greek tragedy. In the plays of Sophocles and Æschylus mortals fulfil their manifest destinies, but Fate is the secret agency which hurries them forward to their ends. So, in this drama of Wagner's, Tristan and Isolde are the victims of a fatal love before the action begins, and the philtre is only the instrument through which all restraints are removed and the unhappy pair hurled into the vortex of their own passion, helpless victims of cruel Destiny.

Upon the deck of the ship bound for Cornwall Isolde lies silent on her couch. From aloft floats down the song of a sailor, crooning of his absent Irish love. Isolde, starting up, demands to know where she is. Before night, Brangäne tells her, the ship will reach Cornwall. "Nevermore! To-night nor to-morrow," exclaims Isolde, a dread purpose in her mind. And then she bursts into rage, she who has hitherto been silent and even has refused food. Brangäne begs her to free her mind. "Air!" cries Isolde. The curtain is thrown back, showing the stern of the ship and Tristan at the helm. Isolde gazes at him and murmurs:

> " To me given ;
> From me riven ;
> Leal and trusted,
> True and trait—
> Death-devoted head !
> Death-devoted heart ! "

In these lines we hear a revelation of Isolde's heart. Tristan was hers; he is not. Both must die. She sends Brangäne to summon him to her presence. He offers excuses. Why? Later he tells Isolde, when she asks him why he has avoided her during the voyage, that it was not meet that he who escorted a bride across seas should go near her. She derides the excuse, knowing its shallowness. The man was afraid of himself. He had once wooed this woman and now in her presence he felt the old fascination. He dared not trust his heart.

Brangäne's persistence arouses the squire Kurvenal, who rebuffs her by singing a popular song about Tristan's victory over Morold. Then Isolde in her rage tells the whole story to Brangäne. She tells how the wounded Tristan, calling himself "Tantris," came to Ireland that she might nurse him when he was suffering from a poisoned wound. She tells how she found the nick in his sword and fitted to it the splinter, taken from the head of Morold, not her uncle, as in the old poem, but her lover — making her wrong a much deeper one. She tells how she stood ready to slay him with that sword, but he fixed his melancholy gaze upon her. "Not on the sword, not on my arm; full to my eyes went his look. His misery pleaded straight to my heart." This look was her undoing, and Wagner made its musical symbol one of the salient themes of his score. Tristan swore truth and thanks eternal, yet no sooner had he returned to Cornwall than he suggested the expedition to Ireland to get Isolde as a bride for King Mark, his uncle. It is this for which Isolde craves vengeance. Tristan, having lightly won her love, would present her as a gift to another. She curses him in her rage, and cries, "Vengeance! Death! Death to the two!" Brangäne vainly strives to soothe her. Staring vacantly into space she murmurs: "Unloved by the noblest of men, must I stand near and see him? How can I endure the anguish?" That is the future she dare not, will not face.

What a vast difference already between the original legend and this wonderful dramatisation of it by Richard Wagner! Brangäne says it is foolish for Isolde to fancy that she can remain unloved. Does she forget her mother's magic art, which has provided her with potions of strange power? No, Isolde has not forgotten. She asks for the casket, and when

Brangäne shows her the love potion she brushes it aside and declares that the drink of death is for her. Reader, keep this death thought always in mind. It is the basic underthought of the entire drama. In the first act it appears first in the mind of Isolde. She will renounce life, for there is nothing in it for her but misery. In the second act both she and Tristan feed upon the dream of death ; and in the third act death unites them.

At last Tristan and Isolde are face to face. She demands revenge for Morold. Tristan offers his sword and bids her slay him. She refuses on the ground that she cannot go before Mark as the slayer of his favourite knight. She invites Tristan to drink atonement with her. He understands, and is ready with her to seek oblivion. Brangäne, bidden to bring the drink of death, hastily substitutes for it the love potion. She will do anything rather than slay her mistress; she condemns her to live and suffer. The words of Tristan as he stands with the cup in hand ready to drink show that he comprehends the situation. He has discovered that Isolde loves him; he knows that he loves her. He prefers death to a life of renunciation or dishonour. He drinks. She seizes the cup and shares the draught. It was not the drink of death. It was for them the drink of hell. Hurled now by the unrestrained passion within them into one another's arms, the man wonders what dream of honour it was that troubled him but a moment ago, and the woman marvels that she trembled at the thought of shame.

Tristan.—" Was träumte mir,
von Tristan's Ehre ? "

Isolde.—" Was träumte mir
von Isolde's Schmach ? "

"What dreamed I of Tristan's honour ? " " What
dreamed I of Isolde's shame ? " I have purposely
dwelt at length on the incidents and dialogue of this
wonderful first act, because they furnish the key to
the entire drama, and because so many persons, even
professed lovers of Wagner, misconstrue the meaning
of the action.   The ill-fated pair are lovers before the
drama begins, but both are labouring under a misunderstanding. She thinks that he does not love her
because he has come to carry her home as a bride for
his uncle. He thinks that she is athirst for vengeance
for the death of Morold. She desires to die rather
than face her future. He is ready to die when he
divines the true cause of her rage. Better oblivion
than a life of misery. Brangäne's unwillingness to
be a party to the suicide of her mistress is the motive
for the administration of the potion, which simply
bursts the bonds of restraint and shows the two
hearts to one another free of all disguise.

The rest is simple.   In the second act Isolde awaits
her lover in the garden. Brangäne warns her of
Melot, but she refuses to accept the warning. Is not
Melot Tristan's friend ? Put out the torch! That is
the signal. The burning woman cannot put out the
flame of her own passion, but she can and does turn
down the torch. What a portentous signal! The
turning down of the spear and the torch from time im-
memorial have meant that death was present. And
so Wagner turns down this torch with the awful
music of the death motive. Tristan rushes to her
arms. They sing to one another in ecstatic accents and

20

in "wrought riddles of the night and day." The
torch was the day; it kept them asunder. Its extinction brought night, the only time when they may be
together. And so in ever-ascending polyphonic utterances of metaphor, they arrive at last at a naked
truth. For them the day is all separation and lies.
Only night eternal, the night of death, can make them
free. Isolde sings:

> " Dem Licht des Tages
> wollt' ich entfliehn,
> dorthin in die Nacht
> dich mit mir ziehn,
> wo der Täuschung ende
> mein Herz mir verhiess,
> wo des Trug's geahnter
> Wahn zerinne :
> dort dir zu trinken
> ew'ge Minne,
> mit mir—dich im Verein
> wollt' ich dem Tode weih'n."

**Mr. John P. Jackson makes this read in English
thus :**

> " Day would I flee,
> Away to the Night
> Take me with thee
> To end the deception
> For me and for thee !
> Where end should all lies
> That our hearts could sever,
> Where together we 'd drink
> Of rapture forever—
> And in love united there
> Death all-everlasting share ! "

Tristan responds that he drank eagerly what he
thought was the draught of death. Isolde complains

that the draught was deceitful, for instead of sweeping them both into night, it left them in the cold glare of day, where was only separation for them. Tristan answers that with honour and fame both destroyed in the glare of day, their hearts can have but one vast yearning, the yearning for night. Then he leads her to the embowered seat, and there they sing together that marvellous duet beginning :

> " O sink' hernieder
> Nacht der Liebe,
> gieb Vergessen
> dass ich lebe."

"O sink around us, night of love ; grant forgetfulness that I live." From the tower floats down the warning of Brangäne. The lovers heed it not. Wrapped in each other's arms, they prate of odious day and love-giving night, the night of eternity. Then comes the awakening. Mark, led by Melot, surprises them. Tristan murmurs : " Der öde Tag zum letzten Mal " ("The hated day for the last time "). A moment later he raves at Mark and his courtiers as "Daylight's phantoms, morning's dreams." When the King has finished his long and pathetic address, Tristan turns to Isolde and asks her whether she is willing to follow him to the land where the sun never shines, the wondrous abode of night. Well she knows his meaning, and as he hesitated not on the ship, so she hesitates not now. Melot's sword is ready, and Tristan hurls himself upon it. The wound becomes a consecration, a deed of expiation and release. It takes the solemnity of the loftiest tragedy, leaving, a comet-flight below its elevation, the melodramatic wound of the legend whence Wagner drew his materials.

This is the wound that will not heal without the aid of Isolde's art. There is no jarring note in the Wagnerian version, no libertine Tristan aiding another in a rude liaison, no Isolde of the White Hand. There is only the one master passion. There is only one tragedy. In the third act we find the wounded, wasting, visionary man lying under a linden tree in the courtyard of his own castle at Kareol in Brittany, whither the faithful Kurvenal has borne him. A shepherd draws a melancholy wail from his pipe, and, in answer to Kurvenal's anxious question sighs, "Lone and bare is the sea." For these two are watching for the ship which shall bear the healer, Isolde, to the side of the stricken man. Kurvenal whispers words of encouragement to his lord, but Tristan shakes his head. He has awakened once more to the glare of sunlit noon, and once more the old fantasies of day and night rush through his brain.

When will the blazing of the torch cease to keep him sundered from Isolde ? When shall it be night for these two ? Kurvenal reveals that he has sent a ship to bring Isolde. The thought is new strength to Tristan. He bursts into a delirium of joy. He sees the ship, the flag waving at the mast. "Kurvenal, siehst du es nicht?" ("Kurvenal, seest thou it not?") Kurvenal sees no sail upon the sea. Again the weary man sinks back upon his rude couch. He relives the story of his love. He raves again as he curses the magic draught, which was not the drink of death. He faints, and for the moment Kurvenal thinks him dead. But no, he revives. He asks again if the ship

is in sight. Kurvenal says to-day it must surely come.
"And on it Isolde!" cries Tristan. Once more the
waning spirit mounts a mighty billow of emotion.
"Isolde, how holy and fair art thou! Kurvenal, man,
art thou blind? Dost thou not see what I see? The
ship! The ship! Isolde's ship! Seest thou it not?"

A new tune peals from the shepherd's pipe. The
ship is sighted! The flag of good tidings streams
from the mast, the flag which means that Isolde is on
board. Fly thou, Kurvenal, to the strand to help her.
To-day shall the lovers be united. Frenzy for the last
time seizes Tristan. Once, wounded and bleeding,
well-nigh slain by Morold, Isolde found him and
nursed him back to life. Again shall she find him so.
Off, then, foolish bandages. Let the red blood flow
merrily. Isolde comes! He hears her calling.
What is this? "Do I hear the light? The torch!
The signal! It is extinguished! To her! To her!"

And so the hero sinks dying in her arms, and for
him at last the longed-for night of total oblivion has
come. Isolde prostrates herself upon his body. A
second ship is sighted, bearing Mark. Kurvenal, misunderstanding the purpose of the King, resists the
entrance of his guard and is slain, after himself giving
a fatal wound to the false Melot. Mark has learned
the secret of the potion. He recognises the truth that
the unhappy pair have been the victims of Fate, and
he has come to unite them. Alas, too late! The
mightiest of monarchs, Death, has come before him.
Isolde, her soul spreadings its wings for flight, sings
out her apostrophe to her dead hero, a marvellous
pæan of praise, the echo of the duet of love, and
sinks lifeless on his insensate form. Night and

eternal oblivion have come for both.   The tragedy is over.

That is the marvellous poem which Wagner made of the old story of Godfrey, a poem in itself worthy, despite its rugged diction, to stand beside the best dramatic literature of Germany, and never once to be thought of as an opera libretto.   I have briefly noted some of the points at which Wagner has separated himself from the sources of his story.   The manner in which he has in all his poems utilised the original suggestions stamps him as a dramatist of the highest rank, a poet of lofty gifts.   In none is this more beautifully demonstrated than in " Tristan und Isolde."   It is true that in some of the later versions of the old poem, when possibly the early faith in love philtres was fading, the idea exists that Tristan and Isolde loved one another from their first meeting ; but, as Miss Weston properly notes, " there is little doubt that the Minstrel held the fatal passion of the two lovers to be due to the Minnetranc alone."   The frequent appearance of magic drinks in old legends is familiar to all students of folk-tales and sagas.   Wagner himself gives us another instance of it in the drinks administered to Siegfried by Hagen, an idea which he obtained from the old tales.   In his " Studies in the Wagnerian Drama " (which I have been forced to parallel in rehearsing some parts of the story of " Tristan und Isolde ") H. E. Krehbiel calls attention to the fact that the existence of the love before the incident of the potion provides that element of guilt which all the ancient dramatists required in order that too much sympathy might not be excited by the sufferings of the hero or heroine.   On the whole, then, Wagner's treatment of this much-discussed drink is perfectly clear. There is no excuse for misunderstanding it. And it raises the tragic element of the drama far beyond the level of the early poems.

Another element of the classic tragedy preserved in this work is that of the inevitable doom of the unhappy pair. They are victims of Fate from the outset, and Wagner has kept the prophecy of death constantly before our minds by making it appear to the lovers themselves as the only avenue of escape from their misfortunes. Furthermore, this forethought of death develops in the second act into a conviction and a passionate desire. The exclamations "Let me die" ("Lass' mich sterben") of the lovers are not mere bursts of sensual rhapsodising, but are expressions of their souls' yearning for the plunge into oblivion at the moment of perfect ecstasy. For both dread the turning of the light of day upon them ; both foresee a future of separation and misery.

The pessimism of this second act is the feature of Wagner's drama which has aroused the largest amount of discussion. Its peculiarly illogical deduction from a turbulent, passionate, soul-consuming love like that of Tristan and Isolde has frequently called forth unfavourable comment. Yet we are bound to admit that in his treatment of this element of his work the master has been dramatically ingenious. In summarising the story I have indicated his poetic treatment of the cessation of the desire for life and the yearning for death. That he has made it poetic is not to be denied, but it is not consistent. If the lovers had sworn renunciation and had suffered from the enforcement of their vow, there would have been consistency in their desire to die. But in the midst of unbridled indulgence in their passion they would have wished to live, unless there had been surfeit and the subsequent moral reaction. But of this we have no hint. The yearning for death, however, is an outcome of Wagner's absorption of the philosophy of Arthur Schopenhauer. This writer was a subjective realist and regarded extant phenomena as the products of the will—that is, the world exists because man wishes to think so. The highest ethical destiny of man is the nullification of the will by the practice of an asceticism which shall remove from him all desire for the objects of sense. These, then, being but creations of the will, shall disappear, and the will, the only reality, shall quietly renounce itself and vanish into the infinite. The doctrine is closely allied to that of the Buddhist Nirvana. Wagner's endeavour to reconcile it with the dramatic ideas of "Tristan und Isolde" was not successful. Asceticism and adultery are not companions. But from the Schopenhaureian pessimism he drew the long-continued harping upon night and death, which is considerably more poetical than the thoughts of the philosopher. In the second act the music of the duet breathes all the pulsing and the languors of consuming passion, and the score effectually masks the dramatic ineffectiveness of the dialogue.

Otherwise the second act is a wonderful conception. In no other part of Wagner's writings is his perfect command of his own union of the arts tributary to the drama more beautifully demonstrated. The picture, the action, the music, combine to create a poetic effect upon the mind of the auditor. The dramatic instincts of Wagner led him to centralise in one meeting of the lovers all the long-drawn passion of the old legend. In the drama we have but one meeting, which brings about the catastrophe. And whatever we may think of the undramatic character of the Schopenhaureian pessimism, which, as I have written elsewhere, is dragged into the story by the neck, it affords ground for a poetic dialogue rich in mysticism and not shocking in suggestion of mere fleshly desire. The dwarf Melot of the legend becomes the faithless friend of Tristan in the drama. He is merely a sketch, for his one action is but a piece of mechanism in the movement of the story.

The substitution of a long harangue for a swift blow of the sword has caused the proverbial finger of scorn to be pointed at King Mark, who comes upon the stage in this act to discover his bride in the arms of his knight. But he is certainly a vast improvement on the Mark of the legend, who was constantly hesitating, who even saw the guilty pair asleep in the forest, but refused to believe because the naked sword lay between them. This Mark at least does not suspect and confide in turns, send them away and then take them back. The long speech explains certain points which are the best defence of Mark's "sermonising," as it is often called. It tells us that he wed a second time only because his court and his people demanded it, and because Tristan himself declared that he would leave Cornwall unless the King yielded. The fact that it was a political marriage, and that the King was old and weary and not prone to emotional flashes, may serve to explain why he talks instead of slaying Tristan on the spot. At any rate Wagner's conception of the voluntary release of the embrace of life by the guilty lovers is carried out, for when Mark does not cut him down, Tristan throws himself upon Melot's sword.

Miss Weston, who makes much of the authority of the old legends and of resemblances in the folk-lore or mythology of antiquity, regrets that the death of Tristan in the third act is less touching than in the legend, where, deceived by Isolde of the White Hand and believing himself forsaken by his own Isolde, he silently turns his face to the wall and breathes out his life with the name of the loved one on his lips. And she furthermore repeats the criticism of Gaston Paris that the final speech of Isolde contains more philosophy than poetry, a weak criticism as one reading of the text will show. Mr. Krehbiel more aptly notes that the elimination of the second Isolde removes from the character of Tristan a stain which was placed upon it by his loveless second marriage, and saves us the shock of seeing the wife and the mistress in contest about his dying couch. Furthermore, the musical treatment of the act is to my mind the most convincing piece of dramatic writing in the literature of the lyric stage. I say this without forgetting the wonders of the first and second acts. There are certain similarities in the musical plans of the three acts. Each begins with a passage intended to create an atmosphere: the first, with the sailor's song floating down from aloft; the second, with the music of the hunt dying away under the black arches of the forest; and the third with the shepherd's pipe wailing the heart-wrecking song of the empty sea. Nothing in the lyric drama excels the potency of the combined scene, action, text, and music at the opening of the second act except the astonishing effect of the preliminary measures of the third.

And then follows a succession of those emotional waves, mounting in foaming crests of tone and sinking in throbbing refluxes, which no other composer ever wrote as Wagner did. Tristan's fevered mind, yearning for the ship, waxes and wanes in crescendi and diminuendi of passion till the suffering and sympathising spectator fancies that his nature will endure no more. And then at the apex of one of the awful upward flights of delirium comes that tremendous climax made by the changing of the melody of the shepherd's pipe. The ship is sighted. Now comes a period of vehement action, ending with the frenzied man's tearing off the bandage, and sinking into Isolde's arms to breathe out his life. Another burst of action follows this crisis, and then the stillness of death itself prevails while the musical finale of the work, the wonderful "Liebestod," falls upon the audience "like the sound of a great Amen." There is nothing in the old legend to suggest the astounding effects which Wagner has heaped up in this last act. It is all the inspiration of a master genius working without trammels in a field created by its own powers.

III.—The Musical Exposition

Let us turn now to a brief examination of the musical structure of "Tristan und Isolde." It is not practicable to make this examination exhaustive, nor would it be profitable. For those who desire to detect each motive of the score as it passes them in the general panorama of tone there are many handbooks. The present writer does not believe that the dramatic influence of Wagner's music upon the auditor is dependent on the latter's full acquaintance with the terminology of the significant themes. That a certain intellectual pleasure is added to the hearing of one of these dramas by a recognition of the identity of the motives is not to be denied, and that their dramatic purport should always be clear to the hearer's mind is beyond dispute ; but it should never be the purpose of an auditor to concentrate his attention on the themes. Learn their meaning from the text. Then let them alone, and they will do their work.

In "Tristan und Isolde" we come upon the Wagnerian system worked out to its end. Indeed, the composer went even further. In a letter to Francis Villot in Paris in 1860, afterward published under the title of "Music of the Future," the poet-composer said of "Tristan und Isolde":

"Upon that work I consent to your making the severest claims deducible from my theoretic premises ; not because I formed it on my system, for every theory was clean forgotten by me ; but since here I moved with fullest freedom and the most utter disregard of every theoretic scruple, to such an extent that during the working out I myself was aware how far I had outstripped my system."

The composer sought in this drama to free himself from all the restrictions of historical detail, and to centralise the music upon the expression of the emotions of his personage, to make the play of emotions, and not the succession of incidents, the real material of the drama. This had always been his ideal of the lyric drama, but he had not been certain of its practicability. In the letter just quoted he says on this point :

" All doubt at last was taken from me when I gave myself up to the 'Tristan.' Here, in perfect trustfulness, I plunged into the inner depths of soul events, and from out this inmost centre of the world I fearlessly built up its outer form. A glance at the volumen of this poem will show you at once that the exhaustive detail work, which a historical poet is obliged to devote to clearing up the outward bearings of his plot, to the detriment of a lucid exposition of its inner motives, I now trusted myself to apply to these latter alone. Life and death, the whole import and existence of the outer world, here hang on nothing but the inner movements of the soul. The whole affecting action comes about for reason only that the inmost soul demands it and steps to light with the very shape foretokened in the inner shrine."

In beginning the work, he wrote the text without any thought of operatic style. The reader will note that it is written in a freely formed rhymed verse, the rhythms being few, but elastic, and of such a nature that the poetry suggests the form of the melody without hampering the composer. This result could have been achieved only by the procreation of both verse and music by one mind. The organic union of text and tone was conceived in Wagner's brain before pen touched paper. In reference to this he says in the " Music of the Future ":

" Whereas the verses were there [in the Italian opera] intended to be stretched to the length demanded by that melody through countless repetitions of words and phrases, in the musical setting of ' Tristan ' not a trace of word repetition is any longer found, but the weft of words and verses foreordains the whole dimensions of the melody, *i. e.*, the structure of that melody is already erected by the poet."

At a first glance this seems to be a contradiction of Wagner's theory that the poem should not impose its form on the music. But we must bear in mind that this poetry was prepared with the avoidance of text domination in the poet's mind. Wagner wrote to Villot that he found that his melody and its form were wholly freed from the old shackles. He composed with the utmost liberty.

Before noting a few of the most significant phrases of this score, which is a shimmering web of leading motives, let us take a glance at the general plan. Here is a work constructed upon a model diametrically opposed to the familiar one of Meyerbeer, the one regnant in Europe at the date of " Tristan und Isolde's " production. Meyerbeer built entirely for the succession of incidents, musical and pictorial. The dramatic idea had to conform itself to this scheme. Wagner built wholly on the ground of the thought and feelings of his personages, and the action and the music had to place themselves as explicators wholly at the service of these inner governors. Yet we shall find that each act of the drama has a clear and symmetrical musical shape, and that although this form is prescribed by the emotional movement, it is none the less grounded upon the fundamental laws of musical form.

Each of the three acts begins with a musical mood picture, in which the elements of external description and inner feeling are skilfully combined. The first act opens with the quaint, peaceful song of the sailor, which suggests a calm sea and a pleasant voyage. The second begins with the hunting music dying away in the forest, music which establishes a nature mood, a mood of moonlight and rustling leaves. The third is ushered in with the music of the empty sea, a descriptive lament whose profound melancholy is not equalled in any other score. Starting from each of these pictures, Wagner develops an act. The sailor's song in Act I. is followed by a sudden interruption of the peaceful mood. Isolde's passion begins to play. It bursts into tumult. The curtain is thrown back, and to accompany the motionless picture of Tristan at the helm, the sailor's song is repeated. Again the music gradually rises in emotional force, till another climax is reached, when Kurvenal trolls his ditty and the insulted Isolde has the curtain closed. Another point of repose, and again with Isolde's passion the music rises, but sinks to languorous yearning as she tells of the glance that won her soul. The wave mounts again as she curses Tristan and cries for vengeance. The music sinks into impressive depths as Isolde proclaims her purpose to administer the drink of death, and here Wagner relieves the strain and makes a sharp contrast by introducing the cries of the seamen outside. Then follow Kurvenal's boisterous entrance, and at length the entrance of Tristan, which is heralded by an orchestral passage voicing the heroism and the fate of the hero, a passage of extraordinary power. The scene between Tristan and Isolde begins resposefully and rises to a climax of passion at the taking of the drink. Then comes a moment of expectancy, followed by an upheaval, and then each utters the other's name in a phrase of deepest yearning. The sailor's music again affords the necessary relief, and the act comes to an end in a turmoil of tone.

The musical scheme of the second act is simpler because the emotions are less complex. After the opening mood picture, Isolde has a brief scene of contest with Brangäne, and at the extinction of the torch the musical wave, which has been growing, curls and breaks. The next one starts with Isolde's waving her scarf. Now we have a rapid, agitated movement, depicting the wild haste of Tristan, the eagerness of Isolde. The lover enters and this movement becomes tumultuous. When its climax is reached the necessary point of repose is made as Tristan leads Isolde to the seat. We have had an allegro agitato; now follows an adagio appassionata, the love duet. Its long-drawn, melting measures are broken once by the watch-cry of Brangäne—so composed that it does not interrupt, but intensifies the mood—and at last the rude interruption of Kurvenal. The contrast here is short and sharp. The dramatic situation is enough. Then follows another slow movement,—the coda of the adagio,—Mark's speech, Tristan's answer, his appeal to Isolde, her answer. With the few crashing measures of Melot and of Tristan's self-impalement, the musical scheme is completed. Its form is perfect; its organic union with the mood scheme of the act complete.

The musical plan of the third act has again more detail, because the story is more incidental. With the melancholy music of the empty sea as a starting-point, Wagner develops a long adagio, whose wave-crests are the summits of Tristan's delirious outbursts. This adagio ends when the shepherd's pipe proclaims the sighting of the sail. Then enters the allegro agitato of the act, the wild rhapsody of Tristan, the tearing off of the bandages, and the death of the hero. With Isolde's mourning over the body we get a point of repose and contrast. The shepherd announces a second ship. Descriptive music of rapid movement follows, till the fight is interrupted by Mark's entrance, and the final slow movement is begun. This movement comes to its majestic climax with the "Liebestod," and with a few bars of finale by the orchestra the work ends, like Tschaikowsky's sixth symphony, with its adagio lamentoso.

The drama is prefaced by a prelude, in which some of the most significant themes of the work appear. The thought underlying the prelude is the insatiable desire of the lovers, ever rising higher and higher in emotional waves till it sinks exhausted in its vain endeavour to find its own satisfaction. Several themes are combined in the musical structure of the Vorspiel, but the most important are those of Love and the

Glance of Tristan; the glance which, Isolde tells Brangäne, stayed her hand when she had discovered that Tristan was the slayer of Morold and had lifted the sword to slay him. These two marvellously expressive themes are heard frequently throughout the drama. The sailor's song, with which the first act begins, contains the melody of the sea music, heard several times in the course of the act.

THE SEA.

This theme belongs to what Mr. Krehbiel has well described as the music of the scene, or scenic music. It deals with the externals of the drama, not with its emotions. The next significant motive to appear is that of Death, which is first heard when Isolde exclaims, "Death-devoted head! Death-devoted heart!"

DEATH.

Closely associated with this in meaning is the Fate motive, which is first heard in the harmonic scheme of the prelude.

FATE.

We have now before us nearly all the significant thematic material of the first act. Most of the other melodic features are freely composed and do not figure in the subsequent episodes. The repetitions of the motives quoted will explain themselves to the most casual observer. The re-entrances of the Death and Fate motives are unmistakable in purport, while the reappearance of the Love and Glance themes after the drinking of the potion brings back the opening of the prelude with its story of desire insatiable, love immeasurable.

The play upon the contrasting fancies of night and day, which forms the figurative material of the lovers' dialogue in the second act, suggests new thematic devices, and so the act opens with the proclamation by the orchestra of the Day theme.

DAY.

Derived from this is the beautiful motive of the Night, which appears in Tristan's long speech dealing with the fanciful contrast of the two. When he says, "Was dort in keuscher Nacht dunkel verschlossen wacht?" ("What watches yonder darkly concealed in chaste Night?") the theme sings softly in the orchestral accompaniment:

NIGHT.

This luscious, languorous theme plays an important
part throughout the act.   The hearer will note how
beautifully it serves as the introduction to the cantabile of the duo, "O sink' hernieder," and how effectively the composer has made the day and night
variations of the one fundamental musical idea carry
out the thought of the dialogue.   Another theme
which appears in the introductory music of the second
act is that of the Triumph of Love:

TRIUMPH OF LOVE.

From a development of this theme, by the simple
musical device of augmentation, Wagner constructs
the climax of the duo, which becomes again the
climax of the last speech of Isolde over the dead body
of Tristan:

Another significant motive heard in the opening
measures of the act is the Love Call, which is afterward employed frequently in the action:

LOVE CALL.

These are the principal and most significant new motives which appear in the love music of this wonderful
act.   Of course, some of the themes heard in the first
act are employed here again, and nothing in the entire
score is more charged with meaning than the combination of the motive of the Triumph of Love with the
harmonies of that of Death at the instant of Isolde's extinction of the torch.   Such feats of musical depiction
the attentive listener will find on every page of the
score, yet the actual number of motives to which
special meanings have been attached is not large
enough to tax the memory.   The appearance of King
Mark in the action is noted by two motives, one used
to indicate his personality and the other his grief:

The third act opens with music descriptive of bitter
grief and loneliness.   The first phrase, that of grief, is
a remarkable thematic development of the second half
of the Love motive:

The ensuing long ascending passage expresses loneliness most eloquently. This is interrupted by a new
motive, heard frequently in this act, the motive of
Anguish:

ANGUISH.

The melody played by the shepherd's pipe has received various titles, but it speaks its own language
of melancholy. The music allotted to Kurvenal in the
opening scene of the act is similar in character to that
which he sings in Act I., and at one place is a
repetition of it. In the long speeches of Tristan we
hear repeated with powerful dramatic significance the
motives of Day and Night, the Love theme, the Death
theme, the motive of Anguish, and snatches of the love
duo of Act II. The musical material of the entire
act is now woven of what has already been heard.
The motives melt and flow in a stream of marvellous
melody, till at the end Isolde proclaims her hero's
greatness in the "Liebestod," which is a repetition,
with some developments, of Tristan's "So stürben
wir um ungetrennt, ewig' einig' ohne End'," and the
motive of the Triumph of Love :

So stür-ben wir um un- -ge-trennt,
So die that we to-geth- -er blend,

E - wig, ein - ig oh - - ne End'.
Liv - ing, lov - ing, with - out end.

There are other motives in this stupendous score, but, as I have already intimated, it would be idle for the music-lover to burden his memory with them. Many of them are thematic developments of phrases first heard in the germinal form, and it is in the overwhelming eloquence of these developments that the power of the score is largely to be found. With the themes already given the lover of the true lyric drama should readily understand the purposes of the composer. For the rest, the perfect organic union of text, tone, and action in "Tristan und Isolde" makes it the most directly expressive of all the later dramas. Only those who go to hear it with the conception of an old-fashioned opera in their minds fail to receive its message. "Tristan und Isolde" is a drama of human emotions uttered in tones. As such it must be conceded a place among the mightiest conceptions of the poetic brain.

DIE MEISTERSINGER VON NÜRNBERG
Opera in Three Acts.

First performed at the Royal Court Theatre,
Munich, June 21, 1868.

Original Cast.

Hans Sachs	Betz.
Veit Pogner	Bausewein.
Kunz Vogelgesang	Heinrich.
Conrad Nachtigall	Sigl.
Sixtus Beckmesser	Hölzel.
Fritz Kothner	Fischer.
Balthazar Zorn	Weixlstorfer.
Ulrich Eislinger	Hoppe.
Augustin Moser	Pöppl.
Hermann Ortel	Thoms.
Hans Schwartz	Graffer.
Hans Foltz	Hayn.
Walther von Stolzing . . .	Nachbaur.
David	Schlosser.
Eva	Fräulein Mallinger.
Magdalene	Frau Diez.
Ein Nachtwächter	Lang.

Weimar, Mannheim, Carlsruhe, Dresden, Dessau,
1869 ; Berlin, Hanover, Vienna, Leipsic, Stettin, Königsberg, 1870 ; Hamburg, Prague, Bremen, 1871 ;

Riga, Copenhagen, 1872 ; Mayence, 1873 ; Cologne,
Nuremberg, Breslau, 1874 ; Brunswick, 1876 ; Strassburg, Augsburg, 1877; Gratz, Düsseldorf, 1878; Wiesbaden, Rotterdam, Darmstadt, 1879 ; Schwerin, 1881 ;
London, May 30, 1882.

First performed in America at the Metropolitan Opera
House, New York, Jan. 4, 1886.

Cast.

Hans Sachs	Emil Fischer.
Veit Pogner	Joseph Staudigl.
Kunz Vogelgesang . . .	Herr Dworsky.
Conrad Nachtigall	Emil Saenger.
Sixtus Beckmesser	Otto Kemlitz.
Fritz Kothner	Herr Lehmler.
Balthasar Zorn	Herr Hoppe.
Ulrich Eislinger	Herr Klaus.
Augustin Moser	Herr Langer.
Hermann Ortel	Herr Doerfler.
Hans Schwartz	Herr Eissbeck.
Hans Foltz	Herr Anlauf.
Walther von Stolzing . . .	Albert Stritt.
David	Herr Krämer.
Eva	Auguste Krauss (Mrs. Seidl).
Magdalena	Marianne Brandt.
Nachtwächter	Carl Kauffmann.

Conductor, Anton Seidl.

DIE MEISTERSINGER VON NÜRNBERG

"TANNHÄUSER" was finished in April, 1844, and in the summer of that year, while at Marienbad, Wagner made the sketch of "Die Meistersinger von Nürnberg." He designed this comic opera as a pendant to the serious "Tannhäuser" (see Chapter VI. of the biographical part of this work), and no doubt the historical relations of the minnesingers, who figured in the tragedy, with the meistersingers, who provided him with the characters for his comedy, suggested the nature of the humorous opera and the general manner of the treatment of the subject. The first drafts of the comedy were made in the summer of 1844, but the poem was completed in Paris in the winter of 1861–62. The music was begun in 1862, but, as we have seen, was laid aside when the composer fled from his creditors, as narrated in Chapter XI. of the biography. The work was resumed after King Ludwig had become Wagner's protector, and the score was finished on Oct. 21, 1867.

Something of the character of the German minnesinger we have seen in our study of "Tannhäuser," where Wagner gives an idealised picture of one of their courtly contests in poetry and song. These minnesingers were the German companions and imitators of the French troubadours, from whom they took their origin. Their epoch dates from the reign of Conrad III., of the Hohenstauffen dynasty, who ascended the throne in 1138. In 1148, when he undertook a crusade in company with Louis VII. of France, the nobility of Germany were brought into habitual acquaintance with the nobility of France, who at that time were cultivating Provençal poetry and song in the "gay science" of the Troubadour. The German emperors now began the pursuit of the customs of chivalry. They and their nobles threw open their courts with a brilliant hospitality which rivalled that of France. The splendour of their tournaments, the glitter of their festivals, drew visitors in throngs from far and near. With them came the poet and the singer, and thus the German, who in the crusade had caught the infection of the chanson of Provence, found his first rude attempts brought face to face with the more polished productions of the visiting chanteurs and jongleurs.

The minnelied was the outcome, and for more than a century this form of courtly song was prized by the German people. While the Hohenstauffen dynasty remained on the throne (1138-1272), the literature of chivalry was patronised at court and the song of the minstrel was heard throughout the land. These singers were called minnesingers from the old German word "minne," which means "love"—the topic most dear to the minstrel heart. With the death of the first Frederick, the great Barbarossa, the star of the Swabian dynasty set, and the sweet sounds of the Swabian lyre were soon drowned in the turmoil of the internal disorders which beset Germany in the period of the Great Interregnum. This was a time after the death of the last Hohenstauffen, when various minor princes wore the imperial title without exercising its functions or its authority. The customs of chivalry naturally fell into disuse when there was no central home for them, and the minnesinger became a memory. The period of disturbance was ended with the accession to the throne of Rudolf of Hapsburg. This monarch was engaged during much of his reign in putting down the internal disorders, and his chief business was the overthrow of the powerful and independent nobles. He was furthermore largely occupied with quarrels with the Huns. The court language was changed from West Gothic to East Gothic, which was less national, and much of the southern culture which had characterised the reign of the Swabian emperors inevitably disappeared. The customs of chivalry sought shelter in the courts of minor princes, who were unable to give prizes of sufficient value to attract the knightly singers, engaged, as most of them were, in their final struggle for power and privilege.

The field of poetry and song was left to competitors of lower social standing. A versifying mania now began to pervade the lower classes. Blacksmiths, weavers, shoemakers, doctors, and schoolmasters sought to mend their fortunes by making verses. Poetry became dull, mechanical, pedantic; poets, conceited, shallow, and arrogant. The spirit of the age, filled with the instinct of preservation through co-operation against attack from without, led these people to form themselves into corporations, and Charles IV. (1346–78) gave them a charter. They spoke of twelve minnesingers as their models and masters,* and themselves they called mastersingers.

* This explains the meaning of Kothner's question to Walther in the first act, " What master taught you the art ? " To this Walther an-

They held periodical meetings to criticise each other's productions. Correctness was their chief aim, and they seem to have had little real conception of poetry. Every fault was marked and he who made the fewest was awarded the prize and permitted to take apprentices in the meistersinger's art. At the expiration of his apprenticeship a young man was admitted to the corporation and declared a "Meistersinger."

The first mastersinger of whom we know anything was Heinrich von Meissen, called "Frauenlob" because of his fondness for singing the praise of woman. He founded a guild of meistersingers at Mainz in 1311, and by the end of the fourteenth century most towns in Germany had similar bodies. The school reached its highest development in Nuremberg in the time of Hans Sachs (1494–1575). Sachs is an historical character, and there is abundant opportunity for the study of his style, as 6048 of his works are extant.* It was his period which Wagner selected for treatment in his comedy.

The order of meistersingers, however, continued to practise its calling long after this time. At Ulm the institution survived even the changes which the French Revolution effected in Europe. As late as 1830 twelve old mastersingers, after being driven from one refuge to another, sang their ancient melodies from memory in a little inn where the working men used to meet to drink their beer in the evenings.

swers with the beautiful lyric, "Am stillen Herd," in which he declares that Walther von der Vogelweide, one of the minnesingers (see "Tannhäuser"), was his master.

   * Many of these works are now regarded as spurious, but the majority of them are undoubtedly from the pen of the famous cobbler-poet.

In 1839 only four of the singers survived ; and in that year these remnants assembled with great solemnity and, declaring the society of mastersingers disbanded forever, presented their songs, hymn books, and pictures to a musical institution of Ulm. It is said that the last of the four died in 1876.

The meisterlied — mastersong — created by these singers was a lineal descendant of the minnelied, the song of the minnesinger. The latter was constructed in strophes, and each strophe consisted of three parts. The first and second parts were alike in metre and melody, and were called "Stollen." The third part was in a different metre and had its own melody, and it was called the "Abgesang," or aftersong. The minnesingers used three forms: the Lied (song), the Lerch (lay), and the Spruch (proverb). The lay was composed of differently constructed strophes, each with its own melody. The song was in several strophes, all built and set alike. The proverb was in a single strophe. The lied form was that adapted for their use by the meistersingers. Their songs consisted of three "Bars" (staves). Each staff was divided into three "Gesätze (stanzas). The Gesatz was constructed in three sections, the first two being alike in metre and melody and called "Stollen." The third section differed in metre and had its own melody and was called the "Abgesang," or "aftersong." Thus we see that the "Bar" of the meisterlied corresponded to the strophe of the minnelied. The subjects treated in their songs were usually religious, though secular topics were not excluded. Sometimes didactic or epigrammatic themes were chosen. The tunes were all fixed, and the meistersinger's art was purely poetic. The tunes were called tones and had curious names, such as the blue tone, the red tone, the ape tone, the lily tone. In writing his comedy, Wagner, aiming, as he did, to reproduce in a lifelike manner the customs of the time, adhered to the rules of the meistersingers in the matter of song, and, in selecting a theme to designate the guild, used the melody of the "long tone" of Heinrich Müglin, a meistersinger of the early period. For the construction of the song he lays down the law in the address of Kothner to Walther, when the former reads the rules from the "Leges Tabulaturæ." These laws prescribe the form which we recognise as substantially that of the lied of the minnesinger.

Wagner drew his information as to the manners and customs of the meistersingers from the principal source of all our knowledge of them. This is a book entitled "De Sacri Rom. Imperii Libera Civitate Noribergensi Commentatio," written by Johann Christtoph Wagenseil, Professor of Oriental Languages at the University of Altdorf, and published in 1697. Not only did the poet-composer find his facts there, but he took from the volume also the names of his characters, for Veit Pogner, Fritz Kothner, Conrad Nachtigall, Balthasar Zorn, Sixtus Beckmesser, and the rest of Wagner's meistersingers all walked the earth in their day and sang their artificial ditties in imitation of their masters, the minnesingers. Beckmesser, who appears as the "low comedian" of Wagner's work, seems to have been a worthy, though prosaic, person in his time. He was certainly not a butt of derision, such as Wagner's character becomes through his own stupidity and vanity.

The story of "Die Meistersinger" is, of course, Wagner's own. His representation of the characters of the masters is his own. The real Hans Sachs is, perhaps, not so well known as the real Wolfram von Eschenbach, but it is probable that he was only a little better than his fellow meistersingers. His works were more popular, and he was doubtless a man of superior ability. But it is not likely that he excelled the rest in refinement and artistic insight quite as much as he appears to do in Wagner's comedy. The story tells us that young Walther von Stolzing, a Franconian knight, has fallen in love, almost at first sight, with Eva, the daughter of Veit Pogner, the most substantial member of the guild, a man of some means. Pogner has decided that his daughter shall wed a meistersinger, and that she shall be the prize of the winner in the forthcoming contest of song. Her own choice is to operate only in so far as to permit her the liberty of rejecting the winner if she does not like him. But she must, in the end, marry someone chosen by a contest and approved by all the masters. Sachs endeavours to have the voice of the general public added to that of the guild, but Pogner is unwilling to introduce too many novelties into his experiment.

Walther meets Eva at the morning service of St. Catherine's Church, in which the principal meetings of the masters were held. She tells him that she must choose a master, and also that if he be not a master, she will have no other. David, an apprentice to Hans Sachs, arrives with other apprentices to prepare the church for an examination in song, and explains very vaguely to the young knight what he must do to become a master. Pogner and the other masters assemble, and Pogner, declaring that the desire of a knight to become a singer brings back the old times, explains the presence of Walther. He presently announces to the masters for the first time his plan in regard to his daughter's choice, a plan which gravely disconcerts Beckmesser, an aspirant for her hand. Walther is now introduced as a candidate for the degree of master. Kothner instructs him in the rules and appoints Beckmesser marker. The marker was a critic whose business it was to note every offence against the rules. Beckmesser conceals himself in the marker's booth, and Walther, having announced love as his theme, sings his song, which is entirely incorrect according to the laws of the guild, but in which Hans Sachs at once discovers the force of a new genius. In spite of his appeals the youth is declared, according to the formula, "outsung," and the meeting dissolves in confusion, Walther vainly endeavouring to make himself heard, Sachs pleading for him, the other masters objecting, Beckmesser scolding and pointing out more faults, and Pogner deeply troubled lest his daughter's already engaged affections make it impossible for him to carry out his plan.

The second act shows us the street, on one side of which is the house of Pogner and on the other that of Hans Sachs. Pogner brings his daughter home, still troubled in his mind and striving to fathom hers. When he has gone into the house, Magdalena, Eva's companion, tells her of Walther's failure, and she determines to ask Sachs for advice. Presently the shoemaker seats himself at his work in the door of his house. The balmy air of the evening, the scent of the elder tree, turn his thoughts to the poetry which he heard at the trial. What though it outraged the rules of the masters and even puzzled him? Within it lay a real power. The singer sang, not to meet rules, but because utterance was demanded by his feelings. Let the masters rage; Hans Sachs is well pleased. This is the substance of the famous monologue of the second act.

Eva comes from Pogner's house and in a most charming scene with Sachs hints that as an avenue of escape from the possibility of marriage with Beckmesser, who intends to compete for her hand, she would be glad to become Sachs's wife. But he discourages this foolish idea. Then she tries to learn the details of the defeat of Walther, and Sachs, to test her feelings, pretends that he and all the other masters were actuated by mere jealousy in voting against the youth. Eva discloses her real feelings. Sachs leaves her, and the next moment she is in the arms of her lover. They plan to elope. Sachs, who has been listening and watching, throws open his window and lets a flood of light into the street just as they are about to depart. Then Beckmesser approaches for the purpose of serenading Eva. Sachs now brings his bench out into the doorway, and begins to sing lustily at his work. Eva and Walther hide, and Beckmesser inquires the reason of Sachs's outbreak. The cobbler protests that he is trying to finish the pair of shoes which Beckmesser had demanded of him that very day. Magdalena, personating Eva, appears at the window, and Beckmesser endeavours to sing his song to her. Sachs's singing and pounding prevent him.

Then they come to an agreement. Sachs is to act as marker, and correct each error with a blow of his hammer. He vows that the shoes will be finished before the song is. Beckmesser sings and Sachs strikes many blows. The shoes are finished first. Then Beckmesser sings desperately and Sachs shouts lustily. The neighbours, aroused by the outcry, begin to appear at their windows and presently in the street. David, seeing Magdalena, his sweetheart, at the window, and Beckmesser serenading her, attacks the singer with a cudgel. The neighbours take sides, and a general mêlée ensues. Walther decides to cut his way through the throng with Eva and escape, but Sachs intercepts him, sends Eva into the arms of her father, and takes Walther into his own house. At that moment the nightwatchman's horn is heard. The crowd melts. The beaten Beckmesser limps painfully away. The watchman passes up the empty street, startled at his own shadow. The full moon rises over the distant roofs, and as the silent street is flooded with its mild light, the orchestra breathes a passage of perfect peace and beauty while the curtain falls. It is one of Wagner's most potent dramatic and musical achievements.

The third act opens in the interior of Sachs's house. The poet-shoemaker is in a reverie, and the prattling of his apprentice cannot rouse him from it. When he is left alone, he breaks into the second great monologue, "Wahn, Wahn." One must read the entire text of this in order to understand it. At its conclusion Walther descends from the chamber in which he has passed the night, and informs Sachs that he has had a "wondrous lovely dream." Sachs bids him put it into verse, and make a mastersong of it. Walther bitterly asks how he can make a mastersong and one that's good. Sachs reproves him and bids him observe law in his poetry. Walther begins the song which he afterward sings for the prize. At the end of the first stanza Sachs stops him and instructs him as to the nature of a "Stollen." After the second "Stollen" he requires the young knight to make the "Abgesang." Giving him several hints as to the construction of his lay, Sachs writes it down, deeply moved by its beauty.

When Sachs and Walther have left the room, Beckmesser enters, and, finding the newly written song, thinks it is by Sachs and that the shoemaker means to enter the contest. When Sachs returns Beckmesser charges him with this intention, and to his surprise Sachs gives him the song, vowing that under no circumstances will he claim it as his own. Beckmesser departs, almost besides himself with joy. Eva arrives and declares that one of her shoes hurts. Sachs smiles incredulously, but pretends to adjust the shoe. Walther, richly clad, appears and stands spellbound at the sight of Eva. Sachs hints that now the third stanza of the song might be produced, and Walther sings it. Eva, deeply moved, throws herself into Sachs's arms, saying that she has reached a new understanding of him and herself. David and Magdalena enter, and Sachs announces that a mastersong has been made. He promotes David from apprentice to journeyman that he may hear the song, which an apprentice could not honour, and then he invites Eva to speak. Here is introduced Wagner's one quintet in purely lyric style, and it is conceded to be one of the loveliest conceptions of this extraordinary work. The party starts for the field of contest, and the scene changes to an open place on the banks of the river.

The various guilds of artisans assemble, and finally the meistersingers enter in formal procession. Sachs, who is hailed by the people in glad chorus, announces the terms of the contest and Beckmesser is summoned to the singer's stand. Trembling in every limb he makes a futile attempt to sing Walther's song, at which he looks vainly at every opportunity. He makes a farce of it, and is laughed to scorn by the people. In a rage he rushes away, pausing only to declare that the song is by Sachs, and not himself. Sachs, however, says that the song is not his and that it is a good song if correctly sung. He calls for some one who can sing it, and Walther appears. The masters, though they divine Sachs's plan, allow the young knight to sing, and the entire assembly, seconded by the conquered masters, declares that he has won the prize. Eva places the crown of laurel on his head, and with him kneels before the well-pleased Pogner. But when he would hang around Walther's neck the insignia of a mastersinger the youth refuses it. Sachs again intervenes and reads the young knight a little lecture on the importance of honouring what is established in art. Walther yields; Eva places the laurel on Sachs's brow, and the curtain falls as the people acclaim him in joyful chorus.

In a letter to Dr. Franz Brendel, dated Aug. 10, 1862, Liszt quoted a part of a letter from his daughter, Cosima, then the wife of Von Bülow. She said :

"These 'Meistersinger' are, to Wagner's other conceptions, much the same as the 'Winter's Tale' is to Shakespeare's other works. Its phantasy is found in gaiety and drollery, and it has called up the Nuremberg of the Middle Ages, with its guilds, its poet-artisans, its pedants, its cavaliers, to draw forth the most fresh laughter in the midst of the highest, most ideal poetry. Exclusive of its sense and the destination of the work, one might compare the artistic work of it with that of the Sacraments-Häuschen of St. Lawrence (at Nuremberg). Equally with the composer has the sculptor lighted upon the most graceful, most fantastic, most pure form—boldness in perfection ; and as at the bottom of the Sacraments-Häuschen there is Adam Kraft, holding it up with a grave and collected air, so in the ' Meistersinger ' there is Hans Sachs, calm, profound, serene, who sustains and directs the action."

This charming critical view of the work from the woman who was afterward to be the sharer of Wagner's joys and labours is so apt that, although this is not a book of criticism, but rather of exposition, I give it place with pleasure. As a picture of the pseudo-artistic life and influence of the mastersingers the work, as genuine and great a comic opera as "Le Nozze di Figaro," is perfect. Louis Ehlert, in one of his pregnant essays, has disclosed a belief that Wagner was not a natural humourist, and that the fun of "Die Meistersinger" is laboured. This is a somewhat severe judgment, founded chiefly upon observation of the character of Beckmesser. The unfortunate Marker is, indeed, a somewhat artificial figure, but much depends upon his impersonator. He may be made a burlesque by very slight overaccentuation of his peculiarities, and the temptation to gain the applause and laughter of the unthinking is too strong for any but a great artist. The true humour of "Die Meistersinger" lies in its presentation of the shallow, pedantic, poetic art of the time, the futile methods of the tribunal, the homely bourgeois life, the quaint pageantry of the guilds, and the pretty plot by which Sachs overthrows the vainglorious pretender to the hand of Eva, and smooths the path of true love.

Behind this delightful comedy there lies a symbolism which should not be overlooked. The masters represent the tyranny of formalism in art, the dominance of that opinion which mistakes form for substance, and attributes to the outward shape of every work the credit for its merit. Walther von Stolzing, in his efforts as poet and singer, is the embodiment of the free impulse, the desire for untrammelled expression. Sachs, without the creative power of the young knight, is the truer artist. He represents the influence of enlightened and sympathetic intelligence. He discerns at once the innate power of the new poesy which Walther brings into the dusty circle of masters, but at the same time he perceives its need of discipline. It is he, therefore, who induces the new genius to submit itself to the sovereignty of the fundamental laws of form—a vastly different thing from practising mere formalism.

Students of Wagner's works have often been invited to accept Walther as a representative of Wagner himself. This is not justified by anything in the work or in the other writings of its creator. Nevertheless we have ground, and the support of Wagner, for the assumption that he really designed Walther to represent the spirit of progress in music, while the masters embodied that of pure pedantry. Those two powers have always been at war in the world of art and always will. Theoreticians and critics publish rules, which they deduce from the practice of the great artists. The next original genius who arrives has something new to say and says it in a new way. He throws overboard some of the old formulas and invents new ones, as Wagner did, and the theoretical and critical world bursts into an outcry of indignation at the disturbance of settled principles. After a time the two forces become reconciled, and the new rules find their way into the theoretical treatises, while the critics descant upon the additional flexibility imparted by them to art. Wagner, in "Die Meistersinger," has shown us the spirit of progress in its jubilant youth, scoffing at the established rules of which it is ignorant. One of the finest lessons of the symbolism of the comedy is that a musician, or any other artist, must master what has already been learned of his art before he can advance beyond it.

The musical plan of "Die Meistersinger" embraces such a wealth of detail that a complete exposition of it would consist of a full analysis of the score. There are many leading motives, and these are repeated or developed with all of the wonderful skill which was at Wagner's command when he undertook this work. While impracticable to give an exhaustive analysis of the score, it is not too much to invite the reader to observe the general musical development of the drama. The prelude contains several of the most important thematic ideas, and these we may first consider. The Vorspiel begins with the Meistersinger motive:

THE MEISTERSINGERS.

A few measures further on appears the Meister-singers' march:

THE MASTERS' MARCH.
Trumpets and Harp.

These two themes, with their solidity, breadth, dignity, and formality, serve admirably to present all the best musical elements of an art which embodied the glorification of rule and the potency of tradition. The second theme has a special interest for us because Wagner built it on the beginning of a genuine Meister-singer tune (the "long tone" of Heinrich Müglin). This tune begins thus :

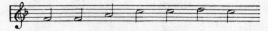

Throughout the drama these Meistersinger themes are employed by Wagner to typify the art represented by his masters, and, as Mr. Krehbiel has very pertin-ently pointed out, their majesty and musical beauty are satisfactory evidence that the composer did not wish us to undervalue the artistic movement of which they are typical. Opposed to these themes we hear in the Vorspiel others associated with the uprising of

emotion, of passion in the young lovers of the play.
These themes, irregular in rhythm, restless in general
style, breathe the leaping aspirations of the romantic
personages, and thus embody the romantic principles
which are constantly urging progress in art. The
first of these is a theme designed to express Walther's
artistic emotion and its search for expression :

WALTHER'S EMOTION.

The second embodies the young knight's love and
its longing, and thus becomes the property also of Eva :

YEARNING OF LOVE.

Two other themes must here be noted, that of the
closing passage of the prize song, and that of Spring.
The latter is employed especially to designate spring
as a period of emotional blossoming rather than a
mere season. It is the springtime of Walther's life
and passion and song:

PRIZE SONG.

SPRING.

To these themes must be added that of Derision,
heard in the last act, when the people are amazed at
the appearance of Beckmesser as a contestant:

DERISION.

Out of this material the prelude is built, and its
character is that of a contest of forces with a final reconciliation, which is, as we have seen, the basis of
the artistic symbolism of the comedy.

The first act begins with a chorale, in which the
old-fashioned style of writing is exhibited.   As the
congregation disperses, Eva and Walther enter into
eager converse, and the themes of Emotion and Spring
are heard.   And here I must ask the reader to note the
wonderful use Wagner has made of this sequence of
tones :

By a very simple change the first three tones are
altered to those of the Spring motive or the closing
strain of the prize song.   It is by such logical musical processes that Wagner makes the development of
his dramas so artistic and so convincing, while at the
same time he fascinates the ear by the purely sensuous
beauty of the varying melodies.   The Spring theme
plays a most important part in the score, and it is
worthy of note that it is so pregnant with meanings
that whether played fast or very slowly it is eloquent,
though with a difference.   Note, if you will, the extraordinary force with which it sings from the orchestra when Sachs's mind, in the second act, is

ruminating on the events of the trial and cannot free itself of the influence of Walther's song. But to proceed with the first act: After the scene of the lovers, with the entrance of David, we begin to hear lively, rhythmic melodies, associated with the youth and gaiety of the apprentices. A portion of this music signifies the chastisement afflicted upon an apprentice by a master, and appears several times in the score to call attention to Sachs's repression of David :

CHASTISEMENT.

When David tells Walther of the art of a master-singer we hear the lovely theme of the Art of Song, plainly enough a variant of the melodic basis of the prize song :

THE ART OF SONG.

All of the music of David's scene with Walther is light and airy, but with the entrance of the masters we hear serious ideas again, the first of them being the motive of the Council :

THE COUNCIL.

The second, a very tender and gracious theme, is that of St. John's Day, the day of the contest for Eva's hand, and it is developed with wonderful eloquence in the address of Pogner:

ST. JOHN'S DAY.

When Walther appears, we hear for the first time the theme of his knighthood :

WALTHER, THE KNIGHT.

This is heard frequently in the score, and when Beckmesser, acting as Marker, shows the slate covered with notes of errors in Walther's song, this theme is heard distorted and caricatured. In answer to Kothner's inquiry as to who was his master, Walther sings the lyric "Am stillen Herd," and its second phrase (marked *a*) reveals its foundation on the Spring theme:

"AM STILLEN HERD."

The subsequent trial song, as will be noted at a single hearing, throbs throughout with the Spring theme. Note the fine contrast made by Kothner's formal statement of the laws of the mastersong, ending with a fine vocal exfoliation in the old style:

The act comes to an end with a general discussion among the masters, while Walther vainly endeavours to make himself heard and the apprentices sing a chorus of derision. As Sachs remains in the foreground, moved by the new music which he has heard, we hear once more its fundamental phrase, the Spring motive.

The music of the second act is simplicity itself up to the dialogue of Pogner and Eva. The score is rich with themes already made known, but when the father tells his daughter how she must on the morrow make her choice before all the citizens, we hear for the first time a peculiarly lovely motive intended to designate the old city itself:

NUREMBERG.

Familiar motives, employed to make a mood-picture of great beauty, illustrate the scene between Sachs and Eva. But here, indeed, we must pause to note the wonderful expressiveness of the monologue of Sachs, preceding his scene with Eva. The orchestral part throbs with the Spring motive, which finally swells into a broad and beautiful cantilena. The lyric of the first act is quoted by the orchestra also, and at length Sachs concludes with a bit of new melody of his own. He, too, is filled with the spirit of the new music:

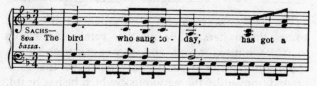

SACHS— The bird who sang to-day, has got a
8va bassa.

throat that right — ly wax - es Masters may feel dis-

may, but well con - tent with him Hans Sachs is!

A prominent part is played in the ensuing scene by the tender Eva motive :

EVA.

Walther's entrance brings back the Knight theme, and others which have been heard before. The music of the summer night, heard when the watchman is approaching, is very beautiful, and its return at the close of the act, punctuated by phrases of Beckmesser's serenade, is still more lovely. A fine contrast is that between Sachs's uproarious song, which is thoroughly good in the old style, and that of Beckmesser, which is bad. The development of the turmoil in the street is worked out with immense contrapuntal skill, and we hear in the midst of it a new theme, that of the Beating, made skilfully out of the fourths used in the lute accompaniment to the Marker's serenade :

THE BEATING.

The gradual building up of the turmoil at the end of the act, when the excited people pour into the streets and the general fighting begins, is wonderfully worked out in the score, in which the Beating motive plays a prominent and humorously expressive part. In the midst of the rumpus, the horn of the returning watchman is heard, its discord making a fine musical effect. After the crowd has dispersed and the watchman has repeated his droning formula, the music of the summer night, as I have already mentioned, steals back in an ethereal whisper, and the act comes to a close with one of those beautiful points of repose which Wagner knew so well how to make after a movement of extreme agitation.

The third act is preceded by an introduction of wonderful beauty and expressiveness. With the chorale of the last scene, the shoemaker song sung by Sachs in the second act, and the "Wahn" motive, the composer paints for us the very soul of the poet-cobbler. The "Wahn" motive is that on which is founded the great monologue of this act, beginning with the words "Wahn, Wahn, überall Wahn"—"Madness, madness, everywhere madness."

"WAHN, WAHN."

The whole scene between Sachs and Walther is surcharged with melody of the most luscious kind, and we hear the beginning of Walther's mastersong, the song which finally wins for him the prize:

THE MASTERSONG

The music accompanying the entrance of the sore and limping Beckmesser is filled with exquisite humour, and perhaps in it all there is nothing more subtle than the use of the "Wahn" motive when the Marker, after his agitated rush about the room, sits on the bench and vainly strives to think of a new song.

The music of the scene following Eva's entrance is built on familiar motives, whose significance here is easily traced, and the quintette, as will be noted at the first hearing, is made from the prize song. The recitation of Sachs preceding the quintette is one of the most beautiful passages in the opera, but it is uncessary to think of it as built of motives. The last scene opens with much freely composed music, the entrance of the guilds and the dance. With the advent of the masters we return to the dignified music associated with them. The rest of the scene is simple. The people sing the beautiful chorale, "Wach' auf," Beckmesser makes his foolish attempt to sing Walther's words to the tune of his own serenade, and then Walther sings the song as it ought to be sung, slightly altering the "Abgesang" in his fresh inspiration.

The principal characteristic of the music of "Die Meistersinger" is its lyric quality. There are no tragic passions to be depicted, no evil thoughts to be expressed. Beckmesser alone has malice, and that is of a petty, foolish sort, best treated, as it is in this exquisite work, with ridicule. The other personages are all lovable; the motives all kindly. The underlying elements which are in contest, the opposing principles, whose workings make the ethical basis of the drama, are artistic, the old against the new, the formal against the free. The expression of each must of necessity be lyric, the one in well-regulated rhythms, the other in rushing bursts of apparently spontaneous melody. But the total result is one great spring ode, throbbing with the very heart-beats of young poesy and song, and sure at all times and in all places to capivate those who have ears to hear and souls to understand.

DER RING DES NIBELUNGEN

A Stage Festival Play

for

Three Days and One Preliminary Evening.

First performed in its entirety at Bayreuth, August, 1876; Munich, 1878; Vienna, Leipsic, 1879; Hamburg, 1880; Berlin, 1881; London, Königsberg, Hanover, Danzig, Breslau, Bremen, Barmen, 1882; New York, Metropolitan Opera House, March 4, 5, 8 and 11, 1889.

DAS RHEINGOLD

Prologue to "Der Ring des Nibelungen."

First performed at the Royal Court Theatre, Munich,
September 22, 1869.

Original Cast.

Wotan	Kindermann.
Donner	Heinrich.
Froh	Nachbaur.
Loge	Vogl.
Alberich	Fischer.
Mime	Schlosser.
Fasolt	Polzer.
Fafner	Bausewein.
Fricka	Fräulein Stehle.
Freia	Fräulein Müller.
Erda	Fräulein Seehofer.
Woglinde	
Wellgunde	Frau Vogel.
Flosshilde	Fräulein Ritter.

This performance was against the wish of Wagner.
The first authorised performance was that at the
Festspielhaus, Bayreuth, August 13, 1876, when the
cast was as follows:

Wotan	Franz Betz.
Donner	Eugen Gura.
Froh	Georg Unger.

Loge . . . . . . Heinrich Vogel.
Alberich . . . . . . Carl Hill.
Mime . . . . . . Carl Schlosser.
Fasolt . . . . . . Albert Eilers.
Fafner . . . . Franz von Reichenberg.
Fricka . . . . . Friedericke Grün.
Freia . . . . . Marie Haupt.
Erda . . . . . . Luise Jäide.
Woglinde . . . . Lilli Lehmann.
Wellgunde . . . . Marie Lehmann.
Flosshilde . . . . Marie Lammert.

Weimar, Vienna, Leipsic, Hamburg, Brunswick, 1878; Mannheim, Cologne, 1879; Frankfort, London, 1882.

First performed in America at the Metropolitan Opera House, New York, Jan. 4, 1889.

Cast.

Wotan . . . . . . Emil Fischer.
Donner . . . . . Alois Grienauer.
Froh . . . . . Albert Mittelhauser.
Loge . . . . . Max Alvary.
Alberich . . . . . Joseph Beck.
Mime . . . . Wilhelm Sedlmayer.
Fasolt . . . . Ludwig Mödlinger.
Fafner . . . . . Eugen Weiss.
Fricka . . . . Fanny Moran-Olden.
Freia . . . . Katti Bettaque.
Erda . . . . . Hedwig Reil.
Woglinde . . . Sophie Traubmann.
Wellgunde . . . Felice Koschoska.
Flosshilde . . . . Hedwig Reil.
Conductor, Anton Seidl.

DIE WALKÜRE

Music Drama in Three Acts.

First evening of the trilogy, "Der Ring des Nibelungen."

First performed at the Royal Court Theatre in Munich, contrary to the author's wish, on Aug. 26, 1870.

Original Cast.

Siegmund	Vogl.
Hunding	Bausewein.
Wotan	Kindermann.
Sieglinde	Frau Vogl.
Brünnhilde	Fräulein Stehle.
Fricka	Fräulein Kaufmann.

First authorised performance in the Festspielhaus at
Bayreuth, Aug. 14, 1876.

Original Bayreuth Cast.

Siegmund	Albert Niemann.
Hunding	Joseph Niering.
Wotan	Franz Betz.
Sieglinde	Josephine Scheffsky.
Fricka	Friedericke Grün.
Brünnhilde . . .	Amalia Friedrich-Materna.
Gerhilde	Marie Haupt.

Ortlinde	Marie Lehmann.
Waltraute	Luise Jäide.
Schwertleite . .	Johanna Jachmann-Wagner.
Helmwige	Lilli Lehmann.
Siegrune	Antoinie Amann.
Grimgerde . . .	Hedwig Reicher-Kindermann.
Rossweisse	Minna Lammert.

Vienna, New York, 1877 ; Rotterdam, Leipsic, Hamburg, Schwerin, 1878 ; Weimar, Mannheim, Cologne, Brunswick, 1879 ; Königsberg, Frankfort, 1882.

First performed in America at the Academy of Music, New York, April 2, 1877.

Cast.

Siegmund	Mr. Bischoff.
Hunding	Mr. Blum.
Wotan	Mr. Preusser.
Sieglinde	Mlle. Canissa.
Fricka	Mme. Listner.
Brünnhilde	Mme. Pappenheim.

Conductor, Adolf Neuendorff.

SIEGFRIED

Music Drama in Three Acts.

Second evening of the trilogy, "Der Ring des Nibelungen.

First performed at the Festspielhaus, Bayreuth,
August 16, 1876.

Original Cast.

The Wanderer	Franz Betz.
Siegfried	George Unger.
Alberich	Carl Hill.
Mime	Carl Schlosser.
Fafner	Franz von Reichenberg.
Brünnhilde . . .	Amalia Friedrich-Materna.
Erda	Luise Jäide.
Forest Bird	Lilli Lehmann.

Hamburg, Vienna, Munich, Leipsic, 1878; Schwerin,
Brunswick, 1879; Cologne, 1880.

First performed in America at the Metropolitan Opera
House, New York, Nov. 9, 1887.

Cast.

Wanderer	Emil Fischer.
Siegfried	Max Alvary.
Alberich	Rudolph von Milde.

Mime	.	.	.	.	.	Herr Ferency.
Fafner	.	.	.	.	.	Johannes Elmblad.
Brünnhilde	.	.	.	.	.	Lilli Lehmann.
Erda	.	.	.	.	.	Marianne Brandt.
Forest Bird	.	.	.		Auguste Seidl-Kraus.

Conductor, Anton Seidl.

GÖTTERDÄMMERUNG

Music Drama in Three Acts.

Third evening of the trilogy, "Der Ring des Nibelungen."

First performed at the Festspielhaus in Bayreuth, August 17, 1876.

Original Cast.

Siegfried	George Unger.
Gunther	Eugen Gura.
Hagen	Gustav Siehr.
Alberich	Carl Hill.
Brünnhilde . . .	Amalia Friedrich-Materna.
Gutrune	Mathilde Weckerlin.
Waltraute	Luise Jäide.
The Three Norns . {	Johanna Jachmann-Wagner. Josephine Scheffsky. Friedericke Grün.
The Rheindaughters . . . {	Lilli Lehmann. Marie Lehmann. Minna Lammert.

Munich, Leipsic, 1878 ; Vienna, Hamburg, Brunswick, 1879; Cologne, 1882.

First performed in America at the Metropolitan Opera House, New York, Jan. 25, 1888.

Cast.

Siegfried	Albert Niemann.
Gunther	Adolf Robinson.
Hagen	Emil Fischer.
Alberich	Rudolph von Milde.
Brünnhilde	Lilli Lehmann.
Gutrune	Auguste Seidl-Kraus.
Woglinde	Sophie Traubmann.
Wellgunde	Marianne Brandt.
Flosshilde	Louise Meisslinger.

Conductor, Anton Seidl.

(The Waltraute and Norn scenes were omitted. They were first given at the Metropolitan on January 24, 1899, when Mme. Schumann-Heink was the Waltraute, and also one of the Norns. The others were Olga Pevny and Louise Meisslinger. "Der Ring des Nibelungen" was first performed without cuts at the Metropolitan on January 12, 17, 19, and 24, 1899.)

DER RING DES NIBELUNGEN

I.—The Sources of the Poems

THE gigantic tetralogy of Wagner must be studied as a single opus, for such indeed it is. A poem in four cantos, a dramatic sequence after the manner of the Greeks, it is the story of a single action, a single crime and its tragic atonement. What that story is we shall presently see. How Wagner conceived and created his new and wonderful version of the Norse mythology, the Volsunga Saga, and the "Niebelungen Lied," is what must first occupy our attention. Wagner's first mention of this work is found in a letter to Liszt, written in June, 1849, when he announces his intention of setting to music his "latest German drama, the 'Death of Siegfried.'" This drama embodied that part of the story now told in "Götterdämmerung," and in the composition of it Wagner found that the necessary explanations of the incidents leading up to the story quickly became too long and complex. He decided that he must write a prefatory drama on the story of the young Siegfried, and in doing this he found himself involved again in explanatory difficulties. Thus he finally decided to make a trilogy with a prologue. In a long letter of Nov. 20, 1851, to Liszt he explains how the completed form of "Der Ring" came into existence.

The books of "Das Rheingold" and "Die Walküre" were finished in the first week of November, 1852. He then set about reconstructing the other two, already written, but now in need of extensive alterations. The story of the completion of the poem in its new form and the beginning of the music has already been told in the biographical part of this work. It is necessary only to recapitulate here that the text was finished in 1853. The music of "Rheingold" was begun in the autumn of 1853 at Spezzia, and finished in January, 1854. He wrote to Liszt on Jan. 14: "I went to this music with so much faith, so much joy; and with a true fury of despair I continued, and have at last finished it." The music of "Die Walküre" was begun in June, 1854, and finished late in the same year. The instrumentation was commenced with the opening of the following year. Then came the visit to London, where the score of the first act was completed in April. The score of the first two acts was sent to Liszt on Oct. 3. Wagner having been delayed in the work by many distractions and by mental depression, it was not till the ensuing year that the score was wholly written.

The music of "Siegfried" was begun in 1857, and the first act was finished in April of that year. The second act was begun, and then came the interruption caused by Wagner's eagerness to return to active touch with the stage, his pressing need of money, and his fear that he would not live to complete his gigantic undertaking. This second act, therefore, was not completed till June 21, 1865, at Munich, "Tristan und Isolde" having been written in the meantime. The third act was finished early in 1869. The music of "Götterdämmerung" was begun at Lucerne in 1870, and completed at Bayreuth in November, 1874. The point at which the work on this tetralogy was suspended for that on "Tristan und Isolde" is designated in a letter to Liszt, dated May 8, 1857. Wagner says: "I have led my young Siegfried to a beautiful forest solitude, and there have left him under a linden tree, and taken leave of him with heartfelt tears. He will be better off there than elsewhere."

Just how Wagner came to take up the subject of Siegfried's death is not known. A recent German writer in one of the Munich newspapers has asserted that the suggestion came from Minna, his first wife. This assertion is in line with the belief of many that Minna was more sinned against than sinning, and that Wagner's complaints of her inability to understand him were intended to divert suspicion from the real causes of the troubles between them. It seems hardly likely, however, that a woman of Minna's simple character would have conceived the availability of the Siegfried legend for Wagner's ideal music drama. The fact that Siegfried had for centuries been the popular mythical hero of the German people and that his deeds and personality had constituted most of the materials of one of the great mediæval German epics, the "Nibelungen Ljed," seems sufficient to have attracted the attention of the master to the subject. He himself says in his "Communication" that even while he was at work on "Lohengrin" he was debating which of two subjects, "Friedrich Barbarossa" or "Siegfried," he should take up next. He adds:

"Once again and for the last time did myth and history stand before me with opposing claims; this while as good as forcing me to decide whether it was a musical drama or a spoken play that I had to write."

It was with the decision to utilise only mythical subjects for his serious dramas that he concluded to lay aside "Barbarossa" and work upon "The Death of Siegfried." This poem in its original form is included in the collected writings of Wagner, and is interesting as being the first attempt of Wagner to embody the legendary tragedy in a drama. A reading of it will show clearly why he was obliged to write three other dramas to lead up to this one and make its meaning comprehensible. In working out the plan as a whole he selected and utilised with his customary skill the salient points of the Norse and German forms of the story, and he found more suitable material in the sagas than in the German epic. And out of the Northern mythology, so beautifully stored in the sagas, he evolved those ethical features which raise "Der Ring des Nibelungen" to a position beside the great Greek tragedies of antiquity.

We must study these dramas chiefly by tracing their sources and showing how Wagner utilised his materials. He himself wrote an article entitled "The Nibelungen Myth as Material for a Drama," and in it may be found the germinal form of the entire story as it first took cognisable existence in his mind. In its completed shape, however, it differs from this embryonic outline in many particulars.

First, then, the age of the legends upon which these dramas are founded is not so great as might appear from their mythological nature, and that will explain some of their curiosities. We are prone, when

watching the actions of Wagner's gods, to think that
these stories date from the antique age of fable, but
the truth is that they came into existence in the modern age of fable, the early centuries of the Christian
era.   Furthermore, although Wagner has used chiefly
the Norse forms of the materials, the great Siegfried
legend was originally the production of the German
people.   The Scandinavian bards obtained some of
their ideas from Germany, and thus came about the
strange mingling of Norse mythology and Teutonic
fable.

When the dominion of Rome in the west of
Europe was overthrown in 476 A.D., the Teutonic
race occupied the country from the banks of the
Rhine and the Danube to the coasts of Norway.   The
invaders who settled in the southern provinces of
Europe soon lost their distinctive speech.   But in
Germany and Scandinavia the old tongues remained,
and consequently poetic recitation, the custom of long
centuries, continued.   Tacitus tells us that the people
of these northern lands were accustomed to store
their history in rhyming chronicles repeated by the
bards.   It was not till the reign of the wise and
heroic Charlemagne (742–814) that these chronicles
were collected.   Nothing remains of the collection
which he made, but it can hardly be doubted that
some of the materials found in the Siegfried legend
formed part of the old stories of the bards, for it has
been traced back as far as the sixth century, when its
germs were recognisable.   In the first preserved form
of the story of this hero's exploits we find recorded
the fabulous history of times not widely separated
from those of the conquest of Rome's western em-

pire, for in the sixth century appeared in tradition the names not only of Siegfried and Dietrich von Bern, but Theodoric the Great and Attila.

This first preserved form of the legend is called the "Heldenbuch" ("Book of Heroes"). In its present shape it dates from the latter part of the twelfth century, but there is evidence that it was in existence long before that period. It is a collection of poems dealing with the events of the time of Attila and the incursions of the German nations into Rome. The principal personages who appear in this book are : Etzel, or Attila ; Dietrich, or Theodoric the Great ; Siegfried, Gudrune, Hagan, and others who reappear in the "Nibelungen Lied." The period of the events which occur in the Wagnerian dramas may be estimated by the formation of a succession of incidents leading back to Attila, an historical personage with an established date. In "The Horny Siegfried," one of the poems of the "Heldenbuch," we find matter which serves as a prelude to the "Nibelungen Lied." In this poem Siegfried appears as the embodiment of manly heroism, beauty, and virtue, as he was known to Teutonic song and story for centuries. From having bathed in the blood of dragons he was invulnerable except in one spot, between the shoulders, on which a leaf had happened to fall. Having rescued the beautiful Chriemhild from dragons (or a giant) and obtained possession of the treasures of the dwarfs, he returns her to her father, King of Wurms, and then marries her.

The "Nibelungen Lied" identifies Chriemhild as the sister of Gunther, the Gutrune of Wagner's version. Chriemhild, in order to obtain revenge for the treachery

24

of Siegfried and Brünnhilde, which I shall recount in the outline of the "Nibelungen Lied," after the death of the former marries Attila. It was twenty-six years after the death of Siegfried when she carried out her plan of revenge. How long this was before the death of Attila is not related, but we know that he died in 453 A.D. He is supposed to have been born about 406, which would have made him forty-seven years old at the time of his death. It was thirteen years after her marriage to Attila when Chriemhild accomplished her revenge. Supposing that Attila's death took place not less than a year later, that would fix the date of the marriage at 439, or when this busy warrior was thirty-three and perhaps ready to rest, and that of the revenge at 452. Therefore, as the "Nibelungen Lied" tells us that the death of Siegfried took place twenty-six years before the accomplishment of the revenge, we may suppose that the hero expired in 426. At any rate, the date of his death must have been in the early part of the fifth century. And equally, therefore, much of the supernatural paraphernalia of "Götterdämmerung" belongs to the store of fable which has come down from that period. If one is curious to establish dates for the earlier dramas he must first discover how long Siegfried and Brünnhilde remained together on the Valkyrs' Hill after the sleeping beauty was awakened by the young hero. The date of "Die Walküre" would be some twenty or twenty-two years earlier, for in the last scene of that work we learn that Sieglinde is to become his mother. As for "Das Rheingold," that must be left to conjecture entirely.

From the *Heldenbuch* the next step in the

German versions of the legend carries us to the "Nibelungen Lied." Here, as I have noted, we find Chriemhild as the sister of Gunther. Siegfried has heard of her beauty and determines to win her as his bride. But all his efforts are in vain. Meanwhile, to the Court news comes of the beautiful Brunhild, Queen of Isenland, a woman of matchless courage and strength. Every suitor for her hand must abide three combats with her, and if vanquished is put to death. Gunther decides to try to win her, and Siegfried accompanies him on his expedition, with the understanding that if they succeed he is to have Chriemhild to wife. Arriving at the Court of Brunhild, Siegfried, in order to increase respect for the standing of Gunther, poses as his friend's vassal. The combats take place, and Siegfried, making himself invisible by the aid of the magic cap which he obtained from the dwarfs, assists Gunther to conquer the Queen.

Gunther weds Brunhild and Siegfried marries Gutrune, but the proud Queen of Isenland does not relish the idea of having for a sister-in-law the wife of a vassal. Gunther tells her that Siegfried is a Prince in his own country, but she disbelieves her spouse, and to punish him for his falsehood denies him her embraces, binds him with her magic girdle, and hangs him on a nail. Siegfried, having pity on Gunther, promises to deprive Brunhild of the girdle and make her a wife in fact as well as in name. So on the following night, disguised by the Tarnkappe, he takes Gunther's place, embraces the unwilling Brunhild, and carries off her magic girdle and her ring. Gutrune misses Siegfried from the chamber, and in the end he is compelled to explain to her. He foolishly gives her the girdle and the ring. The two women subsequently come to hot words on a question of precedence in entering a church (like Elsa and Ortrud), and Chriemhild in her anger charges Brunhild with her relations with Siegfried, producing the ring as evidence. Then Brunhild, discovering the deception of the Tarnkappe, vows vengeance, in the attainment of which Hagen aids her. Having induced Chriemhild to disclose to him the mortal spot on Siegfried's body, he drives a spear into it and slays him. It is to secure revenge for this murder that Chriemhild marries Attila.

This is a very brief and imperfect outline of the mighty epic of mediæval Germany. It breathes the spirit of mediævalism, and it contains few of the mythological features which appear in the beautiful Scandinavian version of the story of Siegfried. Yet it has certain incidents employed by Wagner in the dramas, especially in "Götterdämmerung." The use of the Tarnhelm, the substitution of Siegfried for Gunther in the wedding chamber, the discovery of the deception through the recognition of the ring by Brünnhilde, and the slaying of Siegfried by Hagen's spear-thrust in the back—all appear in the drama in most significant forms.

It is to the Norse forms of the legend, however, that we must turn for the earlier parts of Wagner's story and for the most significant features of the undercurrent of ethical thought. This version in its oldest form is found in the Eddas, some of which are undoubtedly of great antiquity. Yet in these poems we meet with the historic name of Attila. No doubt many deeds performed by earlier and forgotten heroes were attributed to this wonder-worker of the early Middle Ages, and in this way he became a sort of composite figure, and thus was thrust into the later versions of the Eddaic tales. All the other personages in the story are mythical. As Mr. Sparling notes in his introduction to the translation of the Volsunga Saga made by William Morris and Eirikr Magnusson,* only fragments of the Eddaic poems still exist, but "ere they perished there arose from them a saga," that of the race of Volsungs.

How old the original Eddaic stories are can only be conjectured. When the Scando-Gothic races overran Europe they carried at least the germs of these stories with them, but no man knows where they got them. But it is certain that the northern versions of the Nibelung tales, as known to us now, must have originated in the same legends as the "Nibelungen Lied." It was not until the middle of the seventeenth century that the collection of the rhymed Eddas credited to Saemund the Wise was discovered, and the prose Eddas of Snorre Sturleson (born 1178, died 1224) were written a century later than these. For Saemund the Wise was born in 1056 and died in 1131. If he collected the Eddas, it was about 1100. Both the Eddas and the Lied were widely diverging branches of an old trunk, and that accounts in a measure for both their resemblances and their differences. The southern version is more adulterated with inexact history, while the northern embodies more of the fundamental religious mythology of the people.

Far away in the snowy fastnesses of Iceland were

* London, Walter Scott, 1888.

preserved the ancient stories of the hero Sigurd and the heroine Brünnhilde. Even to this day these stories are sung or told by the secluded people of the Faroe Islands. Whence did they procure them? From the scattering of races, which, begun according to religious history at the end of the flood, continued through the Dark Ages. So impressed upon the imaginations of the wanderers were these old tales that they connected historical personages with the actors in them, not only, as we have seen, by attributing fabulous deeds to real beings, but by tracing the descent of actual persons from those of mythical nature. For example, the first King of Dublin was Olaf the White, and, according to tradition, he was the son of Ingiald, son of Thora, daughter of "Sigurd Snake-in-the-Eye" son of Ragnar Lodbrok by Aslaug, daughter of Sigurd by Brünnhilde. And the widow of Olaf was one of the settlers of Iceland. It was in the ninth century that Harold Fairhair determined to conquer all Norway. He fought also in the British Isles, and after a long and bloody struggle made himself master of Ireland as well as of the northern coasts. Many of the vanquished, including Olaf's widow, took refuge in the western islands, and with them went the legends, which had come up from the Rhine valley, and which, safely buried in the fastnesses of Iceland and the Faroes, grew into the sagas known to us as the Elder Eddas. "There also shall we escape the troubling of kings and scoundrels," says the Vatsdoelsaga. In their security they made their wondrous songs.

It was in 1643 that Brynjolf Sveinsson, Bishop of Skalholt, discovered the works attributed to Saemund, and he christened them the "Edda Saemundar hinns froda," or "Edda of Saemund the Wise." The term "Edda," which is Icelandic for "grandmother," had been applied already to the prose tales of Sturleson, though the latter are of later origin than the former. The two works are frequently distinguished as the Elder and the Younger Edda. The Elder is often called the Poetic Edda, because it consists chiefly of songs, while the Younger is often named the Prose Edda. The first part of the Elder Edda gives the mythology of the North, while the lays of the heroes are found in its second part. One of the translators of the Prose Edda has described it as a sort of commentary on the Poetic Edda.*

The poems which contain the story of Sigurd and Brünnhilde are a portion of the second part of the Elder Edda. An important part, recounting the story of Sigurd's life from his meeting with Brünnhilde to his death, has been lost, and for that part of the tale we are compelled to go to the Prose Edda and the Volsunga Saga. In the second part of his Younger Edda, Snorre Sturleson rehearsed briefly in simple prose the story of Sigurd the Volsung, which in the Elder Edda ran through several poems, forming in their natural connection an epic of great power. As one of the historians of Norse literature says:

"The sad and absorbing story here narrated was wonderfully popular throughout the ancient Scandinavian and Teutonic world, and it is impossible to

---

* For the substance of the Elder Edda consult "Asgard and the Gods," by Wägner & McDowall; London, Swan, Sonnenschein, Le Bas & Lowrey, 1886. For the Prose Edda, see "The Younger Edda," translated by R. B. Anderson, Chicago; Scott, Foresman & Co., 1897.

say for how many centuries these great tragic ballads had agitated the hearts of the warlike races of the North. It is clear that Sigurd and Brynhilda, with all their beauty, noble endowment, and sorrowful history, were real personages, who had taken powerful hold on the popular affections in the most ancient times, and had come down from age to age, receiving fresh incarnations and embellishments from the popular Scalds."

It is possible that this is true, but the original history of the personages is quite lost. The story told in the "Skaldskaparmal," the second part of the Younger Edda, is a rehearsal of the contents of the "Short Lay of Sigurd," "The Lay of Fafner," and one or two others in the Elder Edda bearing on the Volsung tale. Wagner has utilised certain portions of these original lays, especially that of Fafner. The words of the Forest Bird to Siegfried come very close to those of the Eagles, who sang to Sigurd in "The Lay of Fafner":

> " There lies Regin,*
> Contemplating
> How to deceive the man
> Who trusts him:
> Thinks in his wrath
> Of false accusations.
> The evil smith plots
> Revenge 'gainst the brother."

Compare this passage with the words of the Forest Bird in Act II. of "Siegfried":

> " O trust not in Mime,
>   The treacherous elf!

> * Mime.

> Heareth Siegfried but sharply
> The shifty hypocrite's words,
> What at heart he means
> Shall by Mime be shown."

But it was in the Volsunga Saga that Wagner found his material in its fullest and most available form. None of the editors of the remnants of Icelandic literature makes it clear whether the Volsunga Saga is older than Snorre's Edda or not, though the former seems to belong to the 13th century. The facts seem to be that most of the sagas, including this one, had come into settled form about 900 A.D., and were written down between 1140 and 1220, or during the lifetime of Snorre. It is probable, therefore, that Snorre's recapitulation of the Volsung story was founded as much upon the Volsunga Saga as upon the poems of the Elder Edda. In all likelihood he knew both, and accepted the definite outline of the saga as a shape into which to put his recital of the contents of the lays.

The value of the Volsunga Saga in relation to the Nibelung tale lies in the fact that its compiler was acquainted with some of the lays of the Elder Edda, now lost, and that he recounted their incidents for us, and that it supplied Wagner with the principal materials for three out of four of the "Ring" dramas. The origin of this saga is not known, but may easily be surmised. The Norse sagaman was a luxury of every Court, as were the Norman minstrel and the Saxon gleeman, and it was frequently his office to glorify his sovereign in song by connecting him with the marvellous heroes of ancient fable. Students of mediæval epics know that it was common for their makers to seek thus to laud their patrons. An

interesting instance of this is the original French story
of the Holy Grail, in which an attempt is made by Kiot
of Provence to show that the sacred vessel was first
consigned to the care of Titural, a mythical Prince of
the Anjou Dynasty. The Volsunga Saga appears to
have been arranged largely for the purpose of glorify-
ing the children of Olaf.

As a corollary to the chief saga there may be mentioned the Thidrek (Dietrich) Saga, which includes
the Niflunga Saga, and was, as its writer states, made
from the German stories. This saga agrees in some
parts with the poems of Eddaic origin, and in others
with the "Nibelungen Lied." There is also the Nornagest Saga, in which Nornagest (the Guest of the
Norns) tells how he witnessed some of Sigurd's deeds
and his death. But the fundamental saga is that
which tells the story of the Volsung race.

The story of the Volsunga Saga is too long to be repeated in full in this volume, but an outline of its
principal incidents must be given. The genealogy of
the Volsung race begins with Odin, whose son was
Sigi, who begat Rerir, the father of Volsung, a mighty
king. In the midst of Volsung's palace, with its
branches piercing the roof, stood the great tree called
the Branstock. Volsung had ten sons and a daughter,
the latter born a twin with the eldest son. Their
names were Sigmund and Signy. King Siggeir of
Gothland wedded Signy, and at the feast there came
into the hall an old, one-eyed man, wrapped in a
robe, and he struck a sword into the Branstock so
that no man save Sigmund could draw it forth. Siggeir was jealous and when he had returned to his own
land with his bride he invited Volsung and his sons

on a visit. When they had come, he fell upon them and slew Volsung and set his sons in a wood to be devoured by wolves. Sigmund escaped and dwelt in the wood. Signy, desiring to avenge the slaughter of her kin, sent her sons to Sigmund to be tested as to their fitness for the task. But he, finding them unfit, slew them. Then Signy put a witch to sleep with her husband and in disguise went to Sigmund's house and asked for shelter. Sigmund saw she was fair and he kept her three nights. Then she went to her home. And she bore another son, whom she called Sinfjotli. And when he was grown she sent him to his father, Sigmund.

In time, Sigmund and Sinfjotli slew Siggeir, and Signy, having revealed the fact that Sinfjotli was a full-blooded Volsung, died with her husband. Sigmund now married Borghild, who hated Sinfjotli and poisoned him. Sigmund divorced her and married again, his second wife being Hjordis, who had rejected Hunding, the son of Lygni. Hunding came with his followers and fought Sigmund, whose sword was broken in the battle by the spear of an old, one-eyed man, wrapped in a mantle. Dying, Sigmund gave the pieces of the broken sword to Hjordis to keep for her son, who was to be the greatest of the Volsungs. Hjordis went to the Court of the King of Denmark and bore the son, who was called Sigurd. Alf, the son of the Danish King, wedded Hjordis, and Sigurd grew up at the Court. His foster-father and instructor was Regin, a famous smith, a man of wisdom. Regin saw that Sigurd would be a hero, and hoped to make use of him. Sigurd was sent to the woods to choose himself a horse, and on the way

he met an old man with one eye, who bade him drive
the horses into the water.   One swam across the river
and that one the old man told Sigurd to choose.   This
horse's name was Grani, and it was of the strain of
Odin's stable.   Now Regin told Sigurd of a dragon,
Fafnir, which lay guarding a mighty store of gold,
and he urged Sigurd to slay this dragon and get the
hoard.   And Regin told Sigurd the story of the gold.

One Hreidmar had three sons—Fafnir, Otter, and
Regin.   Otter was so called because he was wont
to take the form of an otter and go into the lake
called Andvari's Lake to catch fish.   One day Odin,
Hönir, and Loki, three of the gods, came to the lake,
and Loki threw a stone at the otter and slew it.
They took off the skin and went to the house of
Hreidmar, who recognised the skin and bade them
pay him a ransom of so much gold as should cover
the skin as it stood upright.   Now Loki knew that
Andvari had a great store of gold, and, going back
to the lake, he caught Andvari, who was swimming
in the guise of a pike, and refused to release him
unless he gave up all his gold and also the ring by
whose magic power the gold was obtained.   And
in his wrath Andvari cursed the gold and the ring
and declared that they should be the bane of every
man who should thereafter own them.   Loki and
the gods strove to cover the otter skin with the gold,
but Hreidmar still saw one muzzle-hair of the otter,
and they were obliged to add also the ring to hide
this.   Then Loki said to Hreidmar :

> " Thou and thy son
> Are naught fated to thrive,
> The bane it shall be of you both."

"Thereafter," continued Regin, "Fafnir slew his father and murdered him, nor got I aught of the treasure, and so evil he grew that he fell to lying abroad and begrudged any share in the wealth to any man, and so became the worst of all worms, and ever now lies brooding upon that treasure." Sigurd bade Regin make him a sword with which to slay the dragon, but every one which the smith made the youth broke across the anvil. Then Sigurd bade him weld the shards of the sword Gram, which had belonged to Sigmund. And when these were welded Sigurd smote the anvil with the new blade and clove it in twain.

Then Sigurd went to fight the sons of Hunding and slew them to avenge his father's death. Next he went in accordance with his promise to Regin and slew Fafnir, the dragon. And Fafnir told him that the treasure which he would gain would be his bane. At the desire of Regin he roasted the dragon's heart, and in preparing it he wet his finger with the blood and cleansed it with his tongue. Immediately he understood the language of the birds and heard the woodpeckers chattering to the effect that he should slay the treacherous Regin, who desired his death, should secure the gold for himself and ride to Hind-fell, where slept Brynhild, for there he would get great wisdom. Sigurd slew Regin and rode off in search of Brynhild, who lay in a castle on a mountain surrounded by fire. Sigurd rode to her through the fire. He took off her helm and cut the byrny (breast-plate) from her with his sword. And she awoke and asked the name of her awakener. And when she had learned it she sang :

" Long have I slept
And slumbered long,
Many and long are the woes of mankind.
By the might of Odin
Must I abide helpless
To shake from off me the spells of slumber.

" Hail to the day come back !
Hail, sons of the daylight !
Hail to thee, night, and thy daughter !
Look with kind eyes adown
On us sitting here lonely
And give unto us the gain that we long for."

She told Sigurd how she had struck down in battle Helm Gunnar, whom Odin had selected to be victorious. "And Odin, in vengeance for that deed, stuck the sleep-thorn into me and said I should never again have the victory, but should be given away in marriage ; but thereagainst I vowed a vow that never would I wed one who knew the name of fear." Then she taught him all her runes, and they two plighted their troth. He went his way, but they met again and renewed their vows and he gave her a ring, the ring of Andvari. Before he departed again she prophesied that he would wed Gudrun, the daughter of King Giuki.

Giuki ruled south of the Rhine. He had three sons, Gunnar (Gunther), Högni (Hagen) and Guttorm, and one daughter, Gudrun. His wife was Grimhild, skilled in magic arts. Sigurd went to their court and stayed five seasons, and Grimhild perceived how dearly Sigurd loved Brynhild, for he spoke much of her, and she also saw that he was a goodly man and she wished to have him wed Gudrun. So she mixed him a drink which caused him to forget Brynhild and he began to love Gudrun. He married her and swore the oath of brotherhood with Gunnar and Högni. Brynhild was well known to all these persons, and one day Grimhild, seeing that Gunnar was still unwed, urged him to go to court Brynhild, and take Sigurd with him. Gunnar's horse, however, would not go through the fire. Then he mounted Grani, but he would not stir. So he and Sigurd changed shapes after a manner taught them by Grimhild, and Sigurd in the guise of Gunnar rode through the flames and, reminding Brynhild that she had sworn to wed no one except him who pierced the fire, claimed her as his bride, and she, being bound by the oath, yielded. He took the ring of Andvari and her girdle from her, and rode away. And she went to Gunnar's home and was married to him. Sigurd gave the ring and the girdle to his wife Gudrun, and when, some time afterward, the two women fell into a dispute as to which one's husband was the greater, Gudrun declared that it was her own husband, Sigurd, who had overcome Brynhild on the mountain and made her wed Gunnar. And in proof of her words she showed the ring which Sigurd had taken from Brynhild's finger and given to her. Brynhild was now eager for revenge, and conspired with Gunnar and Högni to put Sigurd to death. But they had sworn brotherhood, and so Guttorm, the youngest brother, who had not sworn, was chosen ; and he slew Sigurd as he lay asleep in his bed. And Brynhild, aweary of life and the deceits of it, loving no man but Sigurd, drove a sword into her bosom, and, dying, asked Gunnar to burn her body with Sigurd's. And it was so done.

Such is the story of the Volsunga Saga as far as it

concerns the incidents of "Der Ring des Nibelungen." In the remaining part of it is told how Gudrun became the wife of Atli (Attila) and how he schemed to get possession of the treasure which Sigurd had taken from Fafnir. But Gunnar and Högni sank the gold in the Rhine, and thus it disappeared. Atli slew them, but they had not revealed its hiding-place. I have rehearsed the tale of the Volsungs at more length than that of the "Nibelungen Lied" because from it Wagner obtained much more of his material. It now becomes necessary to review the mythological elements of the dramas taken from the Eddas and connected by Wagner with this story from mere hints in the original. When that is done, we shall be ready to survey the dramas in their entirety and see what use Wagner made of his materials.

The injection into the northern legends of the gods and goddesses of Scandinavian mythology and of the stories of the sins of Wotan and the certainty of future destruction of the gods furnished Wagner with the material for all the early portion of his mighty drama. It provided him with the ethical basis which makes Wotan the real hero of a tragedy, to end in the extinction not only of himself and his associate gods, but of the entire old order of the world, and the establishment of a new one. This last idea is found in the songs of the Elder Edda, "Odin's Raven Song," and "Song of the Way Tamer." These relate to the death of Baldur, the favourite son of Odin, and are dark with the mystery of an unknown terror. The gods are disturbed to the depths of their beings, and Odin mounts his steed and rides to Hell to consult the Wala (Erda) and force from her by means of runes some information as to the death of his son. Compare this incident with the first scene of the third act of "Siegfried." Read the "Havamal," the High Song of Odin, which contains also the rune song and expounds the entire scheme of Norse ethics. As one of the commentators on it has well said, "It shows a worldly wisdom, experience, and sagacity to which modern life can add nothing." The power of runes is explained in this song. It was by runes that the wicked princesses of mediæval tales cast spells over their enemies, that sickness was healed, that flying spears were checked in battle, that ships conquered the storms of Old Ocean. Yet these runes were nothing but letters of the alphabet, and their mysterious power was that of knowledge, denied to many in those dark times and seemingly magical in its use by the few.

In order that we may understand the true plot of "Der Ring des Nibelungen," we must briefly examine the mythological basis of it, as furnished by the Eddas.

According to the Eddas, then, the gods dwelt in Asgard (the place of the Ases or Aesir), in the castle named Walhalla, the abode of slain heroes. These gods were not immortal, but were extraordinary beings gifted with wonderful length of days. But they knew that at some time they must meet in final conflict their enemies, of which the chief were the giants. There was also in the far south a mysterious Surtur, with a flaming sword, and the sons of Muspel, who would join in the last great assault on the gods. Allied with these giants would be the horrible children of Loki—the Midgard Snake, which encircled the earth, and the Fenris Wolf. Loki was the spirit of evil, the god of fire, yet he was received among the gods

25

because of his wonderful cunning. The dwarfs dwelt in the subterranean places and were wondrous makers of weapons for the gods, whom, nevertheless, they hated.

The master of all the gods was Odin, or Wotan, the lord of war and the hunt. Upon the field of battle he was followed by his Valkyrs, Wish-Maidens, choosers of the slain, who consecrated the fallen heroes with kisses and carried them away to Walhalla. There they ate of the feast of the blessed and waited to aid Wotan in his final battle with the powers of evil. The mother of the gods was Fricka, the wife of Wotan, the Juno of the Norse mythology. Freya was the goddess of Love, the Venus of the assembly. Iduna, another goddess, had care of the golden apples of endless youth, which the gods ate. Thor was the wielder of the mighty hammer, made for him by the dwarfs.

The story runs thus : Fear of the giants led the gods to desire to have the mighty burg Walhalla surrounded by a strong wall. By the advice of Loki they swore a great oath to give the goddess Freya and the sun and the moon to the builder of this wall, provided that he had it finished before the coming of summer. If the work was then incomplete, the contract was void. The builder, a Frost-Giant in disguise, asked only the aid of his horse Svadilfare, and this was allowed him. The horse carried such vast stones that the work was almost done several days before the time expired. The gods held a council, ''and asked each other who could have advised to give Freya in marriage in Jothunheim (the giant's land) or to plunge the air and the heavens in darkness by taking away the sun and the moon and giving them to the giant ; and all agreed that this must have been advised by him who gives the most bad counsels,—namely, Loki, the son of Lauffey,—and they threatened him with a cruel death if he could not contrive some way of preventing the builder from fulfilling his part of the bargain." * Loki changed himself to the guise of a mare the next night, and the giant's horse ran after the mare and did no work. The giant, seeing that he was to lose his bargain, resumed his natural form, and the gods called upon Thor, who slew him with his hammer. So, as the "Wala's Prophecy" in the Elder Edda says :

> " Broken were oaths,
> And words and promises—
> All mighty speech
> That had passed between them."

Thus did sin enter among the gods, and by the breaking of the oath they burdened themselves with guilt inexpiable. Evil portents came. Iduna sank with her golden apples of eternal youth to the lower depths, and could not be recalled. Baldur, the second son of Wotan, the holy one, into whose presence no impure thing might come, had terrible dreams. Hel, the goddess of the lower world and of death, appeared to him and beckoned him to come to her.

Now the last scenes begin. Wotan rides to the realm of shades and summons the Wala, who foretells the death of Baldur. Fricka begs all things living or inanimate to swear that they will not injure

* " The Prose Edda "; Translated by R. B. Anderson.

Baldur. She overlooks the mistletoe. Loki, noting
the omission, makes a dart of this wood and gives it
to Hödur, the blind god. He in sport shoots the dart
at Baldur, who is supposed to be safe from harm, and
the bright one falls dead. The death of Baldur is the
foreshadowing of the end of the gods, and the dissolution of the universe. Sin has entered among the
gods, and they and all else must pay the penalty.
Then comes Ragnarök, the German Götterdämmerung, the twilight of the gods. The hostile forces
assemble for the last great battle. The sons of Muspel, led by Surtur with the flaming sword, gallop from
the south. The Fenris Wolf and the Midgard Snake
are loosed. Wotan leads the gods in battle. A
mighty conflict ensues, and all are slain. Surtur's
flames burn the world, and from the ashes arises a
new one, purified by fire. A youth and a maiden,
Lif and Lifthrasir, come out of the wood of Hodd-
mimir, where, in the innocence of childhood, they have
slept through all the battle, and they begin the popula-
tion of the regenerate world. And the gods themselves, purified by the fire, reappear and dwell in
eternal peace on the plain of Ida, on the site where
once stood the mighty Walhalla.

II.—The Story as Told by Wagner

WE may now briefly review the four dramas of
" Der Ring," and trace the connection of their incidents. "Das Rheingold" is the prologue of the
whole, and it is essential that we should thoroughly
understand its story, for it lays down the basis, the
motive, of the entire tragedy. We see the Rhine

maidens sporting around the Rhine gold at the bottom of the river. They are interrupted by the appearance of Alberich, the Nibelung, who comes up from the nether regions of Nibelheim, and is at once overcome with the desire to possess one of the maidens. The rising sun lights up the gold. Alberich's curiosity in regard to it brings out the story of its nature. Here enters Wagner's first original and highly poetic touch. Only one who renounces love can make the ring of gold by which power is to be obtained. That idea is not found in the old legends. Alberich, failing in his attempt to win one of the maidens, forswears love and snatches the gold from its resting-place.

One of the maidens tells us that their father had warned them of a foe to come from the bottom of the river. This parent was old Father Rhine himself. Nor is any light thrown on the origin of the gold itself. In the Volsunga Saga we find it in the water, the possession of Andvari. In the "Nibelungen Lied" Siegfried wins the gold from two brothers, Schilbung and Nibelung, who brought it forth from a cave. It had been stored there for centuries. In the Thidrek Saga Siegfried wins it from a dragon, which he kills. But none of the versions account for the origin of the gold. All agree that it finally returned to the Rhine, and that may have been the source of Wagner's idea. Nor is there any slightest foundation for the proclamation that only he who forswears love will be able to profit by the gold. Wagner has simply allowed his fancy to work with the old maxim that money is the root of all evil, and to represent the gods themselves as ignorant of the power of gold and innocent of wrong till they acquired a knowledge of this power. Wotan, in his desire to save Freia, is ready to yield to the tempter, and his temptation and fall form the subject of the second scene.

In order to get at the full meaning of these Nibelung dramas we must keep ever in mind Wagner's intent to follow in a measure the methods of the Greek dramatists. Æschylos, the greatest of the Greek tragic writers, excelled in showing the inexorable workings of Fate, which in the Greek mind corresponded to the modern conception of the inevitable punishment for sin. Wagner is purely Æschylean in his method of constructing his tragedy, and he sets forth the inflexible processes of Fate with the same high purpose. But as he addressed himself to a modern audience he offered to it that conception of Fate with which it was familiar, namely, the absolute certainty of punishment for transgression of the moral law. That he found in the old Norse legend a foundation for this idea was fortunate. It simplified his work, yet left room for him to introduce striking original matter. The rape of the gold by one who has renounced love is original with Wagner.

In the second scene of the prologue, then, we find Wotan and Fricka before the completed castle of Walhalla, which Wotan salutes in a speech of majestic dignity. Fricka at once reminds him of the price to be paid. When Freia enters, calling upon Wotan to release her from the giants, we quickly learn that it was Loge who devised the bargain and who is depended upon by Wotan to find a way out of it. The giants demand their pay. Wotan tells them they cannot have Freia. Then even the "stupid giant," as he calls himself, warns the god of the consequences of violating the faith by which he rules. Loge arrives in the height of the discussion and at once shows the evil, cunning, flickering nature of his character. The arch-enemy of the gods, trusted only by Wotan who confesses to a lack of cunning, Loge has planned a temptation to work the downfall of the Aesir. He tells the story of his wanderings. In all the earth none values aught more than the worth of woman—save one, black Alberich alone, who has forsworn love, stolen the Rhine gold and made from it a ring to give him the mastery of the world. Donner exclaims that such a ring may make Alberich master of the gods themselves, and Wotan cries that he must have the ring. But the giants have also heard, and they offer to accept the Nibelung hoard, the stolen Rhine gold, in ransom for Freia, whom they carry off till such time as Wotan is ready to pay. Here we see that Wagner has followed none of the original material exactly. In the Eddas the giant is not allowed to complete the burg, and the hoard does not enter into the matter at all. In the Volsunga Saga the gold is paid in ransom for the gods held by Hreidmar for the murder of Otter. The connection of the Rhine gold with the entry of sin among the gods, as narrated in the Eddas, is Wagner's own work, and it adds immeasurably to the strength and poetic beauty of the drama.

Wotan and Loge in Nibelheim, the abode of the Nibelungs, is the next picture. Alberich has welded the ring and is the master of his race. Mime has made for him the Tarnhelm, which is to be the instrument of much evil. He prates of the power which is yet to be his, and even threatens the gods. The dwarfs and the giants are alike hostile to the Aesir. Tempted by Loge's cunning to show the magic of the Tarnhelm, Alberich changes himself first to a serpent and then to a toad, and in the latter form the gods make him a captive and drag him away to the surface of the earth before Walhalla. Then they demand of him as ransom the Nibelung hoard. He gives it, for with his ring he can get more. They call for the Tarnhelm. He gives that, too. Then they demand the ring. Alberich warns Wotan not to rob him of it.

> " Say I have sinned ;
> The sin on myself but falls :
> But on all things that were,
> Are, and will be,
> Strikes this evil of thine,
> If rashly thou seizest my ring."

The dwarf, like the giant, knows what must be the consequence of the infraction by the presiding god of the law above all gods. But Wotan tears the ring from his finger. Then Alberich curses the ring. It shall deal out death, not power. It shall bring misery, not gladness. But this curse is, after all, only a piece of stage property. It makes a theatrical effect, and it marks a climax for the auditor. The real curse already exists the moment Wotan stains himself with crime. The thought of the Norse mythology, as set forth in the Eddas, but lost by the maker of Volsunga Saga, is preserved by Wagner in the prophecy of Alberich. The law will do its own work ; but the curse has an external and incidental value in the construction of the drama. Alberich puts into words the inevitable operation of the law.

The prologue now moves swiftly to its end. The giants return with Freia, and it is arranged that they are to receive for her enough gold to hide her. This is Wagner's adaptation of the incident of the filling of the otter skin in the Volsunga Saga. The hoard proves insufficient, and the Tarnhelm goes to swell the heap. Fasolt, the giant who is smitten by the charms of the goddess, still sees the glorious glance of her eye, and demands that Wotan put the ring on the pile to stop this last cranny. Compare Hreidmar's discovery of the muzzle-hair with this poetic idea! The haughty god refuses. The giants declare the bargain off, and start away again with Freia. Loge's plan is working perfectly. He never loses any opportunity to fasten more firmly upon Wotan his burden of guilt. When the giants demand the ring, Loge interposes, saying that the gods must retain that because Wotan means to restore it to the Rhine maidens. Wotan at once falls into the trap, and says:

> " What pratest thou there?
> The prize so hardly come by
> I shall keep, unawed, for myself."

When Wotan has flatly refused to give the ring to the giants, Erda, the embodiment of the earth itself, the impersonation of primeval elements, arises in pale light and mystery. She warns Wotan to flee the curse of the ring. She declares herself to be the all-knowing prophetess, and says:

> " Alles was ist, endet.
> Ein düsterer Tag
> dämmert den Göttern."

" All that exists, endeth.
A dismal day
Dawns for the Aesir."

This brief scene, so charged with dramatic and musical potency, is Wagner's use of the prophecy of the Wala, as contained in the Elder Edda. That prophecy foretells the end of the gods, but its situation in the story is similar to that of the Erda scene in "Siegfried." It comes near the end of the tragedy. Nevertheless from it Wagner obtained the character of Erda and the prediction made by her in "Das Rheingold." The prophecy of the Wala in the Edda does not touch upon the sin of the gods, but it sets forth in detail the story of Ragnarök, as I have already given it. Wagner, however, connects the Wala's utterance with the ethical basis of his tragedy. Wotan, impressed by the prediction, gives up the ring and ransoms Freia. The curse at once begins to operate. The giants quarrel over the division of the hoard and Fafner kills Fasolt. In the Volsunga Saga, from which this incident is adapted, Fafner slays his father, while his brother Regin plays the part allotted by Wagner to Mime in "Siegfried," as we shall presently see. Fafner goes off to the forest with his hoard, and there, as in the saga, becomes a dragon, by the aid of the Tarnhelm, and lies guarding the hoard, which he does not know how to use, for he is too stupid to employ the power of the ring.

Donner raises a thunderstorm to clear the air after the murder, and when the rain is gone a rainbow is seen spanning the valley of the Rhine. The new castle stands forth in all its glory, and Wotan, inviting Fricka to enter with him, for the first time calls it Walhalla.

The goddess asks the meaning of the name, and Wotan replies:

> " What might 'gainst our fears
> My mind may have found,
> If proved a success
> Soon shall explain the name."

The thought in Wotan's mind is that of raising up a race of free heroes who shall perform vicariously the expiation denied to him.   One of them shall of his own volition rescue the ring and restore it to its rightful owners, thus satisfying the demands of the law and removing the curse.   The conception of the hero in the mind of Wotan is made known to us only by the orchestra, which intones the Sword motive here for the first time.   In recent years, with the sanction of Mme. Wagner, a new idea has been introduced into this scene.   In the hoard is the sword, which is discarded by Fafner as valueless.   When Wotan conceives the hero-thought, he picks up this sword and raises it aloft while the trumpet peals out the motive. This was not Wagner's idea, but it is not an unpardonable concession to the demands of the theatre.   It was just a little too much for Wagner to expect that his auditors would carry the Sword motive in their minds from "Das Rheingold" to the first act of "Die Walküre," and remember when hearing it in the latter how it was used in the former and thus find out what it meant there.

Over the rainbow—Bifröst, as it is called in the Eddas—the gods enter Walhalla, the Rhine maidens vainly pleading from the valley below for the return of their ring, and Loge gloating over the end to which, as he says, the Aesir are even now hastening.   And thus ends the prologue, to which I have devoted much space because it contains the foundation of the tragedy. It presents to us the hero foredoomed to destruction, the crime, and the certainty of its inevitable punishment. That is the subject-matter of the propositional part of a classic tragedy. We are now ready to observe the workings of Wotan's futile plans.

With the passage from "Das Rheingold" to "Die Walküre", we enter upon the struggles of the innocent human beings who have been created by Wotan to work his will. The beautiful drama in which Wagner sets forth the events leading to the birth of Siegfried and the slumber of Brünnhilde on the mountain is built from mere hints in the Volsunga Saga. Volsung is no longer the great-grandson of Wotan, but is Wotan himself. Siegmund and Sieglinde are Sigmund and Signy of the saga, twin children of Wotan. The name Sieglinde is that of Siegfried's mother, according to the "Nibelungen Lied." It is Hunding, not Siggeir, who marries Sieglinde. The fight between Hunding and Siegmund takes place, not because of the former's rejection by the maid, but because of the latter's flight with her. The mysterious one-eyed man strikes the sword into the tree at the wedding-feast, and on his spear the sword of Siegmund is broken in the fight. Siegmund Wagner substitutes for the warrior whom Brünnhilde in the saga once struck down, contrary to Wotan's wishes, and when she is put to sleep on the mountain it is for protecting, not slaying, the wrong man. We find that she is surrounded by fire at her own request, that Wotan rules that she shall marry only the hero who will know no fear and can pierce the fire, and that this hero is to be the offspring of

Siegmund and Sieglinde—Siegfried, the full-blooded Volsung, in whose veins flows the blood and in whose heart, freely and unconsciously, works the impulse of Wotan. Let the reader review the story of the saga, and compare it with that of "Die Walküre."

The first act of the drama is taken up with the mutual recognition of Siegmund and Sieglinde, their strange love for one another, the reception of the sword by the hero for whom it was struck into the tree, and the flight of the lovers. Then comes the deeply significant opening scene of the second act. The Valkyr Brünnhilde, revealed to us in all the glory of her divine beauty and strength, starting to the field, is warned not to carry Hunding to Walhalla. To Wotan now comes Fricka, stirred to the bottom of her nature by the deep affront in the action of Sieg-mund and Sieglinde to her dignity as the goddess of marriage. She demands the punishment of the erring pair. Wotan vainly pleads that the gods need the aid of a hero working of his own free will in their defence. Fricka brushes aside this plea with the declaration that heroes have no powers which are denied to gods. She tells Wotan that it is he who breathes courage into Siegmund, that it was he who struck the sword into the tree, devised the need into which Siegmund should fall, and guided him to the house of Hunding. She stands upon her dignity as the celestial queen and demands that the outrage of her especial laws shall be punished. Wotan must not protect Siegmund in the coming fight and he must forbid Brünnhilde's doing so. By hard-wrung oath she binds her spouse to abandon his own plan and submit to the demands of the inexorable moral law.

Brünnhilde returns to his side only to learn the story of her sire's grief. He tells her the history of the rape of the gold, of the endless scheming of Alberich for the downfall of the gods, of his own plan to fill Walhalla with defenders, of his search for Erda, and her becoming Brünnhilde's mother. If Alberich recovers the ring Walhalla is lost, for only he who forswore love can work evil with the circlet of Rhine gold. The ring must be taken from Fafner, but Wotan dare not take it himself because to do so would be a violation of faith and bring more suffering upon him. Only the free hero can accomplish this end. But Fricka has unmasked the truth. Siegmund is but the slave of Wotan's will. And in his final outburst of grief and impotent rage the god sums up his misery :

> "I have wrested Alberich's ring,
> Grasped the coveted gold !
> The curse I incurred
> Doth cling to me yet :—
> What I love best I must relinquish,
> Slay him I hold most sacred ;
> Trusting belief
> Foully betray !
> Glory and fame
> Fade from my sight !
> Heavenly splendour,
> Smiling disgrace !
> Be laid in ruins
> All I have reared !
> Over is my work :
> But one thing waits me now—
> The ending,
> The ending !
> And for that ending
> Looks Alberich !

Now I measure
The meaning mute
Of what the witch spake in wisdom:—
" When that love's defiant foe
Grimly getteth a son,
The sway of the gods
Full soon shall end ! "
The Nibelung dwarf
I now understand
To have won him a woman,
By gold gaining his hopes.
In lust she bears,
Loveless, a babe,
And hatred's fruit
From her draws life.
The love-scorner well
Can work such wonders ;
But he I long for fondly—
The free one—doth lack me yet !
Then now take my blessing,
Nibelung's babe !
What thus I fling from me
Hold as thy fortune :
Walhalla's sumptuous halls
Shall sate thy unhallowed desires ! "

How Wagner builds upon his material! Hagen, the hatred-born son of Alberich, offspring of gold, shall cause the downfall of the gods. He, the child of evil, shall be the instrument of law ! And all this is original with Wagner. To mere hints in the sources he adds the details of a complete poetic story, and always the development of the fundamental ethical thought on which the whole tragedy rests is his. Yet these scenes, in which the god is revealed to us as so intensely human, are the ones to which the average attendant at Wagner performances give the least thought.

Wagner was much concerned about this scene, and indeed about the whole act. On October 3, 1855, he sent the first two acts to Liszt and wrote to him thus :

"I am anxious for the weighty second act ; it contains two catas-trophes, so important and powerful that there would be sufficient matter for two acts ; but then they are so interdependent and the one implies the other so immediately, that it was impossible to separate them. If it is represented exactly as I intend, and if my intentions are perfectly understood, the effect must be beyond anything that has hitherto been in existence. Of course it is written only for people who can stand something (perhaps in reality for nobody). That incapable and weak persons will complain cannot in any way move me. You must decide whether everything has succeeded according to my own intentions. I cannot do it otherwise. At times, when I was timid and sobered down, I was chiefly anxious about the great scene of Wotan, especially when he discloses the decrees of Fate to Brünnhilde, and in London I was once on the point of rejecting the whole scene. In order to come to a decision I took up the sketch and recited the scene with proper expression, when fortunately I discovered that my spleen was unjustified, and that, if properly represented, the scene would have a grand effect even in a purely musical sense."

The remainder of the drama is taken up with the development of what has been prepared. Brünn-hilde's mind is distracted. She feels that Wotan, against his own inclinations, is about to sacrifice Sieg-mund to the wrath of Fricka. Presently the fleeing and guilty lovers approach. Sieglinde, overcome with shame and terrified at the prospect of Hunding's at-tack, sinks senseless in the arms of Siegmund. Brünnhilde appears, and in the beautiful scene, usually named by its German title, the "Todesverkündigung," announces to Siegmund his coming death. He pas-sionately refuses to die or to go to Walhalla without his bride, and Brünnhilde, overcome by his pleading, promises to aid him in the fight. She does so, and Wotan thrusts his spear between the combatants, so that Siegmund's sword is shattered upon it. Hunding slays Siegmund and is himself stricken to death by the will of Wotan. Brünnhilde flees to the Valkyr's rock with Sieglinde, gives her the pieces of the broken sword, foretells the birth of a son, whom she names Siegfried, and sends Sieglinde to secrete herself in the forest to the eastward, where Fafner lies brooding on the hoard. Wotan arrives in hot pursuit of his disobedient daughter, drives off her frightened, pleading sisters, and sentences her, as already told. And all this Wagner has evolved from a few scattered lines in the saga. The marvellous beauty of the scene between Wotan and his beloved child cannot be described.

But let the reader remember that the punishment inflicted on her is not solely because of her disobedience of a command, but also and chiefly because the salvation of Siegmund would have violated Wotan's oath to Fricka and thus have increased the burden of guilt already upon the conscience of this unfortunate and very human god. Again the ethical basis of the tragedy comes to the front, and the moral law, operating as Fate, demands a victim. Brünnhilde becomes the Sleeping Beauty, so familiar to us in the fairy tales, and waits for her prince to wake her, a prince who shall be without fear, and who shall see no terrors in the point of All-Father's dread spear. This hero will be free, " freer than I, the god," as Wotan tells us, while the majestic pealing of the young hero's motive by the orchestra reveals, what the text does not, that Siegfried will be the awakener.

26

None of the sagas or legends in any way connect Brünnhilde with the fate of Siegfried's parents or the birth of the hero. Wagner's invention is here truly dramatic. He has welded separate incidents into a sequence of beautiful poetry and immense dramatic significance. In doing so he has greatly increased the splendour of the character of Brünnhilde. He has enlarged the aspect of her divinity, and has painted with the hand of a master the strange commingling in her of godhood and womanhood. Her sympathy with the doomed pair is wholly womanly, and it leads to her becoming entirely a woman when Wotan, in the enforcement of the demands of law, kisses the godhood from her. None of the old poems suggest such a Brünnhilde as Wagner's. She is a creation as distinct as Shakespeare's Juliet, as great as his Hamlet. In all dramatic literature there is no more majestic female figure than the Brünnhilde of "Die Walküre" and "Siegfried." In the final drama she diminishes in stature, by reason of the loss of her virginity. Then she is only a weak woman, except in the last scene, when she rises once more on the wings of grief to the proudest heights of self-sacrifice.

And so we pass to the next drama of the trilogy, the second act of the tragedy. The story of this is simple. Few ethical questions arise. All is concerned with the acts of the free hero, working without knowledge of Wotan, while the Nibelungs vainly strive to divert the results of the action to their own benefit. Again we meet with the warring forces,—gods, giants, and dwarfs,—but the gods are passive. Wotan, disguised as a wanderer, watches the progress of events, but does not interfere in it. The first act takes place

ın the cavern occupied as home and smithy by Mime,*
no longer subject to his crafty brother, but now in
business for himself and scheming to make the young
Siegfried his instrument for the recovery of the gold
and the ring.   Sieglinde died in childbirth in Mime's
cavern, and the dwarf, knowing well who she was,
has taken good care of her son.   Mime is an infinitely more picturesque character than the Regin of
the saga, and the cavern a far more romantic home
for the nurture of a forest hero than the Court of the
Danish King.   Wagner keeps clear of historical surroundings and conventionalities and presents to us a
primal, elementary youth, a being whom we cannot
fail to love.   For Siegfried is the free, untrammelled
youth of all time, the young man rejoicing in the
strength of his youth, and arriving at the fundamental
laws of life and love by observation, introspection, and
the mighty workings of natural passion.   He is a type,
freed from every convention of clothes-philosophy
and custom, from every condition of time or place.
Siegfried is Young Manhood.   His every utterance
demands of the impersonator a largeness of conception far and away beyond the requirements of
the ordinary operatic rôles.   These are the petty
puppets of libretto machinists, who cut and fit more
or less dramatic stories according to the specifications

* Wagner obtained the name of Mime from the Thidrek Saga, in
which Mimir is a cunning smith, the brother of Regin.   In this saga
Regin is the name of the dragon.   A naked child comes to Mimir,
and because a hind runs out of the wood and licks the child, Mimir
knows that it is a stray which the animal has cared for.   He takes
the child and rears it and calls it Sigfrid.   This youth slays the
dragon, and then the tale proceeds along the same lines as the other
sagas connected with Siegfried.

of the Meyerbeerian plan. But Siegfried must be conceived along the lines of Brünnhilde's apostrophe :

> " O Siegfried ! Herrlicher !
> Hort der Welt !
> Leben der Erde,
> Lachender Held ! "

"O Siegfried ! Lordly one ! Shield of the world ! Life of the earth ! Smiling hero !" He must be big in every way—big in the brawn of his brandished limbs, big in the bursts of his blithesome enthusiasm, and big in the beauty and bloom of his song. For Wagner, in his "Communication," tells us how, in the endeavour to discover what it was that drew him to the heart of the sagas, he drove into the deeper regions of antiquity,

"where, at last, to my delight and truly in the utmost reaches of old time, I was to light upon the fair young form of Man in all the freshness of his force. My studies thus bore me through the legends of the Middle Ages right down to their foundation in the old Germanic Mythos ; one swathing after another, which the later legendary lore had bound around it, I was able to unloose, and thus, at last, to gaze upon it in its chastest beauty. What here I saw was no longer the figure of conventional history, whose garment claims our interest more than does the actual shape inside, but the real, naked Man, in whom I might spy each throbbing of his pulses, each stir within his mighty muscles, in uncramped, freest motion ; the type of the true human being."

It was the recognition of Siegfried in his perfection, not as belittled in the "Nibelungen Lied," that made Wagner conceive him as the hero of his drama. That conception, once formed, was not lost in the subsequent development which made Wotan the real protagonist. Siegfried, in the first drama in which he appears, stands as the type of the utmost freedom of human impulse and action, the complete foil to the far-seeing, law-constrained god. He represents the complementary element in the ethical basis of the tragedy. He is the pure one, over whom Fate, in the shape of the inexorable moral law, has yet no control. He is himself. He makes his own deeds. He is the free agent for whom the despairing god has yearned.

Thus, then, we see him in the first act of the drama, —an impulsive, discontented youth, eager for larger fields of action, moved by strange emotions which he does not comprehend, and for whose meaning he vainly questions the cunning dwarf. A sword he needs, but none which the dwarf makes will bear the force of his blow. At last he wrings from Mime the true story of his birth, and the pieces of the broken sword, which Siegmund in his hour of need christened "Nothung" ("Needful"), are produced as evidence. These shall Mime weld, declares Siegfried, and then the free youth will make his home in the wide world. But weld that particular sword, the sword which Wotan struck into the tree Branstock, is just what Mime cannot do. Wotan, in his wanderer's guise, comes to prophesy to Mime that only one who never knew fear shall accomplish the task. To him is forfeit the head which Mime has staked on answering Wotan's questions.

The scene of the questions between Wotan and Mime was probably suggested to Wagner by the "Vafthrudnersmal," one of the poems of the Elder Edda, which shows Odin holding a similar conversation with the omniscient giant, Vafthrudner. Odin appears as a poor traveller named Gangrader, and engages in a contest of knowledge with the giant. Gangrader, in answer to Vafthrudner's questions, tells the names of the horses that carry Day and Night across the sky and of the river which divides Asgard from Jotunheim (Riesenheim, the giant's land) and the field where the last battle is to be fought. The giant tells the origin of the earth, the story of the creation of the gods, what the heroes do in Walhalla, what was the origin of the Norns, who will rule after the world had been destroyed and what will be the end of the father of the gods. Finally the god asks : "What did Odin whisper in the ear of his son before he ascended the funeral pile ?" The giant recognises Odin by this question, and says, "Who can tell what thou didst whisper of old in the ear of thy son ? I have called down my fate upon my own head when I dared to enter on a strife of knowledge with Odin. All-Father, thou wilt ever be the wisest." We are not told whether the giant lost his head, but we are led to believe that the whispered word was "Resurrection."

When Siegfried returns, Mime vainly endeavours to teach him the meaning of fear, for he would save his head. Siegfried laughs at the conception, and forthwith forges anew the broken blade of Nothung, cleaving in twain the anvil and shouting in the joy of his strength. As for Mime, he now sees that Siegfried will surely slay Fafner, of whom he has told the youth. Yet the dwarf is in terror, for if Siegfried does not learn fear from the dragon, then the dwarf dies ; and if he does learn it, who is to rescue the hoard from Fafner's grasp ?

To the forest, then, in the second act, we follow the

youth and his scheming preceptor.* Alberich lies in watch outside Fafner's cave, and Wotan comes to warn the giant that his fate draws near. Alberich listens, wondering, while Wotan addresses the dragon in his lair. Anon Mime conducts Siegfried to the spot and leaves him. Alone the hero muses on his life, his birth, his mother's death, his own lack of a mate. He hears the song of a forest bird and thinks, could he but understand it, it might tell him of his needs. He fashions a reed pipe wherewith to talk to the bird, but his effort is futile. The scene is one of strange beauty, the orchestra imitating the weaving of the forest leaves and shadows in a wondrous tone-poem, the "Waldweben." Despairing of success with the reed, Siegfried winds a blast upon his horn, and Fafner, the dragon, emerges from his concealment.

Siegfried attacks and slays the monster. Dying, the giant tells him to beware of Mime. Plucking his sword from the beast's heart, the youth wets his finger with the blood and cleanses it with his lips. At once he understands the language of the bird. And here we meet with one of Wagner's dramatic makeshifts, which has often been ridiculed. Before the hero understands the bird its tones are represented by the clarinet; afterward it sings German text in a soprano voice. This is Wagner's plan for conveying the language of the bird to the audience. It is awkward, but there was plainly no other way to let the hearer into the secret. One needs the help of his imagination here, and must bear ever in mind that he is listening to one of the world's fairy tales. The bird

---

* In the locale of this scene Wagner follows the Thidrek, not the Volsunga Saga. The latter makes the place a heath.

sends Siegfried to get the helm and the ring and warns the youth to be wary, for Mime is treacherous.

And now comes another makeshift. Mime approaches, knowing that Siegfried has slain the dragon and obtained the helm and the ring. The dwarf plans to sink the youth in sleep by a potion, slay him, and secure the treasure. But as he would prattle of his love and fidelity, he unconsciously reveals the inner workings of his mind, and to do this he has to utter them aloud. Siegfried and the audience hear them. It is clumsy, but again there seemed no other way. Siegfried slays Mime, and again lays himself down under the linden tree. The "Waldweben" is heard again, and once more the bird sings to the hero, this time to tell him that Brünnhilde sleeps on the fire-girt rock, where only he who knows not fear can reach her. Siegfried springs forward on the path, the bird showing him the way. The whole structure and fancy of this beautiful act are original with Wagner. The saga gave the dramatist only the facts of the slaying of the dragon and the understanding of the language of the birds, which warned the hero of the dwarf's treachery and told him of the sleeping beauty. The treatment and development in the drama are infinitely more poetic than in the original story.

The third act opens with an interview, suggested by the Elder Edda, between Wotan and Erda at the foot of the Valkyr's mountain. Wotan once more consults the Wala, but she tells him naught of value. The god, now ready to resign the empire of the world and prepared for the ending of the Aesir, awaits the hero's coming. Siegfried, led by the bird, confronts him, and with the sword Nothung smites the opposing spear in twain. I have seen it asked why this sword, which was shattered upon the spear in "Die Walküre," now cleaves the runic haft. The ethical basis of the tragedy explains this. Siegmund was doomed to expiate his crime, a victim to Fricka, the avenger, and to the law behind her. But, welded anew by the hand of a spotless hero, the sword is resistless.* The law has no hold upon it. Crying "In vain! I cannot stop thee," Wotan disappears from the tragedy. We hear of him, but see him no more till the flames of Walhalla reveal him to us in the blazing sky.

Siegfried penetrates the fire, and finds the sleeping beauty. He cuts the byrny from her bosom, as in the saga, and wakes her with a kiss. She sings her hymn to the sun and the light and the earth, and proclaims herself Siegfried's from the beginning. One last struggle for her maidenhood, and she yields herself. The union is made. The old order is done. The new race is to come and rule the world. The drama closes with a duo of passionate beauty, and we are ready for "Götterdämmerung," the last act of "Der Ring des Nibelungen."

No doubt the legend of Sigurd's penetration of the flames was taken from the old story of Freyr, the sun god, who rode through a hedge, guarded by fierce dogs, and a flame-circle within it, to win Gerda for his bride. In the later form of the legend, as told in the Elder Edda, Freyr once saw Gerda afar off and fell in love with her. He pined, and his son told Skirnir,

---

* Rassmann holds that the name "Gram" ("Wrath") was given to the sword in the Volsunga Saga because only Odin's wrath could break it. See Rassmann's "Heldensage," vol. i.

his faithful servant, of this. Skirnir took Freyr's horse and magic sword, rode through the flames, and conquered the unwilling Gerda by means of runes. Among the things she refused before he employed the runes was the magic ring which the dwarfs had made. From it eight new ones dropped each ninth night. Thus we see that the myth is related to both of Sigurd's exploits,—that in which he penetrated the flames for himself, and that in which he represented Gunnar. The ring made by the dwarfs, of course, became in the saga tale the ring of Andvari, carrying its curse, and was given to Brünnhilde after the hero had won her.

The last drama of the series opens with a scene taken directly from the Norse mythology. On the Valkyr's rock sit the three Norns, weaving their rope of runes and peering into the events of the past, the present, and the future. For such is their vocation. They are the Fates of older legend. In the Scandinavian mythology they were called Urd, who looked into the past ; Verdandi, who surveyed the present, and Skuld, the youngest, who gazed into the future. Wagner does not use the names, nor does he discriminate in the occupations of the three. Indeed, the scene has no close dramatic relation to the drama about to be enacted, but is rather a pictorial and musical mood tableau, designed to fill the mind of the auditor with portents. In the narrative of the first Norn we hear how Wotan lost his eye, selling it for a draught from the fountain of knowledge, and how he broke a limb from the great ash Yggdrasil itself to fashion his spear. These are incidents in the old mythology. The ash tree was watered daily from Urd's fountain, and it could not wither till the last battle was about to be fought.   From the first Norn's tale we learn that the tree has withered and the fountain dried.   This is a portent of the end.

From the stories of the other Norns we learn that as soon as Siegfried had broken Wotan's spear the god summoned his heroes to the world's ash tree and cut it down.   From it were hewn fagots, and these were piled high in Walhalla.   Wotan and the heroes sit in state, waiting for the flames which shall consume their abode.   The dusk of the gods is at hand.   While the Norns are trying to fathom the outcome of the curse on the ring, their rope breaks.   With frightened cries they sink into the earth, declaring that the world shall no more hear their wisdom.

Siegfried and Brünnhilde, in the dawn of the new day, come forth from their cavern home.   The young hero has matured into a man.   He is clad in Brünnhilde's armor and wears her cloak.   How long they were together on the mountain no one knows.   It was long enough for the youth to become a man, and to learn all Brünnhilde's wisdom.   She is sending him forth to new exploits, fearing only that she may not hold his heart in absence.   She has taught him all her runes, and surrendered to him her maidenhood's strength.   What these runes were we can learn from the Lay of Sigdrifa in the Elder Edda, but they have no bearing upon the story of Wagner.   The statement that Brünnhilde has lost her maiden strength is of importance, for it helps to explain why Siegfried is afterward able to snatch the ring from her.   With her maidenhood, departed the last vestige of her divinity, her strength.   Henceforth she is all woman.   The decree of Wotan is fulfilled.   She says :

" My wisdom fails,
But good-will remains ;
So full of love
But failing in strength,
Thou wilt despise
Perchance the poor one,
Who, having giv'n all,
Can grant thee no more."

Siegfried gives her the ring with a casual and insignificant remark that he owes all his strength to it.
Brünnhilde gives him her steed, Grani, which has lost
its magic powers together with her. Compare this
with the saga story of Sigurd's choice of a horse.
The hero now sets forth, and as the scene changes
we hear his horn echoing down the Rhine valley, and
the orchestra paints his journey. The second scene
shows us the interior of the home of Gunther, the son
of Gibich, who is seated at a table with his sister,
Gutrune, and his half-brother, Hagen. Gunther is the
Gunnar of the saga, but Wagner uses the name from the
"Nibelungen Lied" because it is German. The name
of Gibich is obtained from the "Lex Burgundionum"
of Gundohar, a Burgundian king of the fifth century,
who in it names, as one of his ancestors, Gibica. The
word is derived from the same root as Giuki, the name
used in the Volsunga Saga. Wagner gets the character
of Gunther from the "Nibelungen Lied," where he is
represented as a weak person, usually under the influence of others. Gutrune is the Gudrun of the saga,
the daughter of Grimhild, who employs magic to win
Siegfried for her child's spouse. In the "Nibelungen
Lied" Chriemhild is Gutrune ; the two personages
have been moulded into one and the magic eliminated.
Wagner, as we shall see, identifies the characters of

Gutrune and Chriemhild as the Lied does, but retains the magic, which is wielded by Hagen in furtherance of the Nibelung's plan to recover the ring. He also retains the fact that Grimhild was Gunther's mother. She was also the mother of Hagen, having been overcome by an elf — an idea which Wagner borrowed from the Thidrek Saga.

This idea was essential to his plan of making Hagen appear in the drama as the son of Alberich. It does not consist with Wotan's statement that the Nibelung had won a woman with gold, but that discrepancy is unimportant. The point is that Gunther's half-brother is a Nibelung, and has been entrusted by his father with the task of bringing about the downfall of Siegfried. Wagner has developed the character of Hagen according to this idea, and not according to the original sources. In the Thidrek Saga and the "Nibelungen Lied" Hagen is represented as a crafty villain, while in the Volsunga Saga he is of noble nature and will have naught to do with the plot against Siegfried. In the other two poems he has no motive but malice, while Wagner raises the character to a high tragic plane by giving Hagen the purpose of the Nibelungs' revenge.

The second scene opens, then, with Hagen telling Gunther that he is too long unwed, and that there sleeps on a mountain surrounded by fire the woman who should be his bride. But she is to be reached only by him who never knew fear. This leads to a narration of the exploits of Siegfried, suggested by the narrative of Hagen in the "Nibelungen Lied," when he sees Siegfried approaching the Court of Gunther. Neither Gunther nor Gutrune learns what Hagen has already been told by Alberich, that Siegfried has wed Brünnhilde ; and so they readily fall in with his suggestion that Gutrune administer a magic potion to bind this great hero's heart to her. Siegfried arrives at the castle, and is welcomed by Gunther, who in the mediæval style says in effect : "All that I have and am is yours." Siegfried answers that he has nothing but his good limbs and his home-made sword to offer in return. Hagen immediately asks him where the Nibelungs' hoard is. The hero replies that he deemed it worthless and left it in the cave, except the Tarnhelm, which he has with him, but does not know how to use. Hagen thereupon explains the virtue of it, and inquires where the ring is. Siegfried says it is worn by a woman, and Hagen mutters, "Brünnhilde." Gutrune proffers the magic draught. Siegfried drinks to Brünnhilde and — forgets her. For the drink, artfully prepared by Hagen, was one of forgetfulness. And here we come upon a weak spot in the drama. The drink does not, as we shall see, make Siegfried forget all the incidents leading up to his winning of Brünnhilde, but only their relations. The only plea that can be entered here is that if we accept a magic drink at all, we must not put logical limitations on its powers.

Siegfried now falls in with Hagen's plan. He agrees to go through the fire and get Brünnhilde for Gunther, provided he, in return for the service, receives the hand of Gutrune. There is no talk of a futile attempt on the part of Gunther to penetrate the flames. Siegfried and Gunther swear blood-brotherhood, and the two start for the Valkyr's rock, where, with the help of the Tarnhelm, they are to exchange shapes, as in the saga. Hagen, left alone, gloats over the fact that Siegfried will bring him the ring. Once more the scene changes to the Valkyr's rock, and we meet with an episode in the story entirely original with Wagner, an episode of great beauty and significance. Brünnhilde hears once again the sounds of the passage of a wind-horse, a Valkyr steed. A moment later her sister, Waltraute, is clasped in her embrace. Why has she broken Wotan's command against visiting Brünnhilde? Waltraute says she has fled hither from Walhalla in anguish. "What has befallen the eternal gods?" asks Brünnhilde, in fear. Then Waltraute gives a majestic description of the last gathering of the gods in Walhalla, as already narrated in the Norns' scene. Deep dismay has fallen on the gods. Wotan has sent his ravens out to seek for tidings. This, according to the Eddas, he did daily. Waltraute, weeping on her father's breast, has heard him say:

> "The day the Rhine's three daughters
> Gain by surrender from her the ring,
> From the curse's load
> Released are gods and men."

This is why Waltraute has come. Wotan dare not act, does not dream of doing so; for the atonement must be the work of a free agent. But a Valkyr is a wish-maiden, Wotan's will, and so Waltraute, like Brünnhilde in "Die Walküre," strives to realise her father's wish. Will Brünnhilde give back the ring? But Brünnhilde is no more a virgin Valkyr, a mere daughter of the gods. She is a beloved and loving woman. The ring is Siegfried's bridal gift. Perish the world; perish the eternal gods; but the ring shall not leave her finger where love kissed it into place. Even as Brünnhilde speaks, the orchestra sings the motive of Renunciation, for, as Waltraute flees in despair, the fire springs up in defence of Brünnhilde and the beguiled Siegfried comes in the Tarnhelm, wearing the face and form of Gunther, to wrest the ring from her and make her the bride of the son of Gibich. This is tremendous tragedy; tenfold more tremendous than anything that entered the minds of the sagamen or the fashioners of the "Nibelungen Lied." The Waltraute scene, accentuating, as it does, Wagner's connection of the Nibelung ring with the burden of guilt resting on the gods, presents in a powerful light the human tragedy leading to the restoration of the ring to its rightful owners. Furthermore, the scene is essential to a complete understanding of the character of Brünnhilde in the final drama of the series. The last despairing appeal of Waltraute for the Aesir meets with an answer which fully exhibits the change wrought in Brünnhilde. When Wotan put her to sleep, saying, "So küsst er die Gottheit von dir," he was the familiar Wotan of the trilogy, planning, but seeing only half the issue of his plan. When Siegfried laid the kiss of human love upon the virgin lips of the Valkyr, he it was who truly kissed the godhood from her, and left her with a wholly human disregard for the fading Aesir. All she has given for love, and now comes a second claimant for her. Stricken with horror and shame, she is driven into the cavern. Siegfried, following, announces that his sword shall lie between them.

The second act brings us back to the castle of

Gunther. Hagen, still watching, is visited by Alberich, who urges him to persistence. Alberich's speeches impress upon us two important points, namely: that the curse cannot fall upon Siegfried, because he is ignorant of the powers of the ring, and therefore does not use them; and, secondly, that if he should give the ring back to the Rhine maidens no art could fashion a new one. Both of these ideas are Wagner's. The first is a natural outgrowth of the ethical basis of the drama; the second was doubtless suggested by the old legends, which always finish the story of the hoard by returning it to the waters. Siegfried returns and announces his success, quieting the fears of Gutrune by telling her that his sword lay between him and Brünnhilde. Here we have an alteration of the original stories to suit modern taste. In the legends there was no question of the relations of the disguised Siegfried and Brünnhilde, and they existed with the consent of Gunther. But in Wagner's drama it is made plain to us that Siegfried was loyal in the modern sense, though he used an ancient symbol of honour, the sword.

Gunther arrives with Brünnhilde, and she, seeing Siegfried there with Gutrune, at once suspects treachery. She perceives the ring on Siegfried's finger, and demands an explanation as to how he came by the circlet which Gunther had wrenched from her hand the previous night. This episode of the ring is entirely different, as the reader will note, from those of the Volsunga Saga and the "Nibelungen Lied." But it had to be so, because Wagner had already omitted the incident which, in the sources of his story, led to Siegfried's presenting the ring to his wife. Brünnhilde's questions about the ring evoke no satisfactory answers, and she bursts out with the charge that not Gunther, but Siegfried married her. "He forced delights of love from me!" she cries. Siegfried avows that his sword lay between them. But Brünnhilde is talking of a night long previous to that just passed, a night of which only she and Siegfried should know, but which he, under the influence of the drink, has forgotten. Brünnhilde knows that her hearers are ignorant of that night, but she is bent upon implicating Siegfried, and she lets the assembly believe that she is speaking of the night just passed. Much good ink has been spilled over this scene, one party contending that Brünnhilde was guilty of deceit, and the other that Siegfried had been false to his trust. The intent of the scene is, it seems to me, perfectly plain, but to quiet all doubts we may go to Wagner's own sketch, "The Nibelung Myth as Sketch for a Drama." He describes this point thus:

"Siegfried charges her with shamelessness: faithful had he been to this blood brothership,—his sword he laid between Brünnhilde and himself:—he calls on her to bear him witness. Purposely, and thinking only of his ruin, she will not understand him."

In a speech of double meaning, she declares that the sword hung in its scabbard on the wall on the night when its master gained him a true love. Siegfried swears to his truth on the point of Hagen's spear, calling upon it to pierce him if he is false. This is a purely theatric touch. This spear does pierce him, yet was he not false. Brünnhilde swears upon the same spear that Siegfried has committed perjury. Thereupon Siegfried lightly says that she is daft, and bids the guests to let the festivities proceed. Brünnhilde now suspects some deviltry, but her runic wisdom is gone and she cannot fathom it. But she can and does confide to Hagen that she had made her hero invulnerable, except in the back. Gunther discerns that he has been dishonoured, yet he is loath, for his sister's sake, to be revenged upon Siegfried. This makes Brünnhilde all the more furious, and she readily assents to Hagen's proposition that Siegfried must die. The vacillating Gunther is overcome. Hagen shouts in triumph ; the ring and the power will soon be his.

The last act shows the Rhine maidens sporting on the surface of the water in a little cove of the river. Siegfried, hunting and strayed from his party, appears on the rocks above them. They beg him to return the ring, and he is almost on the point of doing so when they warn him of its curse. He refuses to be scared into parting with it. This meeting with the Rhine maidens is not found in any of the old stories, because the ring which causes the trouble in "Götterdämmerung" is not in any way associated in the legends with the end of the gods. In both the Thidrek Saga and the "Nibelungen Lied," Hagen is warned of an evil by mermaids, and this may barely have suggested this scene, which so accentuates the immediately succeeding tragedy of Siegfried's death.

The hunting party arrives, and to cheer the gloomy Gunther Siegfried volunteers to tell the story of his youth. All this is original with Wagner. The hero narrates the incidents of the drama "Siegfried" to a wonderful epitome of its music, up to the slaying of Mime. Then Hagen administers an antidote to the drink of forgetfulness, and the hero reveals his discovery of Brünnhilde. Gunther is shocked as he realises Hagen's perfidy. Wotan's ravens fly past, and Hagen calls on Siegfried to interpret their tones. As the hero turns his back, Hagen drives the spear into it. Siegfried dies apostrophising his Valkyr love. To the strains of the great funeral march, the body is borne back to the home of the Gibichs, and laid at the feet of Gutrune, who is told, as in the Thidrek Saga, that a wild boar slew her lord. She accuses Gunther, who promptly denounces Hagen. The Nibelung demands the ring; Gunther opposes him; they fight, and Gunther is slain. Hagen reaches for the ring, but the dead hand of Siegfried rises in solemn warning, and sends him staggering back in terror. At this juncture Brünnhilde, who, as we vaguely learn from the text, has heard the truth from the Rhine maidens, enters the hall, a picture of outraged majesty.

After informing Gutrune that she was never the real wife of Siegfried, Brünnhilde sums up the dénouement of the entire tragedy in a speech which must be carefully read by anyone desiring thoroughly to understand Wagner's design. She perceives the whole of Wotan's plan, and upbraids him for throwing on a guiltless man the curse of his own crime. Let the ravens tell Wotan that his plan is accomplished. And let the weary god have rest. She takes the ring from Siegfried's finger, and places it upon her own. When she is burned with him on the funeral pyre, the Rhine maidens may get the ring again. And now fly home, ravens. Pass by the Valkyr's rock and bid the flickering Loge once more visit Walhalla, for the dusk of the gods is at hand, and with this torch will the bride of Siegfried fire the towers of Asgard. Then she addresses the wondering retainers and bids them, when she is gone, to put aside treaties and treacherous bonds as laws of life, and in their place to let Love rule alone. With her steed, Grani, she mounts Siegfried's funeral pyre. The flames rise to heaven. Upon the Rhine are seen the three maidens, one of them holding aloft the ring. Hagen madly springs into the water after the accursed bauble, and is drawn under by the maidens and drowned. The sky blazes and we see the assembled gods, as described by Waltraute, sitting in the burning Walhalla. It is the "Götterdämmerung."

So ends the tragedy. Nothing in the final scenes closely resembles the original legends except the burning of Walhalla. In the legends the gods are destroyed in battle with the powers of evil. Here they die in solemn atonement for sin. And their punishment, which is their release, is accomplished by the voluntary sacrifice of a woman through love. Brünnhilde, wiser in the end than Wotan himself, perfects and completes his plan. The death of the hero, innocent and unoffending, was not enough. The intentional sacrifice, hallowed by love, accomplishes what all Wotan's schemes failed to achieve. The ethical plot of the drama is finished. "The eternal feminine leadeth us upward and on."

This glorious Brünnhilde of Wagner is a grander figure than any conceived by the sagamen. Dimly, indeed, may her sacrifice be connected with the death of Nanna, the wife of Baldur, the bright one, who could not outlive her husband. But that death was merely from a broken heart. This one is a magnificent atonement.

Baldur's horse, fully caparisoned, was led to his

master's pyre. Wotan placed on the pile his ring, Draupner, which every ninth night produced eight other rings. But none of these incidents have the enormous significance of Wagner's final scene. His reconstruction of the story of the end of the gods, of their release from the burden of sin by a voluntary, vicarious sacrifice, raises the poetic issue of his drama to a plane far above the conceptions of the old Norse and Teutonic skalds. With "Der Ring des Nibelungen," in spite of its defects, Wagner set himself beside the Greek dramatists.

III.—The Music of the Trilogy

In "Der Ring des Nibelungen" the leitmotiv system is found at its best. In this gigantic and complex drama it provides a musical aid to an understanding of the intent of the dramatist. It is a running commentary on the action, a ceaseless revealer of inner thoughts and motives. And, owing to the development of plot and character, the musical device of thematic development is employed with admirable effect in this work. Unfortunately for the credit of Wagner, the typical handbook of these dramas, and the fashionable "Wagner Lecture," which consists of telling the story and playing the principal motives on a piano, have gone far to convey wholly erroneous ideas of this unique musical system. The hearer of the lecture and the reader of the handbook are led to suppose that the score consists of a string of disconnected phrases, arbitrarily formed and capriciously titled, and that this is the whole result of the system. The truth is that the score becomes symphonic in

scope. The various motives are invented with a profound insight into the philosophy of musical expression and are repeated or developed according to the
principles of musico-dramatic art formulated in the
mind of Wagner when he had fully elaborated his
theory of the organic union of the text and the music.
Reading the handbooks or hearing the lectures and
afterward recognising the motives as they appear in
the dramas, even when their significance is known, is
not all that Wagner asks of one who attempts to understand his system. It is necessary to study the
scores very thoroughly, to note the intimate union of
text and music, to observe the changes which motives
undergo when new shades of meaning are to be expressed, to grasp the treatment of rhythm and tonality
and the formation and expansion of themes, and generally to follow the composer through the various
ramifications of the most elaborate plan for dramatic
expression in music ever invented.

On the other hand, none of this study is essential to
a mere enjoyment of these dramas. For that, only a
perfect comprehension of the text is necessary; if you
know what the characters are saying and doing, the
music will do its own work. It will create the right
mood for you, though you do not know the name of
a single leading theme. But the thematic system is
there, and to understand it will add enormously to
your intellectual and artistic pleasure and give Wagner
a far higher position in your estimation than he would
otherwise occupy. Only, if you intend to study it, do
not treat it as if it were nothing more than a thematic
catalogue. What I am about to put before the reader
cannot claim to be more than some pertinent hints.

An exhaustive study of these scores would fill a volume.

Let the reader refer to the classification of mot.ves given in Chapter III. of " The Artistic Aims of Wagner " (page 193), and apply it to the themes now to be considered. He will find in these scores all the classes there enumerated and will note that they are used and developed with extraordinary skill.

After the preliminary measures of the introduction to "Das Rheingold," we hear the first guiding theme of the drama, the motive of the Primeval Elements:

PRIMEVAL ELEMENTS.

This motive plays an important part in the trilogy. When Erda rises from the earth in the last scene of the prologue we hear this same theme in the minor mode, and we at once perceive that by this simple process of musical development Wagner associates her with the primeval elements (earth, air, and water), but emphasises the sadness of her character and her peculiar office in the tragedy as a prophetess of woe. When she utters the words, " Ein Düst'rer Tag dämmert den Göttern " (" A dismal day dawns for the Aesir "), we hear her motive first in its natural form, and then inverted, and we then learn that this inversion has an especial meaning, the end of the gods, the " Götterdämmerung ":

A—ERDA.   B—GÖTTERDÄMMERUNG.

Ein düst'-rer Tag dämmert den Göttern

Now let us turn to the scene in which Waltraute comes to tell Brünnhilde how Wotan has had the ash cut down, hewn into faggots, and assembled the gods to wait for the end. In the accompaniment to her words appears the Erda theme, originally that of the Primeval Elements which surrounded the Rhinegold, transformed into a stately progression of octaves. Presently over these we hear the Walhalla theme, and then the octaves descend in a new development of the "Götterdämmerung" theme:

WALTRAUTE.

The stem in sticks...... he bade them to
stack and ar-range in a bulk, 'round the Aesir's sanctified

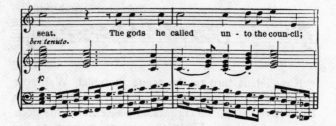

Turn next to the last scene of all, to the entrance of Brünnhilde. We find that the music is this:

Brünnhilde has come to fulfil the prophecy of Erda; the dusk of the gods is at hand. And so when she commands the retainers to erect the funeral pyre, which is kindled at Walhalla, we hear once again the "Götterdämmerung" theme as it was introduced to us in the Waltraute scene:

This is an excellent demonstration of the leitmotiv system in its fullest expansion, and it should warn the reader against accepting these themes as merely arbitrary labels. Let him always seek for their musical philosophy and their relations to one another.

When the Rhine maidens appear swimming around the rock in which lies the gold, they sing these cabalistic words and this melodious music :

RHINE DAUGHTERS.

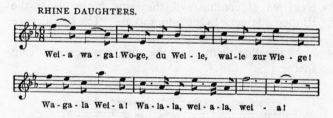

Wei - a wa - ga! Wo-ge, du Wel - le, wal - le zur Wie - ge!

Wa - ga - la Wei - a! Wa - la - la, wei - a - la, wei - a!

Presently, as narrated in the story, the gold discloses itself, and we hear the ascending theme of the Appearing Gold :

THE APPEARING GOLD.

Trumpet.

But when the maidens burst into song in its praise, they sing this :

THE GLEAMING GOLD.

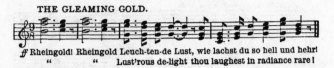

_ff_ Rheingold! Rheingold Leuch-ten-de Lust, wie lachst du so hell und hehr!
"   "   Lust'rous de-light thou laughest in radiance rare!

The first measures of this melody are employed throughout the drama to signify the gold. Examination will show that the words "Rheingold! Rheingold!" are sung to precisely the same melodic form as "Weia" at the beginning and the end of the phrase quoted from the Rhine daughters' music. Here, again, we see how Wagner persists in preserving the musical associations of allied themes, and of deriving one from the other in the symphonic style. In the last act of "Götterdämmerung," when the maidens warn Siegfried of coming evil, they sing his name to the Rhinegold theme in the minor mode. The significance of this is unmistakable.

At the first mention of the ring, we hear the Ring theme :

THE RING.

This theme is subjected to so many developments that they cannot be enumerated in a work of this kind. A single glance, however, will show the reader how closely related it is to the "Götterdämmerung" motive. In certain passages, as in the scene between Brünnhilde and the disguised Siegfried in "Götterdämmerung" this theme and the Walhalla theme are combined, by an ingenious use of the rhythm and melodic sequence of the one with the melody and

harmony of the other, to identify Brünnhilde's personality with possession of the ring. Other important
motives introduced early in the "Rheingold" are the
following :

RENUNCIATION.

Nun wer der Minnie Macht ent-sagt, nur wer der Lie - be Lust ver-jagt
But he who passion's power forswears and from delights of love forbears

WALHALLA.

Brass. *p*

COMPACT.

f Trombones.

GIANTS.

The Renunciation theme is employed throughout the
tragedy to signify renunciation without regard to its
original connection with the ring. The Walhalla motive indicates not only the place, but the origin of
persons who come thence. In this sense it is sometimes applied to Brünnhilde, as well as to Wotan.
The next theme of significance is that of the Tarnhelm
(see page 195). Here, again, we meet with a theme
for which there is a companion closely associated
with it in form and in the action of the drama. This
is the theme of Forgetfulness, heard in "Götterdämmerung" when Siegfried takes the drink offered him by
Gutrune. The close relationship in the meaning of

these themes is best displayed in the scene of Sieg-
fried's arrival at the Valkyr's rock in the guise of
Gunther.   Brünnhilde says : " What man art thou ? "
And, as Siegfried stands at the rear and begins his
answer, we hear these three motives in succession—
Forgetfulness, Gibichung, and Tarnhelm.

The meaning is clear, and the kinship of the Forgetfulness and Tarnhelm themes unmistakable.   Siegfried
uses the Tarnhelm but this once in the whole tragedy,
and uses it because of the forgetfulness and in the
guise of a Gibichung.

When Freia has been carried off by the giants to

wait for Wotan's decision as to the ransom, Loge taunts the gods with their pallor and failing glory. As part of the accompaniment to his speech, we hear the motive of Departing Divinity :

DEPARTING DIVINITY.

Now turn to the last scene of "Die Walküre," and when Wotan tells Brünnhilde that he will plunge her into unbreaking sleep we hear this same motive in this form :

The theme is heard again in its fullest harmonies when the god kisses her eyes and she sinks to sleep. Here, again, Wagner uses uncertainty of tonality to produce an effect of mystery in his music.

At the entrance of Loge we hear another important motive, that of the fire-god :

LOGE.

From this is developed the magic fire music of "Die
Walküre," and the theme is heard frequently throughout the trilogy.   Sometimes it ascends, and again it
descends, and at times it becomes purely melodic in
the diatonic scale and the major mode, but it never
loses its flickering, wavering character.   When Wotan
and Loge descend into Nibelheim, we hear the important theme of the Nibelungs, the smiths :

NIBELUNG SMITHS.

This is heard very often in the tragedy, and always
signifies the Nibelung race.   Alberich's appearance,
driving before him the Nibelungs, who have become
his slaves through the power of the ring, introduces
the theme of Alberich's mastery :

ALBERICH, MASTER OF THE NIBELUNGS.

As it was the Rhinegold which made him lord of
the Nibelungs, the theme is compounded of the Rhinegold motive and that of the Nibelungs, the latter being
brought to a firm and definite close with a major
chord.   With the entrance of the dwarfs carrying the
gold, we hear the theme of the Hoard :

THE HOARD.

The Dragon motive appears when Alberich transforms himself for the first time :

THE DRAGON.

This theme is employed again in " Siegfried " for the transformed " Fafner."   The motive of the Nibelung's Hate is used very often in " Siegfried " and " Götterdämmerung," as well as in the prologue :

THE NIBELUNG'S HATE.

The instrumentation of this theme, the lower part being given to strings and the upper to clarinets, is especially expressive.   It has a snarl and a sneer.   The next important theme introduced in the prologue is that of the Curse :

THE CURSE.

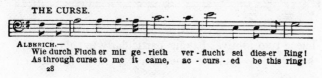

ALBERICH.—
Wie durch Fluch er mir ge - rieth   ver - flucht sei dies-er Ring!
As through curse to me it came,   ac - curs - ed be this ring!

28

This is heard when Fafner kills Fasolt, and throughout the drama at points where the curse is especially
significant, as at the death of Siegfried. The Sword
theme (see page 195) appears when Wotan conceives
his plan. I have not given the minor themes, which
are heard only in the "Vorabend," such as those of
Fricka, Froh, and Freia. Donner's theme is of little
import, being heard again only in the storm music in
"Walküre." There is a long list of minor themes,
but their significance can always be learned from the
text.

In "Die Walküre" a number of significant motives
not heard in the prologue are brought forward. The
first of these indicates the gentle and sympathetic personality of Sieglinde:

SIEGLINDE'S SYMPATHY.

Next comes the Love motive, a melody of some length,
written for celli, and full of feeling:

LOVE.

These two motives belong particularly to this drama;
they do not figure in the other works. In the first

act, however, appear two themes which are used thereafter throughout the tragedy, the themes of the Volsungs' sorrow and the Volsung race :

SORROW OF THE VOLSUNGS.

THE VOLSUNG RACE.

The reappearance of the Sword motive (see page195) in this act should be noted for its pregnant meaning. Siegmund calls upon his father and says, "Where is the promised sword?" The firelight at this instant strikes the hilt of the sword in the tree, and the orchestra gives out the Sword theme with almost startling effect. It would be superfluous to trace the manifold treatment of the various melodic fragments through the score. The hearer of the works cannot fail to become acquainted with their import. The motive of the Volsung race is especially touching in its noble dignity and melancholy. It epitomises in a fragment of music the nature and suffering of the unhappy

Volsungs.   Much of the music of the first act is freely composed, the love song and most of the duet being thus written.   A motive indicative of the personality of Hunding will be easily recognised when heard. With the opening of the second act we make the acquaintance of two motives associated with Brünnhilde in her character of Valkyr:

THE VALKYR'S CALL.

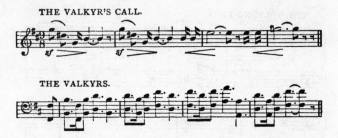

THE VALKYRS.

The second of these is afterward used whenever the nature of the Valkyr is of significance in the drama. The theme, it will be noted, is designed rhythmically to suggest the motion of the Valkyr steed. When Fricka imposes upon Wotan the oath to honour her rights, we hear the theme of Wotan's Wrath, a wrath in which there is a deep note of pathos:

WOTAN'S WRATH.

When Wotan informs Brünnhilde that only a free hero can make the atonement, we hear this theme beautifully combined with the Erda theme and a suggestion of the "Götterdämmerung" motive:

WOTAN.

Nur El—ner könn-te was Ich nicht darf: Ein
But one may compass what I must leave, A

Held, dem helf—end nie .... ich mich neigt—e,
he—ro held by none........... of our num—ber,

It is by such wonderful combinations of the guiding themes that the scores of these dramas become so rich in variety, beauty, and meaning. The significance of this passage is clear and eloquent. The plan must fail and the dusk of the gods must come. The phrase marked A is usually designated the theme of the "Gods' Stress." It is plainly, however, the Erda theme and a variant of the "Götterdämmerung." When Siegmund sits on the rock with Sieglinde fainting in his arms, we hear for the first time **the motive of Fate**, often used afterward:

FATE.

The treatment of the "Todesverkündigung" is free,
the theme being heard only in that scene. Motives
already made known form the warp of the score to
the end of the act, and the third act opens with the
familiar "Ride of the Valkyrs" built on the Valkyr's
Call and the Valkyr theme. When Brünnhilde informs Sieglinde that she is to be the mother of the
"highest hero of worlds," we hear for the first time
the magnificent Siegfried theme, which is to play such
an important part in the remainder of the tragedy:

And in response to this announcement Sieglinde
sings thus:

This theme is heard again at the close of the last scene of "Götterdämmerung," and there we instantly recognise its significance as an embodiment of the glorious divinity of Brünnhilde, the divinity of ideal womanhood, ennobled by love and sanctified by sacrifice. Another significant motive heard in this scene is that of Slumber:

SLUMBER.

This, with the Fire and Siegfried themes, forms the magnificent closing passage of this drama. The melody of Wotan's farewell, though it can hardly be described as a leitmotiv, reappears with beautiful effect in Waltraute's narrative, when she tells of Wotan's sadness.

In "Siegfried" we meet with a score which contains a great amount of freely composed music. There is so much that is external and incidental in this work that the constant employment of guiding themes was unnecessary. The result is that we enter an atmosphere of buoyant, jubilant out-door life, full of the vigour and sweetness of spring and young manhood. The whole of the scene of the forging of the sword is sung in music aglow with the flame of the forge, alive with the rhythm of the bellows and the hammer. The forest scene gives us the bird music and the "Waldweben," freely written, the latter a mood picture, using only the Volsung theme as a reminder. Wotan's splendid summons to Erda is free music, and in the matchless scene of the awakening we hear much that is new and belongs only to "Siegfried."

The first of the important new themes is that intoned by the young hero's horn.   It is the theme of Siegfried, the buoyant, fearless, militant youth:

SIEGFRIED, THE YOUTH.

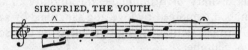

Out of this theme and that of the Sword, the melodies and rhythms being combined perfectly, is made the brilliant motive of Siegfried, the hero who welds and wields the sword:

SIEGFRIED, THE SWORD WIELDER·

This is heard often in the early part of the work. Wotan, disguised as a wanderer, is indicated by a theme without tonality, which, therefore, belongs to the same class as the Tarnhelm and Departing Divinity motives:

WOTAN, THE WANDERER.

In the second act, while Siegfried is alone in the forest, is heard this beautiful and significant theme:

YEARNING FOR LOVE.

After this, till the first scene of the third act, the listener will not hear any motive of high import. All is either free music or the employment of themes whose significance has been previously made known. But in the opening of the last act appears the splendid melody of the Heritage of the World, which is used to embody the readiness of Wotan to resign himself to his approaching fate and to hand over his kingdom to the new race:

Wonderful, too, are the strains which accompany the arrival of Siegfried at the top of the Valkyr's mountain, but most wonderful is the music of Brünnhilde's Awakening:

This is only a fragment of it, but it contains the pregnant phrase of marvellous beauty which returns with such agonising eloquence in the final speeches of the dying Siegfried in "Götterdämmerung." When the Valkyr maid is awake and has recognised Siegfried, their voices unite in the passionate measure of a duet, founded on the motive of Love's Greeting:

LOVE'S GREETING.

In "Götterdämmerung," when Siegfried raises the drink of forgetfulness to his lips, he drinks to the memory of Brünnhilde and intones the words to this very theme. That is one of Wagner's most poignant strokes of musical pathos. The drama of "Siegfried" comes to its end with a sweep of overmastering passion. The themes are peculiar to this work, but most of them are heard in the lovely "Siegfried Idyl," so often played in concert.

"Götterdämmerung" opens with a repetition of known themes in the Norn scene. In the second scene we meet with two new ideas, the themes of Brünnhilde, the woman, and Siegfried, the mature hero :

BRÜNNHILDE, THE WOMAN.

SIEGFRIED, THE MAN.

The first of these expresses very beautifully the loving, clinging nature of the transformed Valkyr. The second is a thematic development of the motive of Siegfried, the youth. The change is chiefly one of rhythm. Siegfried, the youth, is depicted musically in six-eighth measure, a rhythm buoyant and piquant. For Siegfried, the mature hero, the melodic sequence is preserved, but the rhythm is changed to a dual one. The change is one founded on the nature of music, for the dual rhythm is firm, square, and solid. The injection of minor harmony at the end is heard in the first announcement of this theme and serves to indicate approaching sorrow. This motive rises to its grandest development in the funeral march after Siegfried's death, when the orchestra passes in review, in a composition of wonderful beauty and power, the themes most closely associated with him. This theme forms the climax of the march and is pealed forth by the brass in this form :

Two other new themes heard in "Götterdämmerung" are worthy of note. They are that of Gutrune and that of Brünnhilde's Despair, the former appearing in the third scene of the first act and the latter in the second act:

BRÜNNHILDE'S DESPAIR.

There are also themes for Gunther, the Gibichung (already quoted), and for Hagen. But "Götterdämmerung" is most wonderful, musically, for the manner in which the themes of the earlier dramas are repeated in it. The expressiveness of the system is nowhere more forcibly illustrated than in the hero's narrative of his youthful days, when the most significant themes of "Siegfried" pass before us, bringing the whole story back in all its vitality. And in the death of the hero and the wonderful apostrophe of Brünnhilde again we find that the recapitulation or development of familiar themes knits for us the substance of the long tragedy into a perfect texture of poetry. And with the use of the many-voiced orchestra Wagner weaves these motives into a glittering web of counterpoint, which cannot be copied even faintly by the piano arrangement. Several motives are sometimes heard at once, and by the aid of the device of instrumental colouring their expressiveness is greatly heightened.

Thus the orchestra becomes an actor in the drama, continually commenting on the passing action, revealing to us the hidden well-springs of emotion, explaining thoughts to us and flooding the whole drama with the light of its eloquence. Not by the mere cataloguing then of these themes are we to arrive at a full understanding of the composer's intent, but by a careful study of their repetitions and developments. The knowledge thus gained will add immeasurably to the intellectual pleasure of the hearer ; but, as I have already said, Wagner's music makes the right mood pictures even for him who does not know the guiding themes. And that is one of the most satisfying proofs of his greatness.

PARSIFAL

A Sacred Stage Festival Play in Three Acts.

First Performed at Bayreuth, July 26, 1882.

Original Cast.

Parsifal	Winkelmann.
Amfortas	Reichmann.
Titurel	Kindermann.
Klingsor	Hill.
Gurnemanz	Scaria.
Kundry	Materna.

The copyright of this work is still held by the Wagner family, and hence the drama has not yet been performed outside of the Festival Playhouse at Bayreuth.

First performance in the United States, Metropolitan
Opera House, December 24, 1903.

(This was also the first performance anywhere outside of Bayreuth.)

Kundry	Milka Ternina.
Parsifal	Alois Burgstaller.
Amfortas	Anton Van Rooy.
Gurnemanz	Robert Blass.
Titurel	Marcel Journet.
Klingsor	Otto Goritz.
First Esquire	Miss Moran.
Second Esquire	Miss Braendle.
Third Esquire	Albert Reiss.
Fourth Esquire	Mr. Harden.
First Knight	Mr. Bayer.
Second Knight . . .	Adolph Muehlmann.
A Voice	Louise Homer.

Conductor: Alfred Hertz.

Anton Fuchs, of Munich, was brought over as stage
manager, and Carl Lautenschläger as technical director.

First performance in English, given by Henry W.
Savage's Company, Tremont Theatre, Boston,
October 17, 1904.

Kundry	Mme. Kirkby-Lunn.
Parsifal	Alois Pennarini.
Amfortas	Johannes Bischoff.
Gurnemanz	Putnam Griswold.
Titurel	Robert K. Parker.
Klingsor	Homer Lind.

Conductor: Walter H. Rothwell

PARSIFAL

I.—The Original Legends

THE last of the great music dramas of Richard Wagner began to occupy his mind as early as 1857. Professor William Tappert says: "Wagner told me (in 1877) that in the fifties, when in Zurich, he took possession of a charming new house, and that, inspired by the beautiful spring weather, he wrote out the sketch that very day of the Good Friday music." A letter to the tenor Tichatschek defines the year as 1857. The poem was completed in 1877, and on May 17 of that year was read to an assembly of Wagner's friends at the house of Mr. Edward Dannreuther, in Orme Square, London. It was read to the delegates of the Wagner Societies at Villa Wahnfried, Bayreuth, on Sept. 16, and was published in December. Wagner was in his sixty-fifth year when he set to work to write out the music. The sketch of the first act was finished in the spring of 1878. The second act was completed on Oct. 11, and the sketch of the third, begun after Christmas, was finished in April, 1879. The instrumentation was begun almost immediately afterwards, and was completed at Palermo, Jan. 13, 1882.

As we have already seen, it was while gathering the materials for "Tannhäuser" and "Lohengrin" that the character and writings of Wolfram von Eschenbach became known to Wagner. His famous epic, "Parzival," is the immediate source of Wagner's drama, but the origin of such a remarkable art-product cannot be dismissed with this simple statement. Wagner's drama opens to us the entire field of Arthurian romance and the whole circle of legends of the Holy Grail. These old tales have played so important a part in the literature of our own time, as well as in that of the Middle Ages, that it seems fitting and proper that we should seize this opportunity for a glance over the whole ground. Wagner, as we shall find, has in this work, as in his others, taken hints from all the sources, and has introduced special and highly significant ideas of his own.

Wolfram's history I must recount but briefly, for little is known of his life. We learn from his name that he was probably born (about 1170) at Eschenbach in Bavaria, and it is certain that he was buried there; for toward the end of the seventeenth century his tomb, with an inscription, could be seen in the Frauen-Kirche of Ober-Eschenbach. He tells us that he was of the knightly order and with some humour refers often to his poverty. It does not appear, however, that he was obliged to roam about, reciting his verse for a living. He was extremely proud of his knighthood, and his entire poem breathes the spirit of chivalry. It was probably written—or dictated, for Wolfram was ignorant of writing—in the early years of the thirteenth century, and it was published in 1477.

According to Wolfram, the source of his work was a story of the Holy Grail by one Kiot of Provence. No such poem is now known. According to Wolfram, Kiot found at Toledo an ancient black-letter manuscript in Arabic, and learned from it that Flagetanis, a heathen, born before Christ and celebrated for his acquaintance with occult arts, had read in the stars that there would at some time appear a thing called the Grail, and that whosoever should be its servitor would be blest among men. Kiot set out to ascertain whether anyone had ever been worthy of this service, and, as the house of Anjou was then in power, he had no difficulty in discovering that one Titurel, a very ancient king of this dynasty, had once been the keeper of the Grail. Of course this story was invented by Kiot to do honour to his sovereign liege. Wolfram declares that Kiot related the tale incorrectly, and at any rate his version, so far as reported by Wolfram, contains nothing about Parsifal. And this brings us to an important point.

How far back the legends of the Grail go, is unknown. No matter how far we trace them, we always find references to a source. But it seems almost certain that in their earliest forms they had no relation to the tale of Perceval, or Peredur, the Parsifal of later versions. The story as it is now known to us is a union of two originally separate legends. There is good ground, according to all the folk-lorists, for believing that in its original form the Celtic, or, more exactly, Kymric, legend of Peredur was independent of the Grail stories. The latter appeared between 1170 and 1220, and constituted a large body of literature, dealing with a talisman not at first distinctly Christian. For half a century poets sang this legend enthusiastically and then suddenly dropped it. A few scattered

and worthless Grail romances date from a later period,
and, with Mallory's "Morte d'Arthur," written 300
years later,—a noble fragment, indeed,—they came to
an end. Mr. David Nutt, in his "Studies on the
Legends of the Holy Grail," holds, with apparently
excellent reason, that the Grail was originally a Pagan
talisman, and that a history of the legend is the history
of the development of this talisman into a Christian
symbol. He further shows that the legends may be
divided into two classes, one dealing entirely with the
talisman itself, and being largely influenced by
Christian ideas, and the other treating of the quest of
the Grail. Somewhere or other in the stories of the
adventures of Peredur was found a resemblance to
some legend of the search after the Grail, and thus
the Kymric folk-hero became the protagonist of the
Grail-drama.

The Arthurian legends are British; the Grail stories
are French. Let us see how they came together.
Undoubtedly the former went first from France to
England, and the latter followed them. To understand this we must bear in mind that France was
ancient Gaul, and that a large part of the ancient popu-
lation was Celtic. The Celts fairly filled all that part
of France extending from the Garonne River to the
Seine and the Marne. In this land dwelt the Celtae
proper, but their speech and their influence spread
beyond its confines. For these Celts in France were
but a surviving and compressed fragment of the
great vanguard of the Aryan race, which, issuing from
its forest cradle in Asia Minor, and carrying in its
bosom the nursling star of empire, swept westward
toward the Atlantic. It peopled most of Europe and

the isles of the sea, and it planted among the sunny fields of the Midi and the verdant vales of Britain the seeds of the Arthurian legends, the Nibelung tales, the Norse Sagas, all garnered first from some great parent stem of folk-lore in the Eastern jungles. How it chanced that the Arthurian tales blossomed into full fancy in England first no one knows, but it is equally inexplicable how the Grail legends were first developed in France. For the Grail was originally a vessel in which was offered a draught of wisdom or youth, and its transformation into a sacred cup dates from a period considerably later than the time of Christ.

In Gaelic chants descended from remote times we read of a vase or basin which conferred upon its possessor superhuman power. This basin was always placed by the legends in the hands of some famous warrior by a giant or a dwarf, or both, emerging from the waters. The possession of the vase caused him to be envied, and so arose many fierce combats. Not unlike the hoard of the Nibelungs was this famous basin. It is not difficult to see how, as Christianity spread, the wondrous powers of the vessel were attributed to its connection with the Saviour. Wolfram von Eschenbach does not agree with older writers as to the origin of the Grail. He accepted the version of the mediæval poem called the "Wartburgkrieg."

According to this, sixty thousand angels, who wished to drive God out of Heaven, made a crown for Lucifer. When the archangel Michael struck it from his head a stone fell to the earth, and this became the Grail. In the latest mediæval French version the Grail was the cup in which was received the sacred blood from the wounds of the dying Saviour. Indeed, the etymology of the word itself has been a subject of inquiry and dispute. In the Middle Ages it was thought that the name "san-gral" was a corruption of the words "sang real," "blood royal," referring to the office of the cup. Dr. Gustave Oppert has written a long and ingenious argument to prove that "coral" was derived from "cor-alere," and this theory consists well with Wolfram's story of the origin of the Grail as a precious stone. The word, however, is most rationally derived from the Provençal word "grial," a vessel. This derivation accords best with the finest of the early versions of the story, that written by the remarkable French poet, Chrétien de Troyes; and the word "grial" in its several forms is still used in Provence to signify a vessel.

Efforts have been made by tracing the derivation of "Perceval" to show that he was connected with the earliest forms of the Grail legends. One writer derives the name from "perchen," a root signifying possession, and "mail," a cup. The latter word by inflection becomes "vail," and we get as a result "Perchenvail" or "Perchenval,"—whence Perceval,—a cupholder or Grail-keeper. This derivation is of little value in face of the undeniable fact that in the Mabinogi version of the Peredur story he is not the holder of the Grail. Indeed, the Grail itself appears here only in one of its early forms, that of a charger on which lay a bleeding head. This head was afterward decided to be that of John the Baptist. Peredur becomes a searcher after this, and that is the foundation of his connection with later forms of the legend.

We may now review briefly the manner in which

the Grail entered the Arthurian romances, and then take a glance at the principal versions which were of value to Wagner. In 1154, died Geoffrey of Monmouth, a learned Welsh monk, who is celebrated for his work entitled "The History of the Britons." In this we find set forth in full for the first time the account of King Arthur and the Knights of the Round Table. Fact and fiction were, of course, curiously mingled in this work, and historical personages were accredited with some of the deeds narrated in the ancient legends. But here, at any rate, we find the Arthurian cycle in its earliest recorded form. The old Welsh collection of romances known as the Mabinogi, which is sometimes said to be the oldest version of these tales, shows too many evidences of influence from the Grail stories. It must be of a later date than the work of Geoffrey, and certainly much later than the fundamental utterance of the Perceval legend.

In the year in which Geoffrey died, Henry II. of Anjou ascended the throne, uniting under his sceptre the sovereignty of England, Normandy, Anjou, and a great part of Southern France. In this reign flourished Walter Map, or Mapes, the great son of Hertfordshire, who, under Richard I., in 1197, became Archdeacon of Oxford. His chief work seems to have been the introduction of the Holy Grail into the legendary romances. He systematised the Arthurian tales by spiritualising them and making them essentially Christian. This he accomplished largely by the employment of the Grail, an element which he undoubtedly obtained from French sources through the unification of the kingdoms under Henry. Map created Sir Galahad, the stainless knight, and it is regarded as probable that he wrote the Latin original of the "Romance of the Saint Grail." It is accepted as certain that he wrote the original of "Lancelot of the Lake," "The Quest of the Grail," and the "Mort Artus."

German scholars accept as the next version of the story the Provençal poem, written by Robert Borron, a trouvère, born near Meaux. Borron's labours consisted in introducing into the Breton Epic, as it is called, — namely, the French version of the Arthurian tales, — the active workings of the Holy Grail. His labour seems to have been precisely the same as that of Geoffrey, and he has even been credited with liberally helping himself to the Latin works of the British writer. In his "Joseph of Arimathea" he makes the Grail the vessel in which Joseph received the blood of Christ on the cross. This vessel was none other than the cup used at the Last Supper, and had been given to Joseph by our Lord himself. French savants have pretty thoroughly proved that Borron's work was not written about 1170 or 1180, as the Germans believe, but something like forty-five years later. It gives, in fact, one of the latest French versions of the Grail legend and is valuable for that reason. Gaston Paris, a high authority on French mediæval literature, has taken the ground that this version belongs to the thirteenth century, and his views have been supported by other French investigators. The French version which lies nearest to the works of Geoffrey is that of Chrétien de Troyes, who died about 1195.

Little is known of the life of Chrétien, except that he was a native of Champagne and spent most of his time in Courts. About 1160 he wrote his lost "Tristan," which he followed with "Erec," a Bre-

ton legend. Then he wrote his "Cligés," on an
Oriental legend dealing with the abduction of a wife
of Solomon (with her own assistance). About 1170
he wrote his "Lancelot of the Lake," and soon afterward "Ivain; or, The Chevalier of the Lion." About
1175 he wrote "Perceval the Gaul; or, The Story of the
Grail." This he tells us he adapted from a book lent
to him by Philip of Alsace, who, in 1172, fought in
England against Henry II. It seems altogether probable that this book was either Geoffrey's, or one util-
ising its materials.

According to Chrétien, Perceval is the son of a
widow, Kamuellés, whose husband has been slain in
a tournament and who therefore is desirous that her
son shall never hear of the allurements of knighthood.
She retires with him to a forest and seeks to bring
him up in ignorance of all the customs of chivalry.
But one day in the depths of the wood Perceval sees
five knights, and from them learns what knighthood
and the Round Table are. He returns to his mother
and tells her what he has learned. Now he will not
rest till he may be a knight. The poor mother, knowing that it is useless to oppose him, tells him how to
be knightly and sends him forth on his travels. Utterly
ignorant, almost foolishly simple in mind, the youth
makes many errors, and at the Court of Arthur is ridiculed by the knights. But he engages in combat with
one and slays him with a single blow. Equipped
with this knight's arms, he sets out again.

He falls in with an aged and wise man, named
Gonemans de Gelbert, who for nearly a year instructs
him in the use of arms and in other matters. Then
Perceval, whose foolish mind is gradually becoming

enlightened, begins to feel the emotion of pity for his mother, and he goes forth once more, hoping that he may see her again. His wanderings and adventures are numerous and not especially significant. He fights with the King of Deadly Castle. He meets and consoles Gonemans's niece, the beautiful Blanchefleur, who tells him of her many sorrows and bids him rescue the knights and ladies imprisoned in Gringaron. He does her bidding. He is constantly riding on knightly errands, and his nature is expanding and his wisdom deepening.

At length he comes to the Court of a king who is suffering from an incurable wound. While seated at the bedside of this king, he sees for the first time the Grail and a bleeding spear, but gazes upon them in silent wonder, not asking their meaning. The next morning he is ready to ask, but to his amazement he finds the castle deserted. He departs, but as he crosses the drawbridge it is raised, and his horse has to leap. He turns and asks who raised the bridge, what the Grail is, and why the spear bleeds, but no one answers. After he has travelled some distance he meets a maiden, his cousin, who tells him of the death of his mother, and of his error in not asking about the things he had seen. Now Perceval falls in love, with whom we are not told, and his nature becomes tender and affectionate.

He returns to Arthur's Court, where he is visited by a strange wild woman. She tells him that if he had asked the needed question about the Grail, the sick king would have been healed. She also tells him of knights and ladies imprisoned in Castle Orguellous. Perceval and other knights swear to release them, and

Perceval vows that he will never rest till he knows what the Grail is, and finds the bleeding lance. He goes to seek a certain wise hermit, who gives him much advice about seeking for the Grail and the spear. A little further on the story comes to an end unfinished. The tale of Perceval's finding of the Grail was told by others, or it may be that Chrétien completed his work and the latter part was lost. Chrétien's successors, however, provided the conclusion of the story, no doubt adding many unessential details, but preserving the vital point of the original.

For example, according to Borron, Bron, the brother-in-law of Joseph, received the Grail into his care and became the head of the line of Grail-warders. Bron remained on the Continent, but his son Alan settled in Britain, and was the father of Perceval. This youth was to see the Grail, but only after many trials. He made two journeys. On the first he saw the sacred relics, but asked no question. The second time he did ask, and learned the mysteries of the Grail, of which he became the keeper. Other writers, who followed Chrétien, narrated how Perceval found the castle of the sick king again, and asked the vital question, thus restoring the sufferer. Out of these materials Wolfram von Eschenbach made his version of the story, the completest and most beautiful that has come down to us, and the direct basis of Wagner's work.

Wolfram's first two books are introductory to the story of his hero.* In the first, however, it may be noted that he devotes some space to the praise of true womanhood as contrasted with merely external beauty.

* See "Parzifal," translated by Jessie L. Weston, London, David Nutt, 1894; Book V., "Anfortas."

This reminds us of the position taken by Wagner's Wolfram in "Tannhäuser." The main portion of the first two books is taken up with the adventures of Parsifal's father, here called Gamuret. This knight is not slain in a tournament, but is killed through treachery while serving in the army of the Caliph of Bagdad. The widow, Herzeleide, tries to bring up the son, Parsifal, in ignorance of everything pertaining to chivalry, but one day he sees three knights and is entranced. The story now follows closely that of Chrétien, and is filled with interesting details well worth reading, indeed, but not germane to the subject-matter of Wagner's drama. It is well to bear in mind, however, that in this version, as in Chrétien's, Parzifal is so simple-minded and so ignorant as to be fitly described as a "guileless fool." His mother in Wolfram's tale dresses him in fool's clothes, and in these he appears at Arthur's Court and asks to be made a knight. His immediately subsequent adventures are the same in all the legends. He slays a knight, obtains his armour and equipments, and reaches the castle of an old knight named Gurnemanz, the Gonemans of Chrétien. From him he receives much instruction, being particularly warned against asking too many questions.

Setting out again, Parzifal arrives at a city which is besieged. He aids the besieged people, and when they have won their victory, he marries their Queen, the beautiful Conduiramour. After a time he leaves her to seek his mother, of whose death he is ignorant, and to find new adventures. He comes to the bank of a lake where some men are fishing, and asks for shelter for the night. He is taken to a magnificent castle, and shown into a great hall where there are four hundred knights. The master of the castle invites Parzifal to recline beside him on a couch. A squire enters, bearing a bleeding lance, whereupon all burst into loud wailings. Then a steel door opens and there enters a procession of twenty-four beautifnl women, splendidly attired, bearing various articles seemingly of import and value. Finally appears " our lady and queen," Repanse de Schoie, bearer of the Holy Grail, for which exalted office we learn she has been designated by the Grail itself. The Grail is placed on a table before Parzifal and the master of the castle, Anfortas, whose face shows that he suffers intense pain, both bodily and spiritual. There is a feast, for which the food is provided by the power of the Grail. Anfortas presents to Parzifal a magnificent sword, his own. Through all the guileless fool, remembering that Gurnemanz had told him not to be too " swift to question," asks nothing, but thinks that if he stays there long enough he will learn without asking. Whereupon Wolfram moralises:

" But he who his story aimeth at the ear of a fool shall find
His shaft go astray, for no dwelling it findeth within his mind."

Parzifal retires to his sleeping apartment, but in the morning he finds no attendants, and the castle is apparently empty. He mounts his horse and departs, but as he goes a squire scolds him for not asking a question, on which depended the recovery of the afflicted Anfortas and his own happiness. Still confused in mind, Parzifal rides away. Again his adventures have no relation to the Wagnerian drama, though they are extremely interesting. Some of the incidents in this part of the story rise to high beauty. One of these is the effect of a bird's blood on the snow, which so forcibly reminds Parzifal of the red lips and fair brow of his wife that he is overcome. Finally, however, he returns to the Court of Arthur, and while a feast is in progress there appears a woman of dreadful appearance, called Kondrie the Sorceress. She fiercely denounces Parzifal for not asking the essential question at Monsalvasch, the castle of the Grail. Parzifal renounces the Round Table, believes himself unworthy, despairs of mercy in the hereafter, and declares that his wife's love is henceforth his only shield.

Parzifal is now for some time relegated to the background of the story, which occupies itself with the adventures of Gawain, another of the Knights of the Round Table. Finally, we learn how Parzifal meets with an aged knight and his wife, walking barefoot through deep snow, on a pilgrimage to the dwelling of an holy hermit. They reproach Parzifal for not remembering the season. The words of Wolfram's poem here are nearly the same as those of Chrétien, which are these:

> " Knowest thou not the day, sweet youth?
> 'T is holy Friday, in good sooth,
> When all bewail their guilt."

Parzifal arrives at the cell of the hermit, whose name is Trevrezent. The hermit tells Parzifal the story of the Grail and the bleeding spear. Anfortas had yielded to the temptation of lust, and as a punishment he had received in combat a wound from a poisoned lance, and this wound would not heal, while the sight of the Holy Grail kept him from dying. A prophecy finally appeared on the Grail itself, announcing that if a knight came and asked of his own accord the cause of the King's sufferings, they should end, and the inquiring knight should become the Grail king. Parzifal confesses that he once went to the castle, but did not ask the question. Trevrezent now gives him further instruction, absolves him of his sins, and sends him on his way.

We now read of many struggles between the Knights of the Round Table, as representatives of Christianity, and the agents of the evil one. Gawain frees the maidens imprisoned by the magician Klingsor in Chateau Merveil. But Gawain goes no further than this. Parzifal, being the more pious of the two, is permitted after many adventures, including a fight with Gawain, whom he does not recognise, to ride to Monsalvasch, ask the cause of the King's suffering, free him from his agony, and receive the crown. Now his wife arrives with his two sons, one of whom is Lohengrin, and destined to succeed his father as the keeper of the Grail. The story of Lohengrin and Elsa is told, and there are other details, which, fascinating in themselves, have no bearing on the materials used by Wagner.

II.—The Drama of Wagner

Let us now briefly review the story of the drama. According to Wagner, the castle of Monsalvat, as he calls it, stands upon a mountain just above the valley in which is situated the castle of the magician, Klingsor. Monsalvat is the temple of the Holy Grail and the dwelling of its knights. Klingsor's castle is the abode of temptation. The magician represents the powers of evil.   He rages against the servants of the Grail, because he for his sinfulness has been refused admission to their number.   Therefore he spends his life in trying to corrupt them and for this purpose he has a garden of wonders, the chief of which is a company of fascinating women.   Amfortas, the keeper of the Grail, once succumbed to the allurements of one of these, whereby he lost the sacred lance and was wounded by it.   This lance is that which was thrust into the side of the Saviour on the cross and was placed in the keeping of the knights of the Grail.   The touch of the spear which gave the wound alone can heal it.   But the spear is in the hands of Klingsor.

All this we learn from the conversation of Gurnemanz and several esquires in the first scene.   Kundry, the strangest and most potent character of the drama, sometimes the repentant servant of the Grail, at others the unwilling and agonised slave of Klingsor, appears with balsam for the King, but it can give him only temporary relief.   Gurnemanz tells us that the King will be healed through the instrumentality of a sinless fool, enlightened by pity.   This person presently appears in the character of Parsifal.   He shoots a wild swan and when he rejoices in the accuracy of his aim Gurnemanz reproaches him.   The aged knight asks him whence he came, who is his father, who is his mother, and what is his name, but to all of these questions he can only reply, "I do not know." Gurnemanz, astonished at his ignorance, questions him further, and finds that he remembers his mother and her goodness.   He tells how he saw the knights in armour, and followed in the hope of becoming like them.   Kundry, who is an interested listener to the conversation, contributes some items of information, and finally informs Parsifal that his mother is dead. He flies into a rage, and attacks Kundry, but is withheld by Gurnemanz. And now Kundry is suddenly overwhelmed by a mysterious sleep. This is the result of a spell which has been cast upon her by the magician Klingsor. When she is herself, she struggles always for good; but when Klingsor's power is operating, she becomes the most seductive of his agents. This is one of Wagner's most striking ideas. It is his own, for although in a way Kundry is a composite of characters found in the old epics, she is, in Wagner's drama, a new creation. But of that I shall speak further.

Gurnemanz surmises that Parsifal may be the pure fool destined to save Amfortas, and therefore escorts him to the castle of Monsalvat. There he sees the ceremony of the unveiling of the Grail. Amfortas, dreading the ordeal, prays most pitifully for release from his sufferings, but the voice of his father Titurel, too weak to sustain the duties of Grail-warder and living a kind of life in death, bids him face his duty. Amfortas unveils the Grail, and the ceremony of the Lord's Supper is performed. Gurnemanz invites Parsifal to partake of it, but he stands dumbfounded and silent. The Grail is borne away again, and when the knights have disappeared, Gurnemanz pushes the still stupefied Parsifal out of the hall, saying:

> " Letting in future the swans alone,
> Go seek thee, thou gander, a goose."

The rising of the curtain on the second act reveals to us the chamber of Klingsor in a tower of his castle.

He is there awaiting the arrival of Parsifal, who he knows has been cast out of Monsalvat and is approaching his domain. He summons Kundry, calling her she-devil, rose of hell, and Herodias, the daughter of Herod. She arises in a cloud of vapour, apparently in the sleep into which we saw her sink in the first act. Klingsor orders her to tempt the pure fool, whose very foolishness makes him dangerous to the powers of evil. Kundry struggles in vain. Her will is mastered by Klingsor, for she is not pure. The scene changes to the magic garden. Parsifal is standing upon the wall lost in amazement. Beautiful maidens, half clad, changing presently to something almost like flowers, allure him with blandishments of the most seductive kind. These are the servants of Klingsor and they do his bidding. But the pure fool does not understand them. Presently from a thicket comes the voice of Kundry, calling, "Parsifal."

It is the first time the name has been uttered, and he remembers it as in a dream. He now sees Kundry, who has changed from the wild, dishevelled, weeping creature of the first scene to a young woman of surpassing beauty. She tells Parsifal the story of his origin, of his mother's woes and death, and, when his heart is touched, bids him learn the mystery of love. She presses her lips upon his in a long kiss. The result is startling; Parsifal springs up in terror and appears to suffer suddenly intense pain. Then he cries: "Amfortas! The wound, the wound!" He has received the needed enlightenment, through the pity for his mother. His own breast is now torn with the anguish of Amfortas, and with the terrible self-accusation of his own failure to save the sufferer. He realises that the seductions aimed at him are those to which Amfortas succumbed, and he bids the accursed sorceress begone. In her rage she discloses to Parsifal that it was Klingsor who wounded Amfortas with the sacred spear. The magician comes to aid Kundry in her struggle with Parsifal. Klingsor, enraged, hurls the spear at Parsifal to slay him, but the sacred weapon remains suspended above his head. He grasps it, and, making with it the sign of the cross, bids the castle disappear. At once the whole is wrecked, and, as the curtain falls, Parsifal, standing on the ruined wall, tells Kundry that she knows where she may find him again.

The third act shows us Gurnemanz, now very old, living as a hermit in a little hut at the edge of a forest. It is Good Friday, and the loveliness of spring is in the land. To Gurnemanz comes Kundry, clothed in the garb of a penitent, and without her early wildness of mien. She begs leave to serve, and goes about it at once. Parsifal, clad in black armour with closed helmet visor, and bearing the holy spear, approaches. He plants the spear in the earth, takes off his helmet, kneels, and prays before the lance. Gurnemanz, amazed, recognises him. Parsifal expresses his gratitude at finding the aged man once more, and we learn from his speech that he has passed through many experiences since he left the garden of Klingsor. Now he has only one thought, to return to the castle of the Grail and release Amfortas from his sufferings. Gurnemanz tells him that Titurel has died and Amfortas has refused longer to perform his office as Grail-warder.

No more is the sacred vessel revealed, for thus Amfortas hopes to win release by death. Parsifal is deeply moved by the consciousness that he might have prevented all this. He almost faints, and Kundry eagerly brings water to revive him. She bathes his feet, and at his request Gurnemanz baptises him. Kundry produces a phial of ointment and anoints his feet. Again at his request, Gurnemanz anoints his head. Then Parsifal, with water from the spring, baptises Kundry, bidding her trust in the Redeemer. Kundry weeps. Parsifal is clad in the mantle of a knight of the Grail, and with Gurnemanz and Kundry he goes to the great hall at Monsalvat. The body of Titurel is borne in, followed by Amfortas on his litter. The knights conjure him once more to reveal the Grail, but he, in desperate agony, discloses his terrible, unhealing wound, and beseeches the knights to bury their swords in it.

At this moment Parsifal, accompanied by Gurnemanz and Kundry, advances. Parsifal says solemnly that but one weapon will suffice, the spear which made the wound. With it he touches Amfortas's side, and the wound is healed. Parsifal declares the identity of the spear and holds it aloft, while all gaze upon it in rapture. Parsifal commands the pages to uncover the Grail, which he takes out and swings gently before the kneeling knights. Kundry sinks expiring to the floor. Gurnemanz and Amfortas kneel in homage to Parsifal, while from the dome above voices are heard singing, "O heavenly mercy's marvel, redemption to the redeemer!"

No other drama of Wagner shows wider departures from the original material or more condensation of it

than this, the last of his works. Here, as in other
dramas, he has not rested upon any one foundation,
but, using the story of Wolfram as his chief guide, he
has selected from other versions of the Grail legend
such ideas as were in harmony with his own poetic
purpose. Thus he discards Wolfram's conception of
the Grail as a stone from the crown of Lucifer and
goes back to the Provençal idea of it as the vessel in
which Joseph of Arimathea, the rich man who bought
the body of Christ from Pilate, received the precious
blood from the wounds. From Wolfram he took the
idea that the knights who dwell in Monsalvat, and
who went forth to aid the needy in distress (as in
"Lohengrin"), were fed and strengthened by the
Grail itself. The significance of the bleeding spear he
obtained from Chrétien de Troyes. Wolfram, it will
be remembered, made it simply a poisoned lance, with
which an unknown pagan, in the strife for the Grail,
had wounded Amfortas. Chrétien described it as the
spear with which Longinus had pierced the side of the
crucified Saviour. This idea could not fail to attract
Wagner, for it gave him an opportunity to strengthen
the ethical basis of his drama. Amfortas, yielding to
the seductions of Kundry, the temptress, becomes the
prey of the powers of evil, represented by Klingsor,
is robbed of the sacred lance, and wounded with it.
Such a wound is more than physical; it is a mortal
hurt of the soul. The cure comes only through the
touch of the spear itself in the hands of one who
is pure. The wounded King exists in all the versions
of the legend, and is always to be made whole by the
expected knight, who is to ask the essential question.

But in Wagner's version the question is not asked.

It has no dramatic value. As Wolzogen has well
noted, for an audience a visible and symbolic act is far
more effective; and so, instead of hearing Parsifal say,
as in Wolfram's epic, "What ails thee, uncle?" we
see him touch the wound with the spear and bid Amfortas " be whole, forgiven, and absolved." By this
simple change of the original story the conclusion of
the drama is infinitely improved. But the alteration
goes farther than that, for it touches the character of
Parsifal. He is in, Wagner's book, the same guileless
fool as he is in the original legends, but his enlightenment comes to him in another way. Wagner has
subjected his hero to the temptation which in Wolfram's story is undergone by Gawain.

The psychologic plan of the garden scene is subtle,
but not at all difficult of comprehension. Parsifal has
known but one love; he remembers but one tenderness. The sorest spot in his conscience is that where
dwells the memory of the dear mother whom he left.
Kundry, acting as the agent of the evil powers, seeks
to touch that spot. She awakens in her intended victim the divine spark of pity, akin to love, and then
she strives to lead him onward to love itself by the
imprint of a passionate kiss. But the influence of pity
has enlightened the inexperienced heart of the guileless fool, and the kiss which would draw his soul
from him serves but to reveal to him the nature of the
sin for which Amfortas suffers. He cries out with the
anguish of the very wound itself, and bids the temptress begone. This is a conception of unusual kind,
and for the purpose of exposition through music it is
most admirable, in that it centralises the dramatic action entirely upon the play of emotion. Here we find

the Wagnerian theory of the music drama working in its fullest freedom and completeness. Parsifal needs no question. He never hears of one. His awakened soul has already given him the necessary information, and when, after long and weary wanderings, he once more finds the domain of the Grail he is ready to heal the sufferer by the only means capable of performing that merciful act.

Kundry is entirely Wagner's creation. In Wolfram's story Condrie is the messenger who upbraids Parsifal for not healing the sick King, and Orgeluse is the beautiful woman who tempts Gawain. Wagner has united the two, but has created a personality of his own. According to one of the legends, Kundry was Herodias, the daughter of Herod, and had been cursed for having laughed at the head of John the Baptist on a charger. Wagner makes her a woman who had laughed at the suffering Christ and had been condemned by him to endless laughter. Thenceforward she wanders through the world in search of her redeemer. This wandering is common to heroines of the old German legends, and shows us that Kundry had certain traits in common with the Valkyrs of the Northern mythology. One of the names applied to her by Klingsor, Gundryggia, we find also in the Eddas as that of a Valkyr, and we further recognise the Valkyr nature in the union of hostile and helpful traits which was characteristic of the Choosers of the Slain.

Wagner's Kundry seeks to expiate her sin by serving the Grail, but the curse prevents her. Through it she becomes the slave of the powers of evil, represented by Klingsor, and, when under the spell, exercises her entire force in seducing the defenders of the

right. Not until one of the righteous resists her can
the power of the evil one be overthrown, and not till
then can she be released from the burden of her sin.
In other words, through resisting her, Parsifal becomes her redeemer, and it is thus natural and proper
that he should baptise her, and that in the scene of the
baptism the laughter-cursed woman should receive
the blessing of tears.

The relation of Kundry and Parsifal as temptress
and tempted was one which had long dwelt in Wagner's mind. When in 1852 he revived the idea, conceived in 1849, of writing a drama on incidents in the
life of Jesus, he told Mrs. Wille, his Zurich friend, that
he thought of showing Christ as beloved by Mary Mag-
dalene and resisting her. Again in "The Victors," the
Buddhistic drama, which he only sketched, we find
that Ananda, the hero, renounced love and was perfectly pure, while Prakriti, the heroine, after loving
him in vain, herself renounced love and was received
by him into the true faith. It was with these plans
still in his mind that Wagner developed the suggestions of the original sources of his drama into the wonderful scene of the temptation in "Parsifal," and their
influence also was potent in the composition of the
character of Kundry. Mr. Kufferath, in his interesting study of "Parsifal," says that Kundry was to
Wagner's mind simply another incarnation of the eternal woman, of whom Mary and Prakriti were earlier
embodiments. And, indeed, the extraordinary capacity of Kundry's nature makes this theory more than
merely plausible. Another fact which adds to the value
of Mr. Kufferath's idea is that, according to one of the
earlier German legends, the real cause of the enmity of

Herodias for John the Baptist was his refusal of her love. When the head was presented to her on a charger, she wished to kiss the dead lips, but from them was breathed upon her a blast of breath so fierce that it sent her wandering through the world as the unfortunate Francesca flew through the Inferno forever. This stormy wandering was a peculiarity of the Valkyrs, and thus with the union of so many elements in the history and nature of Kundry, we come easily to a belief that Wagner intended to make her one of the aspects of the "eternal feminine." Beautifully he gives her rest when the same blessing is conferred upon the man whose life she ruined. She has repented, but till her victim is freed from the consequences of the joint sin, she, too, must suffer her punishment.

In the character of Parsifal himself certain traits are accentuated by Wagner. These are the complete innocence and the compassionate nature. With compassion Wagner had a deep sympathy. He was so tender to dumb animals and to animate creatures in general that he felt readily the essence of pity which plays so important a part in the old legends. But the older Parsifals, when on their travels, were warriors; they fought their way through life, felling ruthlessly all who opposed them. Wagner's Parsifal is all tenderness and pity. Here, again, we meet with the powerful influence on Wagner of Schopenhauer. Enlightenment by pity is the ethical principle of Schopenhauer's philosophy. Something, too, must be attributed to Wagner's interest in religion. Liszt, an emotionalist in worship, inspired Wagner with emotionalism in sacred matters, and we may infer that certain rapt states of mind, not uncommon to thinkers of the hysteric sort, worked in the formation of "Parsifal."

For the rest there is little to say. Gurnemanz combines the persons and acts of the Gurnemanz and Trevrezent of the epics. Klingsor follows the outline provided by the earlier stories, but Wagner has added one feature not found in them. This magician, with his soul tainted with some unknown sin, was unable to slay the lust which ever burned in his bosom, and in order that he might win the Grail he mutilated himself. Here we come upon another resemblance between this story and that of the Nibelung hoard. To win the gold Alberich renounced love. We have already seen how the Grail resembles the hoard, and this incident in the life of Klingsor, added by Wagner, brings the two stories even closer together.

In telling the story, Wagner has pushed to the front all the most beautiful elements, and has accentuated the Christianity of the tale. He has preached a sermon on the necessity of personal purity in the service of God, on the beauty of renunciation of sensual delight, on the depth of the curse of self-indulgence, and on the nature of repentance. But let it not be supposed that the influence of "Parsifal" rests wholly on the ethical truths contained in it. Its real power is in Wagner's perception of the emotional force of the action of certain ethical ideas upon human nature. By centralising the action of his drama on these emotions, he has put before us a tremendous play of the inner life of man's soul when struggling with its most formidable problems, its own most irresistible passions. "Parsifal" is a religious drama, but it is one for the same reason that the "Prometheus" of Æschylus

was. It is a problem play also, and for the same
reason as any modern French social drama is. Its
boldness lies in the fact that it readopts the stage as
the medium for the publication of tenets of religious
belief and for the exhibition of the naked soul besieged by lust and tried by the moral law. That use
was common in the time of the Greek tragedians. It
is an exemplification of Wagner's theory that the
theatre ought to be an artistic expression of the
thoughts and the aspirations of a people. The author
has therefore striven to suppress personal opinion and
explain exclusively the Wagnerian point of view.

III.—The Musical Plan

The musical plan of "Parsifal" is one of peculiar
power and its outward aspects are of great beauty.
The first act is almost wholly devoted to an exposition of the fundamental thoughts of the drama. We
are introduced to the realm of the Grail, the suffering
of Amfortas, the eagerness of Kundry to serve and
her enslavement to the will of Klingsor, to the "guileless fool" and his failure to ask the question, and to
the solemn ceremony of the Last Supper. The second
act is devoted to a presentation of the working of the
evil element. Klingsor through his flower-maidens
strives to seduce the guileless fool, who is saved
largely by his own guilelessness. Here we have all
the most sensuous and freely composed music. The
first act teems with the fundamental and significant
motives of the score. The second is rich in luscious
melody, spontaneous, dance-like in form and colour,
and asking of the hearer nothing but self-relaxation.

The third act again becomes solemn, but in its first scene the solemnity is charged with the deep and quiet joy of Good Friday. With the return to the castle of the Grail, the fundamental motives are once more brought into action and the development of themes reaches its climax.

The prelude to the drama sets forth some of the principal musical ideas and attunes the mind to the key of the first act. It opens with the solemn strains of the theme of the Last Supper.

THE LAST SUPPER.

This theme becomes one of the principal elements of the score, being utilised throughout the drama to signify the sacredness of the association of the knights of the Grail. The second theme of the prelude is that of the Grail itself, which is here presented to us in a different musical aspect from that of the "Lohengrin" score. There the Grail was celebrated as a potency by which the world was aided, while here it is brought before us as the visible embodiment of a faith, the memento of a crucified Saviour. The theme is, therefore, one of much solemnity.

THE GRAIL.

The Vorspiel next proclaims, in a manner which leaves us no doubt of its purport, the triumphant motive of Belief:

BELIEF.

These three ideas—the Last Supper, the Grail, and Belief—form the materials of the prelude, and become of fundamental importance in the score of the drama proper. They play their parts chiefly in the first and third acts in putting the hearer in the proper mood for the appreciation of the solemn ceremonials in the Grail castle and for a full comprehension of the religious elements of the drama. For the suffering of Amfortas, with which we are made acquainted in the first scene, there is a musical symbol, which is utilised throughout the score at the proper places:

AMFORTAS'S SUFFERING.

A very beautiful answer to this is the music with which the promise of the healing knight is introduced. It is sung by Gurnemanz, and repeated by the young knights who are with him:

THE PROMISE.

Durch Mit - leid wis-send der rei - ne Thor.

By pit - - y 'lightened The guil - less fool.

With Kundry we find associated three principal musical ideas. The first of these is that which places before us the wildness of her nature, the stormy flight, and the curse of laughter:

THE WILD KUNDRY.

The second is a theme designed to represent the element of magic, as exercised by Klingsor in the control of Kundry:

SORCERY.

Lastly, we have one of those simple themes in thirds which always seemed to mean sympathy or helpfulness to the mind of Wagner. It first appears in the score when Gurnemanz asks Kundry whence she brought the balsam:

KUNDRY THE HELPFUL.

The personality of Klingsor himself is indicated by this theme:

KLINGSOR.

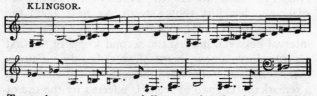

Two themes are especially associated with Parsifal. The first is that of his mother, Herzeleide. This theme has importance because of Kundry's use of the history of the mother to touch the heart of the son:

HERZELEIDE.

The Parsifal theme, however, is used to designate directly the personality of the guileless knight:

PARSIFAL.

Let the reader compare this motive with that of Lohengrin (see page 286), and note the close musical relationship.   This is in part an inversion of that, while the triple rhythm here used robs the Parsifal theme of the militant brilliancy found in that of the rescuing knight of the earlier drama.   At the entrance of Parsifal, who has just shot a swan, we hear again the Swan motive from "Lohengrin" (see page 287).   The interval between the first and second scenes of the first act introduces a new theme of great beauty.   Gurnemanz leads Parsifal toward the castle of the Grail, and a remarkable change of scene is effected by the use of a panorama.   During this change an instrumental passage is built up on the tones of the castle bells, which, at first heard distantly, gradually swell to a grand peal:

THE BELLS.

As we come with the two to the hall of the Grail we hear the musical representation of the cry or lament of the Saviour:

THE LAMENT.

The love-feast scene, which follows, is made up of the principal themes relating to the Grail and the faith of the knights, which are developed in choruses of wonderful beauty. The opening of the second act brings the motives of Klingsor, sorcery, and the suffering of Amfortas all into active use. The music is stormy, passionate, at times furious, till the flower-maidens appear to tempt Parsifal, and then we come to the long passage of freely written melody already described. The significant themes return in the scene between Kundry and Parsifal, but their use is so obvious that it requires no comment. With the awakening of Parsifal's understanding and his recital of his new discoveries, there enters a motive not previously heard, that of Good Friday:

GOOD FRIDAY.

In the first scene of the third act another new theme, that of the atonement, comes forward:

ATONEMENT.

We have now before us the principal musical materials of the score. But in no other of Wagner's dramas is the mere enumeration of themes so unsatisfactory as it is in "Parsifal." The combination of the musical ideas is so subtle, the building of the large mood pictures, of which they are the elements, so masterly, the effect of the general result so potent with the hearer, that in "Parsifal" one may with the most perfect security throw aside all study of the thematic catalogues and abandon himself to the dramatic influence of the music. This does not mean that "Parsifal" is a more artistic work than Wagner's other dramas, but that the moods are so large and so elementary that music very readily embodies them and brings the auditor under their influence. It has been proved that the rarified atmosphere of the Bayreuth theatre was not essential to the creation of proper sympathies in audiences. When performed with sincerity and devotion, the work produces a theatrical impression of extraordinary vividness.

APPENDIX A

THE YOUTHFUL SYMPHONY

MOST of Wagner's biographers have underestimated the historical importance of the juvenile symphony of the master.   Mr. Seidl wrote: " As one takes off his hat in Leipsic before the house in which Wagner was born, in order to honour the spot where a great genius first saw the light, so the musician of the future will take this symphony into his hands with the greatest interest and amazement, since it is one of the foundation-blocks of the structure whose capstones are ' Tristan,' ' Götterdämmerung,' and ' Parsifal.' " The truth is, that most of the biographers never heard the symphony performed.   It was produced by the late Anton Seidl in Chickering Hall, New York, on Friday evening, March 2, 1888, and it was my fortune to hear the performance.   At that time Mr. Seidl wrote to the *New York Tribune* the letter from which the foregoing quotation was taken, and gave an account of the finding of the lost parts of the work.   He said :

" He [Wagner] was continually recurring to a symphony which he had lost sight of after one performance in Leipsic at a concert of the Euterpe, and one performance in Würzburg.   In the latter place it was that the trombone parts were lost.   Letters were written in all directions to all his friends and acquaintances, but no trace of the symphony was found.   Then he requested the littérateur Tappert, of Berlin, a zealous and lucky discoverer of Wagnerian relics, to make journeys wherever he thought it advisable in the interest of the symphony. Tappert, after many inquiries and much reflection, drafted a plan of discovery following lines suggested by the biography of the master, and set out upon a tour through Würzburg, Magdeburg, Leipsic, Prague, and finally Dresden.   In each place he ransacked all the dwellings, inns, theatres and concert-rooms in which Wagner had lived or laboured ; but in vain.   At last in Dresden he visited Tichatschek, the famous tenor, who at this time was already bedridden.   He

knew all the houses in which Wagner had lived while he was Hof-
Kapellmeister, but nothing was to be found in any of them. Tichatschek got a little disgruntled at the much questioning to which he was
subjected and Tappert had to return to Berlin. Before doing so, however, he requested Fürstenau, the flautist, to cross-question Tichatschek thoroughly some day, when he was in a good humour, concerning
the possible whereabouts of some trunks which Wagner had left behind him in Dresden ; for Wagner had once said that when he fled
from Dresden he left all his possessions and did not know what had
become of them.

" The scheme was successful. Tichatschek remembered that in his
own attic were several old trunks belonging to he did not know
whom. Fürstenau looked through them, but soon came down and
declared that, though musical manuscripts were in the attic, they
were only unknown parts and that none bore Wagner's handwriting.
Tappert called for the parts to be sent to Berlin for his inspection. He
recognised at a glance that they were not in his handwriting, but on
carefully examining the separate sheets he found memoranda in lead
pencil which he thought looked like the youthful handwriting of Wagner. To assure himself, he copied the first theme of the first violin
part and sent it to Wagner's wife, who played it on a pianoforte in a
room adjoining that in which Wagner, suspecting nothing, sat at
breakfast. The master listened a moment in silence and then ran into
the room, joyfully shouting that it was the theme of the symphony for
which he was hunting. The discovery was made ! The parts were
sent at once to Bayreuth, and I was called upon to make the score out
of them."

The trombone parts of the last movement were missing, but Wagner
subsequently discovered the key to the leading of these voices in the
elaborately contrapuntal scheme of the movement and rewrote them.
The symphony was then ready for performance. It was Wagner's
original intention to play the symphony on the fiftieth anniversary of
the beginning of his artistic career. But he was unable to carry out
this plan. He subsequently decided to have it given for the Christmas
celebration of 1882, and accordingly it was played under his own bâton
in Venice at the birthday fête of his wife.

The symphony, which is in the conventional four movements, and
is in the key of C major, contains a curious mingling of juvenility in
ideas with maturity of handling. It shows that Weinlig's lessons in
counterpoint were not lost, for its polyphony is masterly, and the close

working out of the last movement, in the style of Mozart's fugal "Jupiter" symphony, may well have aroused the admiration of Rochlitz.

The symphony begins with an introduction marked sostenuto e maestoso, built on this theme.

It will readily be seen that this is a simple and effective theme, designed with a view to contrapuntal treatment. Free modulation, transposition of parts, and alteration of details make up the general treatment of this motive. The first movement, allegro con brio, is built on a first subject, inspiringly vigorous in movement, but quite devoid of originality in melodic form.

This is announced in a forcible manner, copied after some of the Titanic outbursts of Beethoven. There is a short development of this theme, in the course of which the germ of the second subject appears. Thus Wagner early endeavoured to follow the plan of Beethoven in making his second subjects grow out of his first. The second theme, when revealed in its entirety, proves to be this:

The master utilised the rhythmic clearness of this thought in the production of bold, march-like effects. Two episodes are introduced, and in these one hears the voice of the future Wagner. One of them bears a striking resemblance in character to the music of the fight between Siegfried and the dragon. The working out is confined almost wholly to the first subject, with occasional use of the episodes, and the recapitulation is reached by a strenuous climax, in which the orchestral thunderer of the future may be heard.

The second movement, andante, opens with two sustained notes, C and E, given out by the oboes and clarinets, followed by a graceful introductory phrase, prefatory to a lovely melody of folk-song character, which is announced by the violas and gradually spread among the entire body of instruments.

Wagner himself said that this movement could never have been written had not the fifth and seventh symphonies of Beethoven been

known to him, but although his method of construction follows that
of the sovereign of the symphonic world, his ideas and his orchestral
expression of them are his own. The second theme of the andante,
which need not be quoted, is martial, thus giving the necessary contrast to the movement.

The third movement is the scherzo, marked allegro assai. The
movement is decidedly imitative, yet it shows that the youth had attained a remarkable mastery of form and style. The first theme is
this:

This sweeps along in a bright and vivacious manner, full of sunny
simplicity. Then comes the trio founded on this idea:

The working out of the ideas is really very ingenious, and despite the
imitations the movement goes far to demonstrate the possession of
high gifts by the young composer. The last movement, allegro molto
vivace, is the least pleasing to the average hearer, but it is an amazing
exhibition of contrapuntal mastery in one so immature. The principal
theme is this:

Here the model in thought is Mozart, and the same master is followed in the working out. Wagner, in later years, speaking of the boy

who wrote this symphony, said: " He cares no more for melodies, only for themes and their treatment; he delights in the stretti of the fugue, in the combination of two or three motives ; he enters into orgies of counterpoint ; he exhausts every imaginable artifice." This is a sufficient description of this new "Jupiter" movement, which ends with a stirring peroration, presto, closing with as many chords of the tonic and dominant as there are at the finish of the fifth symphony of Beethoven.

APPENDIX B

WAGNER AND THE BALLET

THE difficulties which have always stood in the path of a realisation of Wagner's ideals in regard to the ballet in opera are worthy of some consideration, because they are the results of a high conception of the functions of the dance in the drama. Wagner's troubles in this department began with his "Rienzi." In his "Communication" he says: "I by no means hunted about in my material for a pretext for a ballet, but with the eyes of the opera composer I perceived in it a self-evident festival that Rienzi must give to the people, and at which he would have to exhibit to them in dumb show a drastic scene from their ancient history, this scene being the story of Lucretia and the consequent expulsion of the Tarquins from Rome." He confesses in a note that this ballet had to be omitted from all the stage performances of "Rienzi."

Why? Simply because the pantomimic ballet called for imagination on the part of the ballet-master and mimetic skill in the dancers. If these elements in the ballet were wanting in Wagner's day, they are almost all restored now. Except in cases where the ballet is seen by the spectator to be a mere entertainment for the personages on the stage, as in the garden scene of "Les Huguenots," it ought to have some connection with the drama. That later composers than Wagner have had some desires of this sort is proved by the presence of the Brocken scene in Boïto's "Mefistofele," the inferno scene in Franchetti's "Asrael," and other such episodes. But nowhere is there such an opportunity for a highly significant ballet as in the first scene of "Tannhaüser."

Whoever cares to read it, may find in the essay of Wagner on the "Art-work of the Future" a long disquisition on the nature of the dance. In brief, he says that in the dance the material is man himself, and the method of expression is motion. This motion is governed by rhythm, but its purpose is the communication of the essence of the material to the spectator. In other words — not Wagner's — dance approaches speech from one side just as absolute music does from the other. It is a painter of mood pictures, just as an orchestra is. It therefore reaches its highest form in pantomime, or mimetic action. Again, in "Opera and Drama," Wagner tells us at some length how ballet music as written by the conventional opera composer has cramped the development of this beautiful art of mimetic dancing, the very art, in a sense, from which the drama itself originated at the altar of Bacchus. By writing in the prescribed dance-forms and rhythms the composer compelled the dancer to confine himself to certain conventional steps and figures. Wagner's ideal was a symphonic poem of motion, mimetic in its essence, following the incidents of a story, and moving to the strains of an orchestral background which should free the dancer from formulas and at the same time paint in tone-colours the moods of the pantomime.

The difficulties which confronted Wagner no longer exist. To-day there is a school of ballet which possesses all the qualifications for a full realization of Wagner's ideals. The delineative dance has resumed the place it originally held as a dramatic art, and it will doubtless continue to hold it despite the derangement of the public conception of it by performers who profess to find choreographic plots in Beethoven symphonies and Chopin nocturnes. Without doubt the most commanding influence in the new development of interpretative dancing has been the Russian theatre, and above all the ballet of the Moscow opera under the direction of Begutcheff.

National folk practices, such as the singing and dancing of khorovods (or choral dances), had already led the Russian ballet far from the conventional paths of the French-Italian classic school, and when Begutcheff banished the last remaining foreign elements from his conceptions and turned to Ostrowsky and Tschaikowsky for scenario and music, he led the Russian ballet to the gateway of its promised land, which gave birth to the supremely imaginative achievements of Stravinsky and Michael Fokine. It is unnecessary, and would be apart from the business of this book, to recount the history of the ballet since the composition of Wagner's "Tannhäuser." Enough has been said to remind the reader that the ballet of action and delineation is now the dominating type and that there is a large force of dancers trained in the very art for which Wagner vainly sought. In this, as in some other highly important features of the lyric drama, he was apart from his generation.

INDEX